Shojo Beat

VAMPIRE KNIGHT

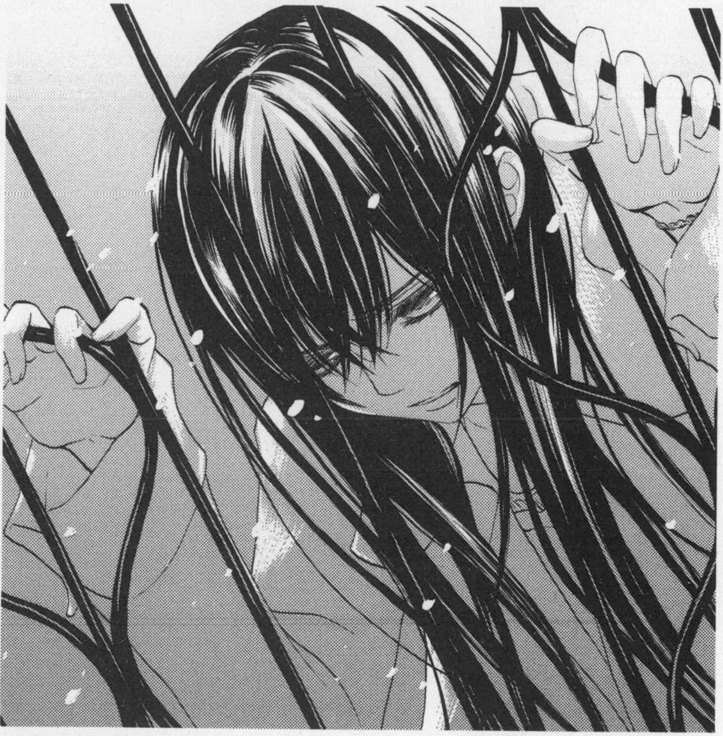

Story & Art by
Matsuri
Hino

Vol. 14

The Story of VAMPIRE KNIGHT

1 Cross Academy, a private boarding school, is where the Day Class and the Night Class coexist. The Night Class—a group of beautiful elite students—are all vampires!

2 Four years ago, after turning his twin brother Ichiru against him, the pureblood Shizuka Hio bit Zero and turned him into a vampire. Kaname kills Shizuka, but the source may still exist. Meanwhile, Yuki suffers from lost memories. When Kaname sinks his fangs into her neck, her memories return!

3 Yuki is the princess of the Kuran family—and a pureblood vampire!! Ten years ago, her mother exchanged her life to seal away Yuki's vampire nature. Yuki's Uncle Rido killed her father. Rido takes over Shiki's body and arrives at the Academy. He targets Yuki for her blood, so Kaname gives his own blood to resurrect Rido. Kaname confesses that he is the progenitor of the Kurans, and that Rido is the master who awakened him!

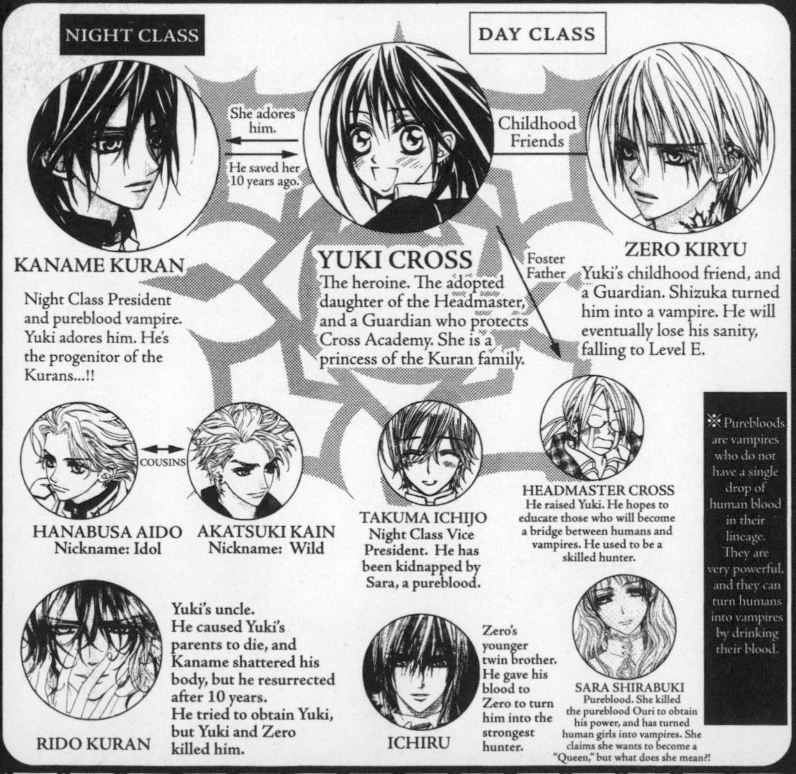

NIGHT CLASS
DAY CLASS
She adores him.
He saved her 10 years ago.
Childhood Friends
KANAME KURAN
Night Class President and pureblood vampire. Yuki adores him. He's the progenitor of the Kurans...!!
YUKI CROSS
The heroine. The adopted daughter of the Headmaster, and a Guardian who protects Cross Academy. She is a princess of the Kuran family.
Foster Father
ZERO KIRYU
Yuki's childhood friend, and a Guardian. Shizuka turned him into a vampire. He will eventually lose his sanity, falling to Level E.
COUSINS
HANABUSA AIDO
Nickname: Idol
AKATSUKI KAIN
Nickname: Wild
TAKUMA ICHIJO
Night Class Vice President. He has been kidnapped by Sara, a pureblood.
HEADMASTER CROSS
He raised Yuki. He hopes to educate those who will become a bridge between humans and vampires. He used to be a skilled hunter.
※Purebloods are vampires who do not have a single drop of human blood in their lineage. They are very powerful, and they can turn humans into vampires by drinking their blood.
RIDO KURAN
Yuki's uncle.
He caused Yuki's parents to die, and Kaname shattered his body, but he resurrected after 10 years.
He tried to obtain Yuki, but Yuki and Zero killed him.
ICHIRU
Zero's younger twin brother. He gave his blood to Zero to turn him into the strongest hunter.
SARA SHIRABUKI
Pureblood. She killed the pureblood Ouri to obtain his power, and has turned human girls into vampires. She claims she wants to become a "Queen," but what does she mean?!

4 Cross Academy turns into a battlefield. After fierce fighting, Yuki and Zero succeed in defeating Rido, but then Zero points his gun at Yuki. No matter what their feelings are, their fates will never intertwine. Yuki leaves the Academy with Kaname, and the Night Class at Cross Academy is no more.

5 A year has passed since Yuki and Zero's parting. Kaname and Zero have become the representatives of each group respectively. It seems that circumstances have become more peaceful, but the pureblood Ouri is thought to have committed suicide at a soirée. (But Sara Shirabuki killed him.)

Pureblood vampires who live forever eventually give up on living. Having seen their pain, Yuki decides to help them avoid involving innocents in their suicides.

6 Kaname gives Yuki his blood to show her his memories of the time when the progenitors existed. Yuki sees a woman with whom Kaname shared a strong bond in the past. But this woman is distressed seeing the vampires taking over...

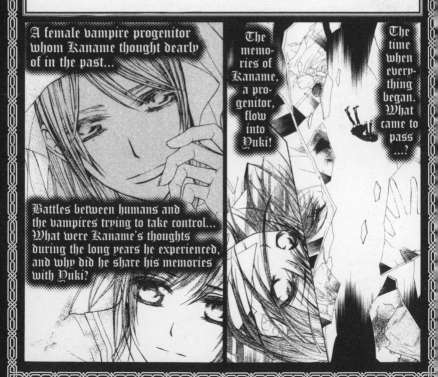

The time when everything began. What came to pass ...?
The memories of Kaname, a progenitor, flow into Yuki!
A female vampire progenitor whom Kaname thought dearly of in the past...
Battles between humans and the vampires trying to take control... What were Kaname's thoughts during the long years he experienced, and why did he share his memories with Yuki?

VAMPIRE KNIGHT

Contents

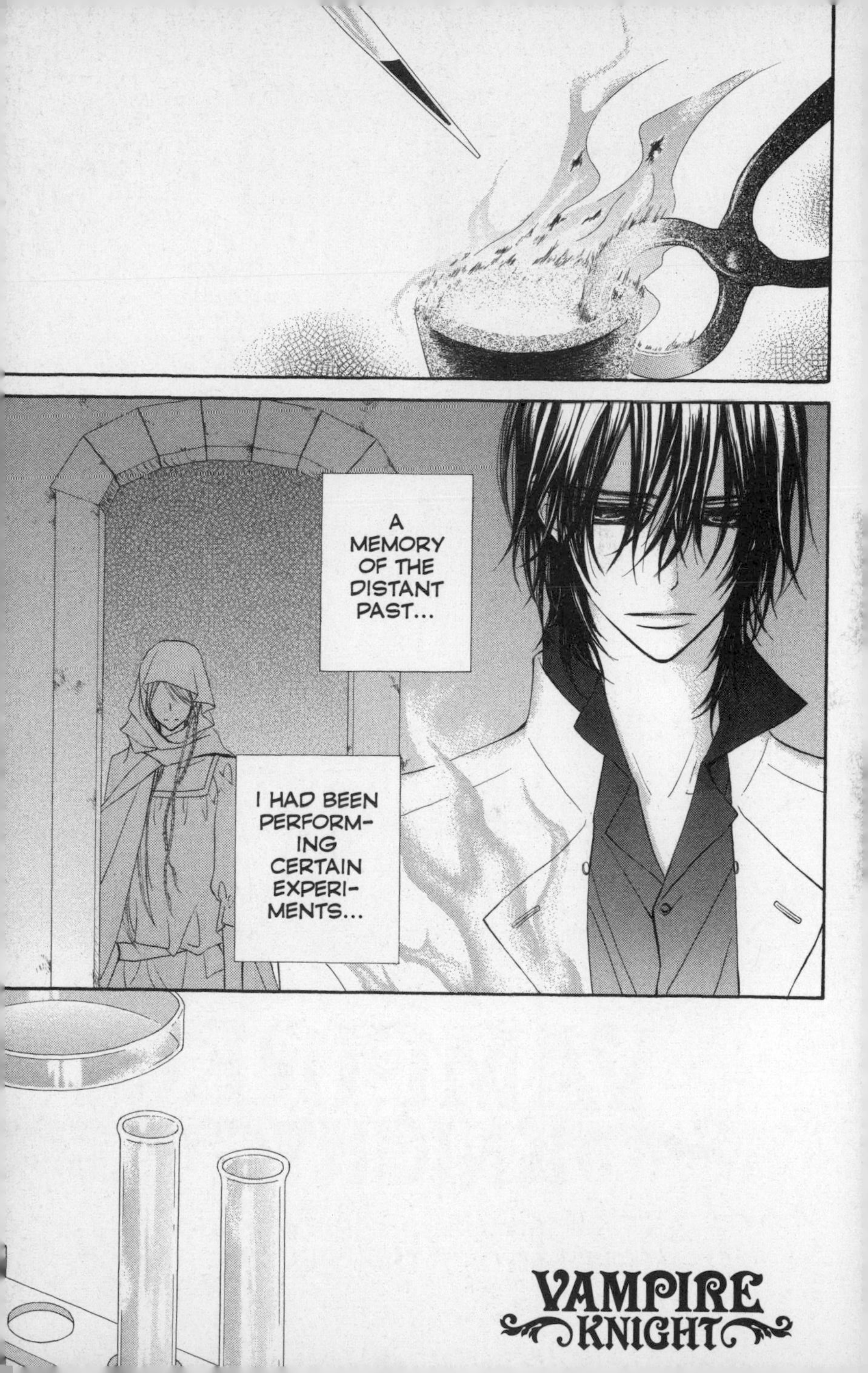
A MEMORY OF THE DISTANT PAST...
I HAD BEEN PERFORMING CERTAIN EXPERIMENTS...
VAMPIRE KNIGHT

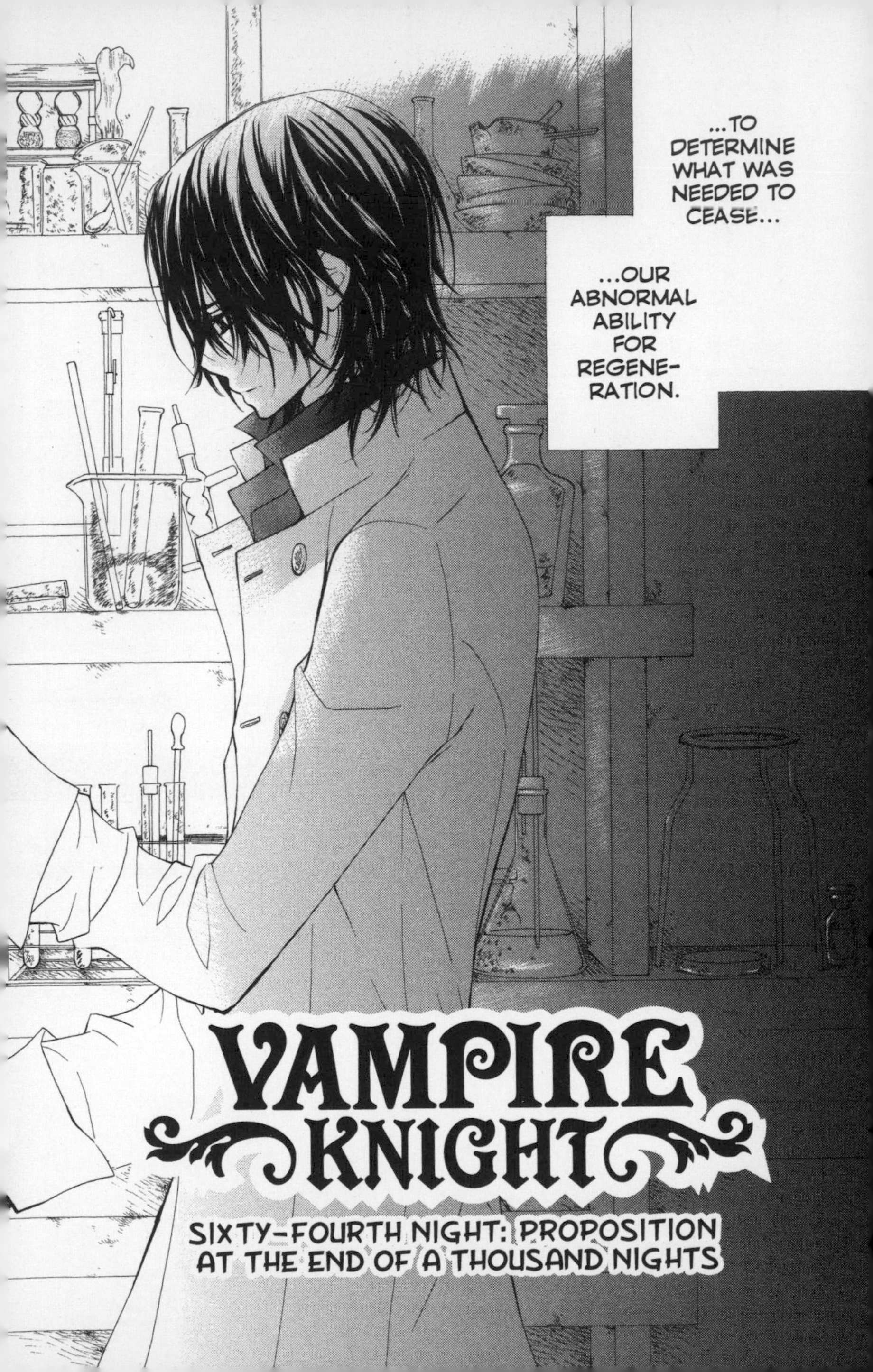
...TO DETERMINE WHAT WAS NEEDED TO CEASE...
...OUR ABNORMAL ABILITY FOR REGENE-RATION.
VAMPIRE KNIGHT
SIXTY-FOURTH NIGHT: PROPOSITION AT THE END OF A THOUSAND NIGHTS

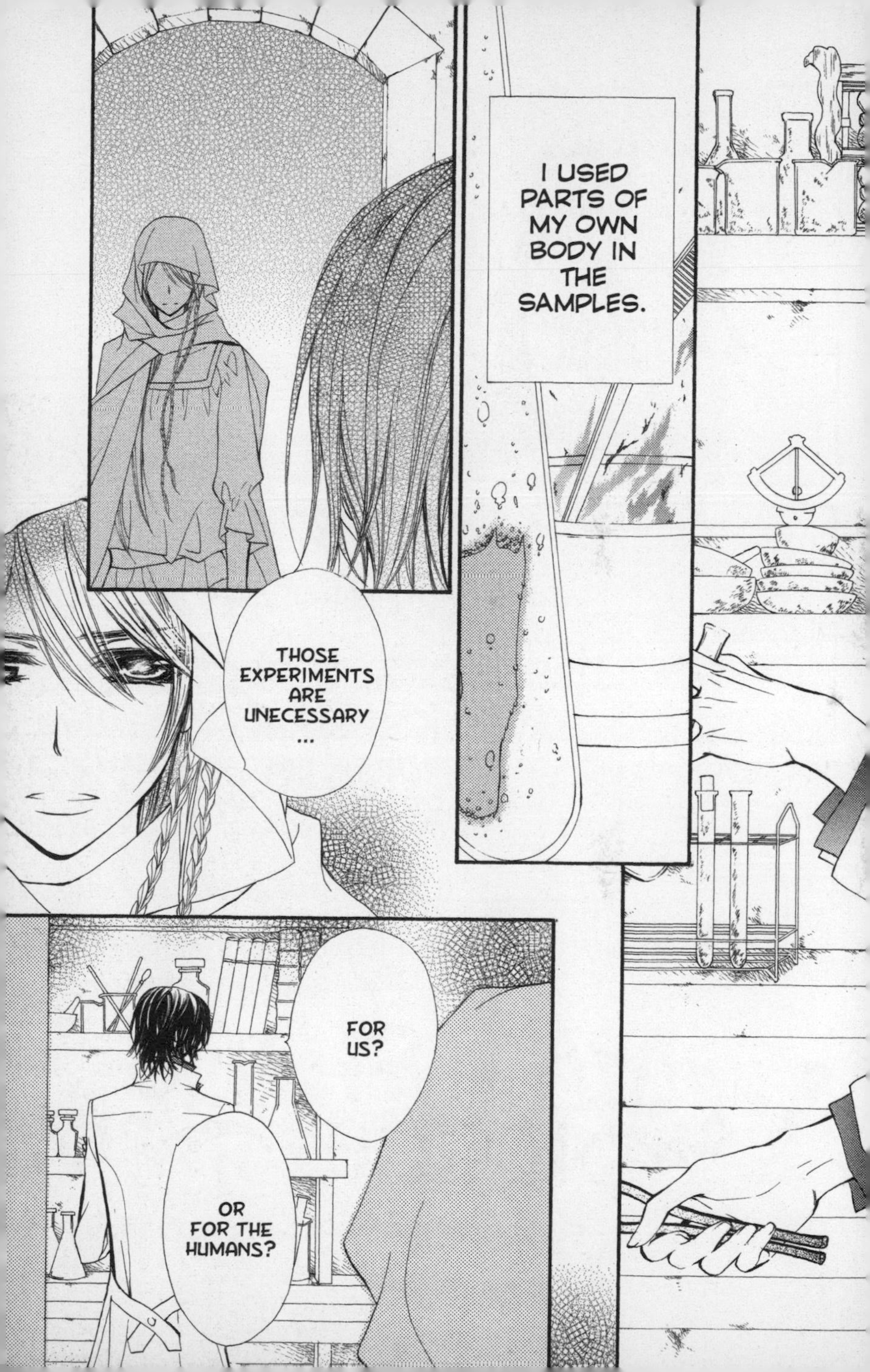
I USED PARTS OF MY OWN BODY IN THE SAMPLES.
THOSE EXPERIMENTS ARE UNECESSARY ...
FOR US?
OR FOR THE HUMANS?

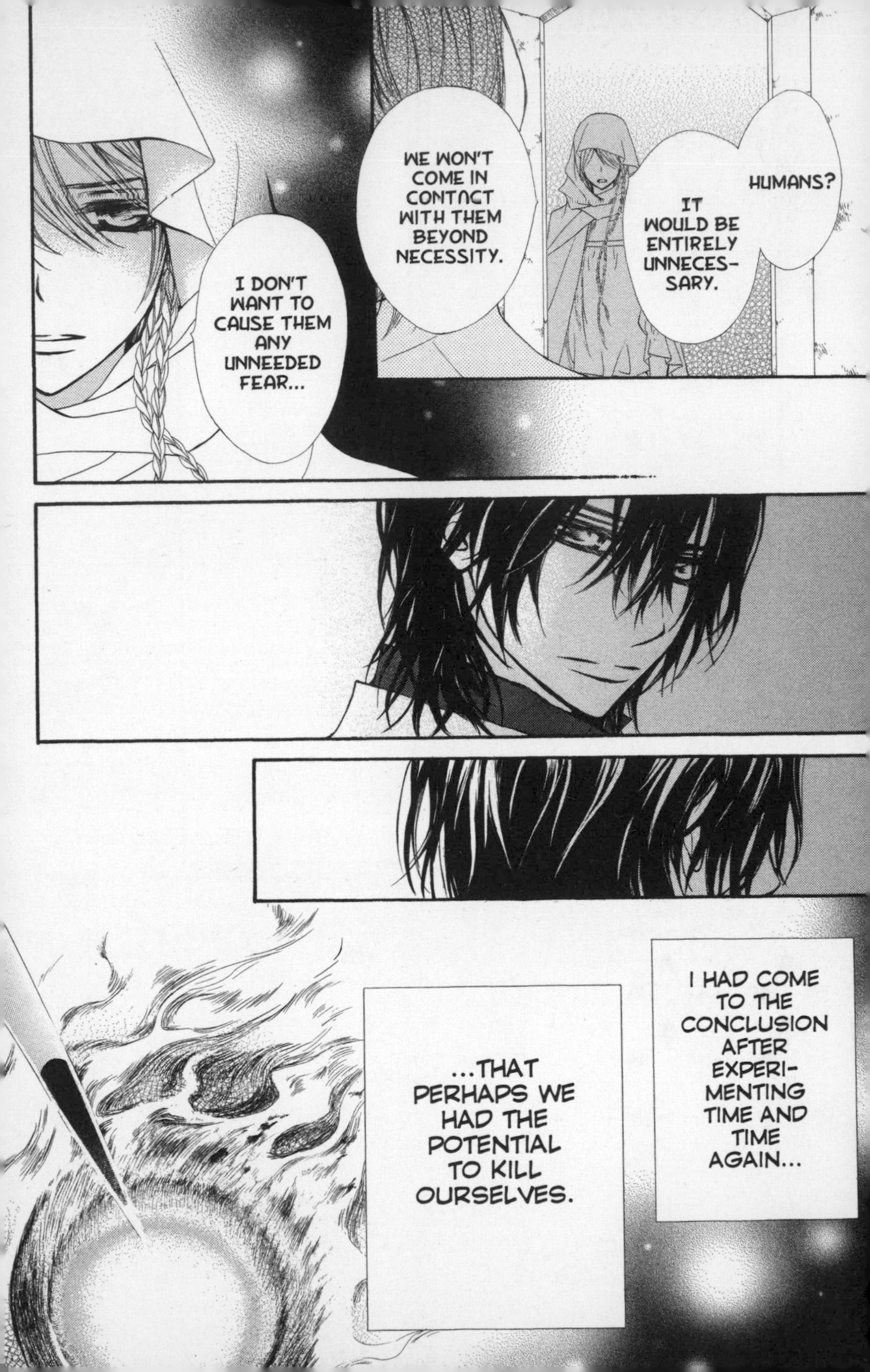
HUMANS?
IT WOULD BE ENTIRELY UNNECES-SARY.
WE WON'T COME IN CONTACT WITH THEM BEYOND NECESSITY.
I DON'T WANT TO CAUSE THEM ANY UNNEEDED FEAR...
I HAD COME TO THE CONCLUSION AFTER EXPERI-MENTING TIME AND TIME AGAIN...
...THAT PERHAPS WE HAD THE POTENTIAL TO KILL OURSELVES.

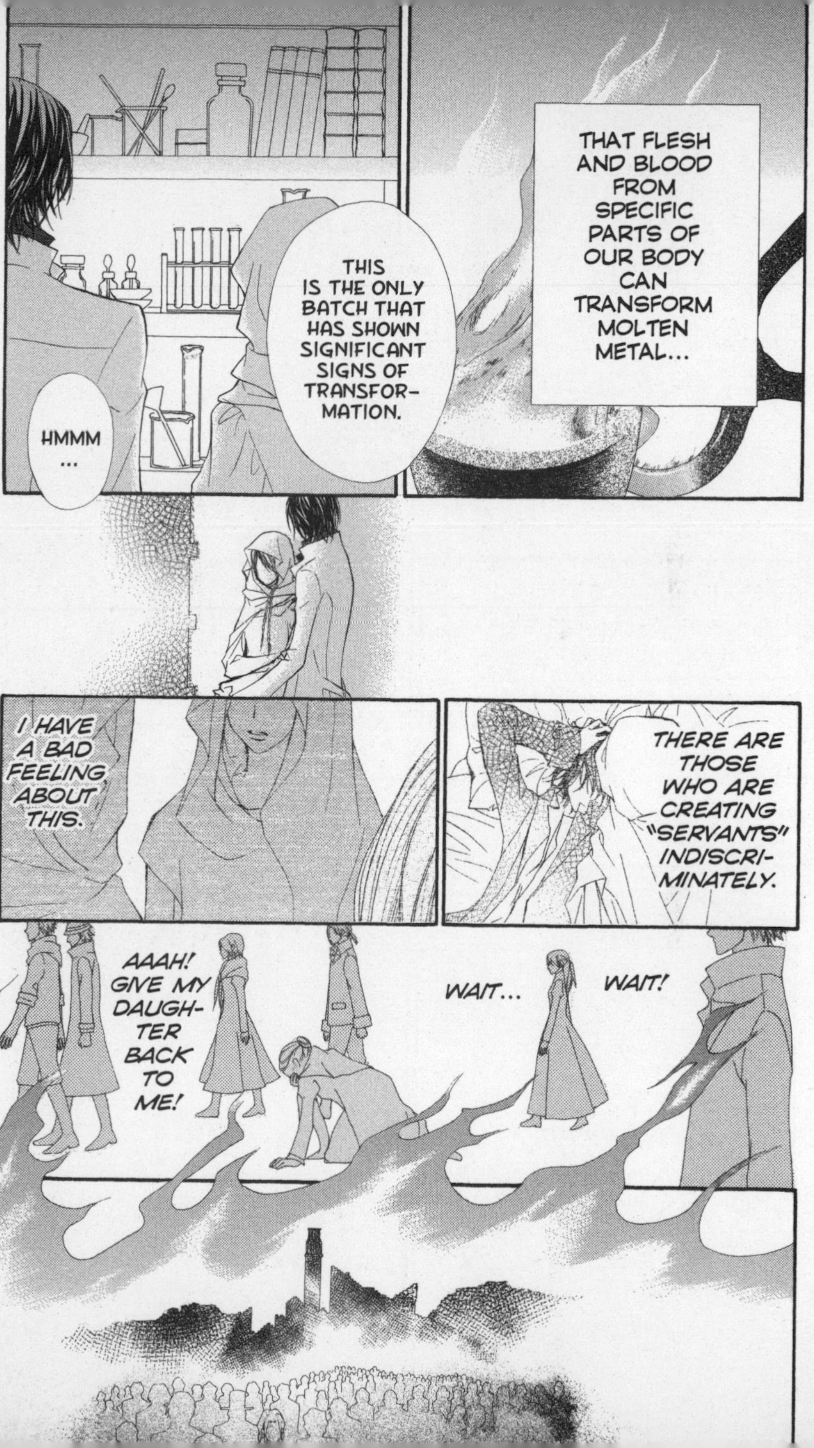
THAT FLESH AND BLOOD FROM SPECIFIC PARTS OF OUR BODY CAN TRANSFORM MOLTEN METAL...
THIS IS THE ONLY BATCH THAT HAS SHOWN SIGNIFICANT SIGNS OF TRANSFORMATION.
HMMM...
THERE ARE THOSE WHO ARE CREATING "SERVANTS" INDISCRIMINATELY.
I HAVE A BAD FEELING ABOUT THIS.
WAIT!
WAIT...
AAAH! GIVE MY DAUGHTER BACK TO ME!

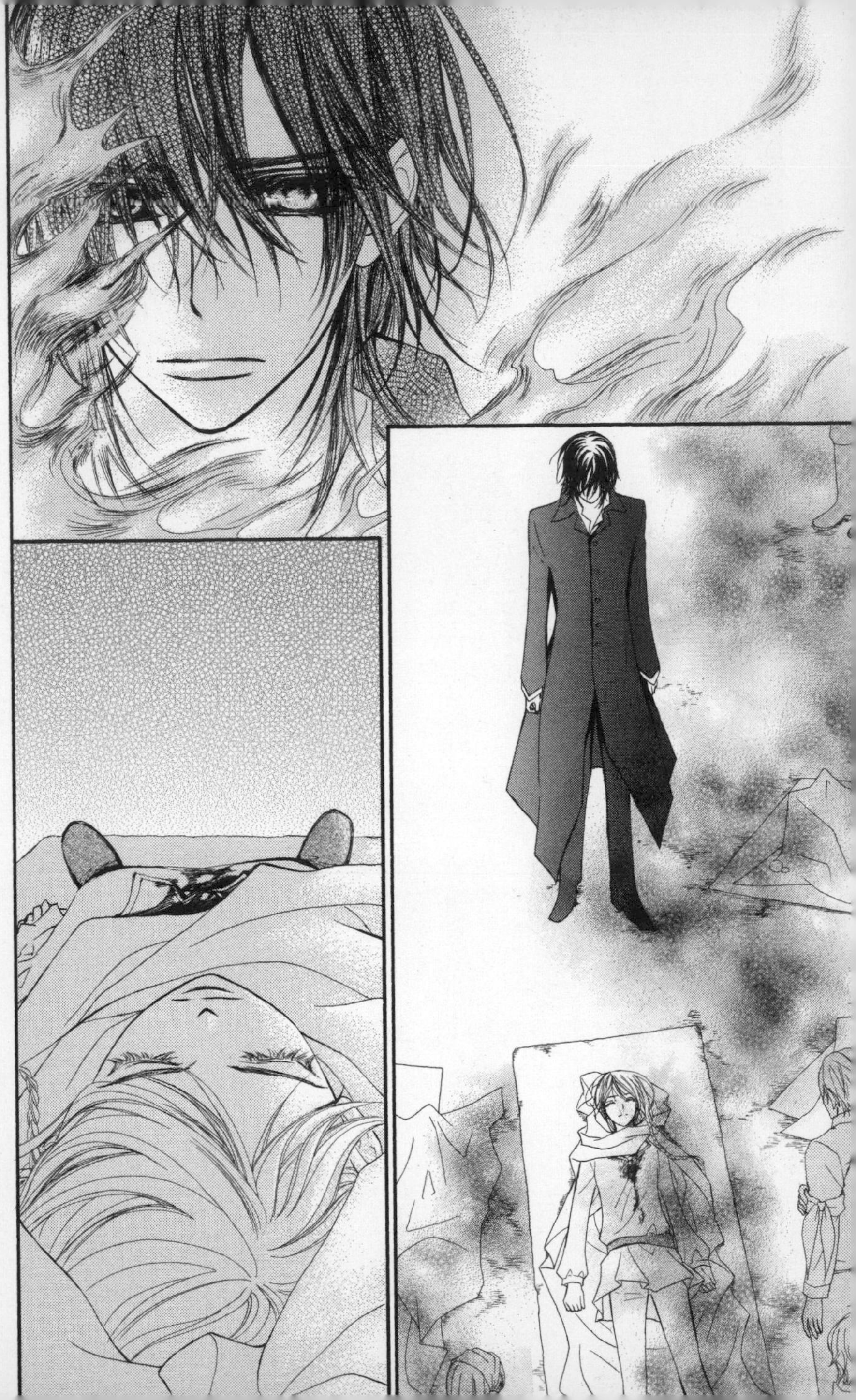

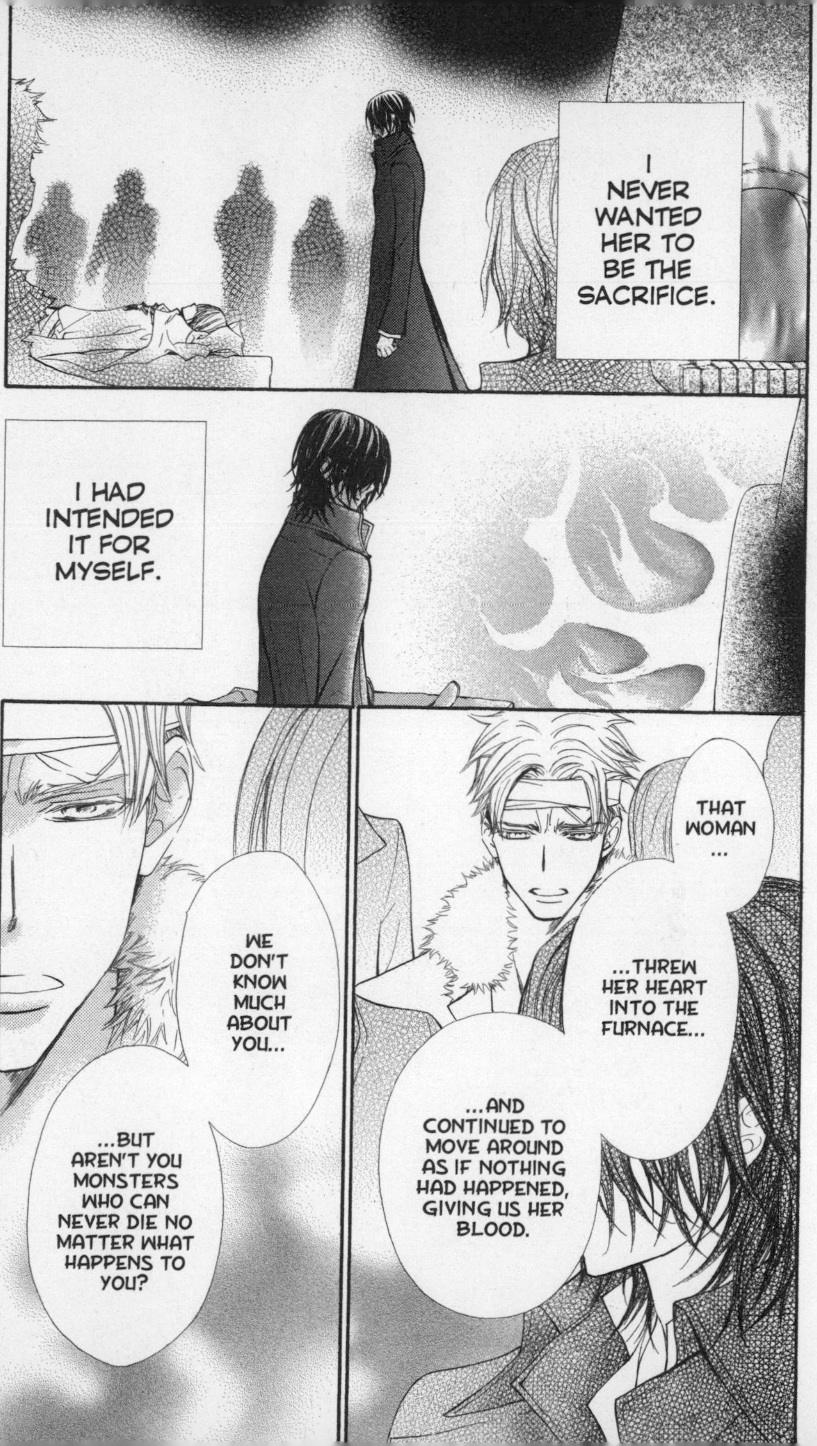
I NEVER WANTED HER TO BE THE SACRIFICE.
I HAD INTENDED IT FOR MYSELF.
THAT WOMAN ...
...THREW HER HEART INTO THE FURNACE...
...AND CONTINUED TO MOVE AROUND AS IF NOTHING HAD HAPPENED, GIVING US HER BLOOD.
WE DON'T KNOW MUCH ABOUT YOU...
...BUT AREN'T YOU MONSTERS WHO CAN NEVER DIE NO MATTER WHAT HAPPENS TO YOU?

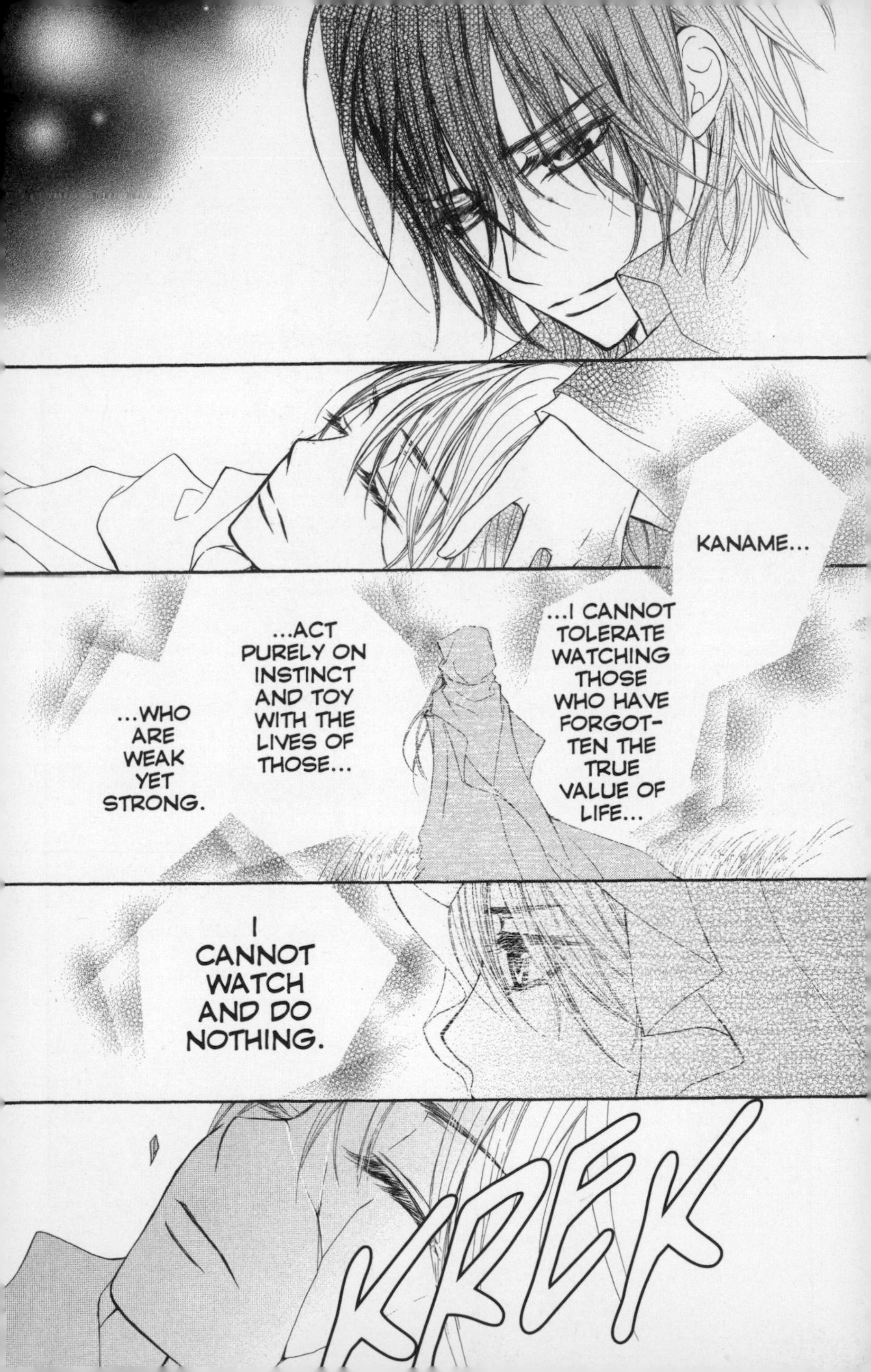
KANAME...
...I CANNOT TOLERATE WATCHING THOSE WHO HAVE FORGOT-TEN THE TRUE VALUE OF LIFE...
...ACT PURELY ON INSTINCT AND TOY WITH THE LIVES OF THOSE...
...WHO ARE WEAK YET STRONG.
I CANNOT WATCH AND DO NOTHING.
KREK

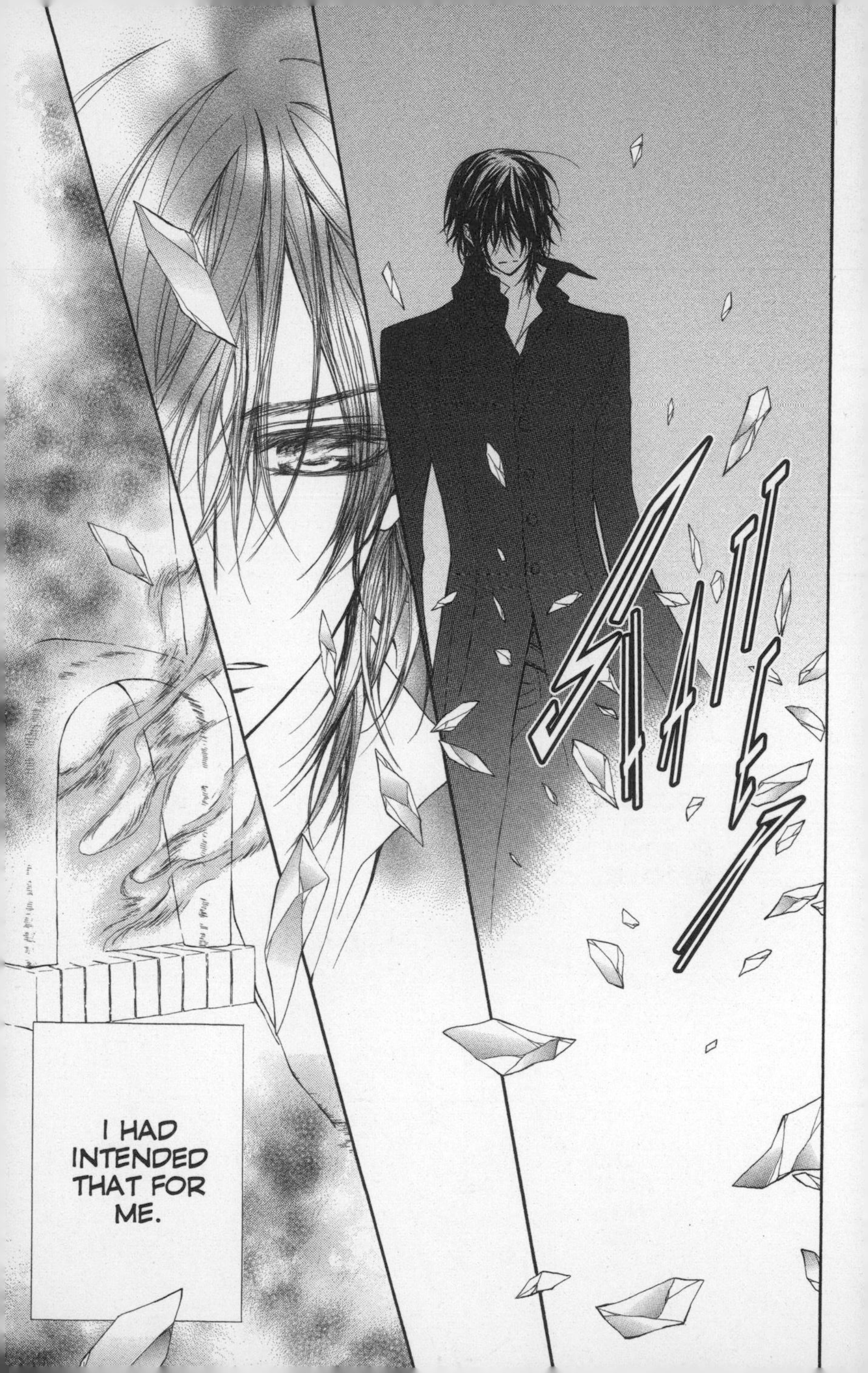
SHATTER
I HAD INTENDED THAT FOR ME.

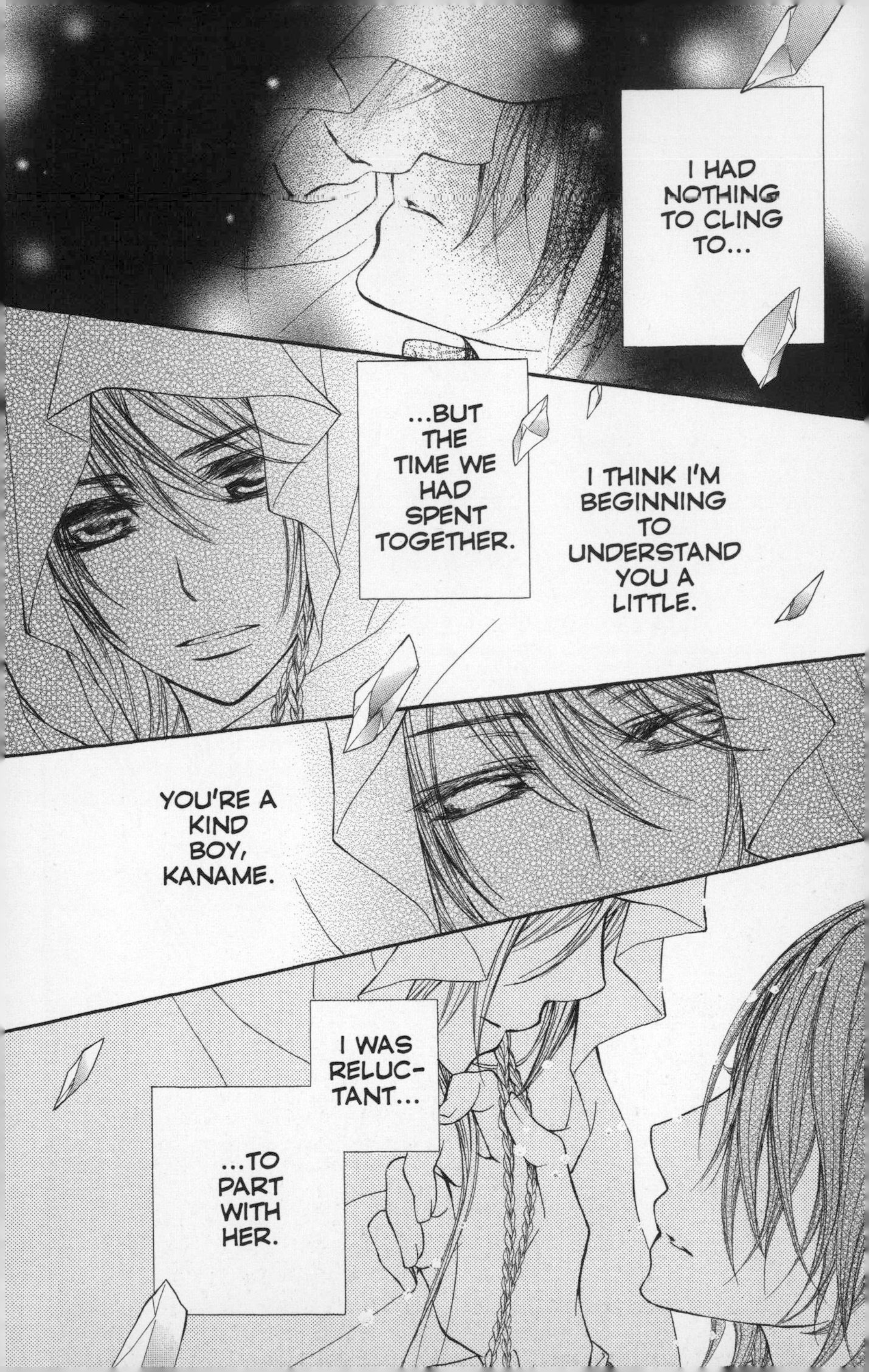
I HAD NOTHING TO CLING TO...
I THINK I'M BEGINNING TO UNDERSTAND YOU A LITTLE.
...BUT THE TIME WE HAD SPENT TOGETHER.
YOU'RE A KIND BOY, KANAME.
I WAS RELUC-TANT...
...TO PART WITH HER.

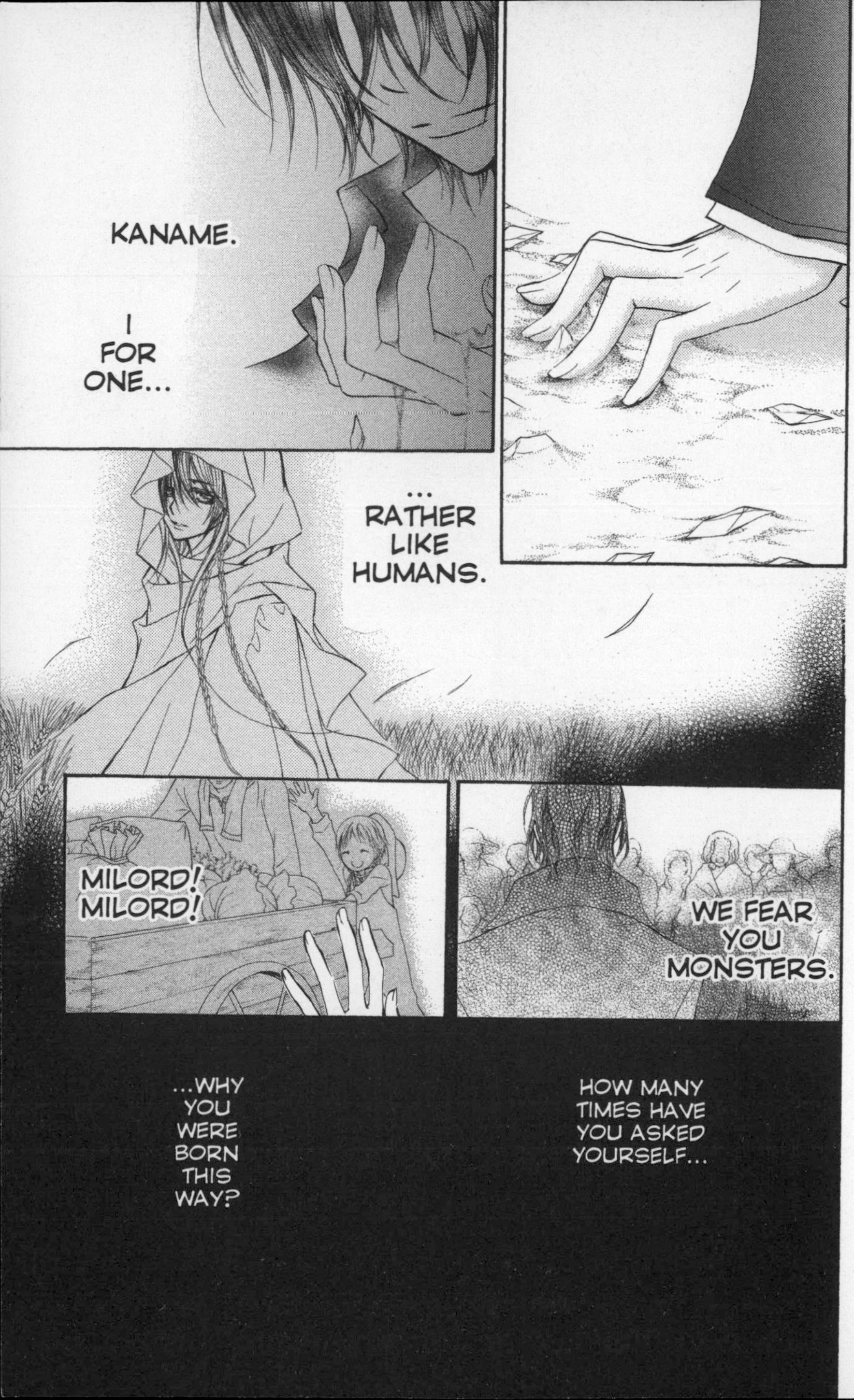
KANAME.
I FOR ONE...
...RATHER LIKE HUMANS.
WE FEAR YOU MONSTERS.
MILORD! MILORD!
HOW MANY TIMES HAVE YOU ASKED YOURSELF...
...WHY YOU WERE BORN THIS WAY?

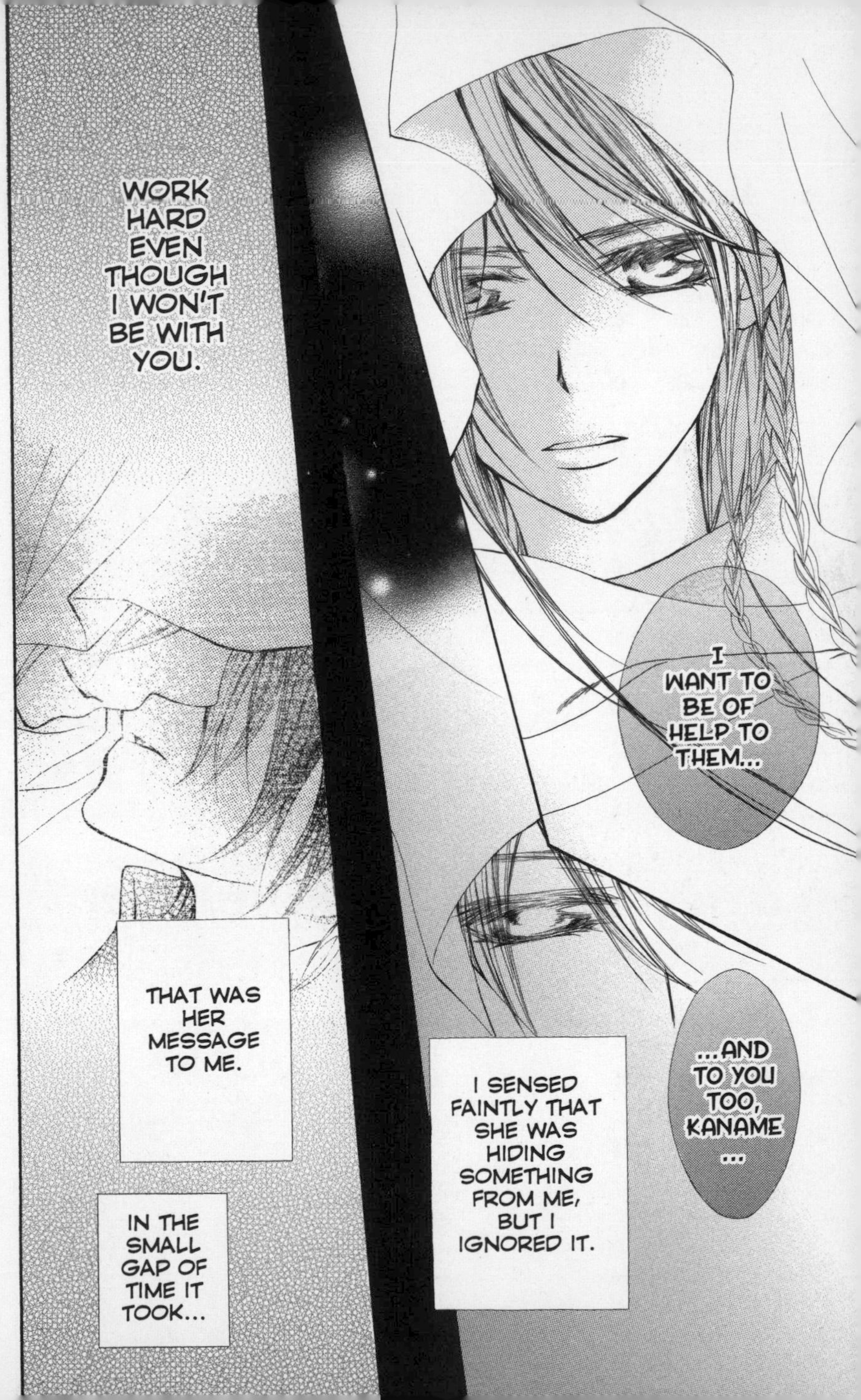
I WANT TO BE OF HELP TO THEM...
...AND TO YOU TOO, KANAME...
I SENSED FAINTLY THAT SHE WAS HIDING SOMETHING FROM ME, BUT I IGNORED IT.
WORK HARD EVEN THOUGH I WON'T BE WITH YOU.
THAT WAS HER MESSAGE TO ME.
IN THE SMALL GAP OF TIME IT TOOK...

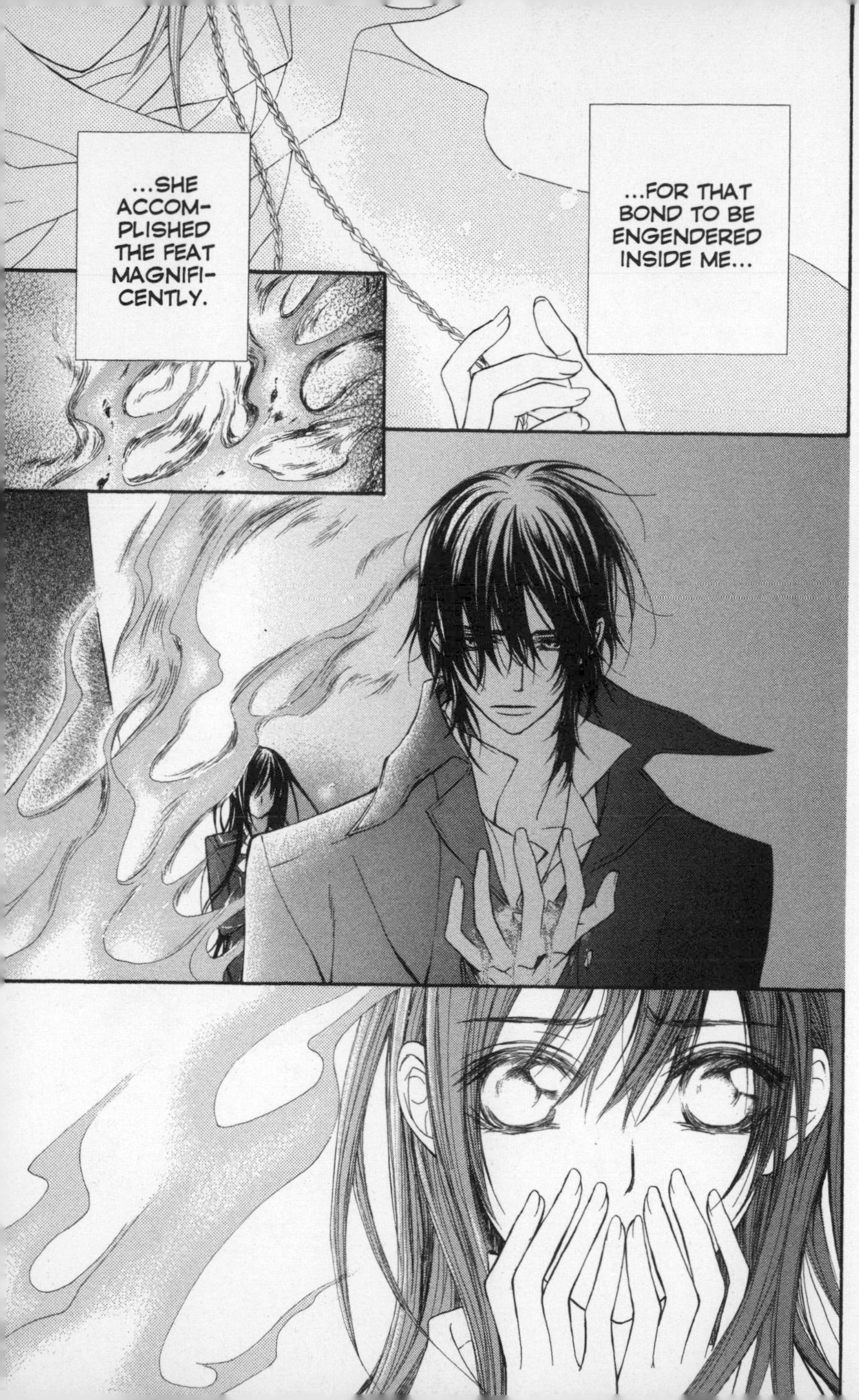
...FOR THAT BOND TO BE ENGENDERED INSIDE ME...
...SHE ACCOMPLISHED THE FEAT MAGNIFICENTLY.

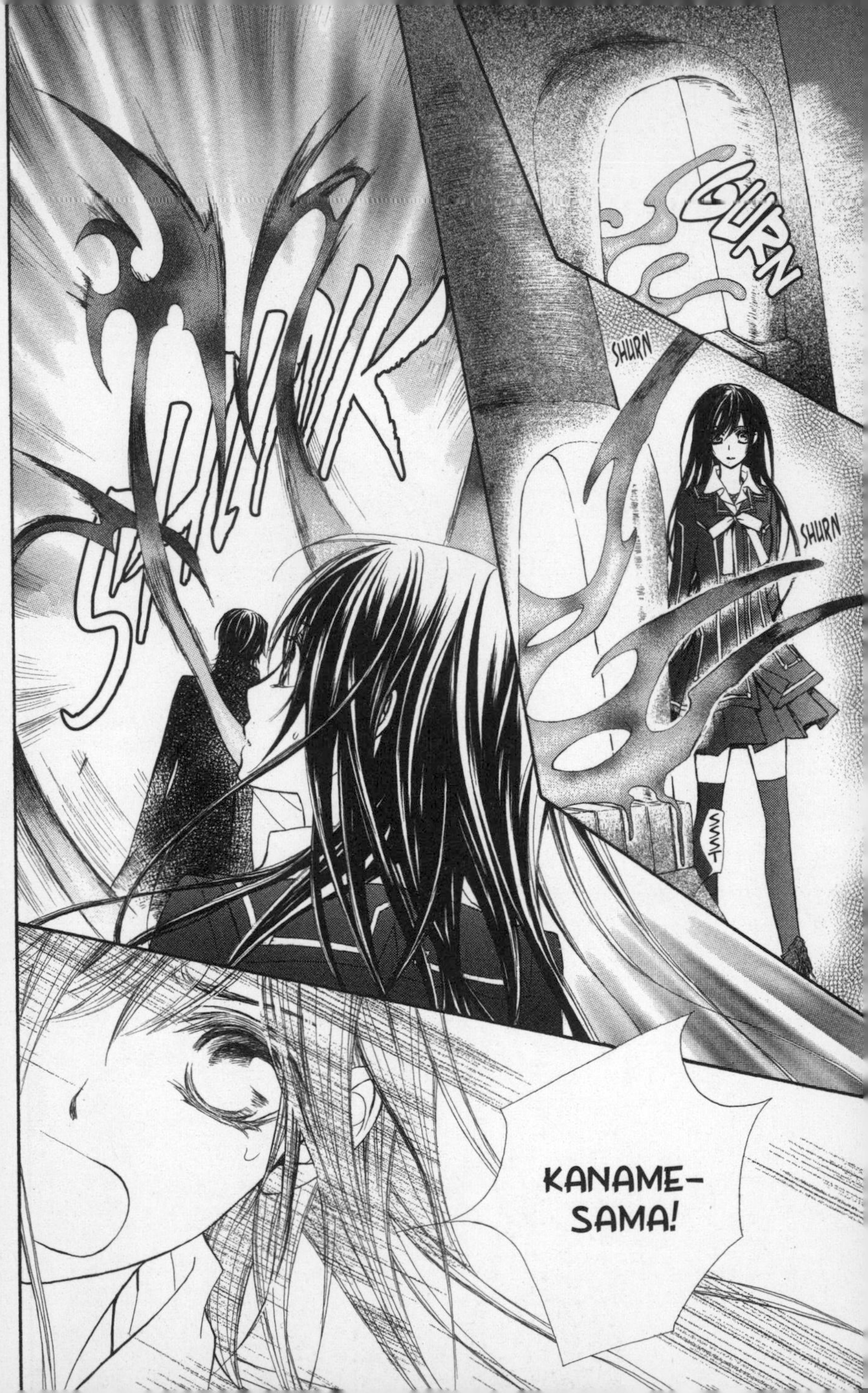
GURN
SHURN
SHURN
SSST
SHUNK
KANAME-SAMA!

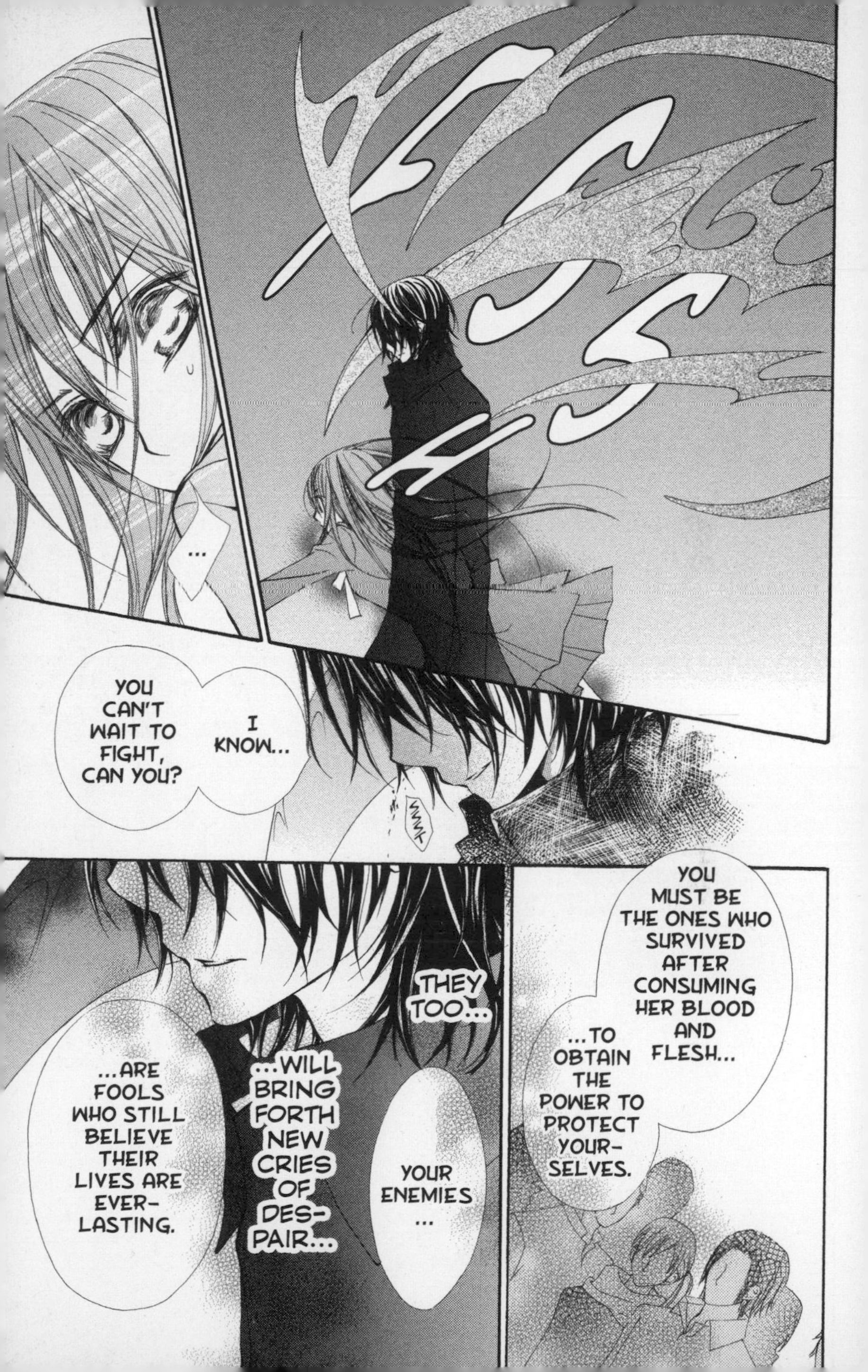
...
I KNOW...
YOU CAN'T WAIT TO FIGHT, CAN YOU?
YOU MUST BE THE ONES WHO SURVIVED AFTER CONSUMING HER BLOOD AND FLESH...
...TO OBTAIN THE POWER TO PROTECT YOUR-SELVES.
THEY TOO...
YOUR ENEMIES ...
...WILL BRING FORTH NEW CRIES OF DES-PAIR...
...ARE FOOLS WHO STILL BELIEVE THEIR LIVES ARE EVER-LASTING.

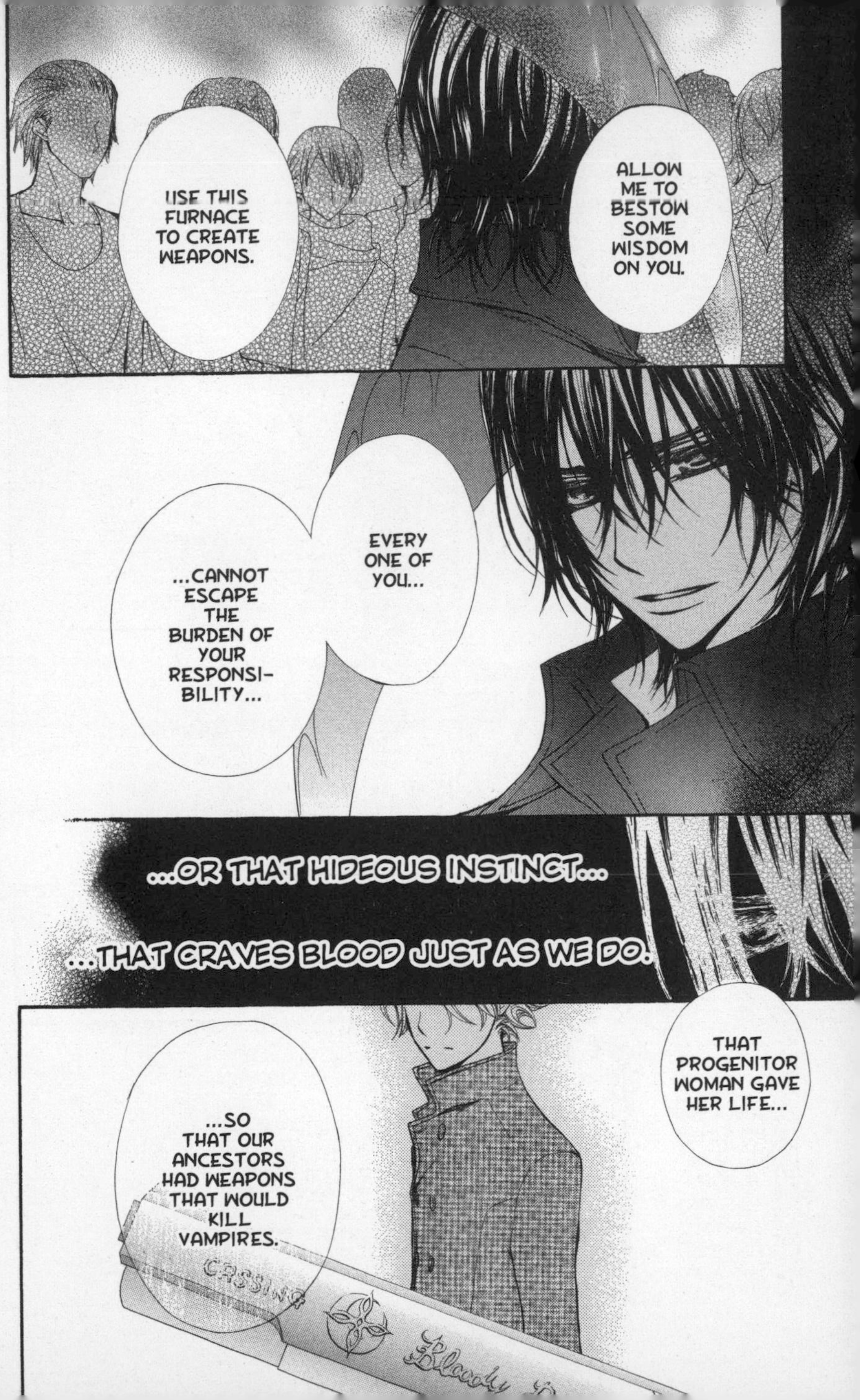
ALLOW ME TO BESTOW SOME WISDOM ON YOU.
USE THIS FURNACE TO CREATE WEAPONS.
EVERY ONE OF YOU...
...CANNOT ESCAPE THE BURDEN OF YOUR RESPONSI-BILITY...
...OR THAT HIDEOUS INSTINCT...
...THAT CRAVES BLOOD JUST AS WE DO.
THAT PROGENITOR WOMAN GAVE HER LIFE...
...SO THAT OUR ANCESTORS HAD WEAPONS THAT WOULD KILL VAMPIRES.

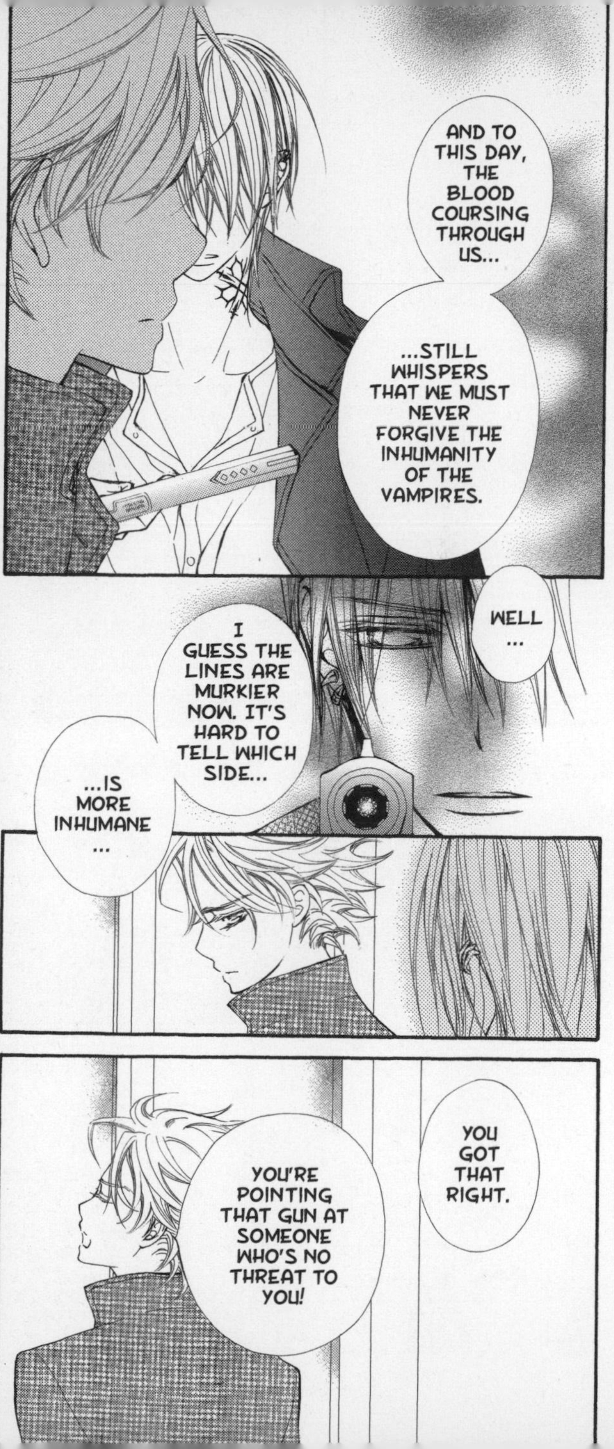
AND TO THIS DAY, THE BLOOD COURSING THROUGH US...
...STILL WHISPERS THAT WE MUST NEVER FORGIVE THE INHUMANITY OF THE VAMPIRES.
WELL...
I GUESS THE LINES ARE MURKIER NOW. IT'S HARD TO TELL WHICH SIDE...
...IS MORE INHUMANE...
YOU GOT THAT RIGHT.
YOU'RE POINTING THAT GUN AT SOMEONE WHO'S NO THREAT TO YOU!

Hino here.

First of all... I would like to express my condolences to all the families of those who lost their lives in the earthquake and tsunami that struck eastern Japan. I hope with all my heart that the people who have suffered so much in that calamity will be able to return to their peaceful everyday lives soon.

And I bring to you volume 14. Thank you very much for picking it up!

I kept running into various walls in this volume. My editor would point out the problems to me, and I kept having dilemmas about whether I had been able to put all the advice I was given to use.

I want to raise my skills to the next level!! Absolutely...

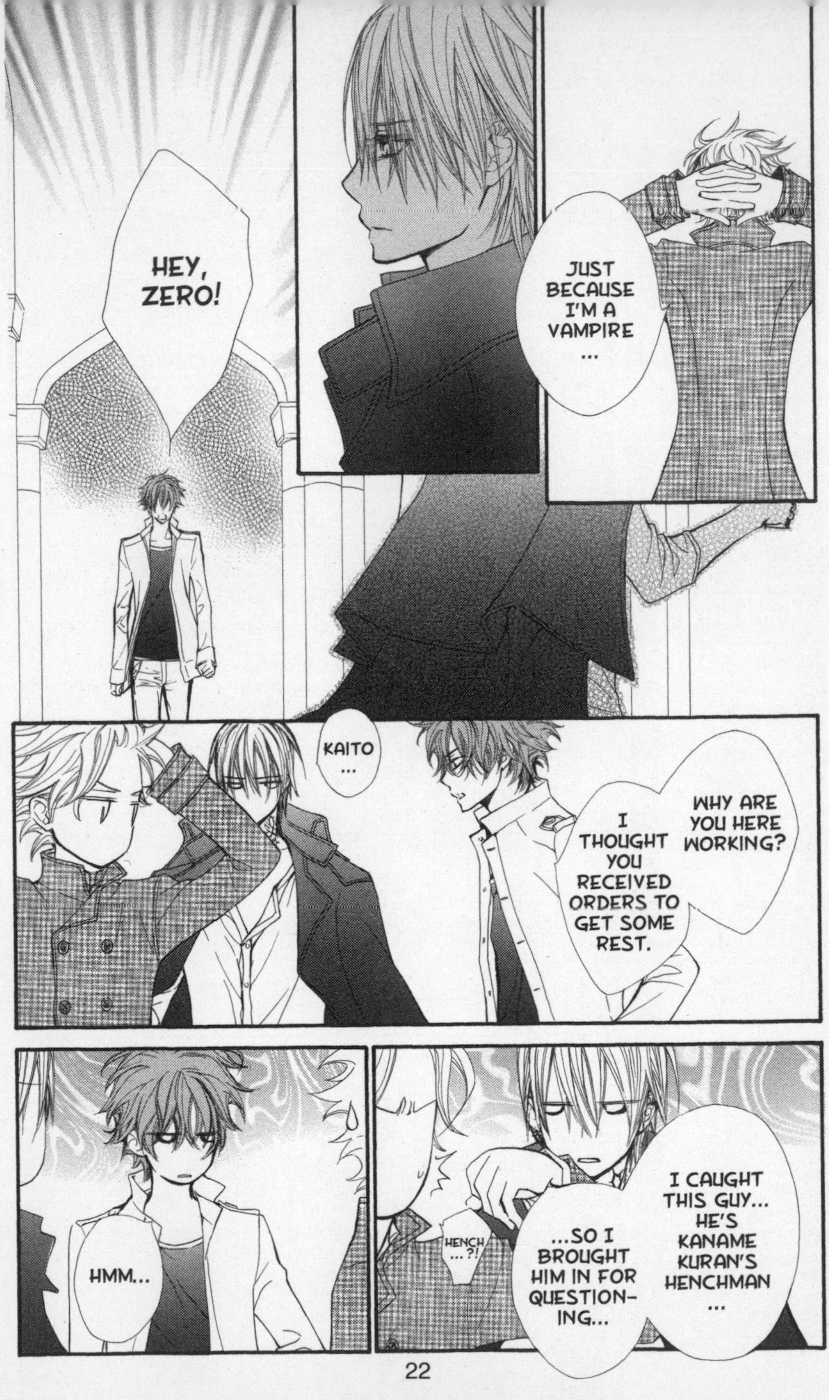
JUST BECAUSE I'M A VAMPIRE ...
HEY, ZERO!
KAITO ...
WHY ARE YOU HERE WORKING?
I THOUGHT YOU RECEIVED ORDERS TO GET SOME REST.
I CAUGHT THIS GUY... HE'S KANAME KURAN'S HENCHMAN ...
...SO I BROUGHT HIM IN FOR QUESTION-ING...
HENCH ...?!
HMM...

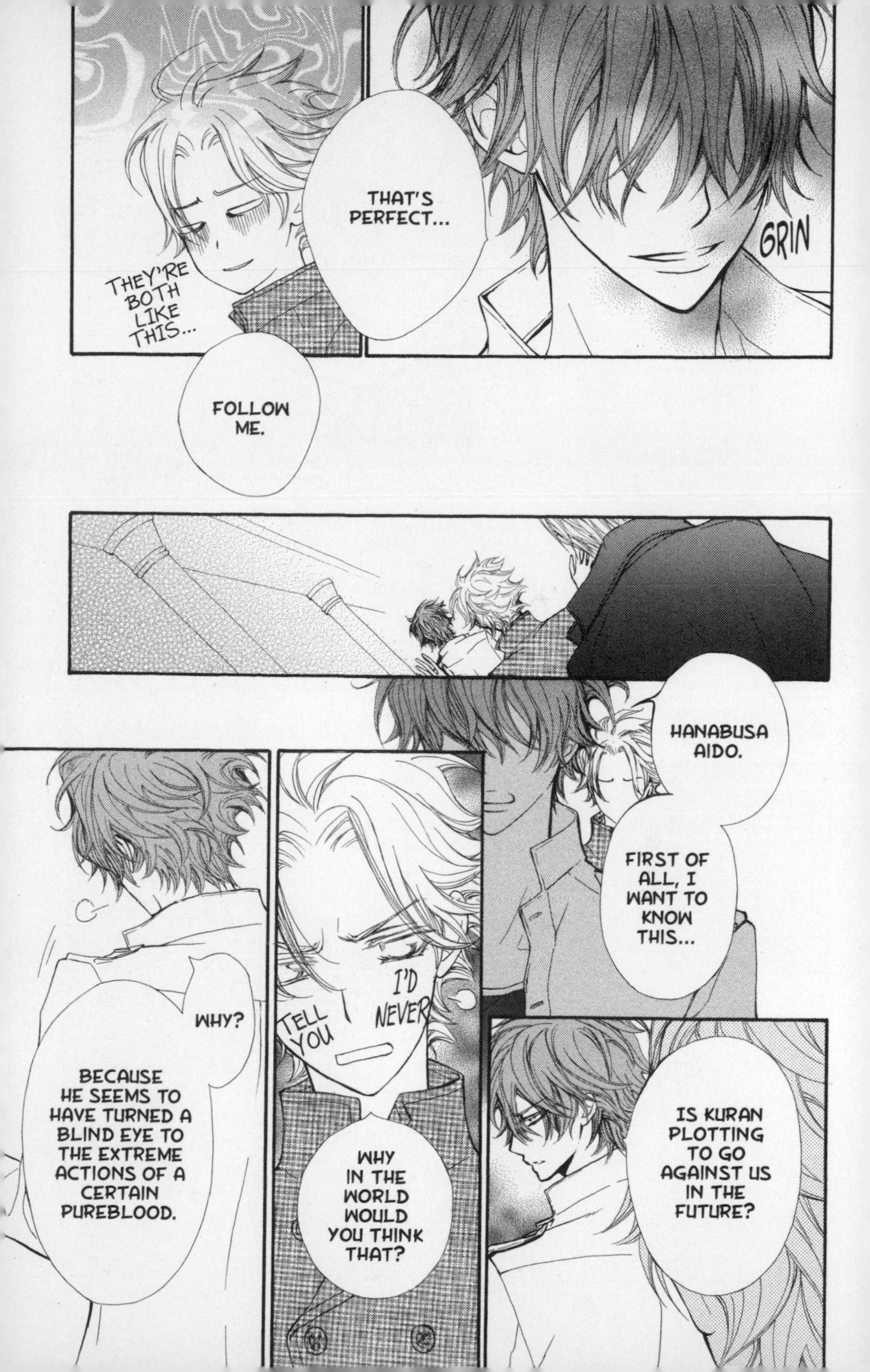
GRIN
THAT'S PERFECT...
THEY'RE BOTH LIKE THIS...
FOLLOW ME.
HANABUSA AIDO.
FIRST OF ALL, I WANT TO KNOW THIS...
IS KURAN PLOTTING TO GO AGAINST US IN THE FUTURE?
I'D NEVER TELL YOU
WHY IN THE WORLD WOULD YOU THINK THAT?
WHY?
BECAUSE HE SEEMS TO HAVE TURNED A BLIND EYE TO THE EXTREME ACTIONS OF A CERTAIN PUREBLOOD.

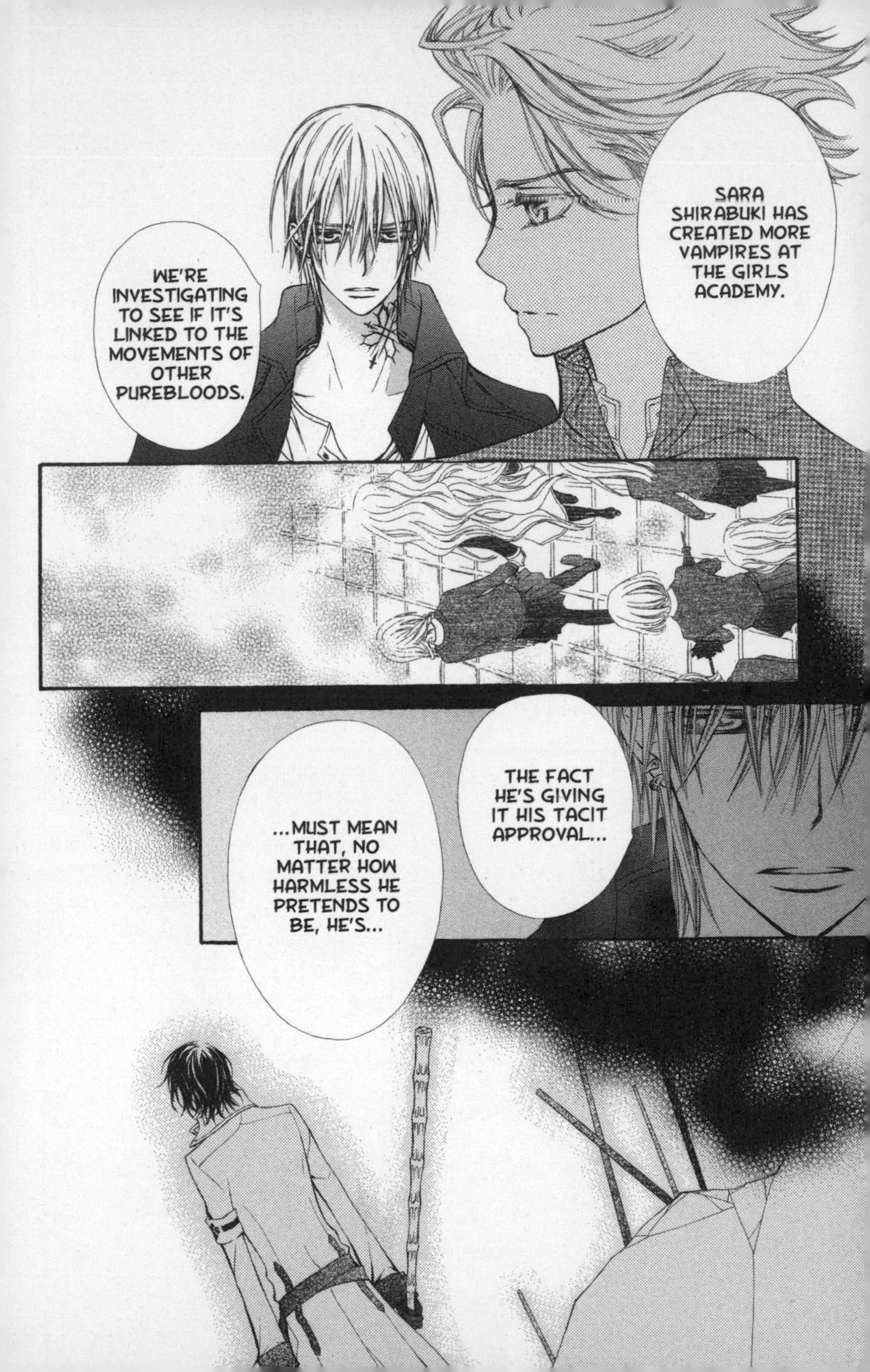
SARA SHIRABUKI HAS CREATED MORE VAMPIRES AT THE GIRLS ACADEMY.
WE'RE INVESTIGATING TO SEE IF IT'S LINKED TO THE MOVEMENTS OF OTHER PUREBLOODS.
THE FACT HE'S GIVING IT HIS TACIT APPROVAL...
...MUST MEAN THAT, NO MATTER HOW HARMLESS HE PRETENDS TO BE, HE'S...

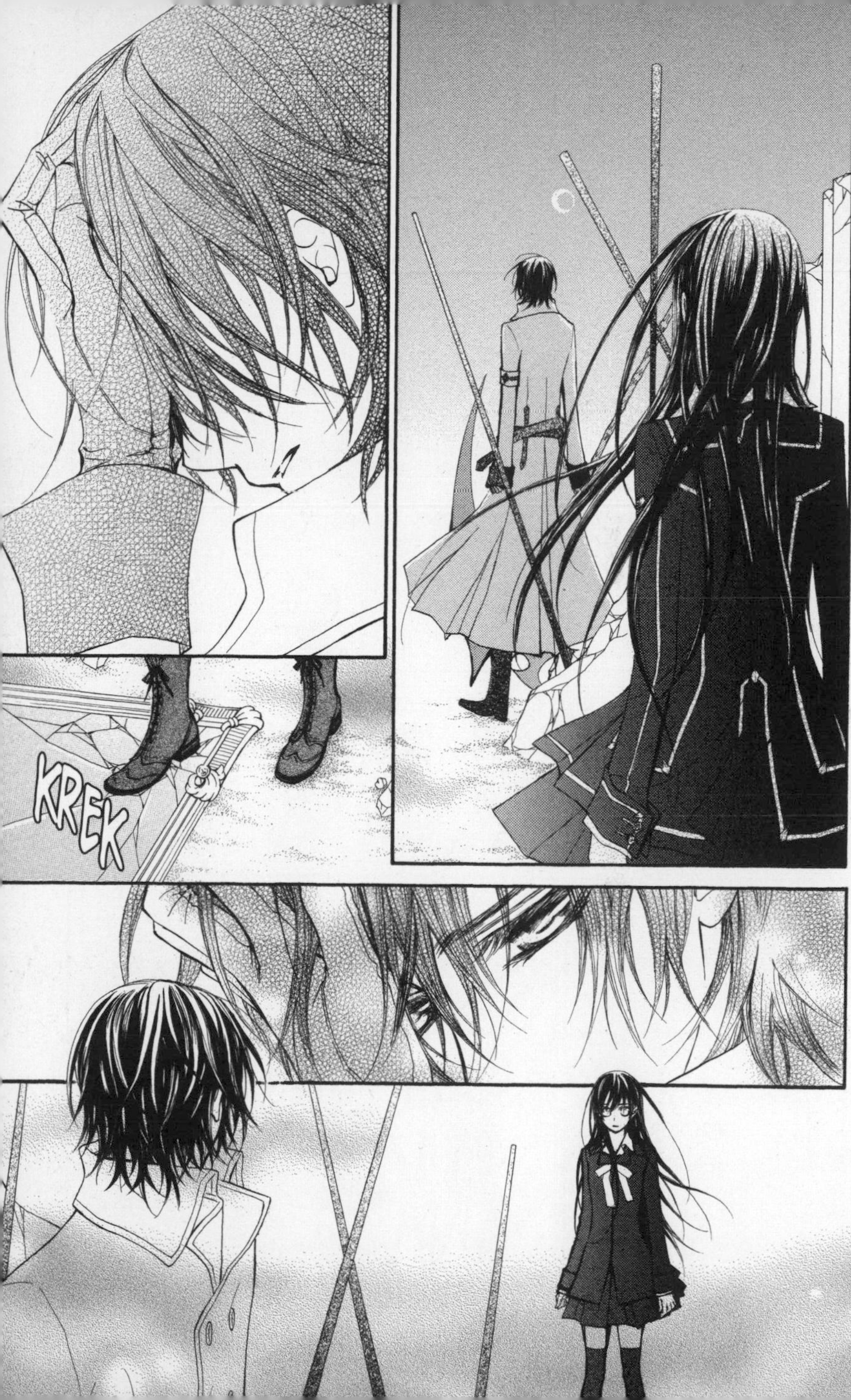
KREK

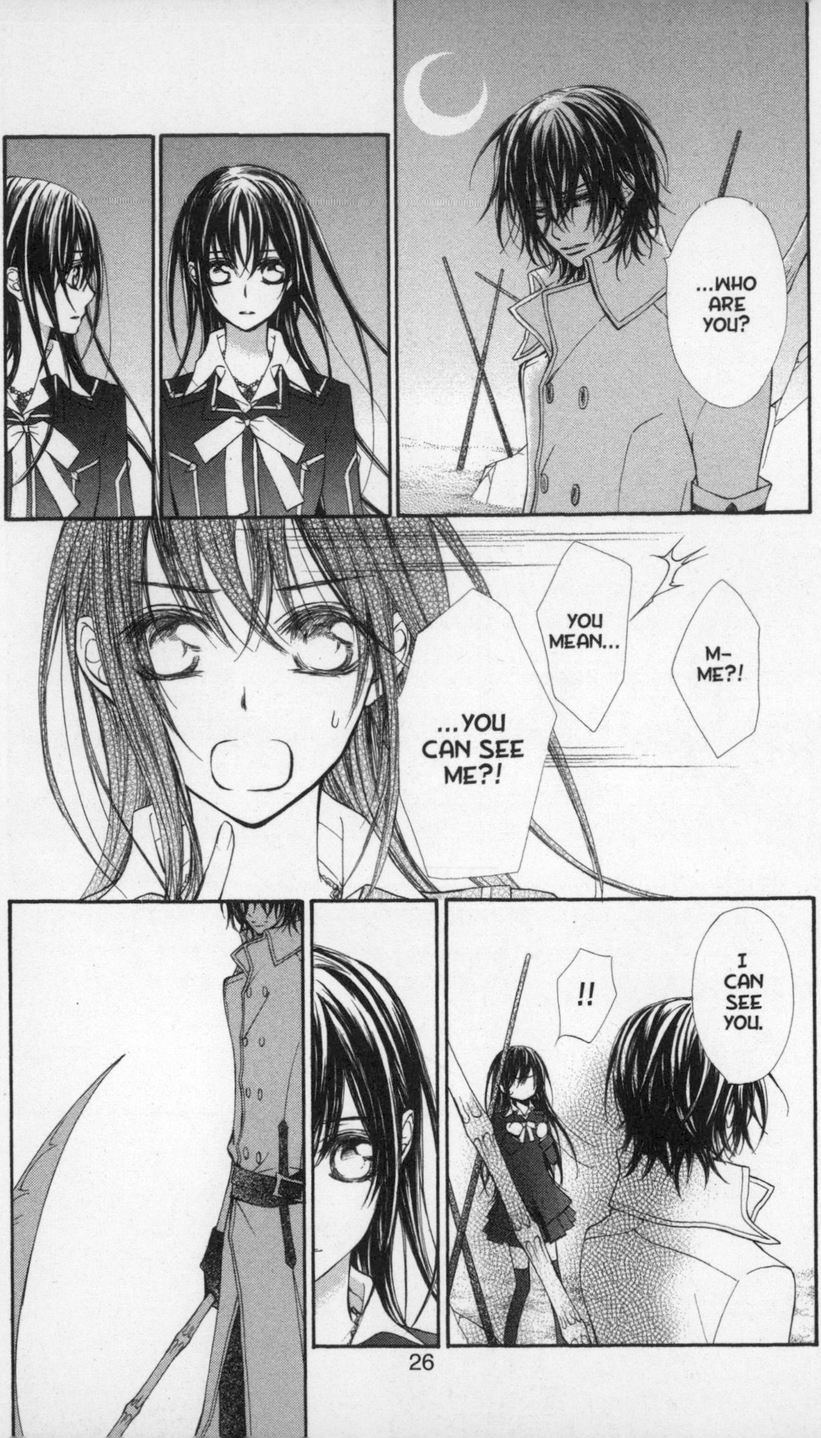
...WHO ARE YOU?
M- ME?!
YOU MEAN...
...YOU CAN SEE ME?!
I CAN SEE YOU.
!!

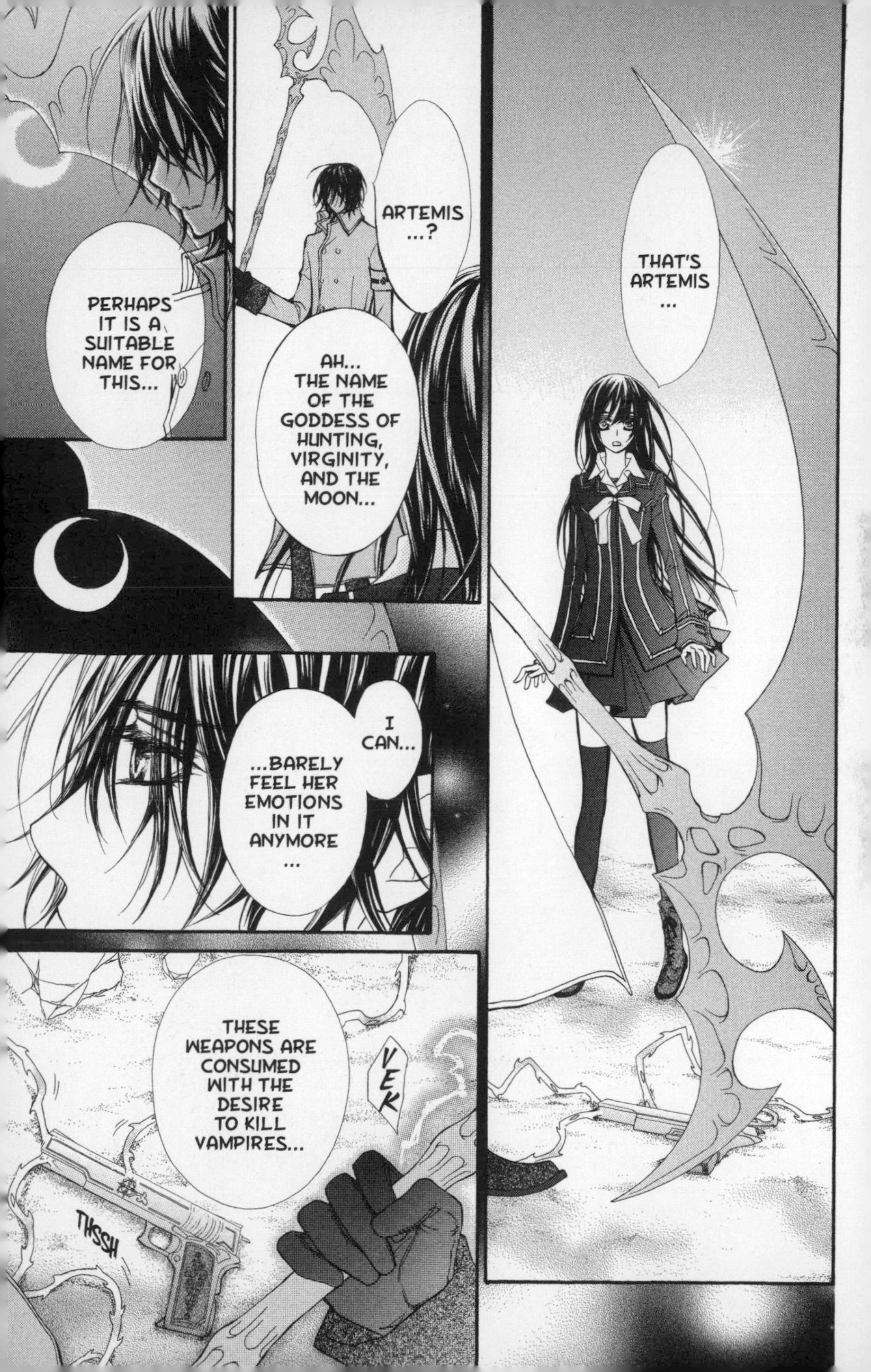
THAT'S ARTEMIS ...
ARTEMIS ...?
AH... THE NAME OF THE GODDESS OF HUNTING, VIRGINITY, AND THE MOON...
PERHAPS IT IS A SUITABLE NAME FOR THIS...
I CAN...
...BARELY FEEL HER EMOTIONS IN IT ANYMORE ...
THESE WEAPONS ARE CONSUMED WITH THE DESIRE TO KILL VAMPIRES...
VEK
THSSH

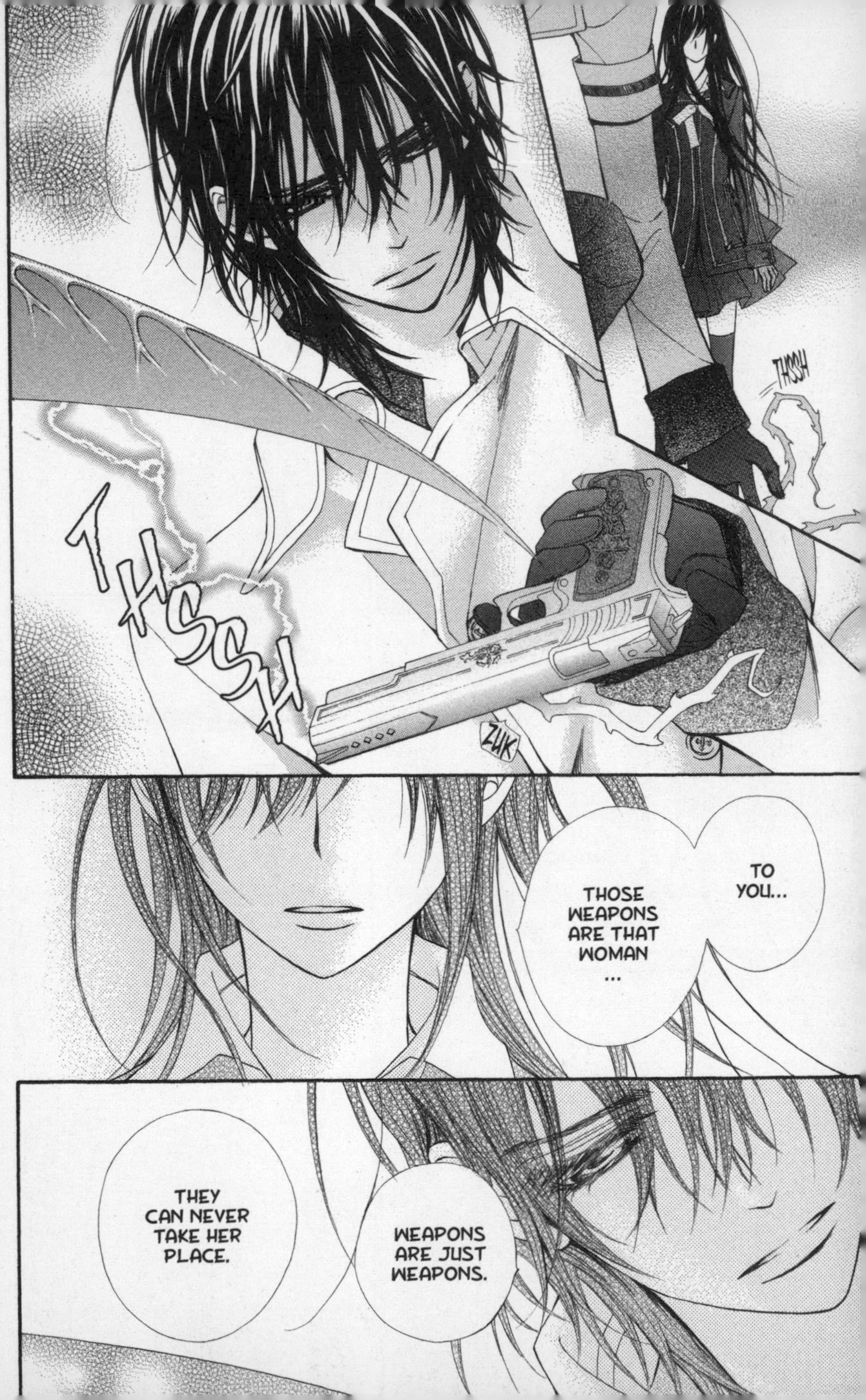
THSSH
THSSH
ZUK
TO YOU...
THOSE WEAPONS ARE THAT WOMAN ...
WEAPONS ARE JUST WEAPONS.
THEY CAN NEVER TAKE HER PLACE.

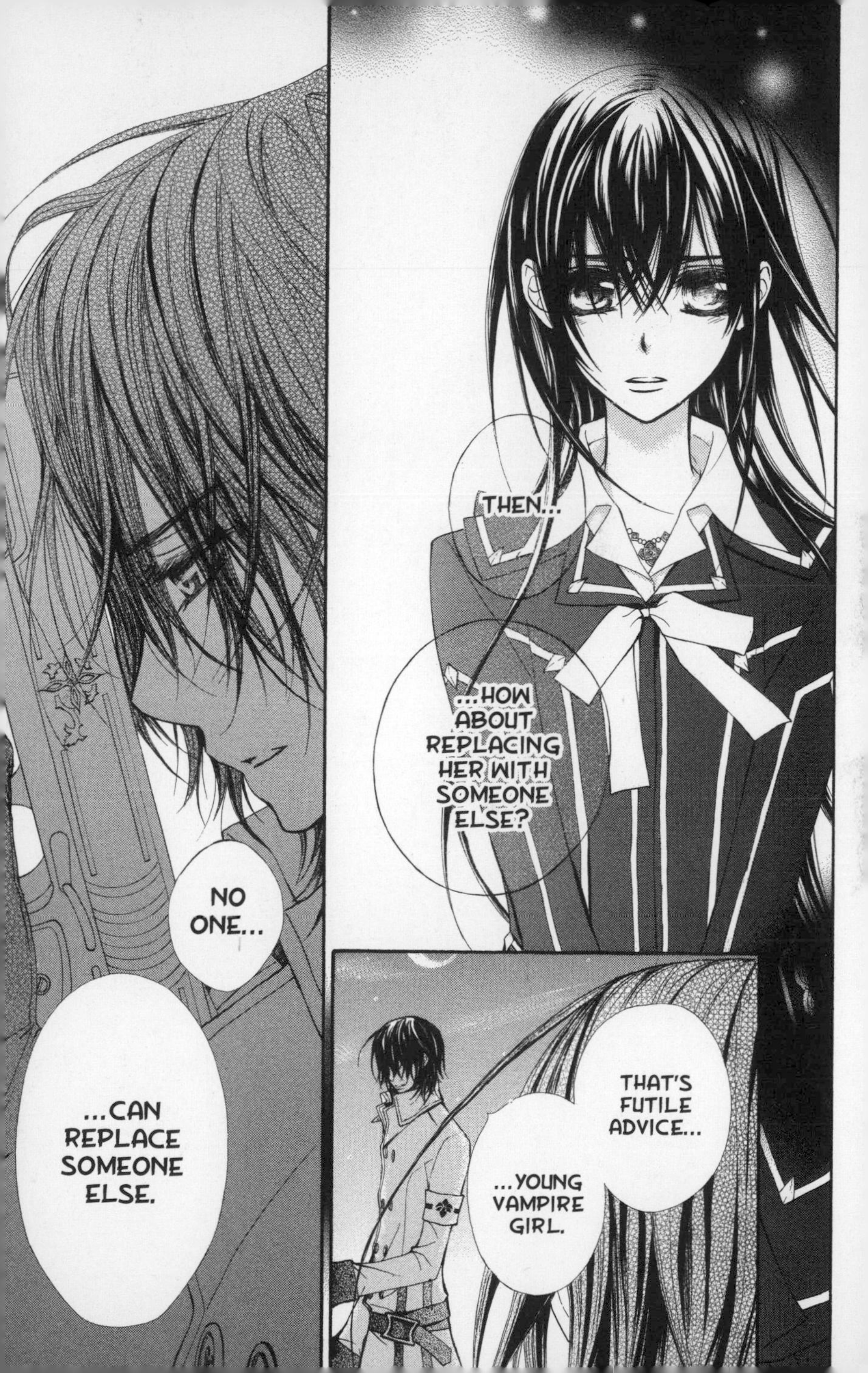
THEN...
...HOW ABOUT REPLACING HER WITH SOMEONE ELSE?
THAT'S FUTILE ADVICE...
...YOUNG VAMPIRE GIRL.
NO ONE...
...CAN REPLACE SOMEONE ELSE.

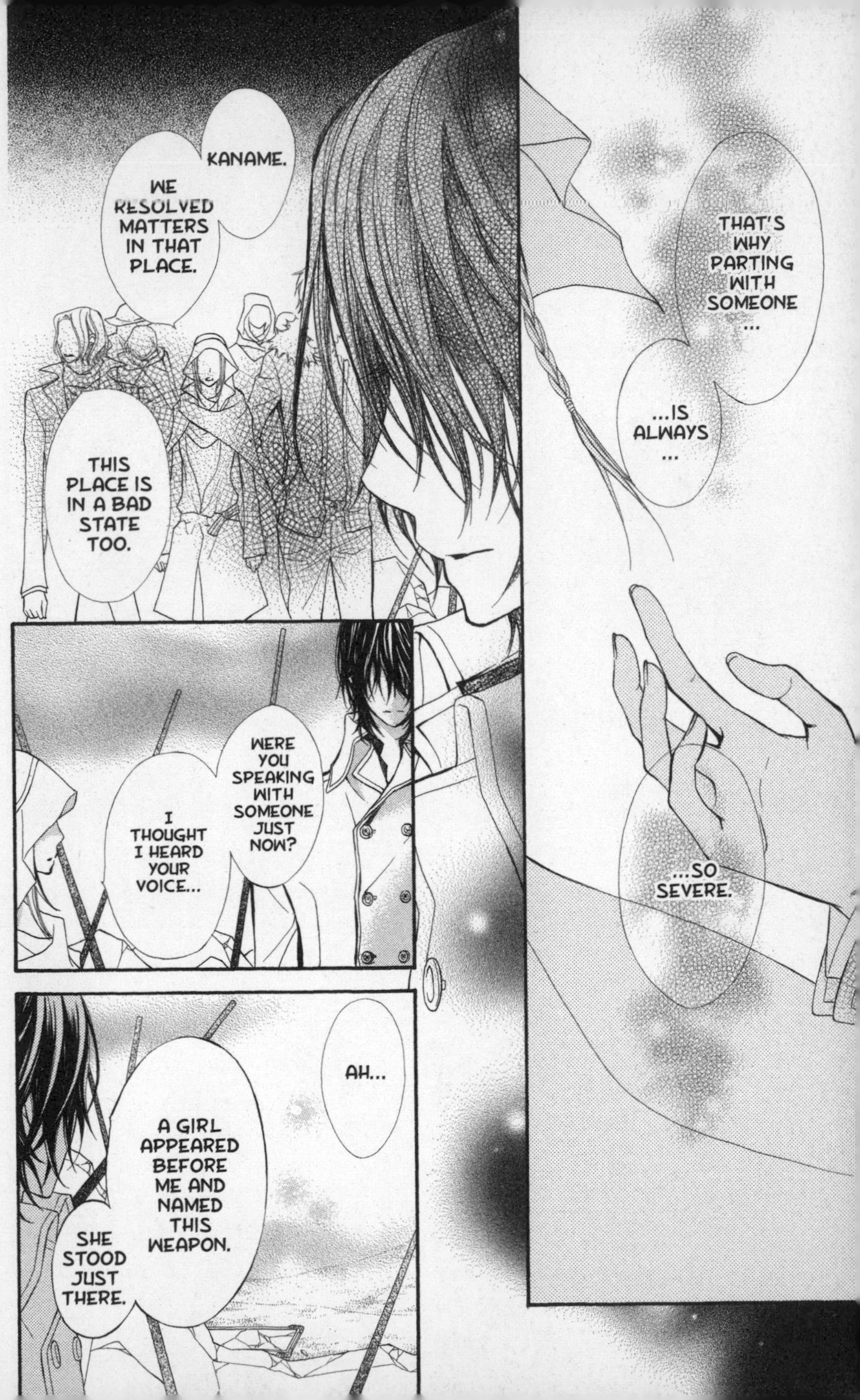
THAT'S WHY PARTING WITH SOMEONE...
...IS ALWAYS...
...SO SEVERE.
KANAME.
WE RESOLVED MATTERS IN THAT PLACE.
THIS PLACE IS IN A BAD STATE TOO.
WERE YOU SPEAKING WITH SOMEONE JUST NOW?
I THOUGHT I HEARD YOUR VOICE...
AH...
A GIRL APPEARED BEFORE ME AND NAMED THIS WEAPON.
SHE STOOD JUST THERE.

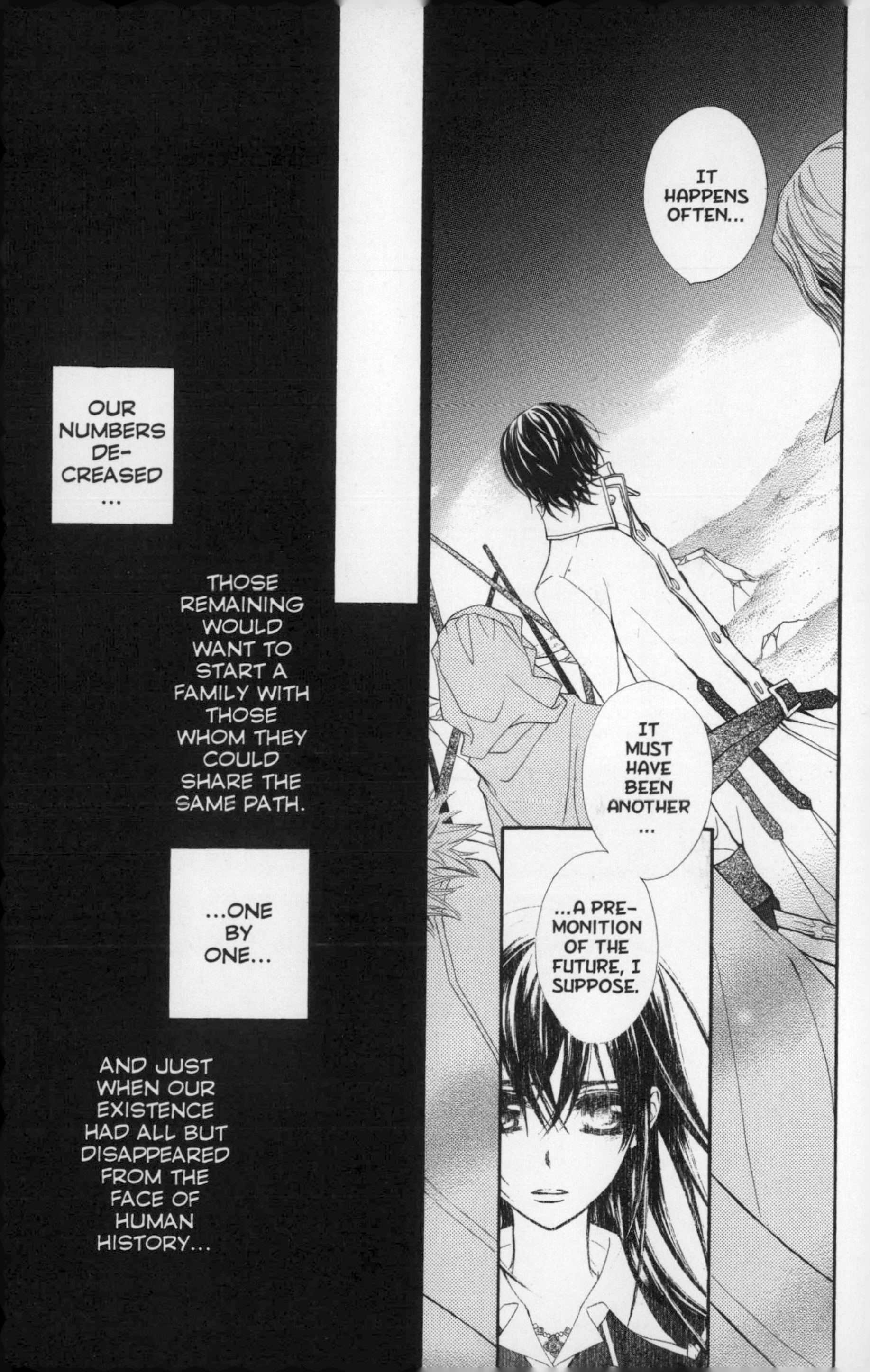
IT HAPPENS OFTEN...
IT MUST HAVE BEEN ANOTHER...
...A PRE-MONITION OF THE FUTURE, I SUPPOSE.
OUR NUMBERS DE-CREASED...
THOSE REMAINING WOULD WANT TO START A FAMILY WITH THOSE WHOM THEY COULD SHARE THE SAME PATH.
...ONE BY ONE...
AND JUST WHEN OUR EXISTENCE HAD ALL BUT DISAPPEARED FROM THE FACE OF HUMAN HISTORY...

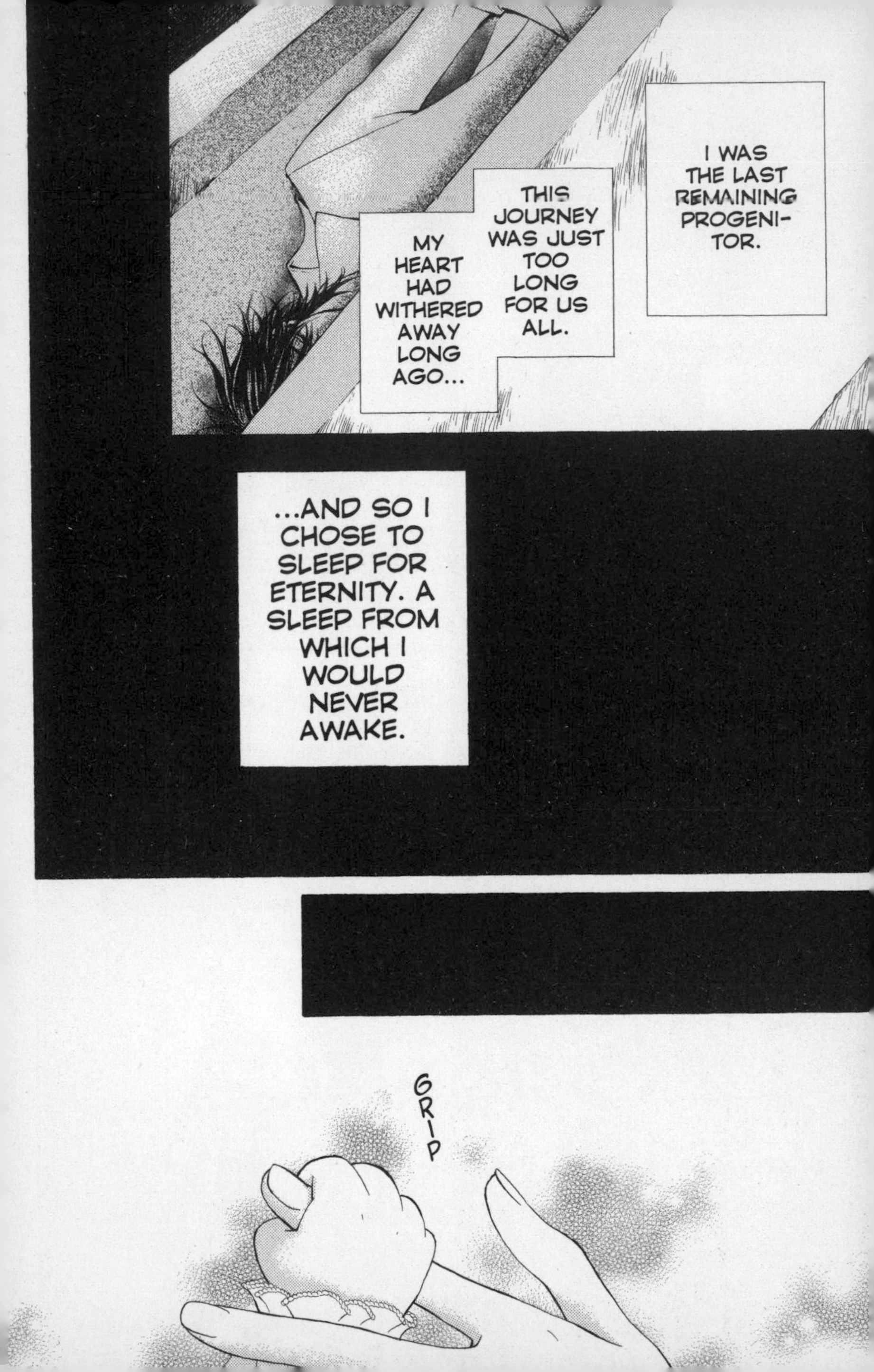
I WAS THE LAST REMAINING PROGENITOR.
THIS JOURNEY WAS JUST TOO LONG FOR US ALL.
MY HEART HAD WITHERED AWAY LONG AGO...
...AND SO I CHOSE TO SLEEP FOR ETERNITY. A SLEEP FROM WHICH I WOULD NEVER AWAKE.
GRIP

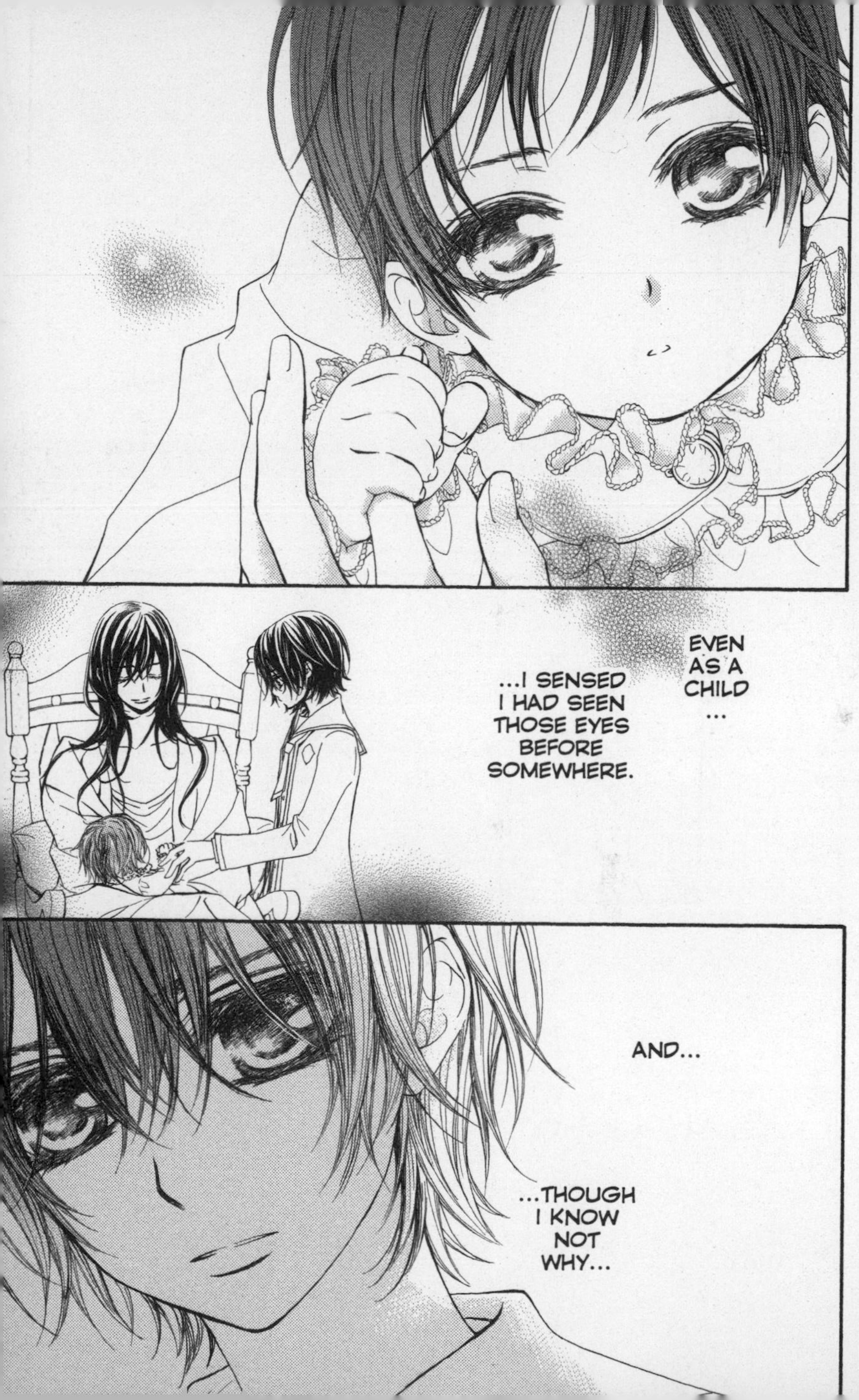
EVEN AS A CHILD...
...I SENSED I HAD SEEN THOSE EYES BEFORE SOMEWHERE.
AND...
...THOUGH I KNOW NOT WHY...

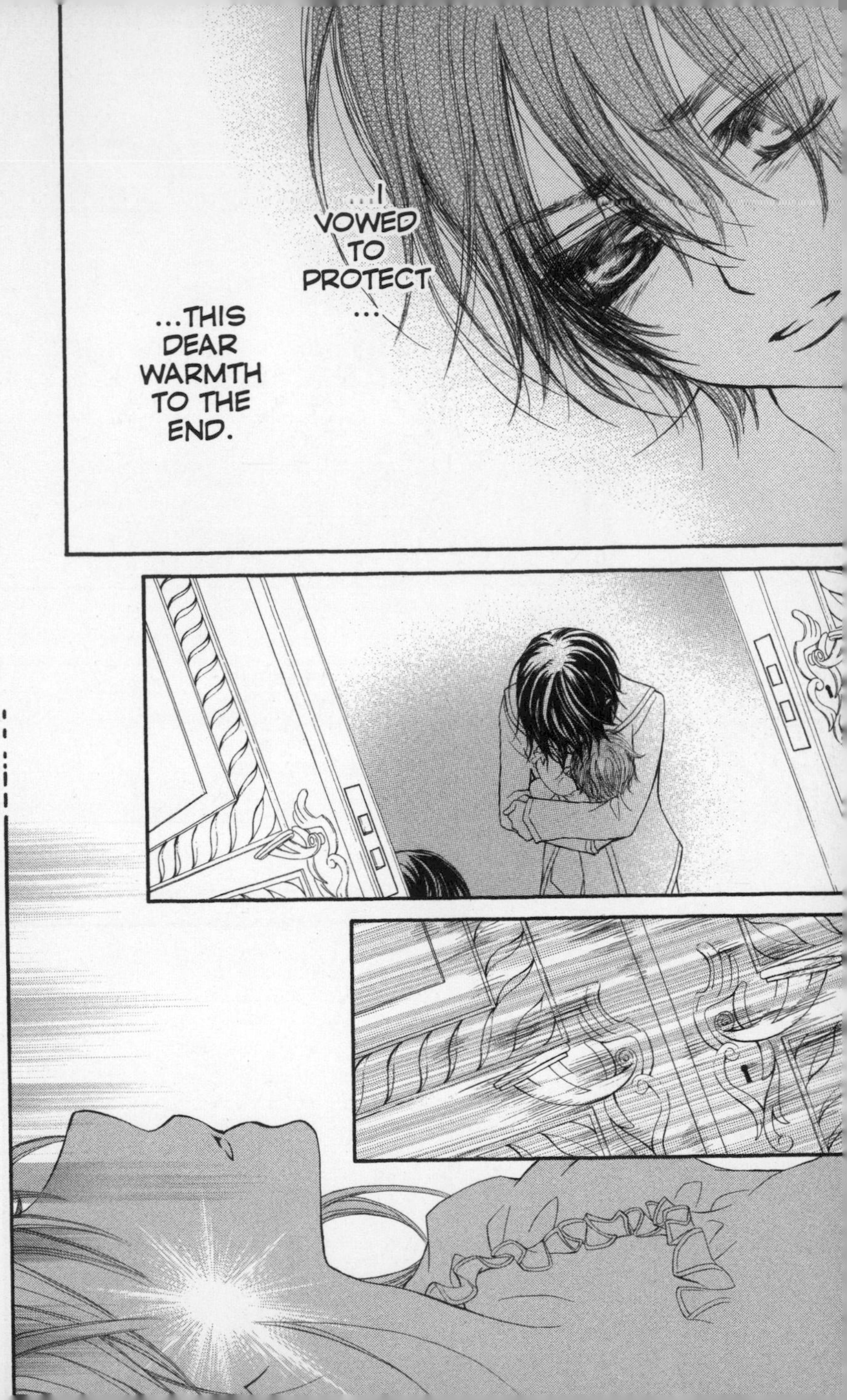
...I VOWED TO PROTECT ...
...THIS DEAR WARMTH TO THE END.

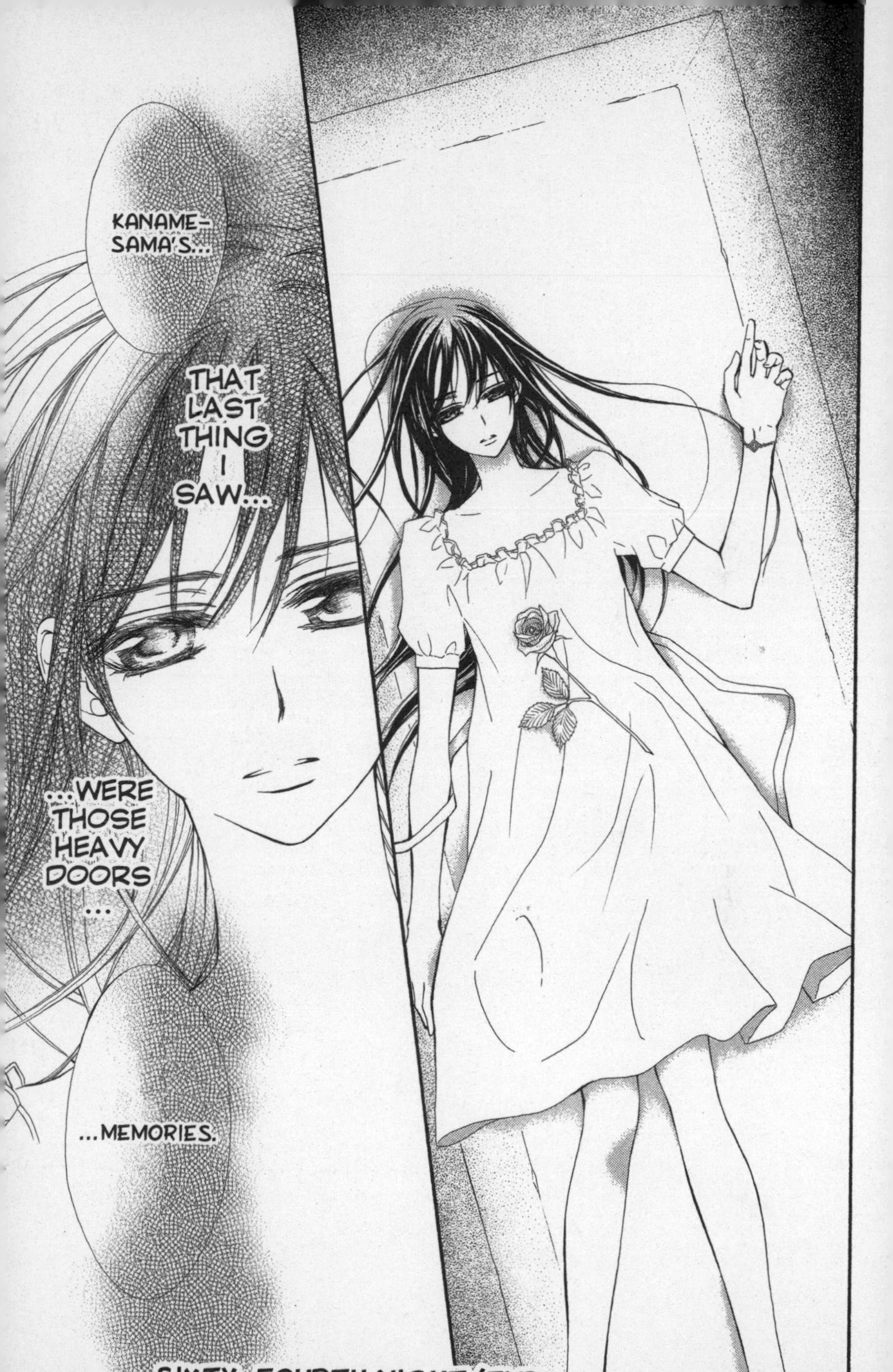
KANAME-SAMA'S...
THAT LAST THING I SAW...
...WERE THOSE HEAVY DOORS...
...MEMORIES.

SIXTY-FOURTH NIGHT/END

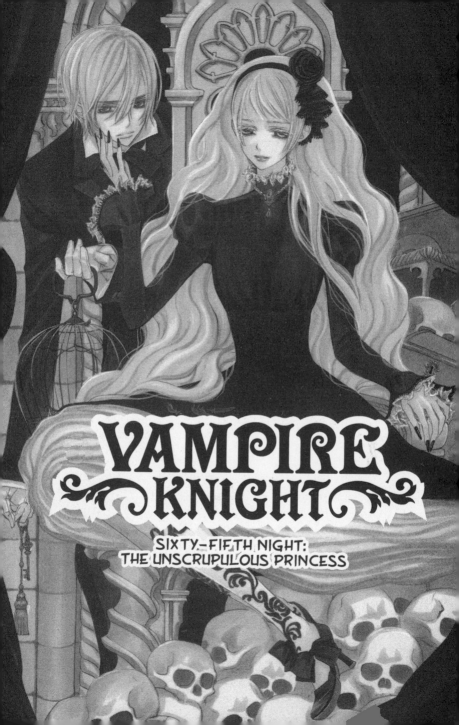

VAMPIRE KNIGHT

SIXTY-FIFTH NIGHT:
THE UNSCRUPULOUS PRINCESS

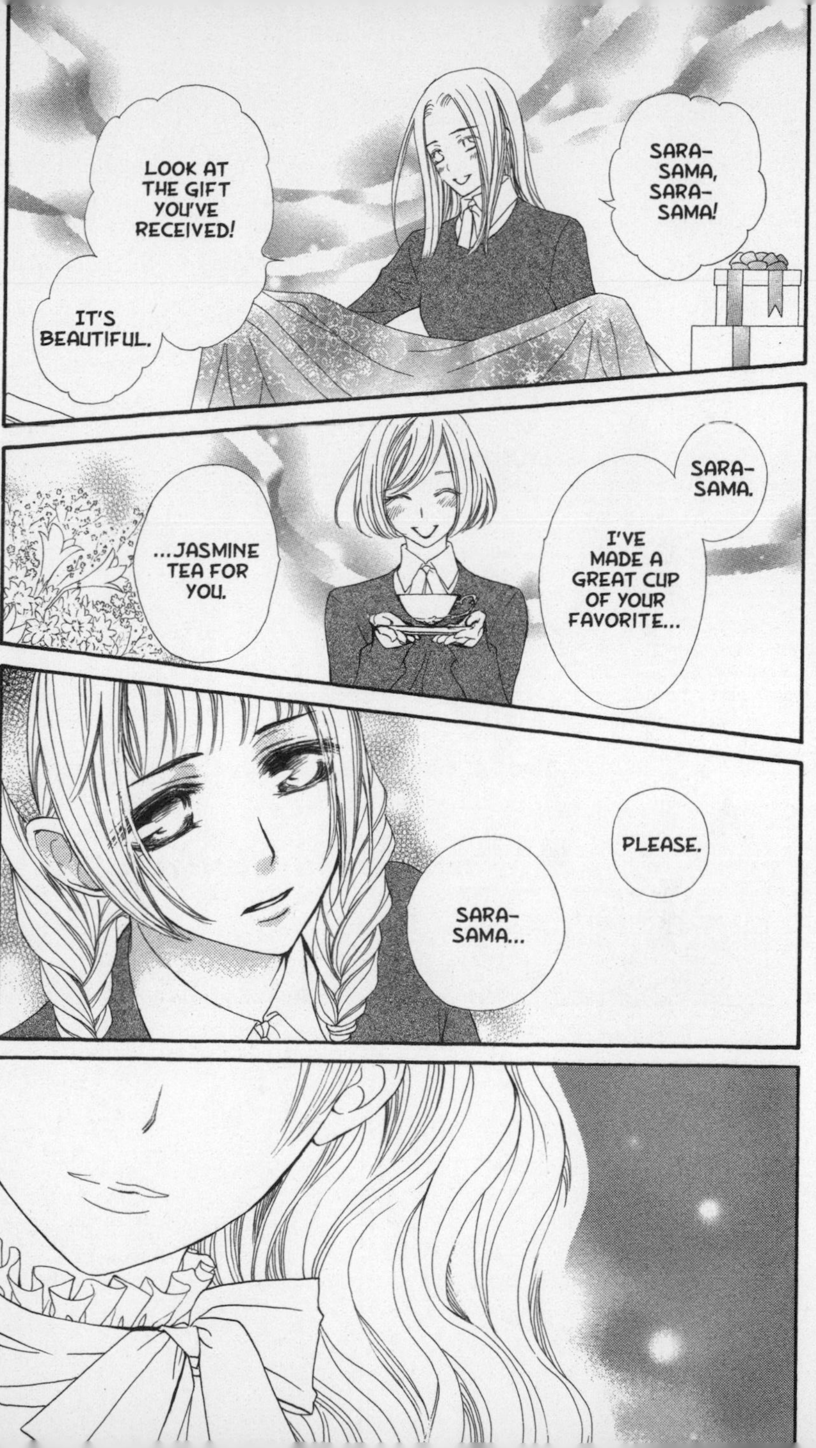
SARA-SAMA, SARA-SAMA!
LOOK AT THE GIFT YOU'VE RECEIVED!
IT'S BEAUTIFUL.
SARA-SAMA.
I'VE MADE A GREAT CUP OF YOUR FAVORITE...
...JASMINE TEA FOR YOU.
PLEASE.
SARA-SAMA...

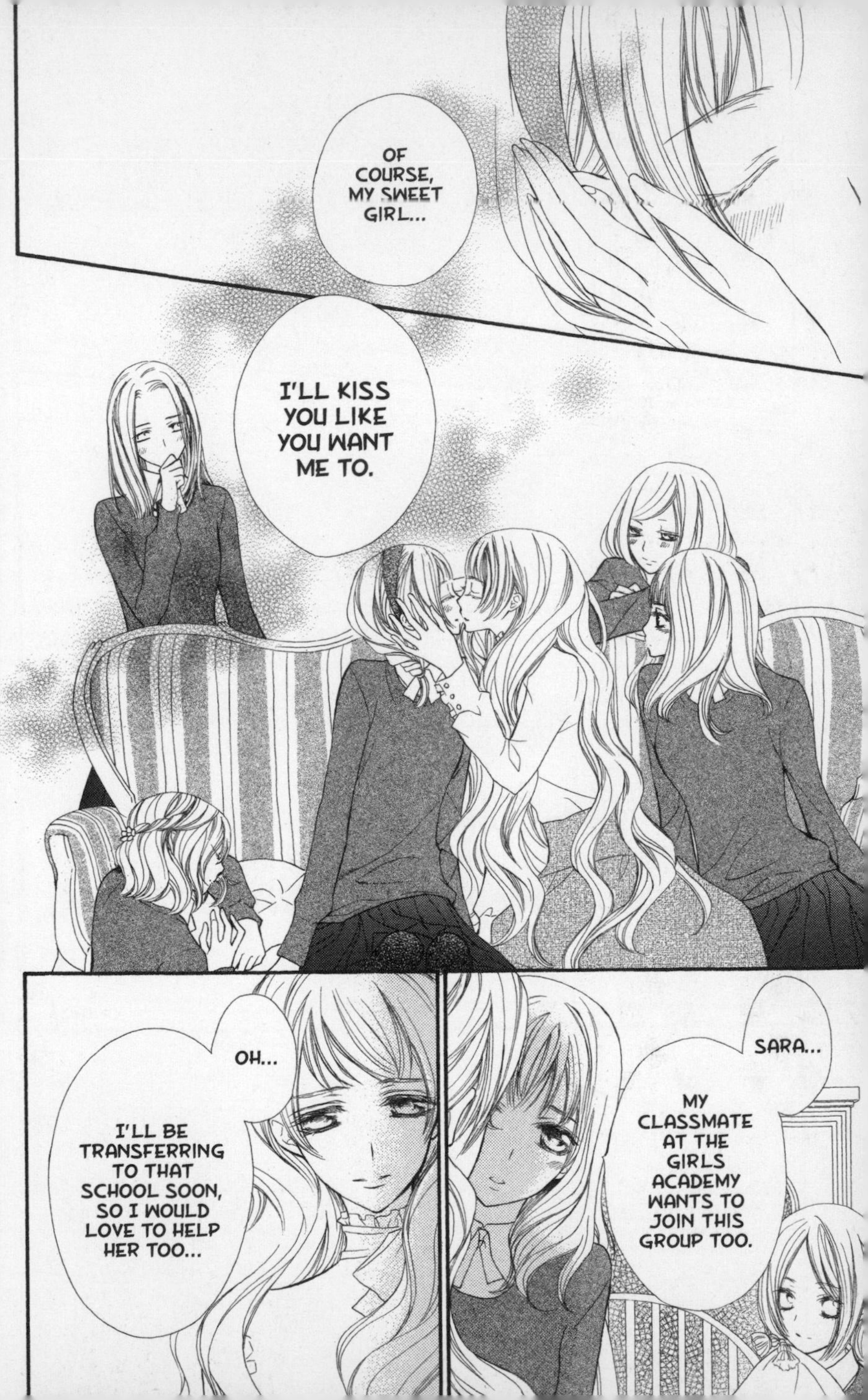
OF COURSE, MY SWEET GIRL...
I'LL KISS YOU LIKE YOU WANT ME TO.
SARA...
MY CLASSMATE AT THE GIRLS ACADEMY WANTS TO JOIN THIS GROUP TOO.
OH...
I'LL BE TRANSFERRING TO THAT SCHOOL SOON, SO I WOULD LOVE TO HELP HER TOO...

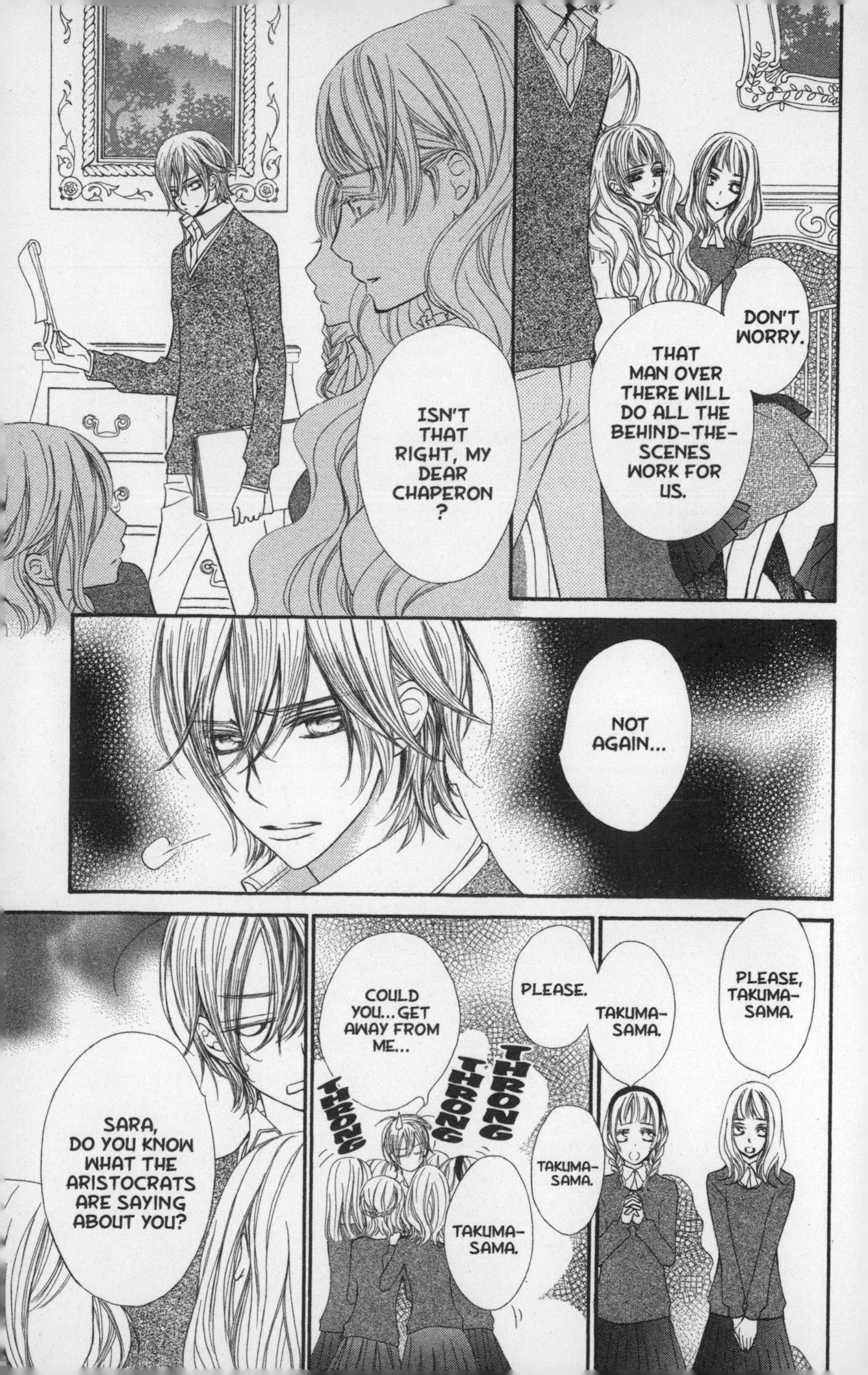

DON'T WORRY.
THAT MAN OVER THERE WILL DO ALL THE BEHIND-THE-SCENES WORK FOR US.
ISN'T THAT RIGHT, MY DEAR CHAPERON?
NOT AGAIN...
PLEASE, TAKUMA-SAMA.
TAKUMA-SAMA.
PLEASE.
TAKUMA-SAMA.
TAKUMA-SAMA.
THRONG
THRONG
COULD YOU...GET AWAY FROM ME...
THRONG
SARA, DO YOU KNOW WHAT THE ARISTOCRATS ARE SAYING ABOUT YOU?

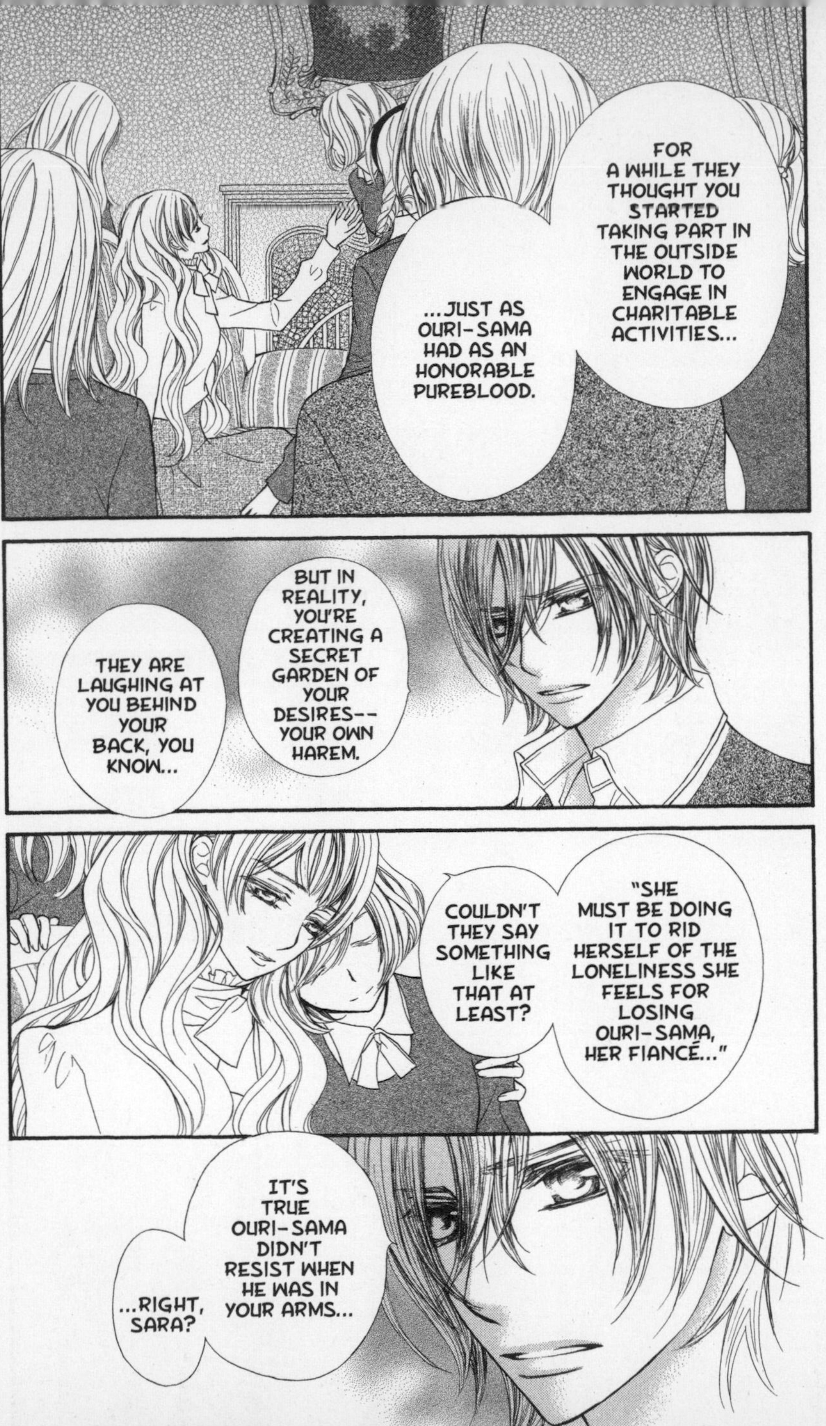
FOR A WHILE THEY THOUGHT YOU STARTED TAKING PART IN THE OUTSIDE WORLD TO ENGAGE IN CHARITABLE ACTIVITIES...
...JUST AS OURI-SAMA HAD AS AN HONORABLE PUREBLOOD.
BUT IN REALITY, YOU'RE CREATING A SECRET GARDEN OF YOUR DESIRES--YOUR OWN HAREM.
THEY ARE LAUGHING AT YOU BEHIND YOUR BACK, YOU KNOW...
"SHE MUST BE DOING IT TO RID HERSELF OF THE LONELINESS SHE FEELS FOR LOSING OURI-SAMA, HER FIANCÉ..."
COULDN'T THEY SAY SOMETHING LIKE THAT AT LEAST?
IT'S TRUE OURI-SAMA DIDN'T RESIST WHEN HE WAS IN YOUR ARMS...
...RIGHT, SARA?

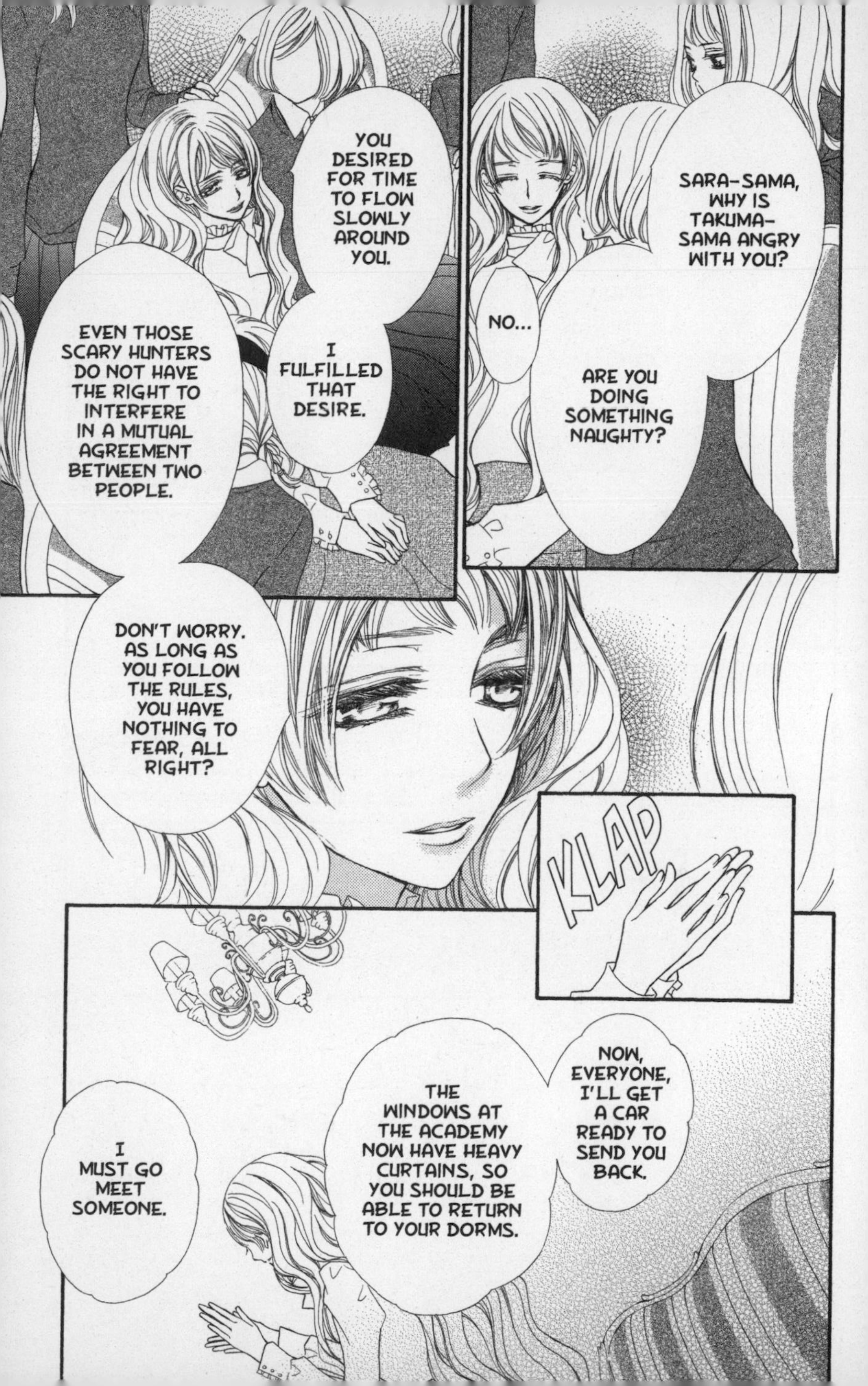
SARA-SAMA, WHY IS TAKUMA-SAMA ANGRY WITH YOU?
ARE YOU DOING SOMETHING NAUGHTY?
NO...
YOU DESIRED FOR TIME TO FLOW SLOWLY AROUND YOU.
I FULFILLED THAT DESIRE.
EVEN THOSE SCARY HUNTERS DO NOT HAVE THE RIGHT TO INTERFERE IN A MUTUAL AGREEMENT BETWEEN TWO PEOPLE.
DON'T WORRY. AS LONG AS YOU FOLLOW THE RULES, YOU HAVE NOTHING TO FEAR, ALL RIGHT?
KLAP
NOW, EVERYONE, I'LL GET A CAR READY TO SEND YOU BACK.
THE WINDOWS AT THE ACADEMY NOW HAVE HEAVY CURTAINS, SO YOU SHOULD BE ABLE TO RETURN TO YOUR DORMS.
I MUST GO MEET SOMEONE.

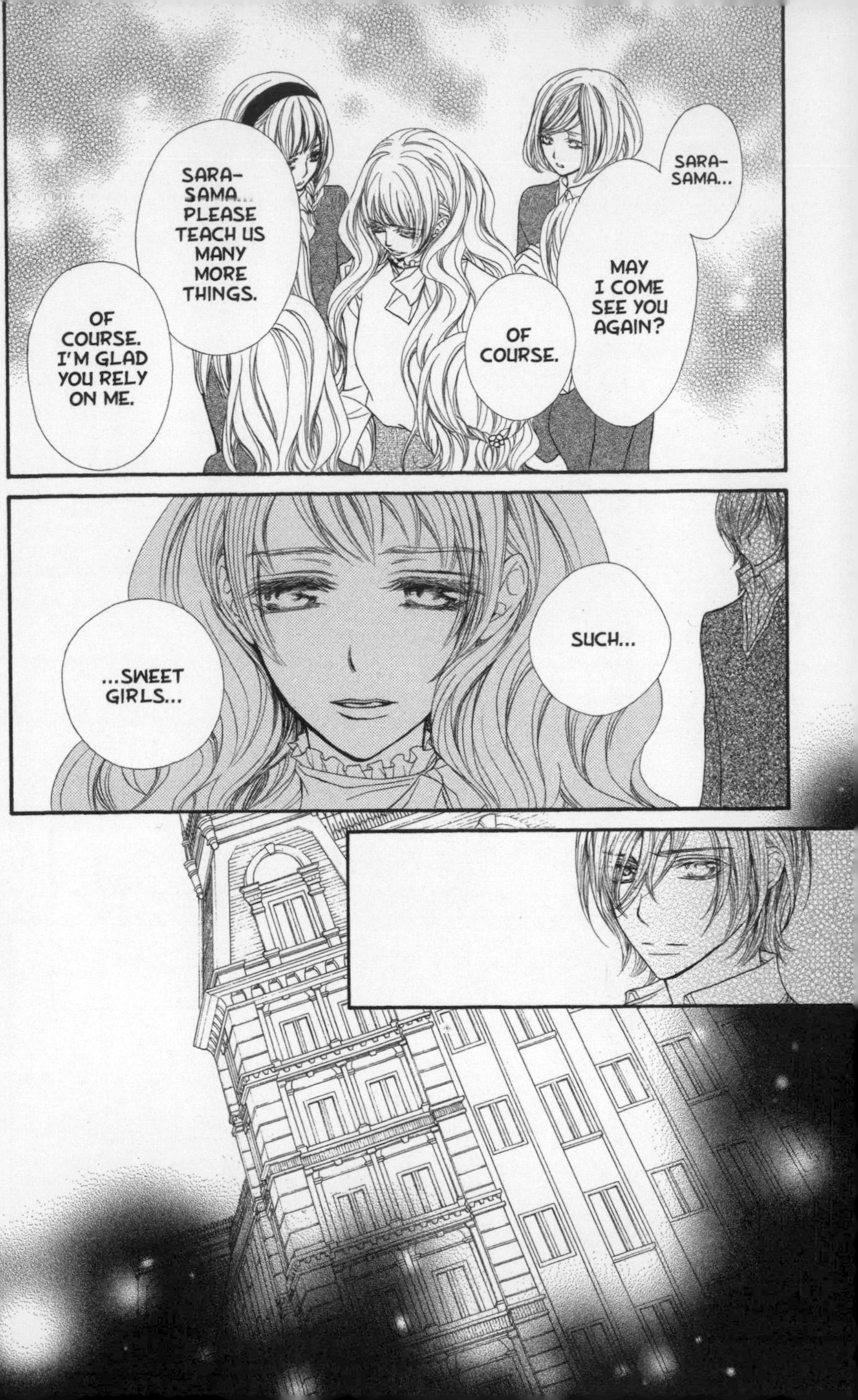
SARA-SAMA...
MAY I COME SEE YOU AGAIN?
OF COURSE.
SARA-SAMA... PLEASE TEACH US MANY MORE THINGS.
OF COURSE. I'M GLAD YOU RELY ON ME.
SUCH...
...SWEET GIRLS...

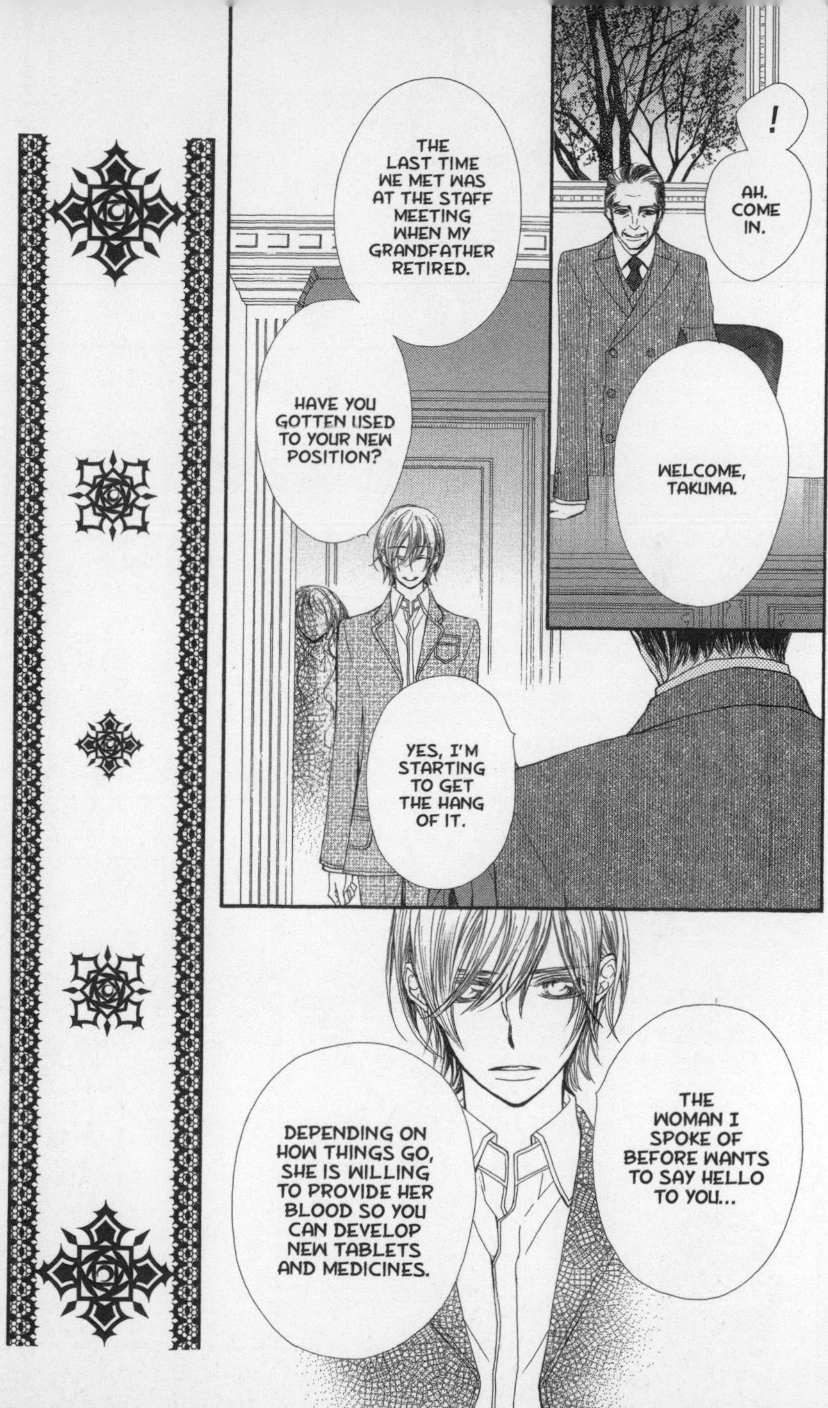
!
AH. COME IN.
WELCOME, TAKUMA.
THE LAST TIME WE MET WAS AT THE STAFF MEETING WHEN MY GRANDFATHER RETIRED.
HAVE YOU GOTTEN USED TO YOUR NEW POSITION?
YES, I'M STARTING TO GET THE HANG OF IT.
THE WOMAN I SPOKE OF BEFORE WANTS TO SAY HELLO TO YOU...
DEPENDING ON HOW THINGS GO, SHE IS WILLING TO PROVIDE HER BLOOD SO YOU CAN DEVELOP NEW TABLETS AND MEDICINES.

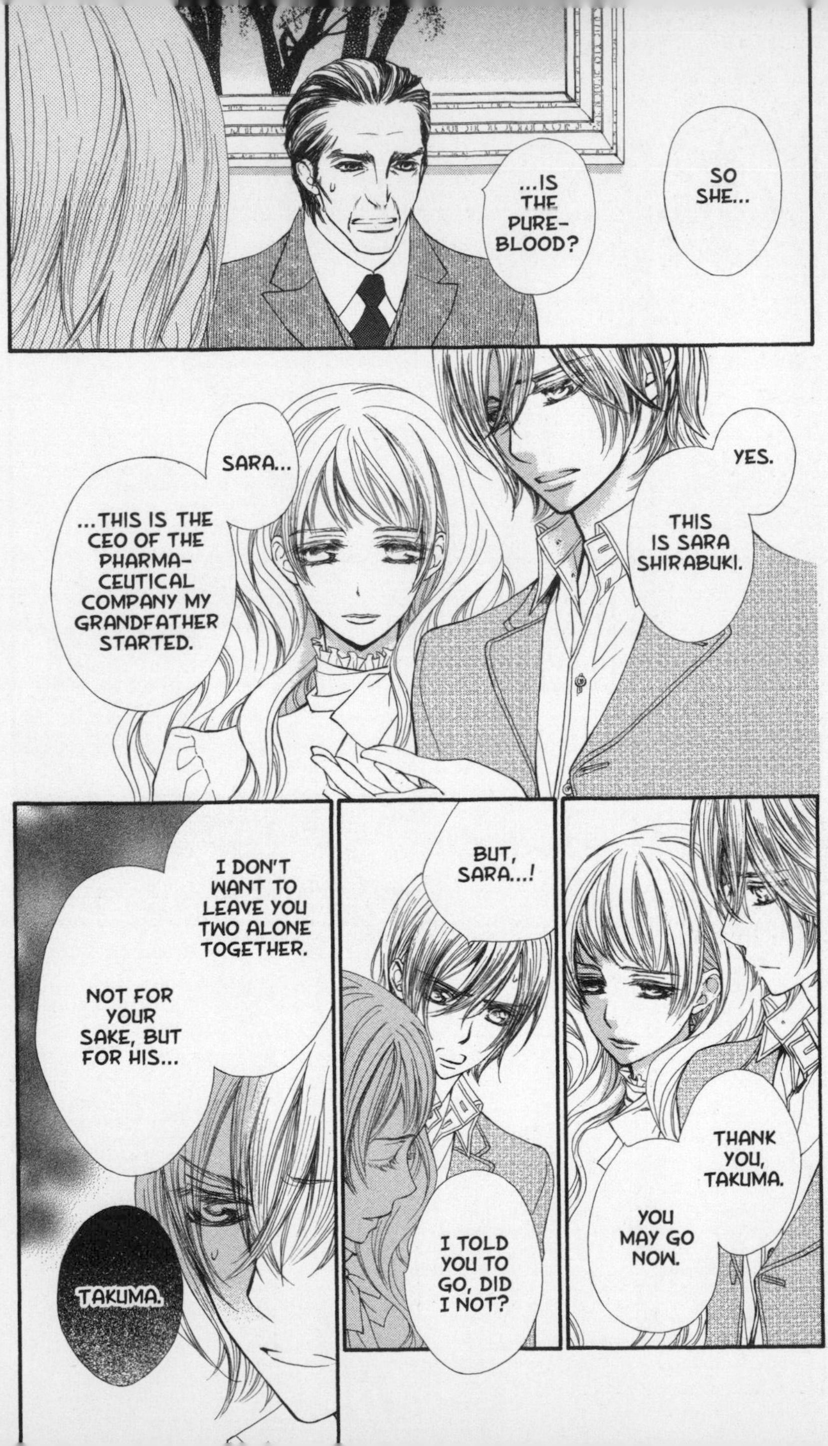
SO SHE...
...IS THE PURE-BLOOD?
YES.
THIS IS SARA SHIRABUKI.
SARA...
...THIS IS THE CEO OF THE PHARMA-CEUTICAL COMPANY MY GRANDFATHER STARTED.
THANK YOU, TAKUMA.
YOU MAY GO NOW.
BUT, SARA...!
I TOLD YOU TO GO, DID I NOT?
I DON'T WANT TO LEAVE YOU TWO ALONE TOGETHER.
NOT FOR YOUR SAKE, BUT FOR HIS...
TAKUMA.

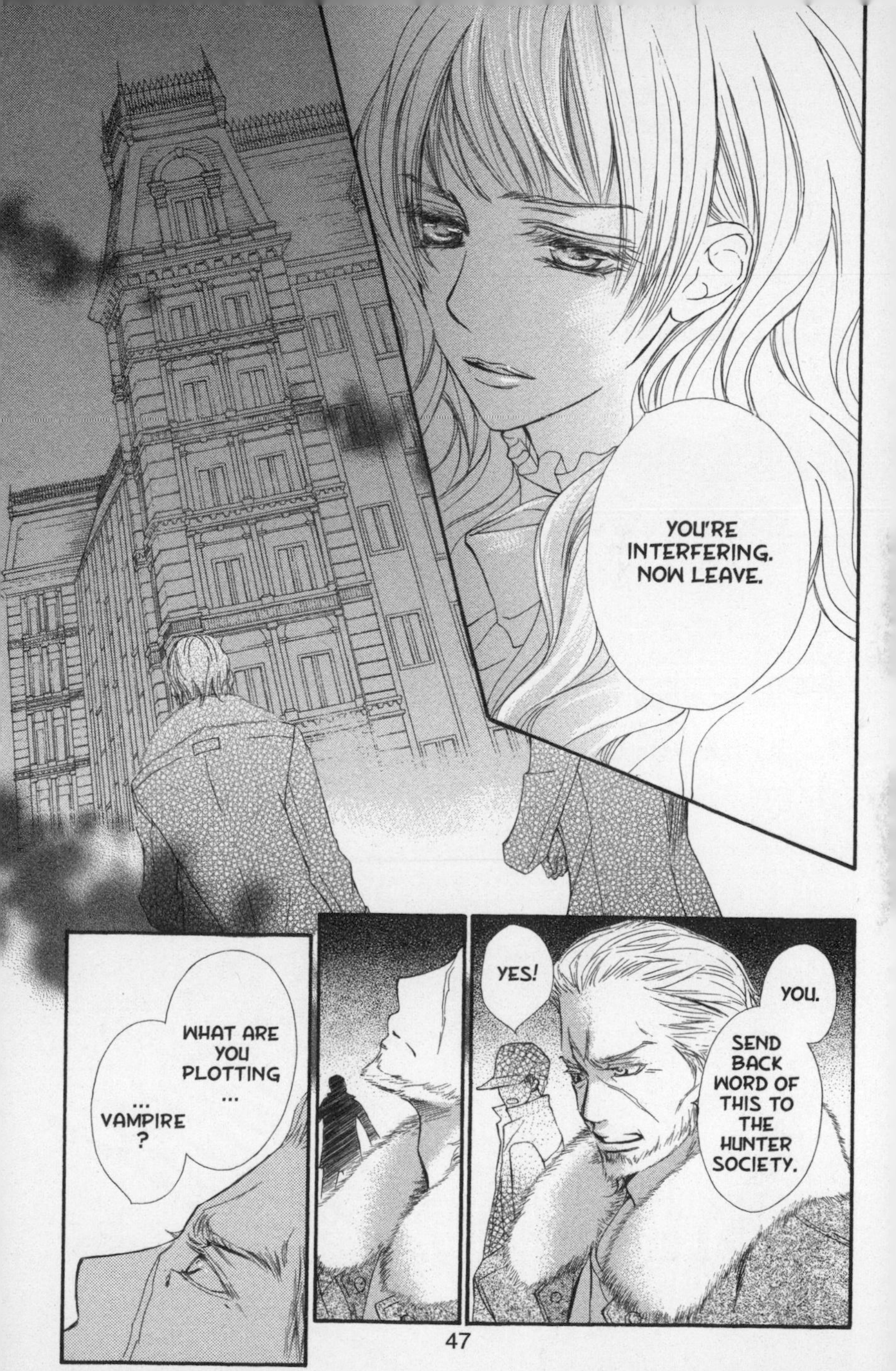
YOU'RE INTERFERING. NOW LEAVE.
YOU.
SEND BACK WORD OF THIS TO THE HUNTER SOCIETY.
YES!
WHAT ARE YOU PLOTTING ... ... VAMPIRE ?

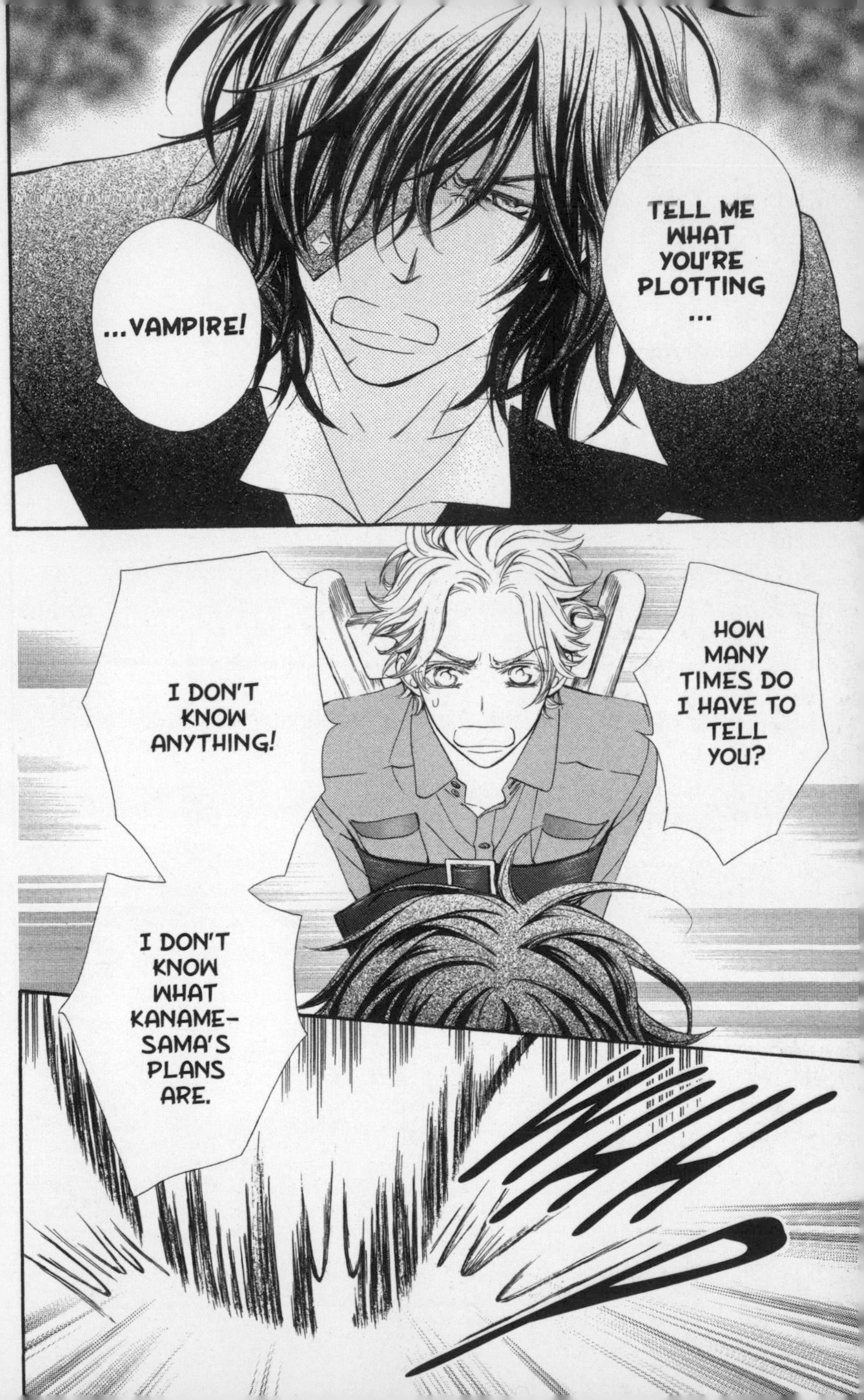
TELL ME WHAT YOU'RE PLOTTING ...
...VAMPIRE!
HOW MANY TIMES DO I HAVE TO TELL YOU?
I DON'T KNOW ANYTHING!
I DON'T KNOW WHAT KANAME-SAMA'S PLANS ARE.

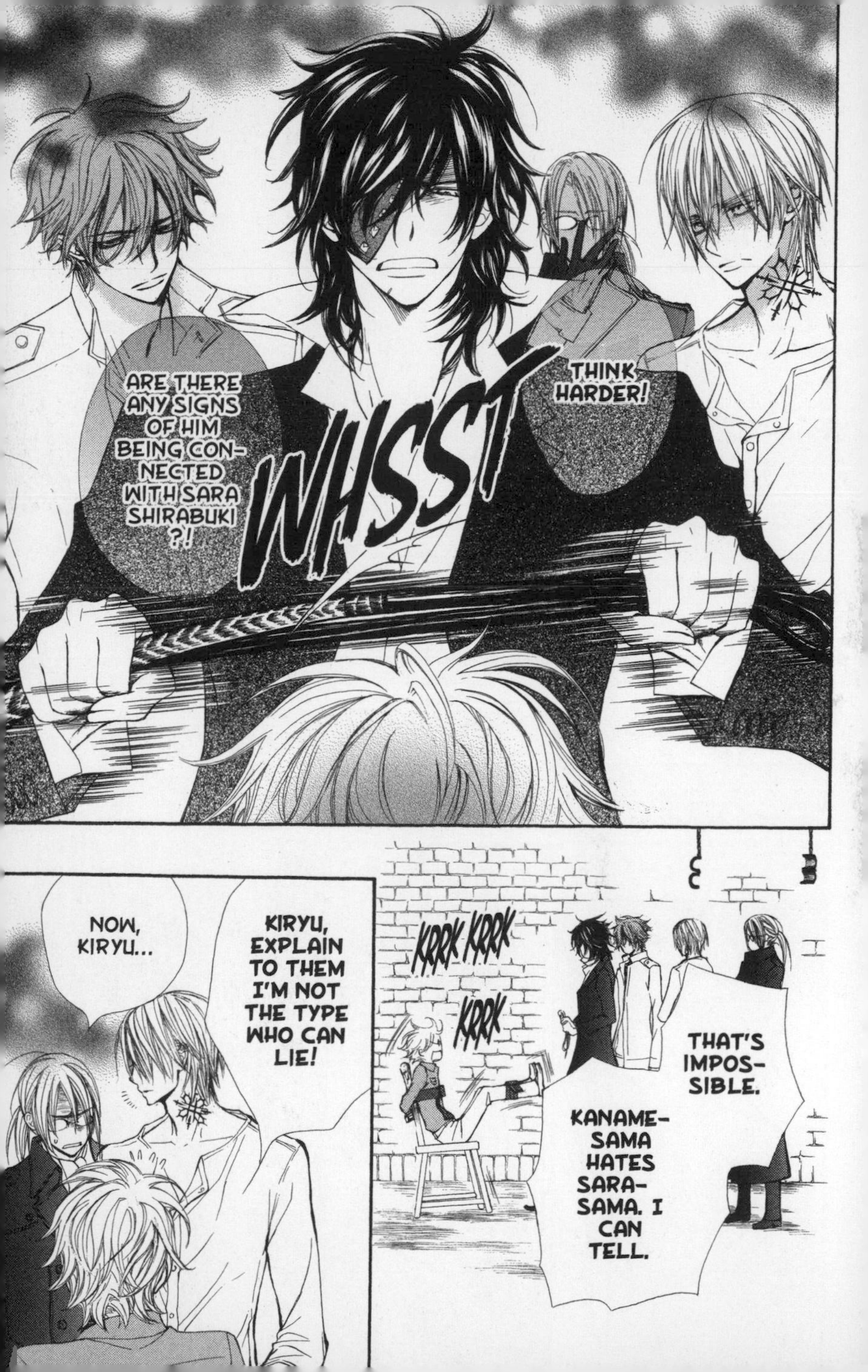
THINK HARDER!
WHSST
ARE THERE ANY SIGNS OF HIM BEING CON-NECTED WITH SARA SHIRABUKI ?!
KRRK KRRK
KRRK
THAT'S IMPOS-SIBLE.
KANAME-SAMA HATES SARA-SAMA. I CAN TELL.
KIRYU, EXPLAIN TO THEM I'M NOT THE TYPE WHO CAN LIE!
NOW, KIRYU...

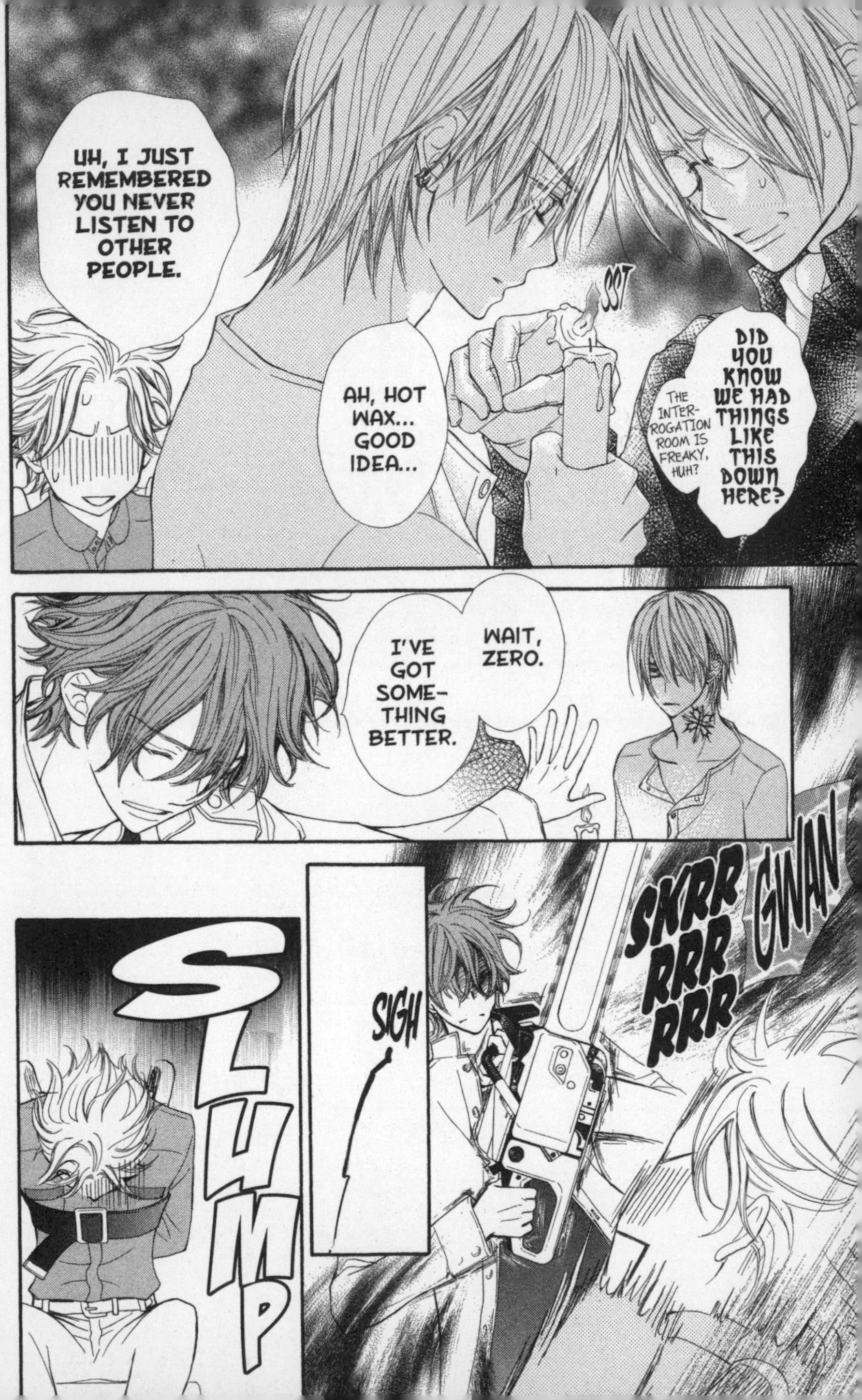
DID YOU KNOW WE HAD THINGS LIKE THIS DOWN HERE?
THE INTER-ROGATION ROOM IS FREAKY, HUH?
SST
AH, HOT WAX... GOOD IDEA...
UH, I JUST REMEMBERED YOU NEVER LISTEN TO OTHER PEOPLE.
WAIT, ZERO.
I'VE GOT SOME-THING BETTER.
GWAN
SKRR RRR RRR
SIGH
SLUMP

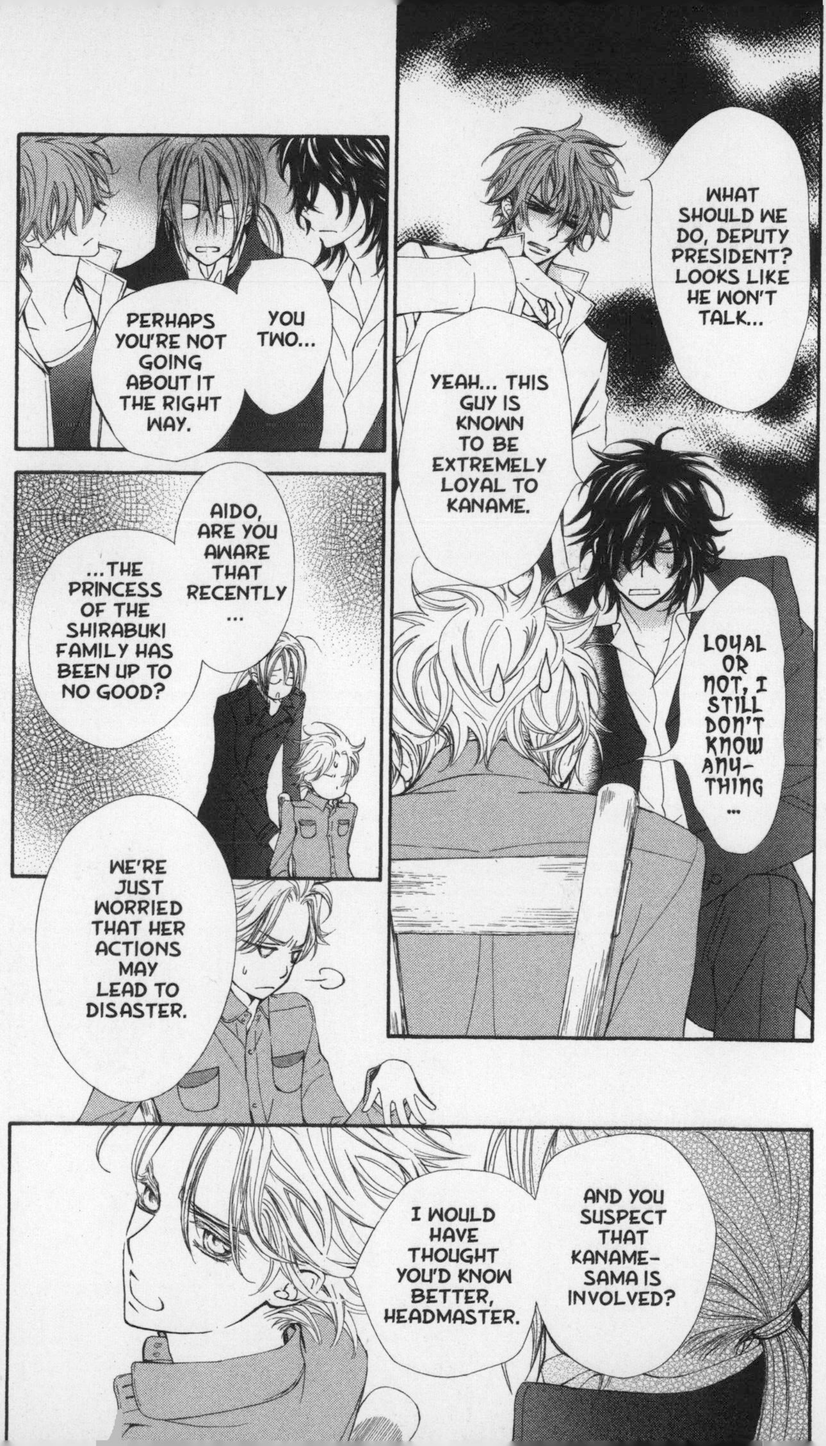
WHAT SHOULD WE DO, DEPUTY PRESIDENT? LOOKS LIKE HE WON'T TALK...
YEAH... THIS GUY IS KNOWN TO BE EXTREMELY LOYAL TO KANAME.
LOYAL OR NOT, I STILL DON'T KNOW ANY-THING...
YOU TWO...
PERHAPS YOU'RE NOT GOING ABOUT IT THE RIGHT WAY.
AIDO, ARE YOU AWARE THAT RECENTLY...
...THE PRINCESS OF THE SHIRABUKI FAMILY HAS BEEN UP TO NO GOOD?
WE'RE JUST WORRIED THAT HER ACTIONS MAY LEAD TO DISASTER.
AND YOU SUSPECT THAT KANAME-SAMA IS INVOLVED?
I WOULD HAVE THOUGHT YOU'D KNOW BETTER, HEADMASTER.

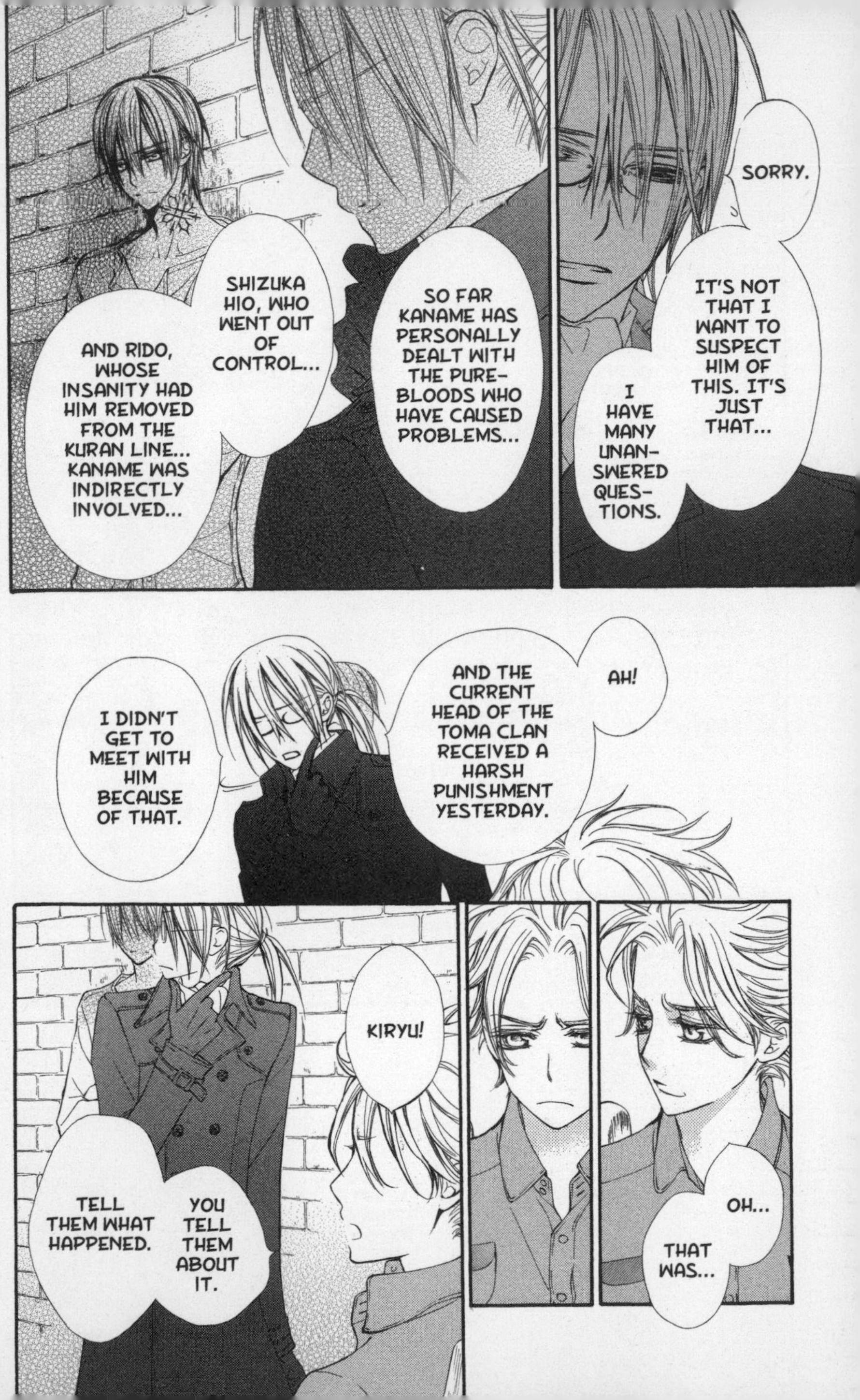
SORRY.
IT'S NOT THAT I WANT TO SUSPECT HIM OF THIS. IT'S JUST THAT...
I HAVE MANY UNAN-SWERED QUES-TIONS.
SO FAR KANAME HAS PERSONALLY DEALT WITH THE PURE-BLOODS WHO HAVE CAUSED PROBLEMS...
SHIZUKA HIO, WHO WENT OUT OF CONTROL...
AND RIDO, WHOSE INSANITY HAD HIM REMOVED FROM THE KURAN LINE... KANAME WAS INDIRECTLY INVOLVED...
AH!
AND THE CURRENT HEAD OF THE TOMA CLAN RECEIVED A HARSH PUNISHMENT YESTERDAY.
I DIDN'T GET TO MEET WITH HIM BECAUSE OF THAT.
OH...
THAT WAS...
KIRYU!
YOU TELL THEM ABOUT IT.
TELL THEM WHAT HAPPENED.

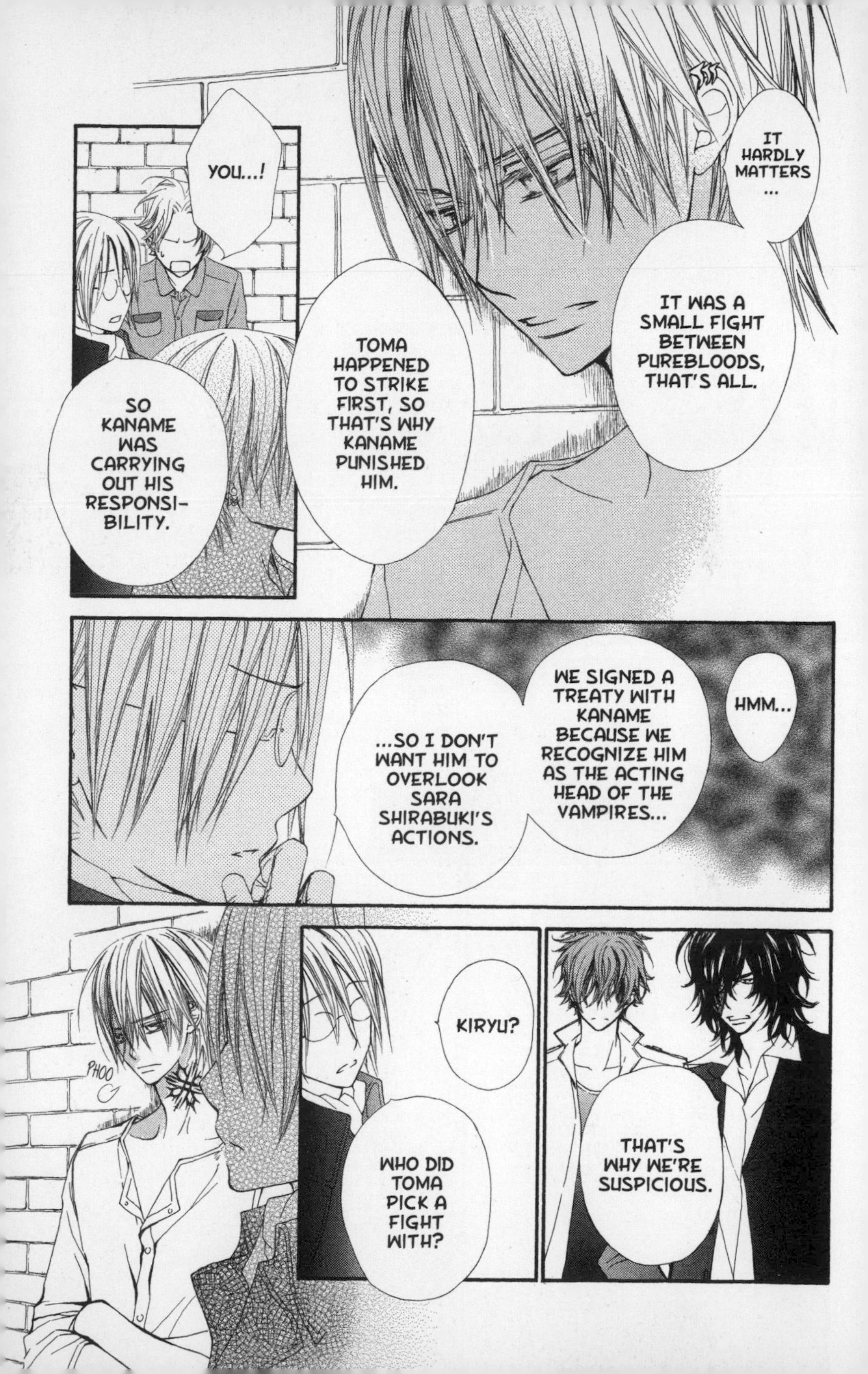
IT HARDLY MATTERS ...
IT WAS A SMALL FIGHT BETWEEN PUREBLOODS, THAT'S ALL.
YOU...!
TOMA HAPPENED TO STRIKE FIRST, SO THAT'S WHY KANAME PUNISHED HIM.
SO KANAME WAS CARRYING OUT HIS RESPONSI-BILITY.
HMM...
WE SIGNED A TREATY WITH KANAME BECAUSE WE RECOGNIZE HIM AS THE ACTING HEAD OF THE VAMPIRES...
...SO I DON'T WANT HIM TO OVERLOOK SARA SHIRABUKI'S ACTIONS.
THAT'S WHY WE'RE SUSPICIOUS.
KIRYU?
WHO DID TOMA PICK A FIGHT WITH?
PHOO

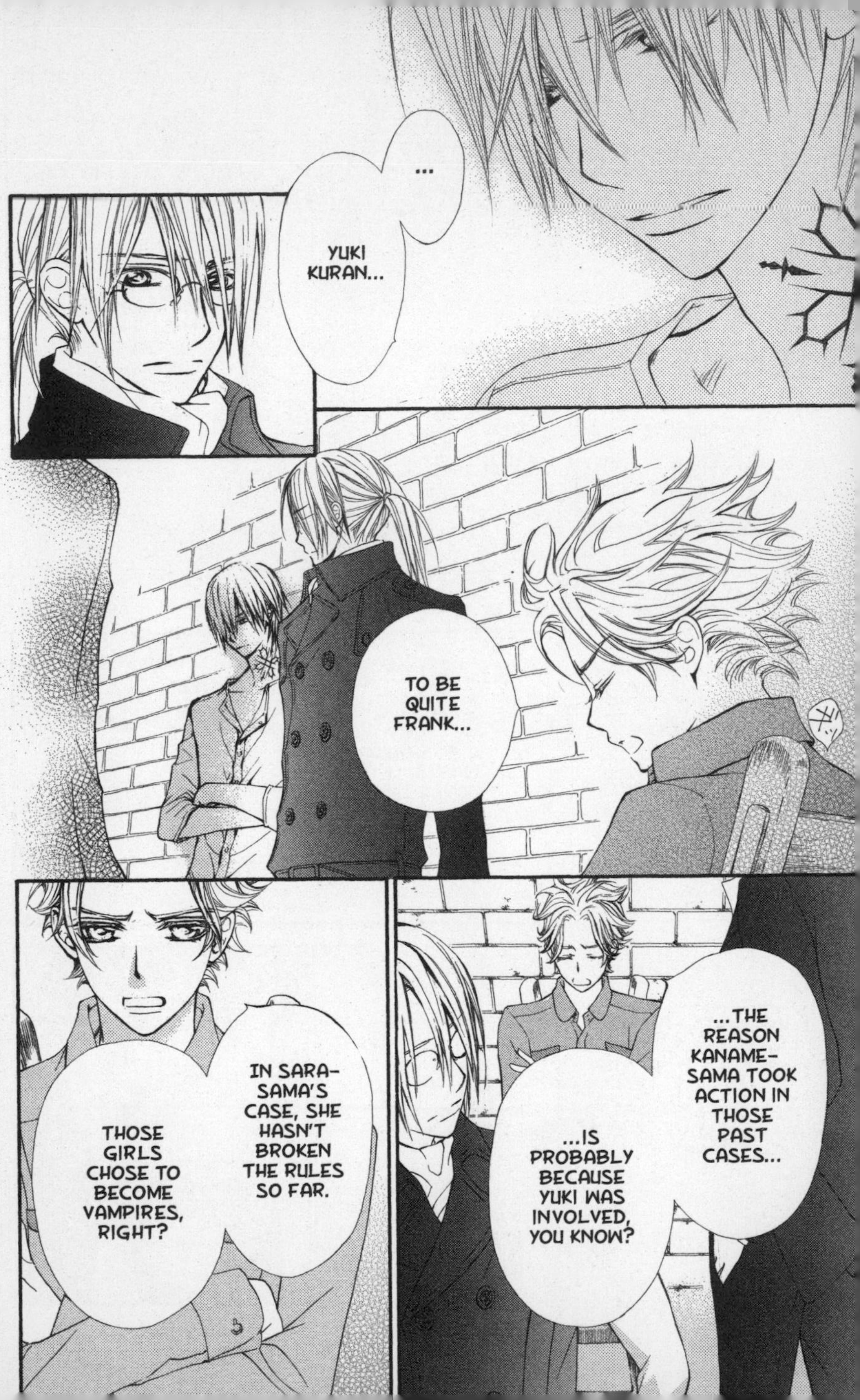
...
YUKI KURAN...
TO BE QUITE FRANK...
...THE REASON KANAME-SAMA TOOK ACTION IN THOSE PAST CASES...
...IS PROBABLY BECAUSE YUKI WAS INVOLVED, YOU KNOW?
IN SARA-SAMA'S CASE, SHE HASN'T BROKEN THE RULES SO FAR.
THOSE GIRLS CHOSE TO BECOME VAMPIRES, RIGHT?

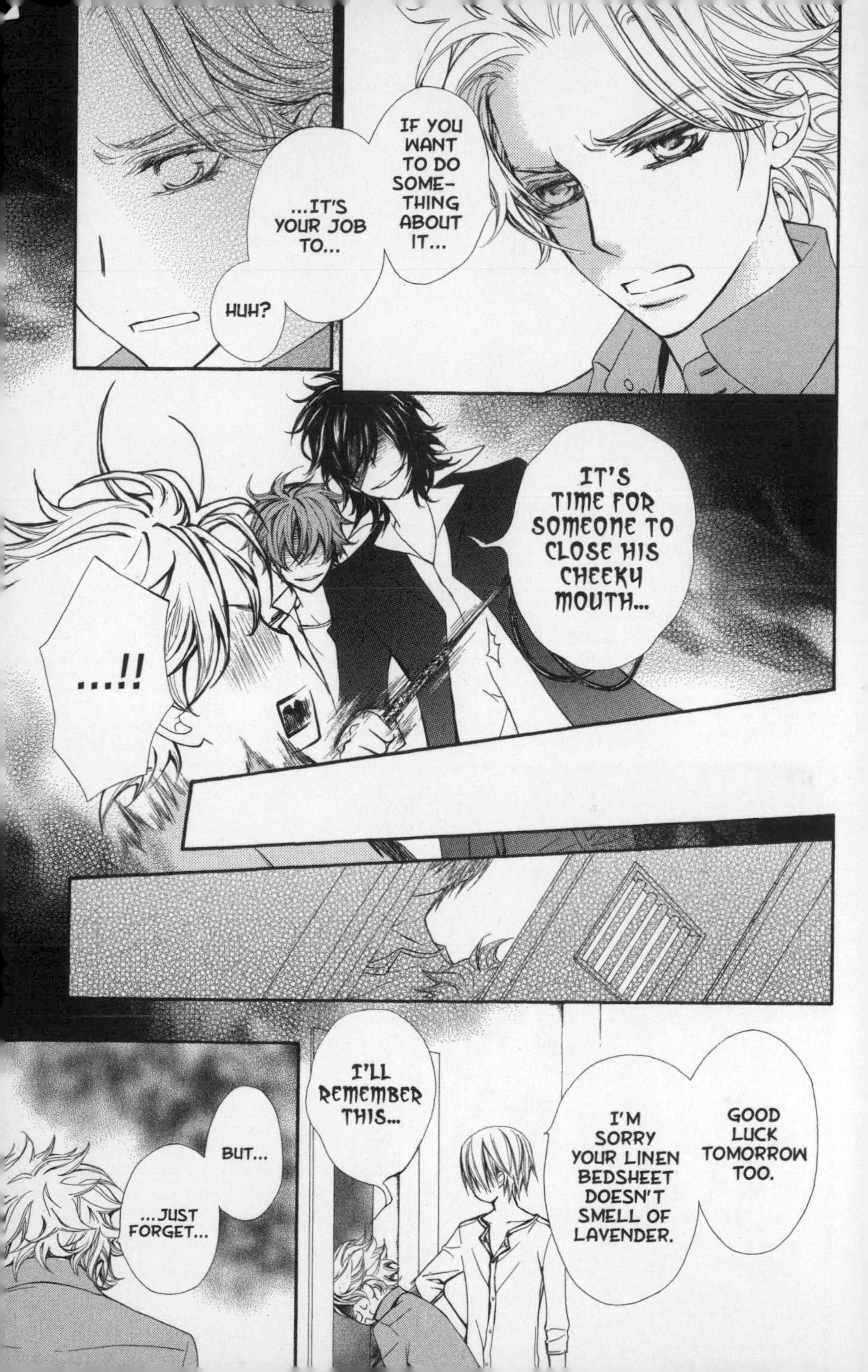
IF YOU WANT TO DO SOME-THING ABOUT IT...
...IT'S YOUR JOB TO...
HUH?
IT'S TIME FOR SOMEONE TO CLOSE HIS CHEEKY MOUTH...
...!!
GOOD LUCK TOMORROW TOO.
I'M SORRY YOUR LINEN BEDSHEET DOESN'T SMELL OF LAVENDER.
I'LL REMEMBER THIS...
BUT...
...JUST FORGET...

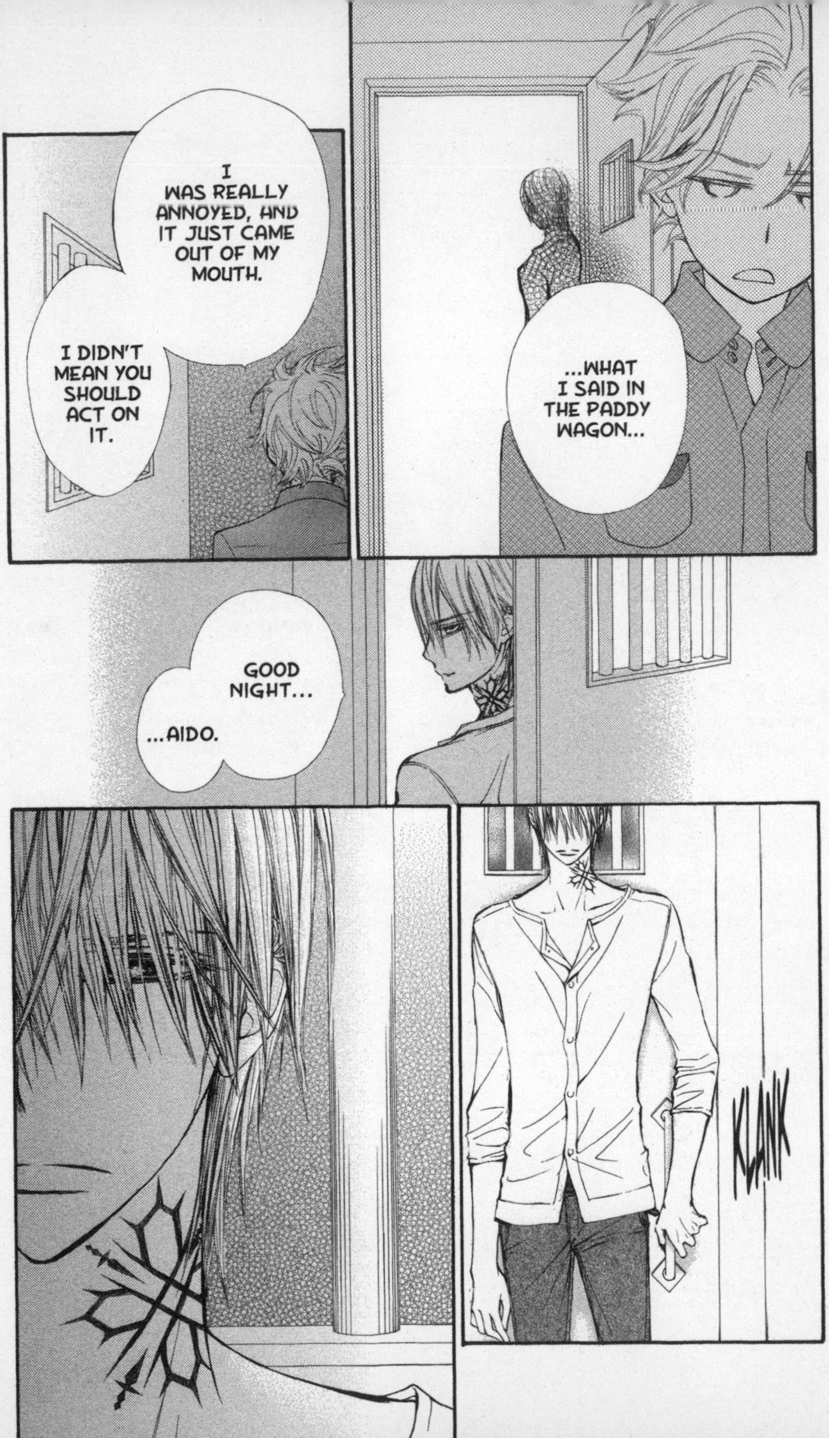
...WHAT I SAID IN THE PADDY WAGON...
I WAS REALLY ANNOYED, AND IT JUST CAME OUT OF MY MOUTH.
I DIDN'T MEAN YOU SHOULD ACT ON IT.
GOOD NIGHT...
...AIDO.
KLANK

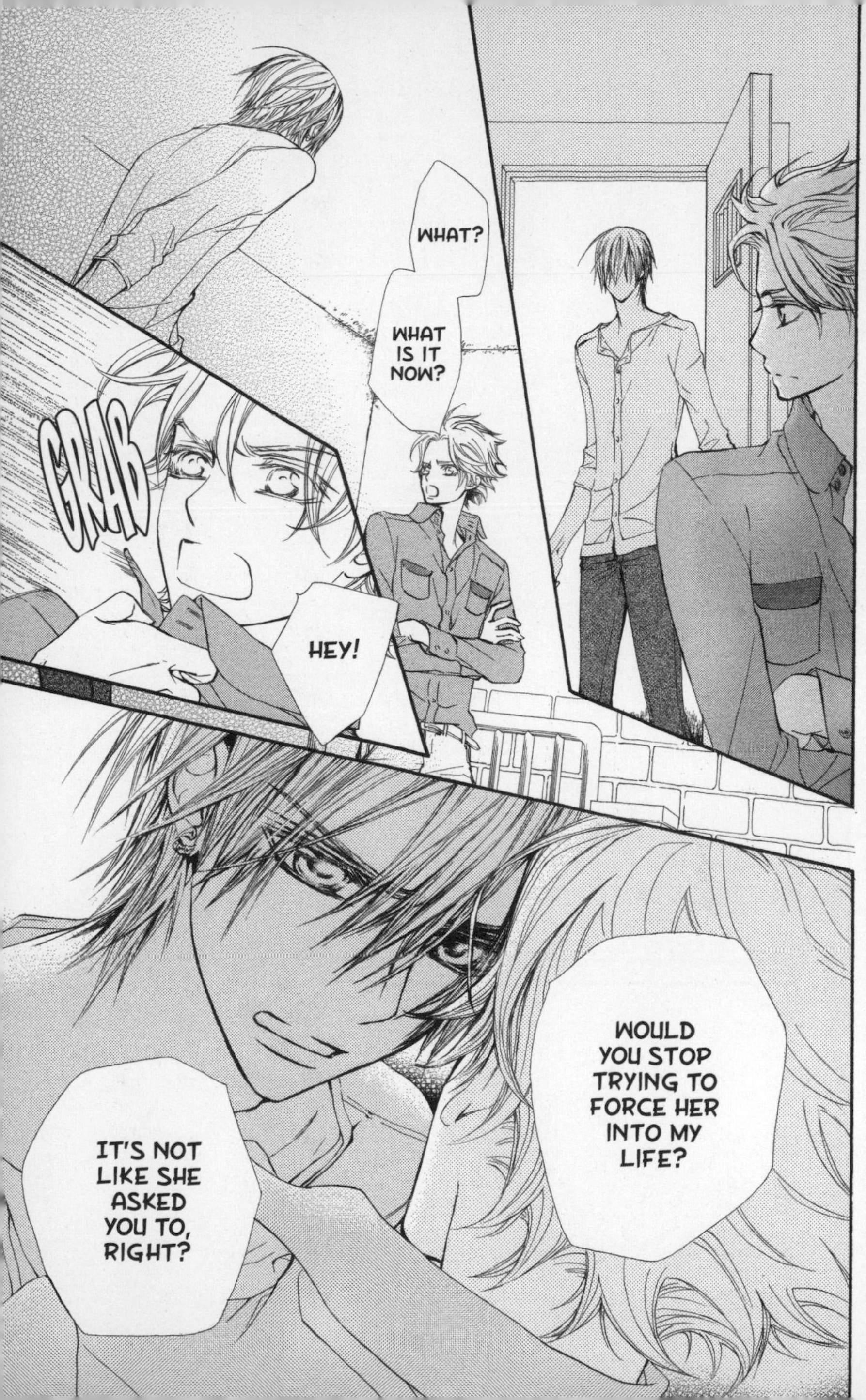
WHAT?
WHAT IS IT NOW?
GRAB
HEY!
WOULD YOU STOP TRYING TO FORCE HER INTO MY LIFE?
IT'S NOT LIKE SHE ASKED YOU TO, RIGHT?

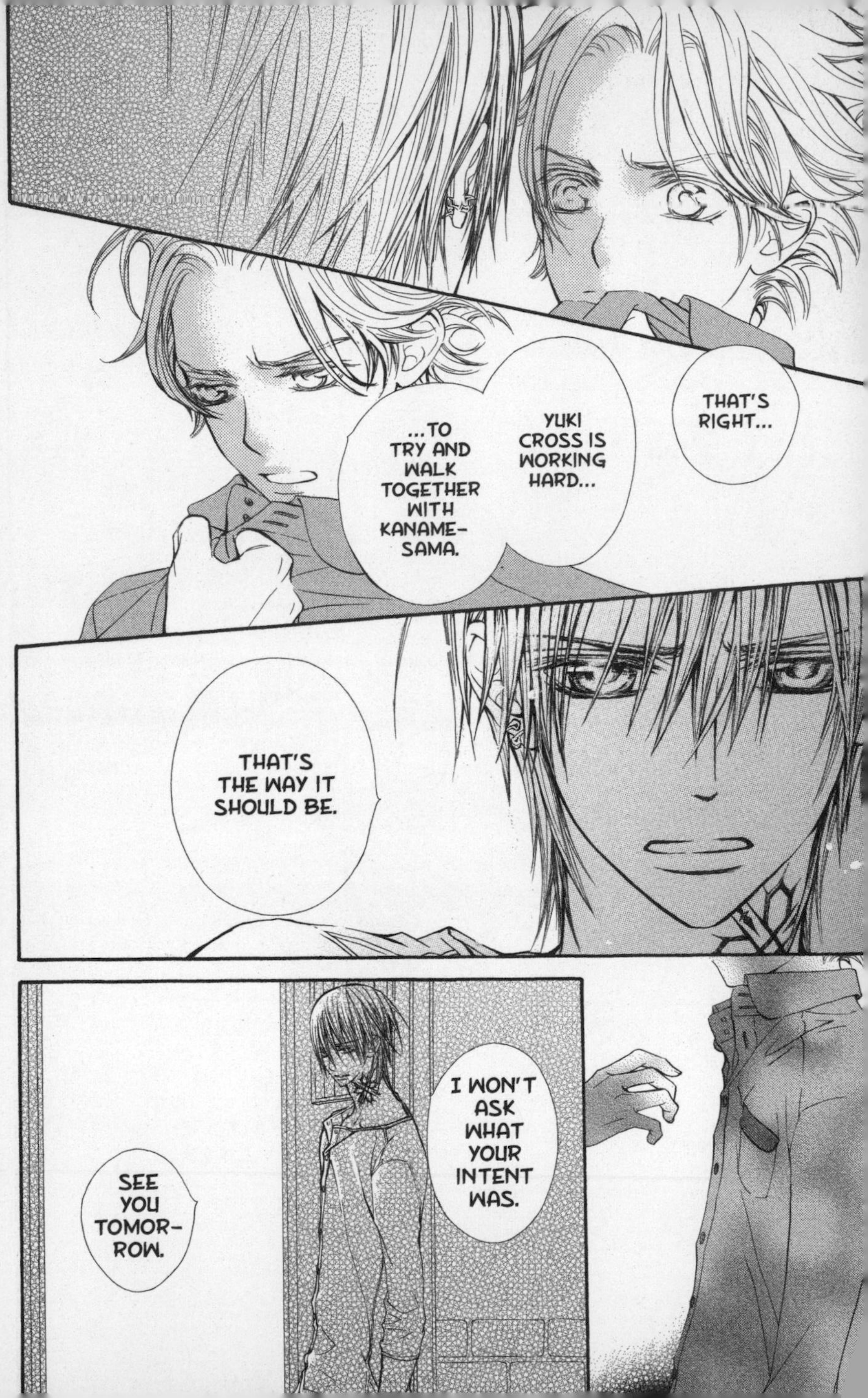
THAT'S RIGHT...
YUKI CROSS IS WORKING HARD...
...TO TRY AND WALK TOGETHER WITH KANAME-SAMA.
THAT'S THE WAY IT SHOULD BE.
I WON'T ASK WHAT YOUR INTENT WAS.
SEE YOU TOMOR-ROW.

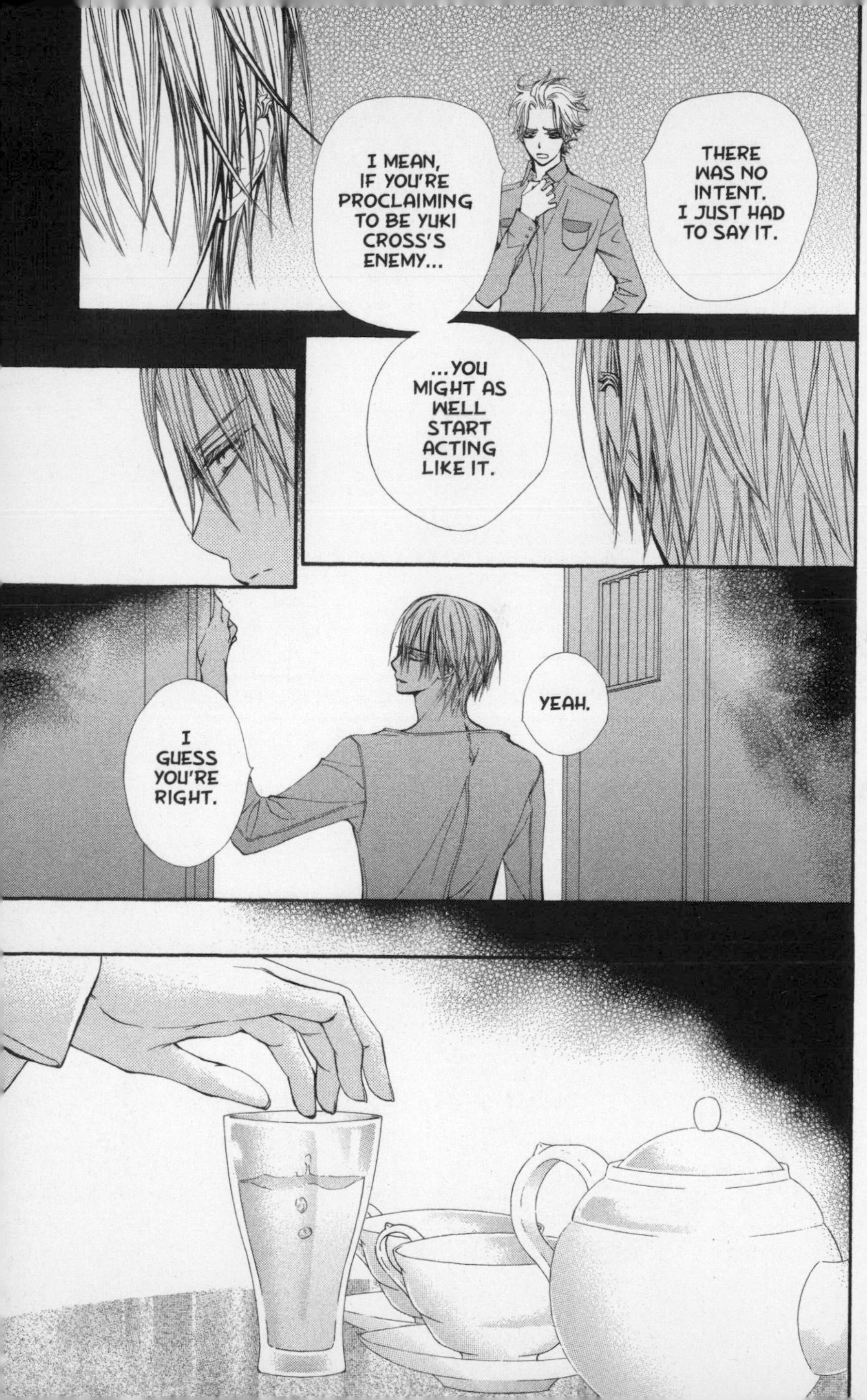
THERE WAS NO INTENT. I JUST HAD TO SAY IT.
I MEAN, IF YOU'RE PROCLAIMING TO BE YUKI CROSS'S ENEMY...
...YOU MIGHT AS WELL START ACTING LIKE IT.
YEAH.
I GUESS YOU'RE RIGHT.

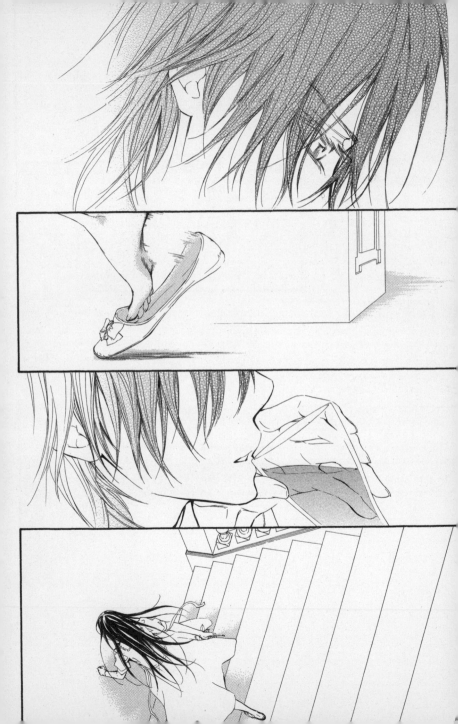

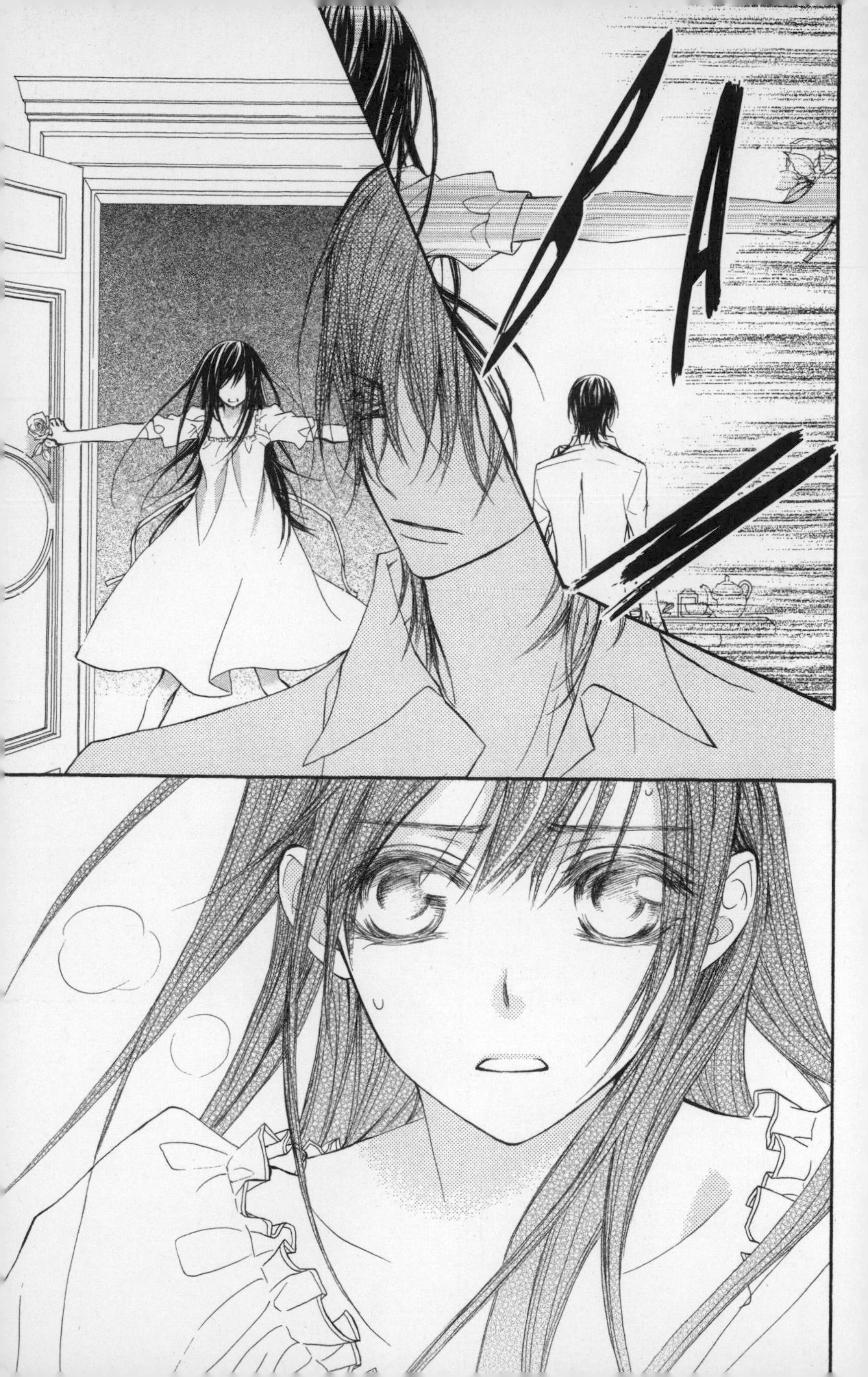
BAM

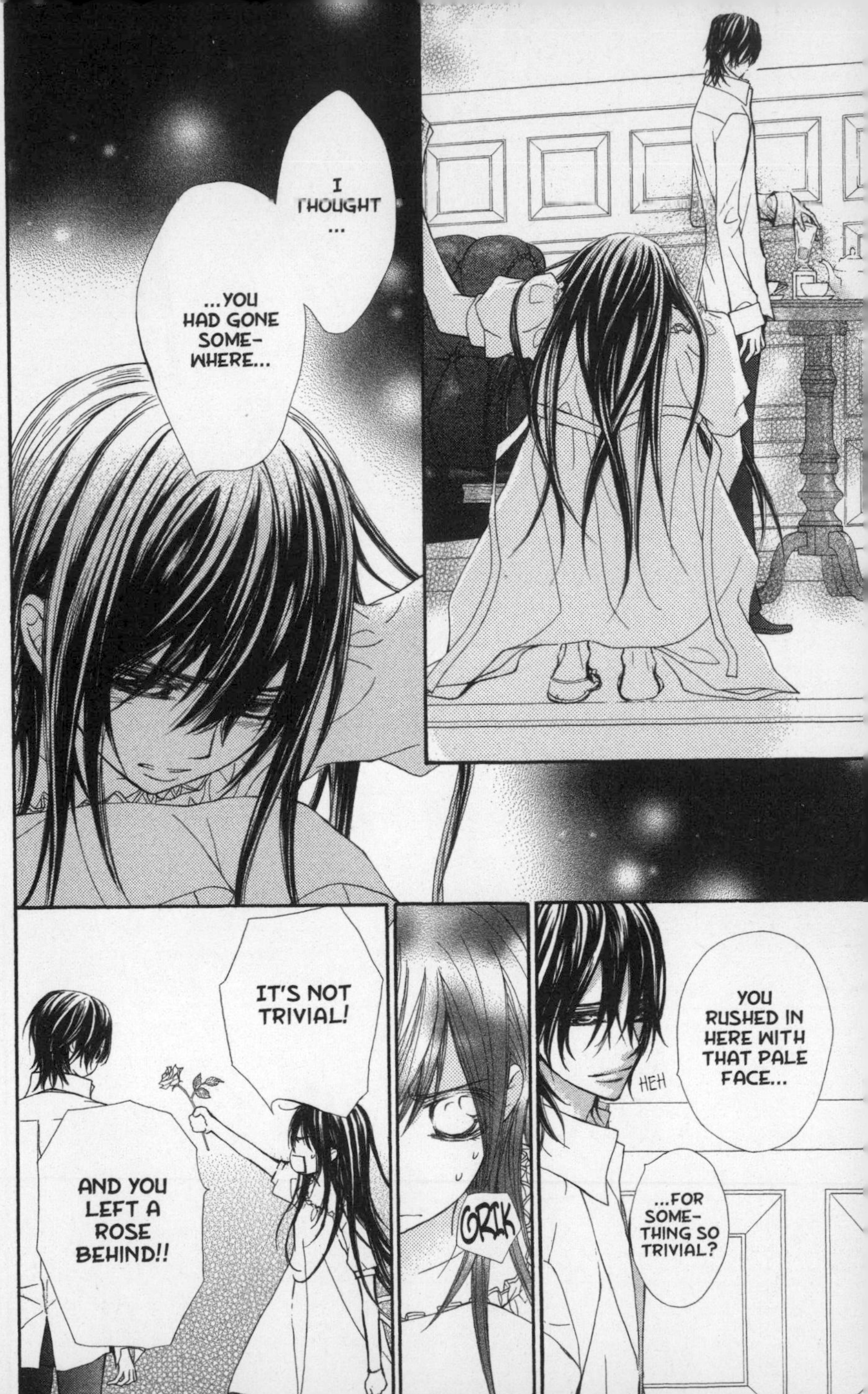
I THOUGHT...
...YOU HAD GONE SOMEWHERE...
YOU RUSHED IN HERE WITH THAT PALE FACE...
HEH
...FOR SOMETHING SO TRIVIAL?
CRIK
IT'S NOT TRIVIAL!
AND YOU LEFT A ROSE BEHIND!!

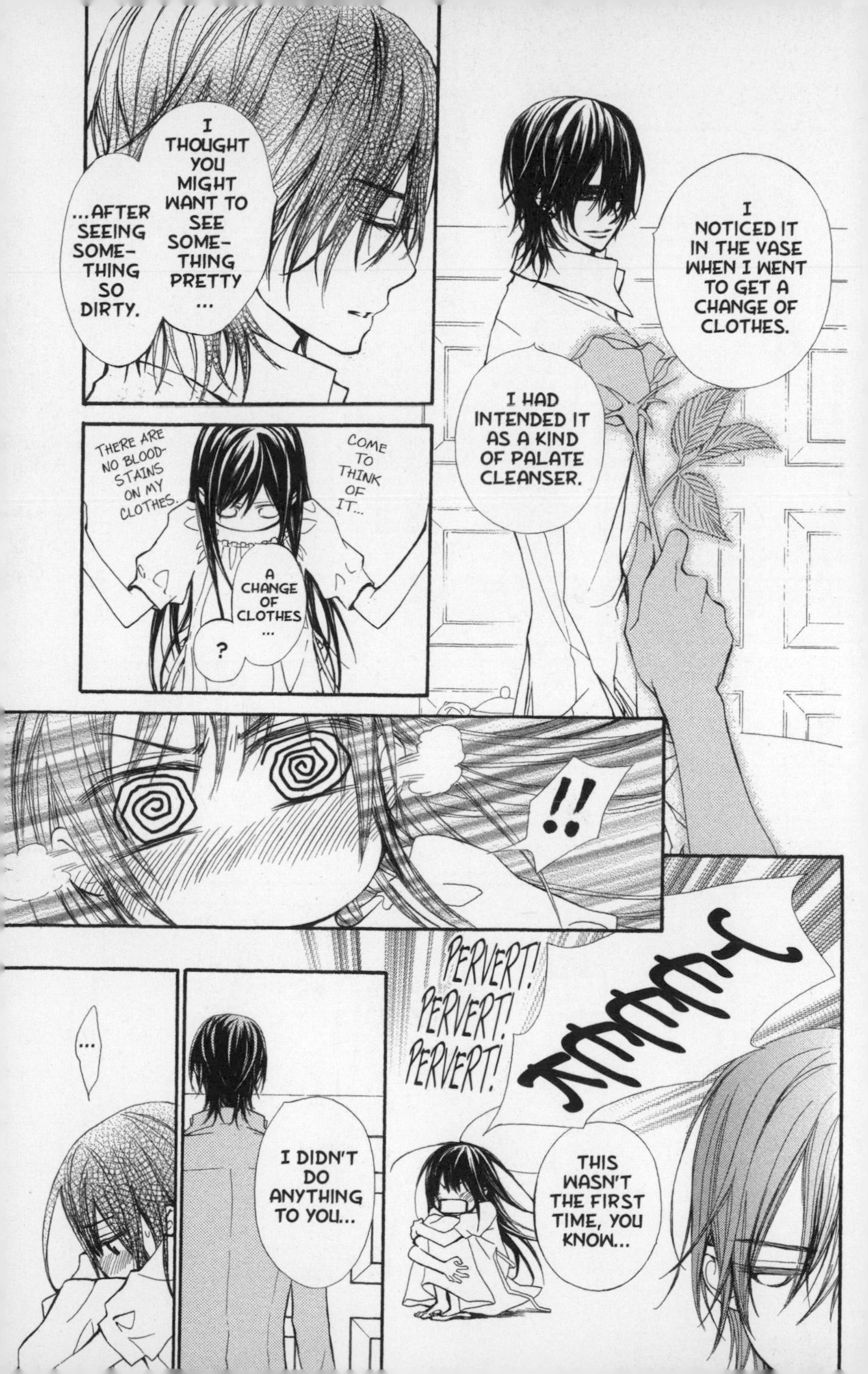
I NOTICED IT IN THE VASE WHEN I WENT TO GET A CHANGE OF CLOTHES.
I HAD INTENDED IT AS A KIND OF PALATE CLEANSER.
I THOUGHT YOU MIGHT WANT TO SEE SOME-THING PRETTY...
...AFTER SEEING SOME-THING SO DIRTY.
COME TO THINK OF IT...
THERE ARE NO BLOOD-STAINS ON MY CLOTHES.
A CHANGE OF CLOTHES...
?
!!
PERVERT! PERVERT! PERVERT!
THIS WASN'T THE FIRST TIME, YOU KNOW...
I DIDN'T DO ANYTHING TO YOU...
...

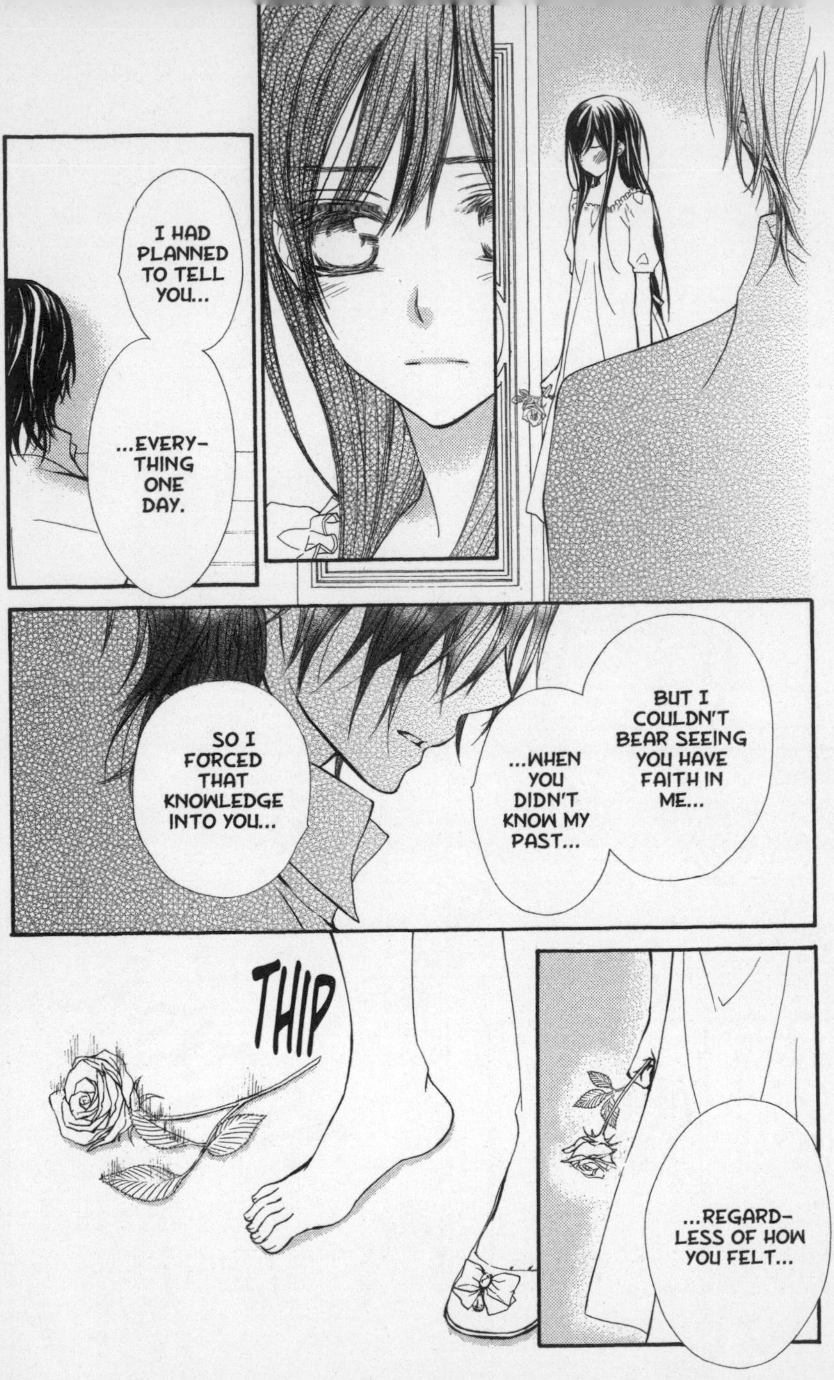
I HAD PLANNED TO TELL YOU...
...EVERYTHING ONE DAY.
BUT I COULDN'T BEAR SEEING YOU HAVE FAITH IN ME...
...WHEN YOU DIDN'T KNOW MY PAST...
SO I FORCED THAT KNOWLEDGE INTO YOU...
...REGARDLESS OF HOW YOU FELT...
THIP

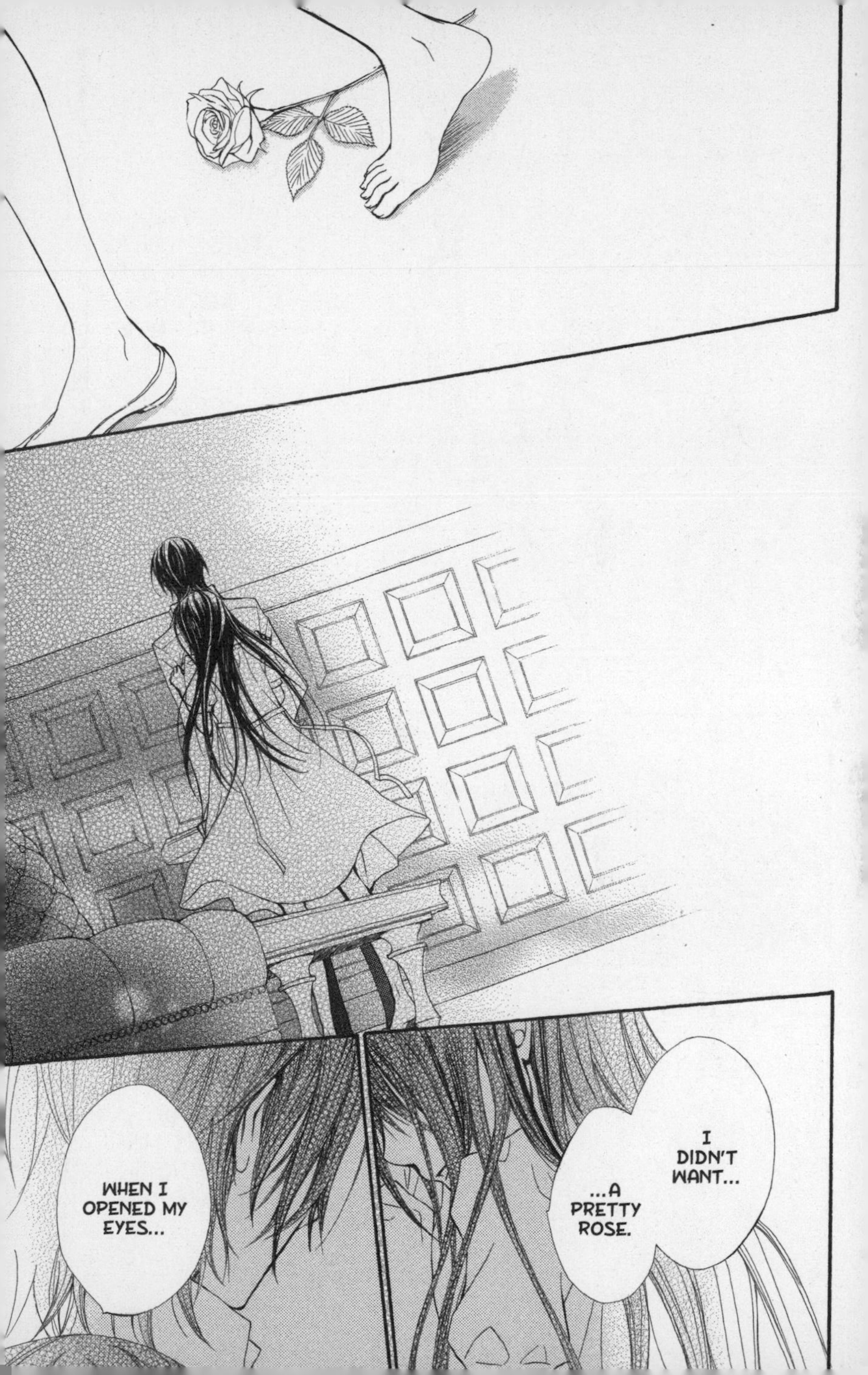
I DIDN'T WANT...
...A PRETTY ROSE.
WHEN I OPENED MY EYES...

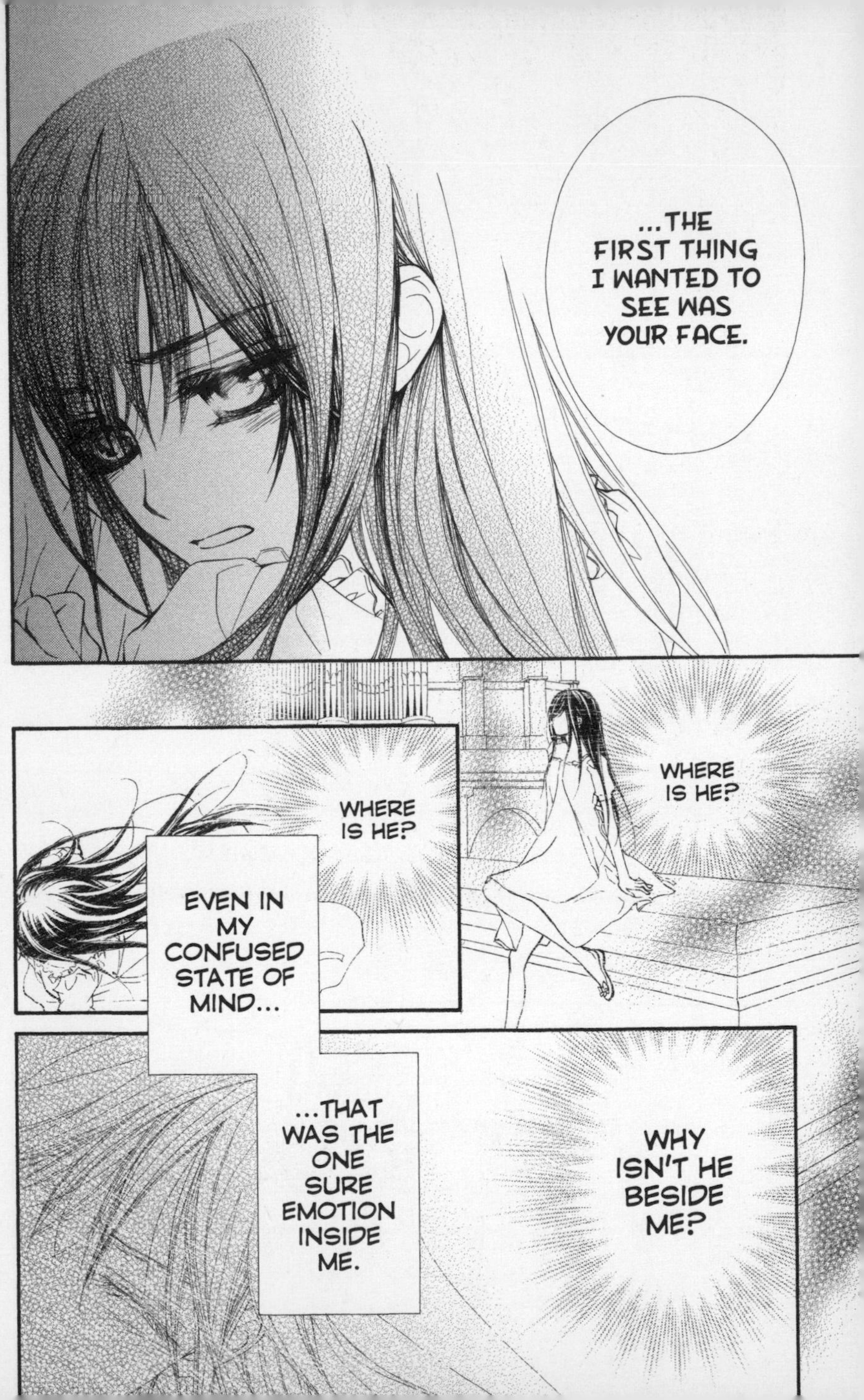
...THE FIRST THING I WANTED TO SEE WAS YOUR FACE.
WHERE IS HE?
WHERE IS HE?
EVEN IN MY CONFUSED STATE OF MIND...
WHY ISN'T HE BESIDE ME?
...THAT WAS THE ONE SURE EMOTION INSIDE ME.

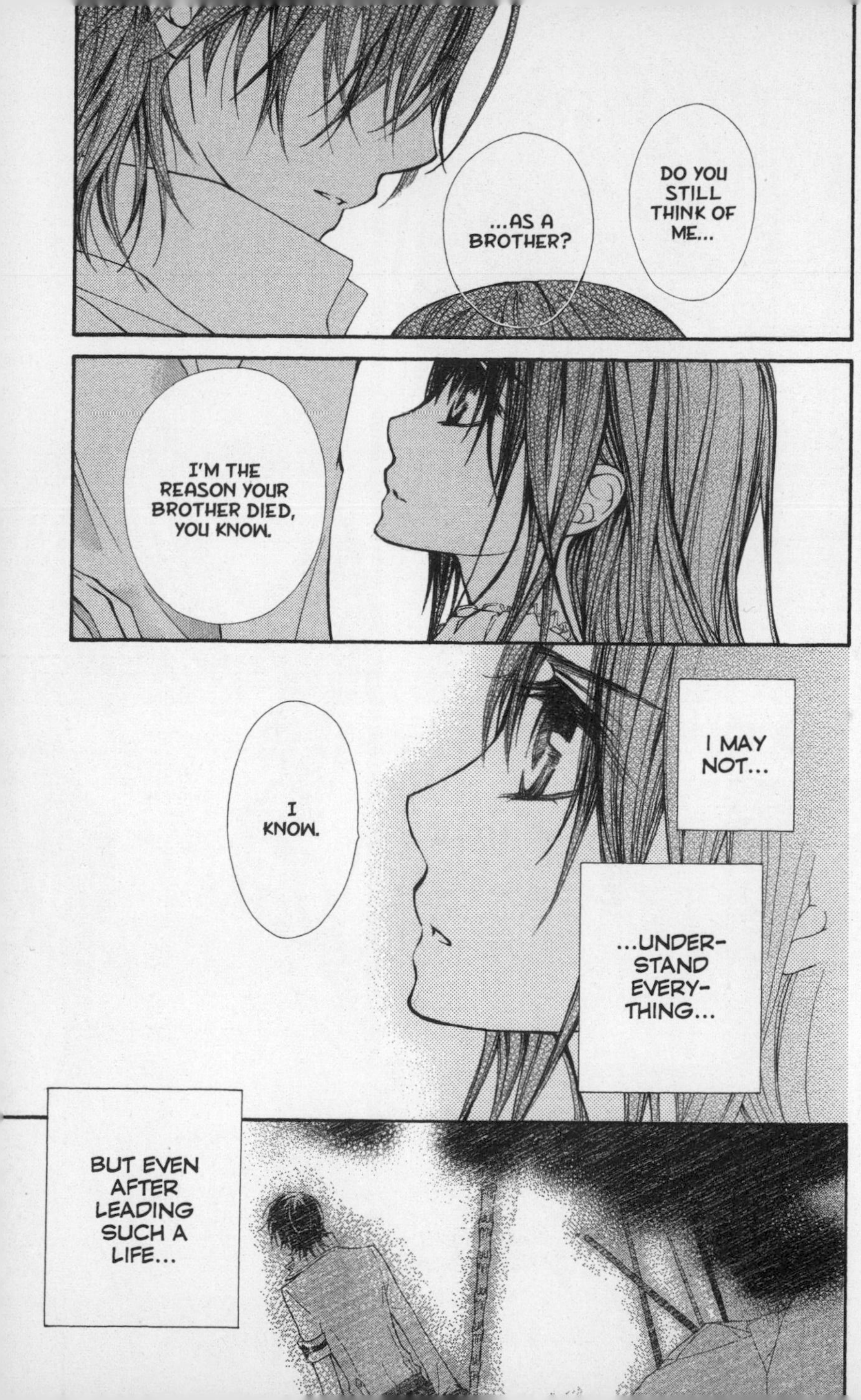
DO YOU STILL THINK OF ME...
...AS A BROTHER?
I'M THE REASON YOUR BROTHER DIED, YOU KNOW.
I KNOW.
I MAY NOT...
...UNDERSTAND EVERYTHING...
BUT EVEN AFTER LEADING SUCH A LIFE...

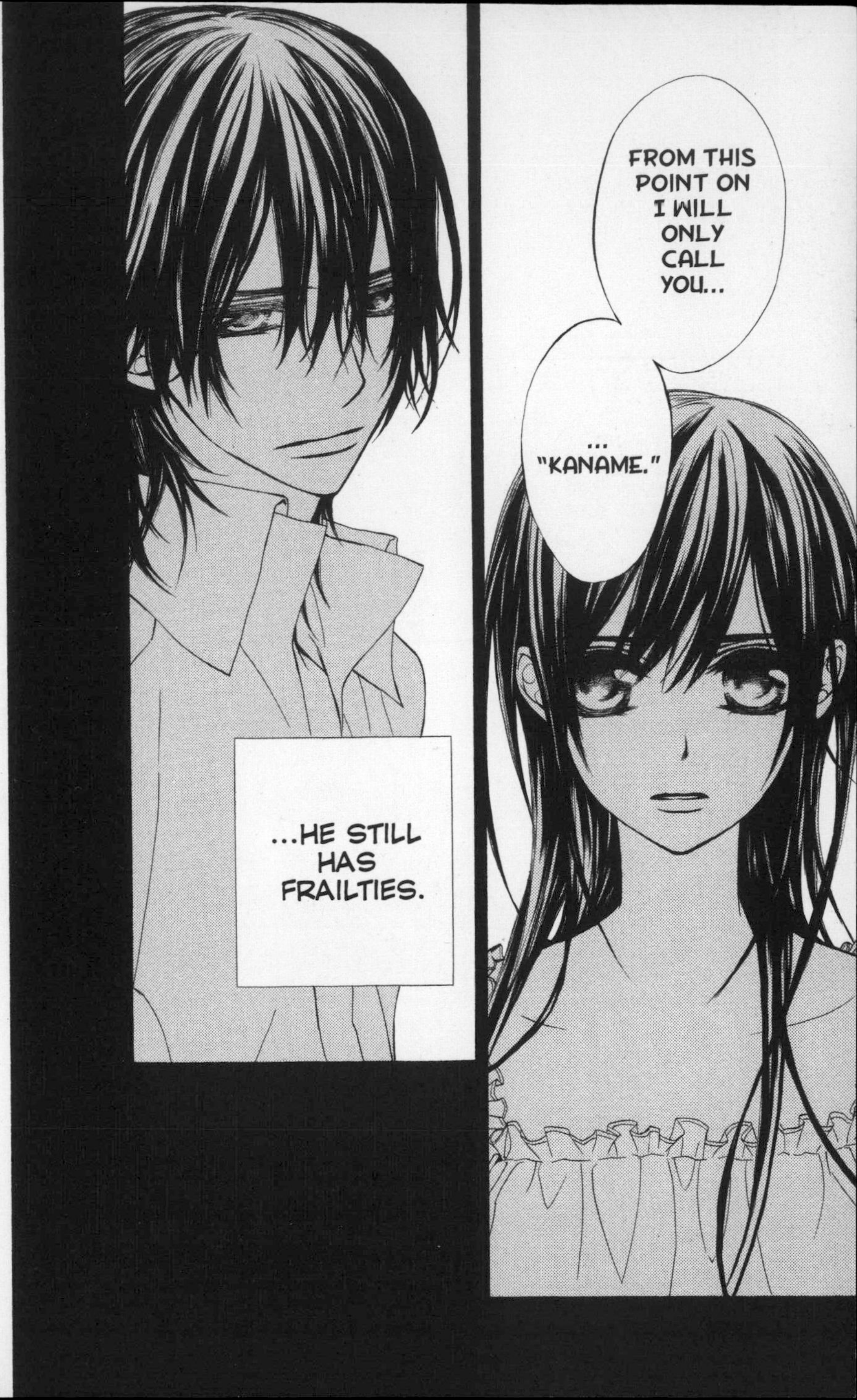
FROM THIS POINT ON I WILL ONLY CALL YOU...
... "KANAME."
...HE STILL HAS FRAILTIES.

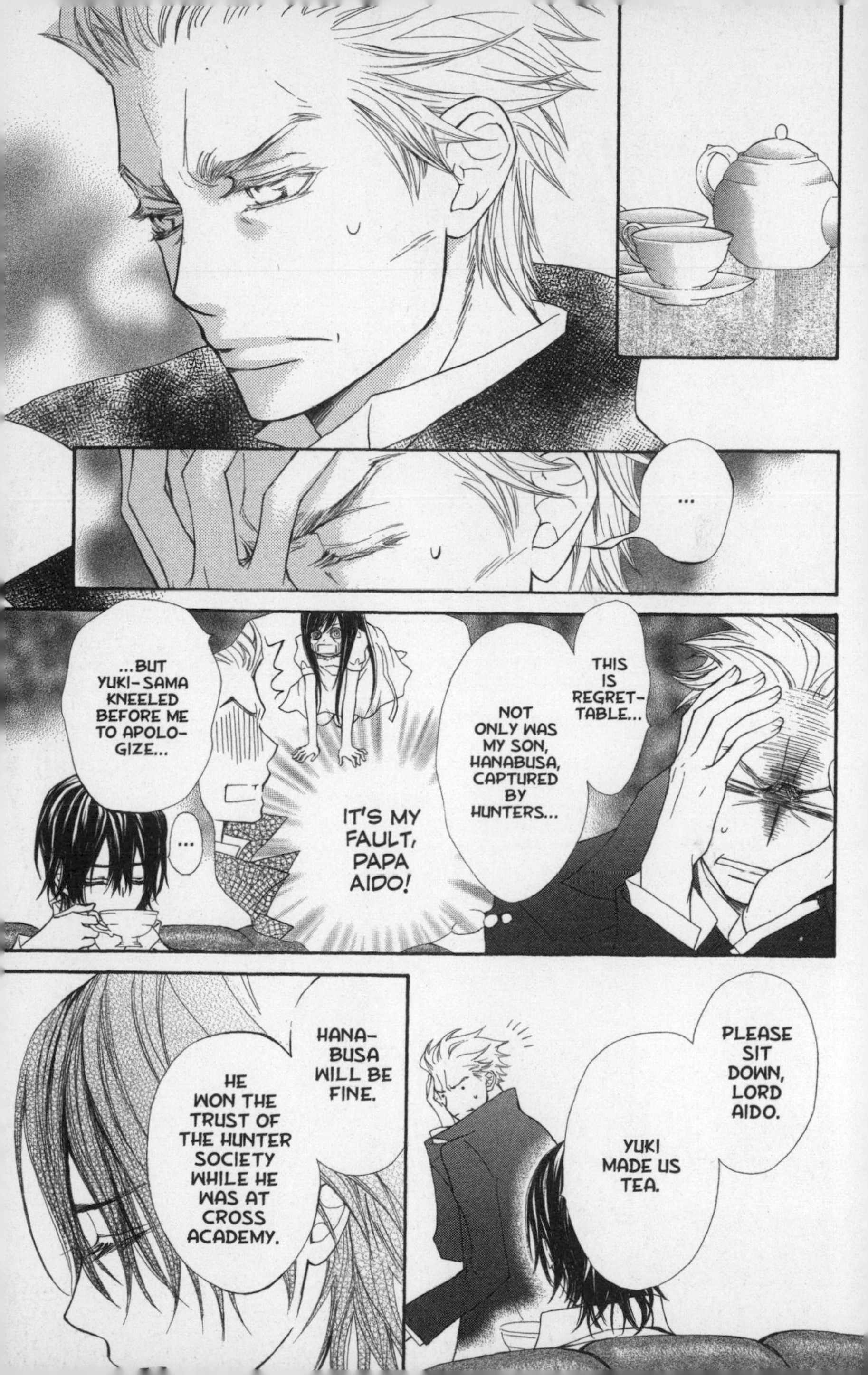
...
THIS IS REGRETTABLE...
NOT ONLY WAS MY SON, HANABUSA, CAPTURED BY HUNTERS...
IT'S MY FAULT, PAPA AIDO!
...BUT YUKI-SAMA KNEELED BEFORE ME TO APOLOGIZE...
...
PLEASE SIT DOWN, LORD AIDO.
YUKI MADE US TEA.
HANABUSA WILL BE FINE.
HE WON THE TRUST OF THE HUNTER SOCIETY WHILE HE WAS AT CROSS ACADEMY.

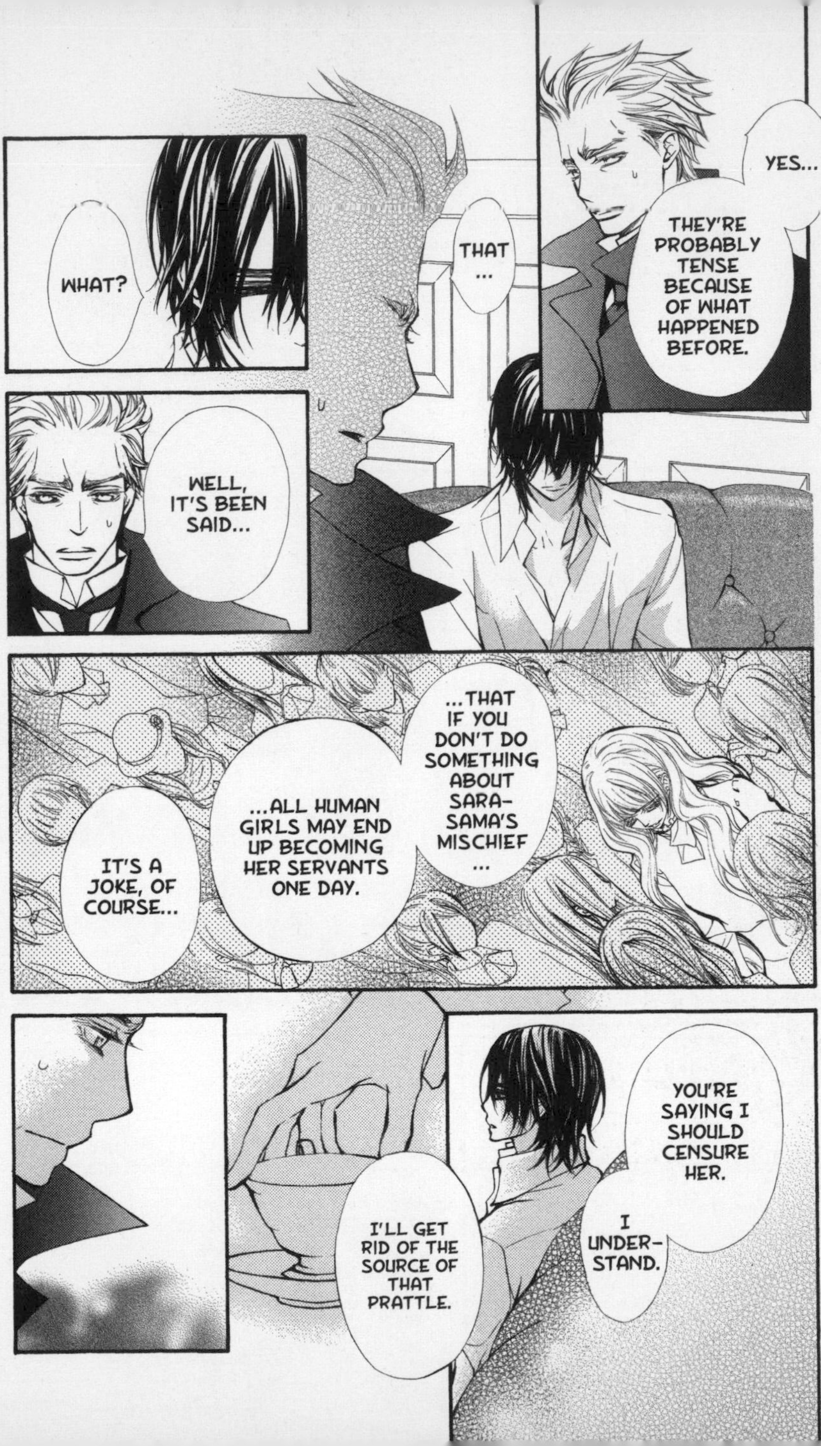
YES...
THEY'RE PROBABLY TENSE BECAUSE OF WHAT HAPPENED BEFORE.
THAT ...
WHAT?
WELL, IT'S BEEN SAID...
...THAT IF YOU DON'T DO SOMETHING ABOUT SARA-SAMA'S MISCHIEF ...
...ALL HUMAN GIRLS MAY END UP BECOMING HER SERVANTS ONE DAY.
IT'S A JOKE, OF COURSE...
YOU'RE SAYING I SHOULD CENSURE HER.
I UNDER-STAND.
I'LL GET RID OF THE SOURCE OF THAT PRATTLE.

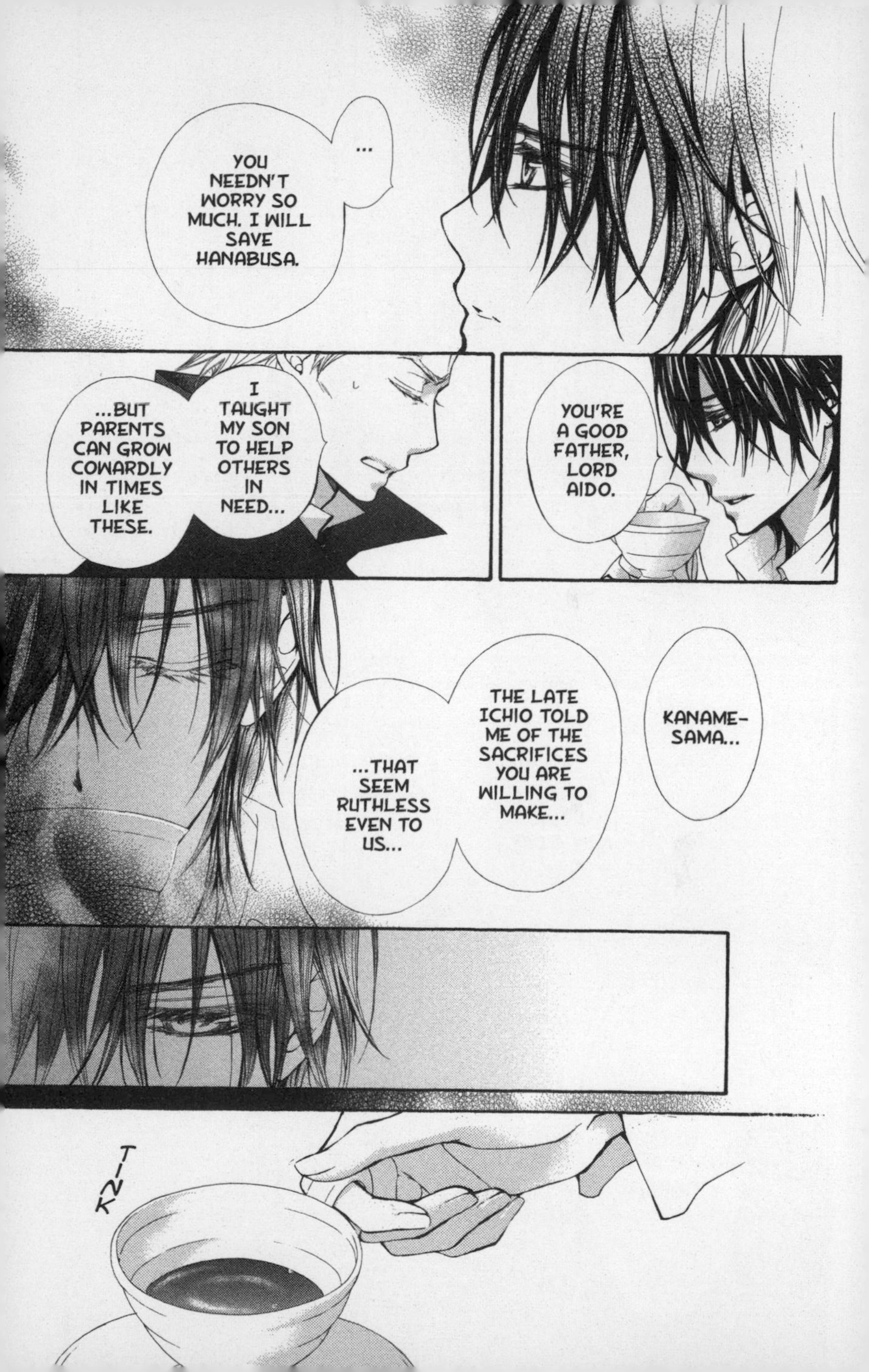
...
YOU NEEDN'T WORRY SO MUCH. I WILL SAVE HANABUSA.
YOU'RE A GOOD FATHER, LORD AIDO.
I TAUGHT MY SON TO HELP OTHERS IN NEED...
...BUT PARENTS CAN GROW COWARDLY IN TIMES LIKE THESE.
KANAME-SAMA...
THE LATE ICHIO TOLD ME OF THE SACRIFICES YOU ARE WILLING TO MAKE...
...THAT SEEM RUTHLESS EVEN TO US...
TINK

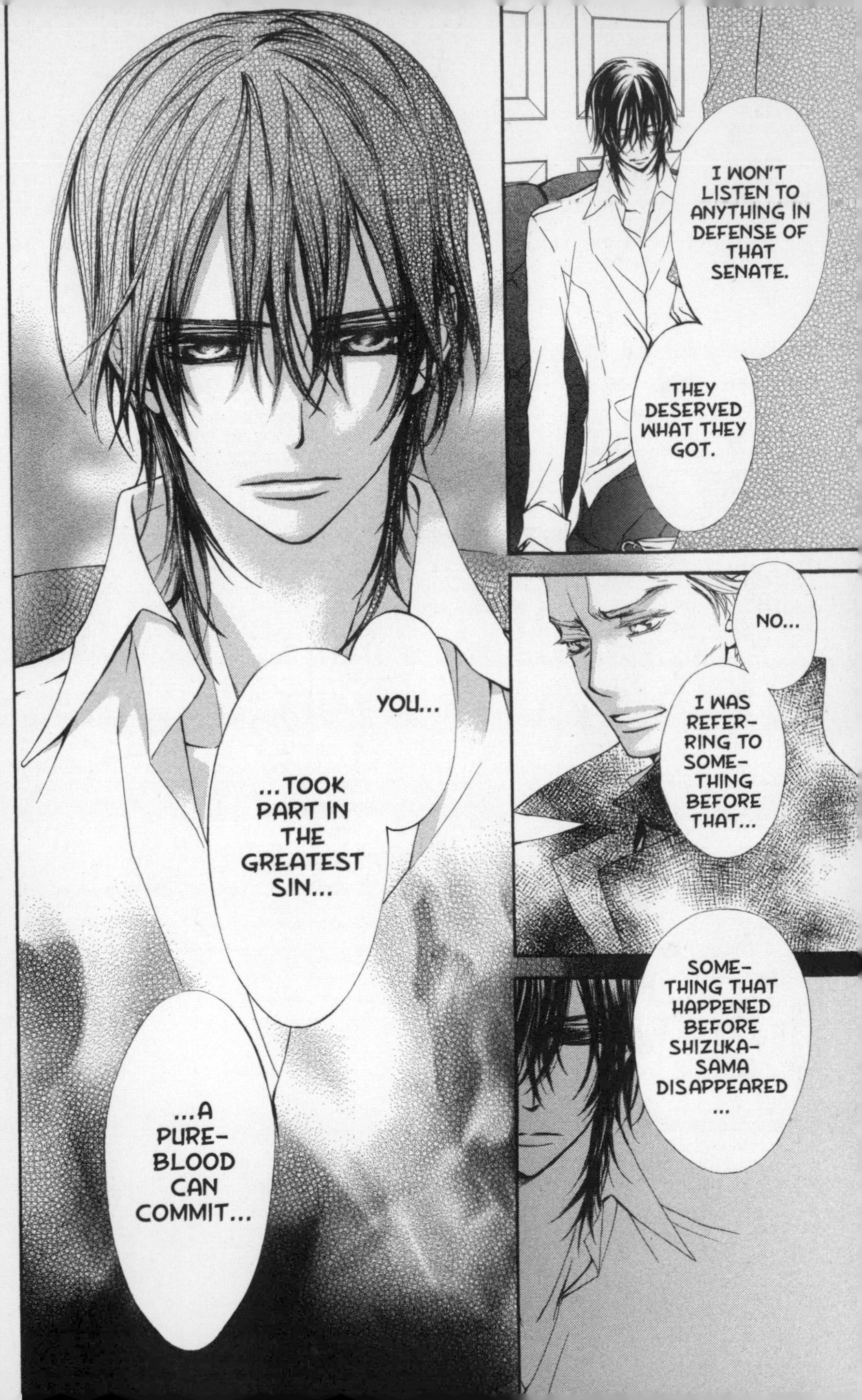
I WON'T LISTEN TO ANYTHING IN DEFENSE OF THAT SENATE.
THEY DESERVED WHAT THEY GOT.
NO...
I WAS REFER-RING TO SOME-THING BEFORE THAT...
SOME-THING THAT HAPPENED BEFORE SHIZUKA-SAMA DISAPPEARED...
YOU...
...TOOK PART IN THE GREATEST SIN...
...A PURE-BLOOD CAN COMMIT...

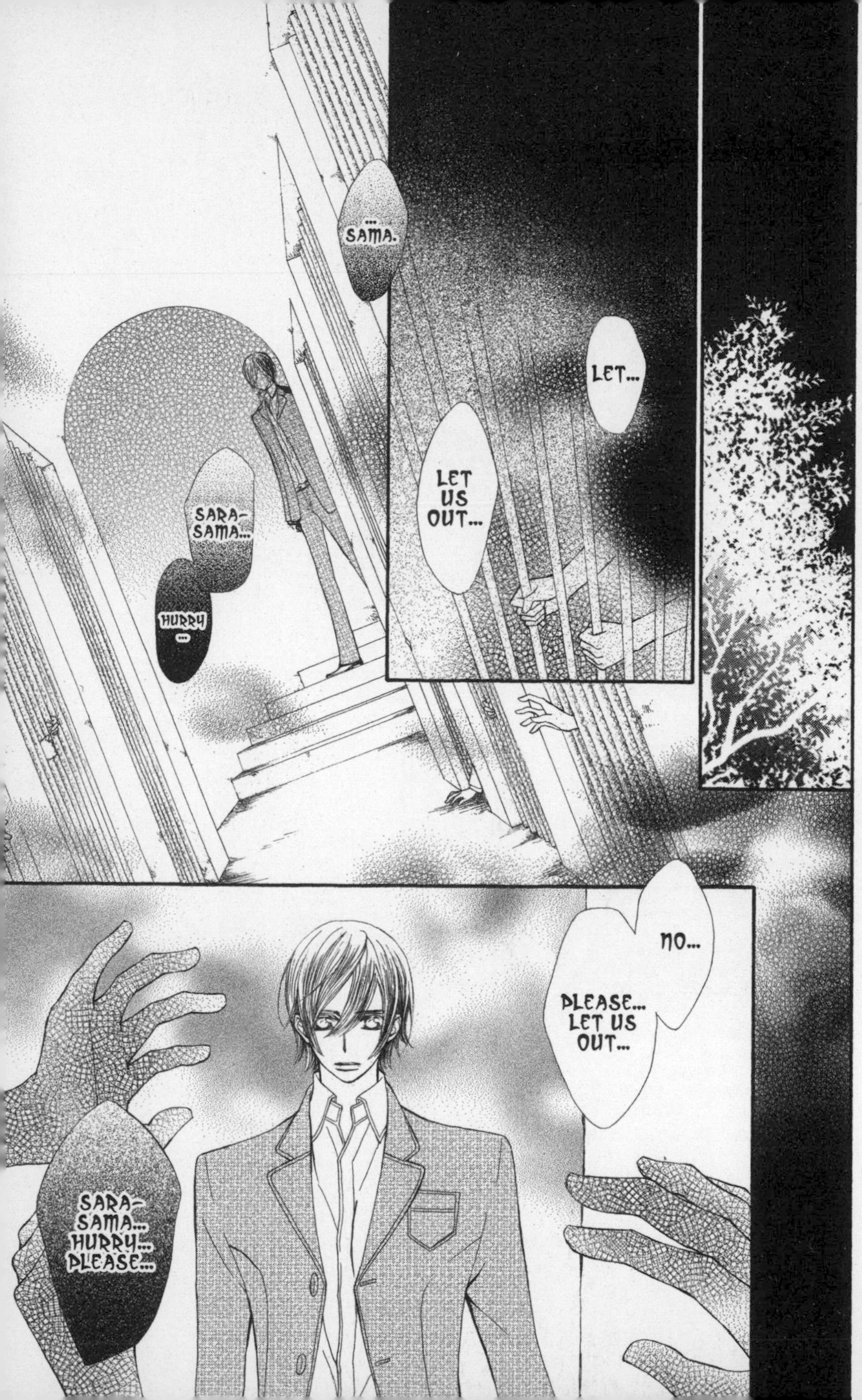
LET...
LET US OUT...
...SAMA.
SARA-SAMA...
HURRY...
NO...
PLEASE... LET US OUT...
SARA-SAMA... HURRY... PLEASE...

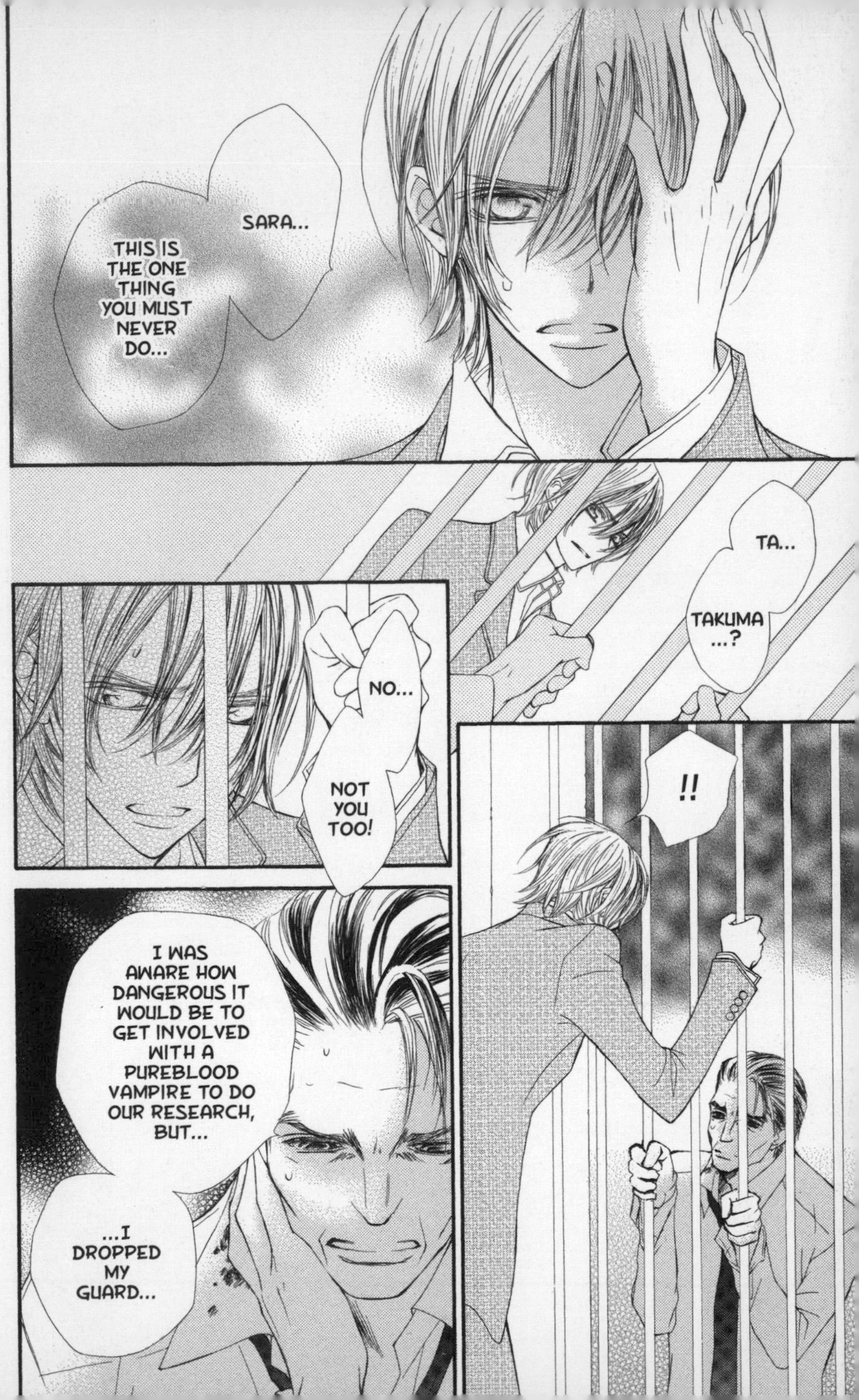
SARA...
THIS IS THE ONE THING YOU MUST NEVER DO...
TA...
TAKUMA ...?
NO...
NOT YOU TOO!
!!
I WAS AWARE HOW DANGEROUS IT WOULD BE TO GET INVOLVED WITH A PUREBLOOD VAMPIRE TO DO OUR RESEARCH, BUT...
...I DROPPED MY GUARD...

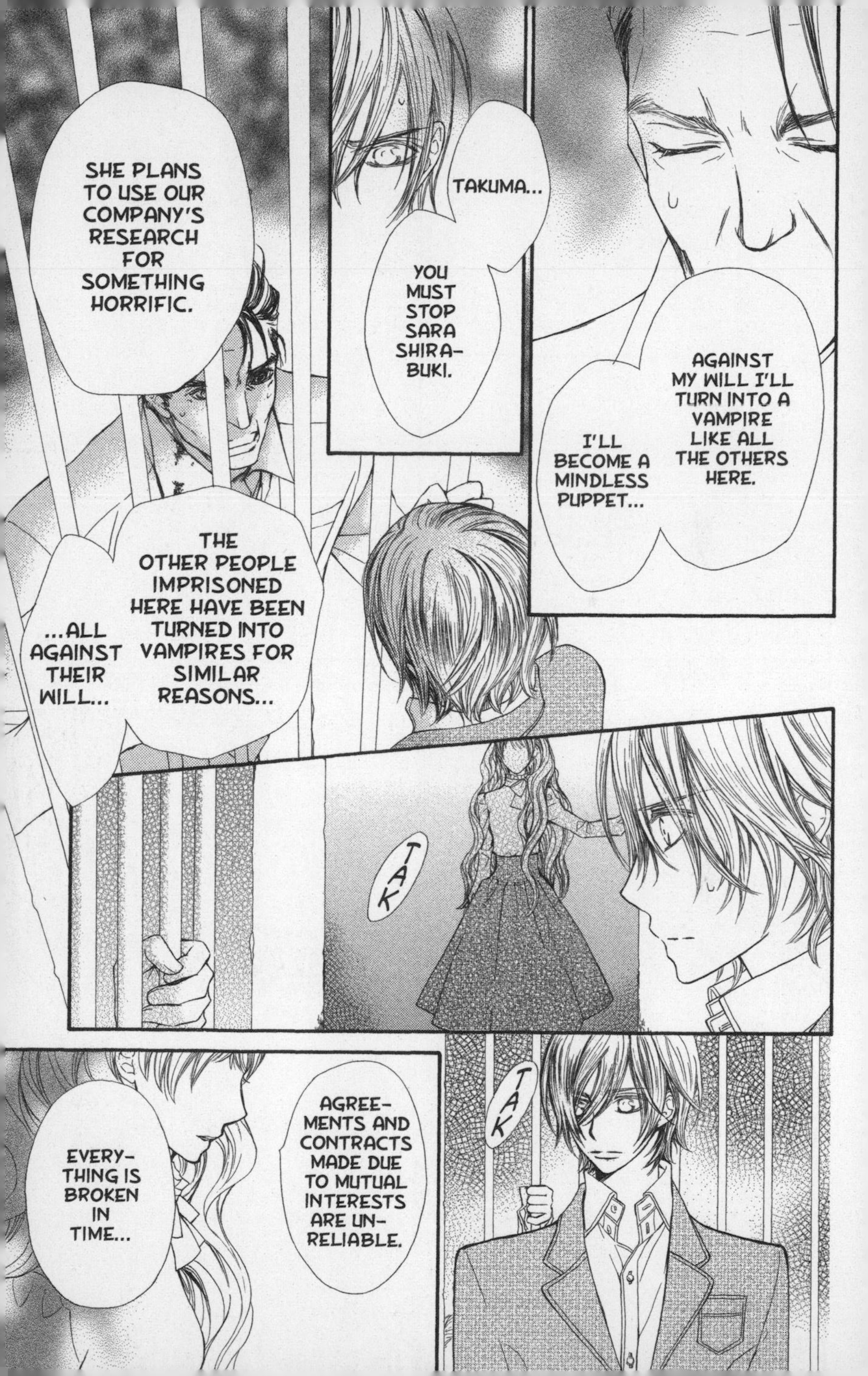
AGAINST MY WILL I'LL TURN INTO A VAMPIRE LIKE ALL THE OTHERS HERE.
I'LL BECOME A MINDLESS PUPPET...
TAKUMA...
YOU MUST STOP SARA SHIRABUKI.
SHE PLANS TO USE OUR COMPANY'S RESEARCH FOR SOMETHING HORRIFIC.
THE OTHER PEOPLE IMPRISONED HERE HAVE BEEN TURNED INTO VAMPIRES FOR SIMILAR REASONS...
...ALL AGAINST THEIR WILL...
TAK
TAK
AGREEMENTS AND CONTRACTS MADE DUE TO MUTUAL INTERESTS ARE UNRELIABLE.
EVERYTHING IS BROKEN IN TIME...

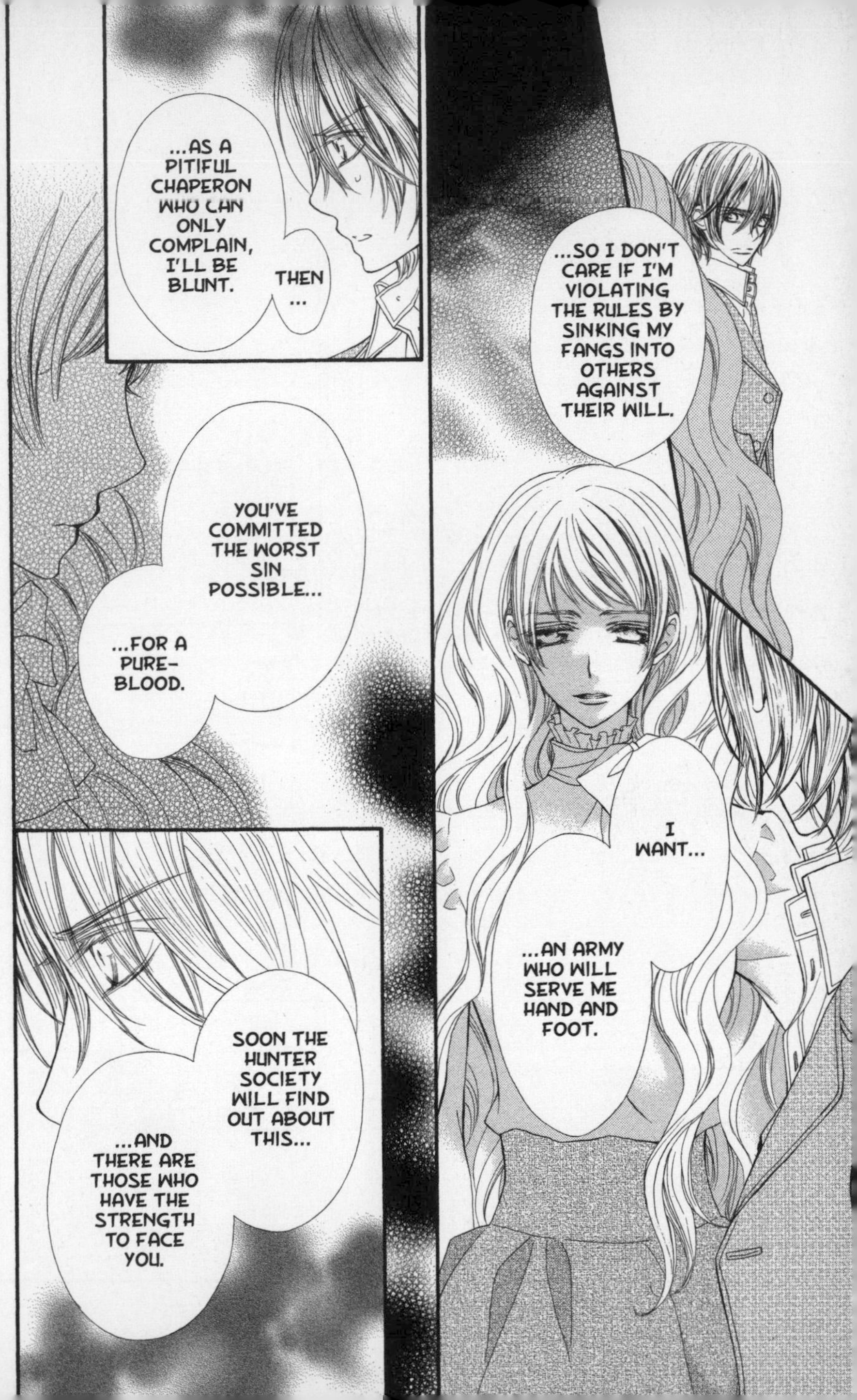
...SO I DON'T CARE IF I'M VIOLATING THE RULES BY SINKING MY FANGS INTO OTHERS AGAINST THEIR WILL.
I WANT...
...AN ARMY WHO WILL SERVE ME HAND AND FOOT.
THEN ...
...AS A PITIFUL CHAPERON WHO CAN ONLY COMPLAIN, I'LL BE BLUNT.
YOU'VE COMMITTED THE WORST SIN POSSIBLE...
...FOR A PURE-BLOOD.
SOON THE HUNTER SOCIETY WILL FIND OUT ABOUT THIS...
...AND THERE ARE THOSE WHO HAVE THE STRENGTH TO FACE YOU.

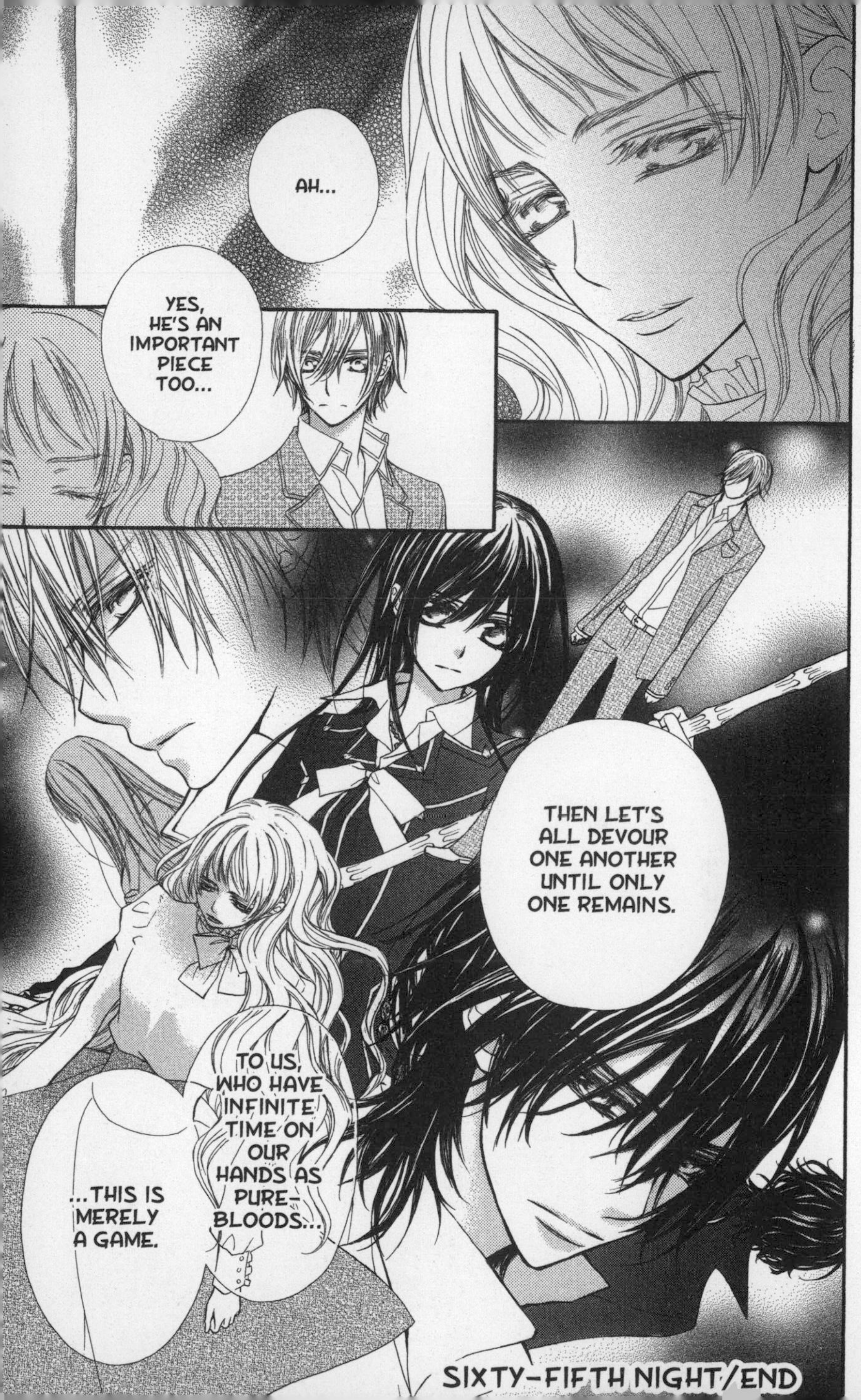
AH...
YES, HE'S AN IMPORTANT PIECE TOO...
THEN LET'S ALL DEVOUR ONE ANOTHER UNTIL ONLY ONE REMAINS.
TO US, WHO HAVE INFINITE TIME ON OUR HANDS AS PURE-BLOODS...
...THIS IS MERELY A GAME.
SIXTY-FIFTH NIGHT/END

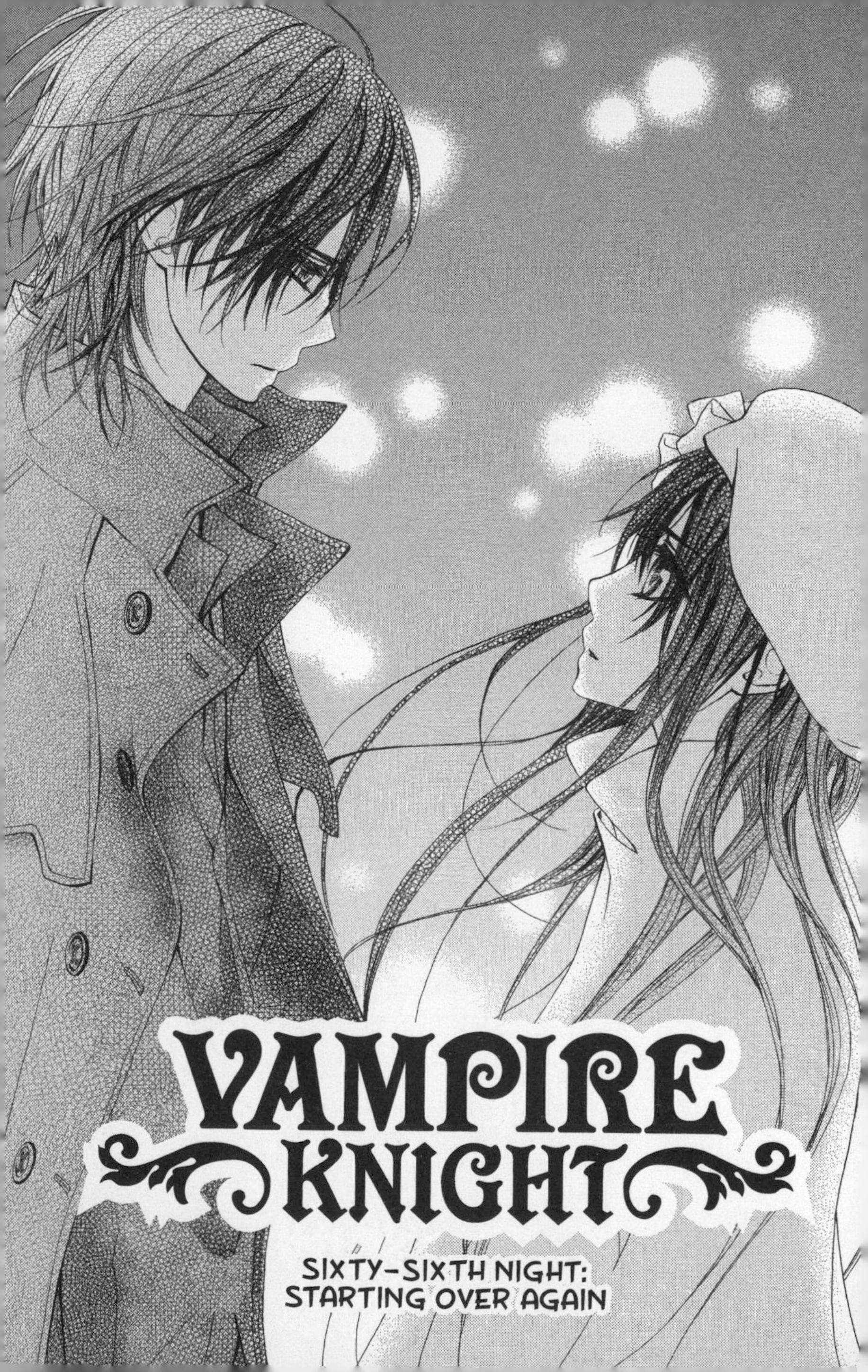
VAMPIRE KNIGHT
SIXTY-SIXTH NIGHT:
STARTING OVER AGAIN

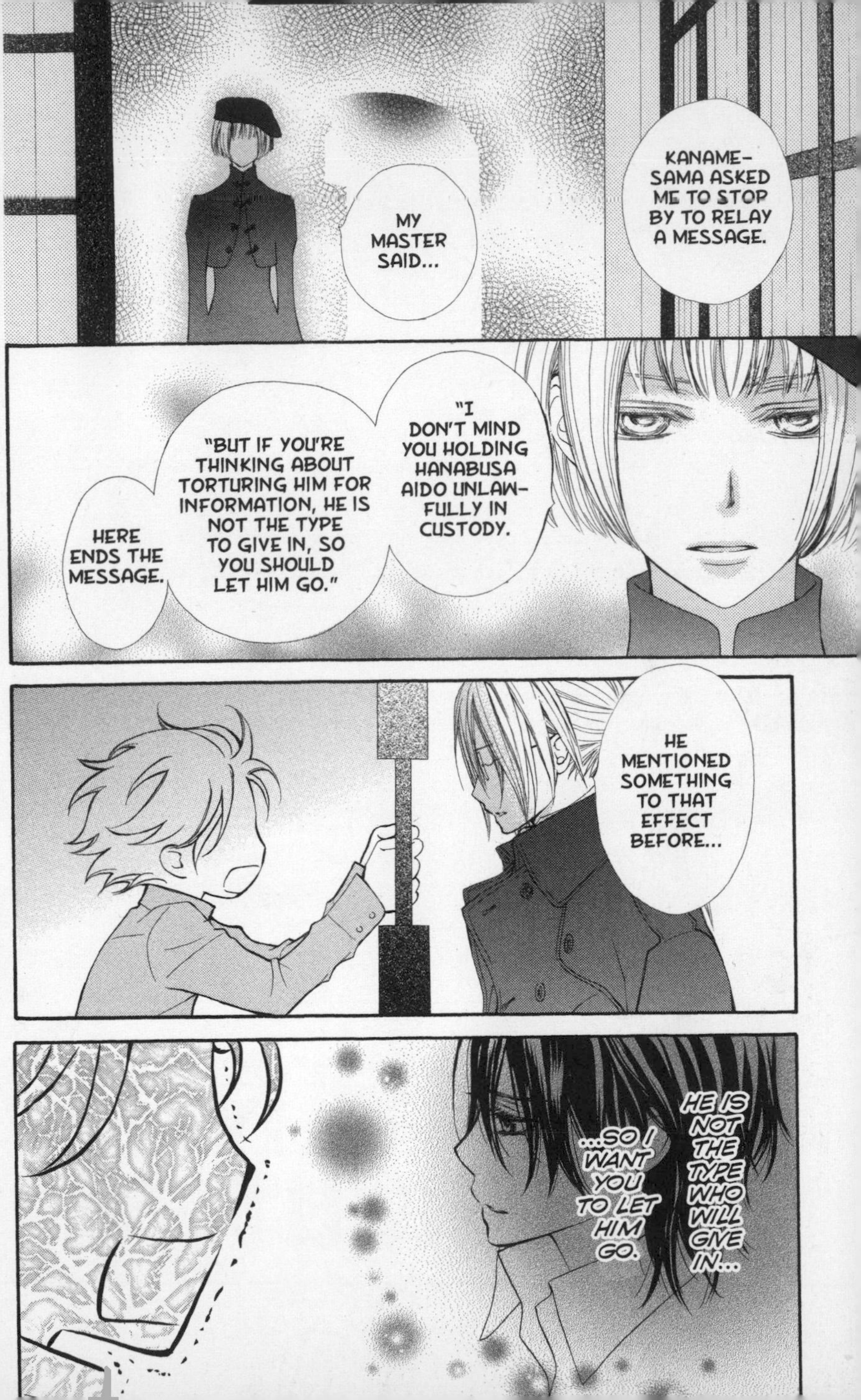
KANAME-SAMA ASKED ME TO STOP BY TO RELAY A MESSAGE.
MY MASTER SAID...
"I DON'T MIND YOU HOLDING HANABUSA AIDO UNLAWFULLY IN CUSTODY.
"BUT IF YOU'RE THINKING ABOUT TORTURING HIM FOR INFORMATION, HE IS NOT THE TYPE TO GIVE IN, SO YOU SHOULD LET HIM GO."
HERE ENDS THE MESSAGE.
HE MENTIONED SOMETHING TO THAT EFFECT BEFORE...
HE IS NOT THE TYPE WHO WILL GIVE IN...
...SO I WANT YOU TO LET HIM GO.

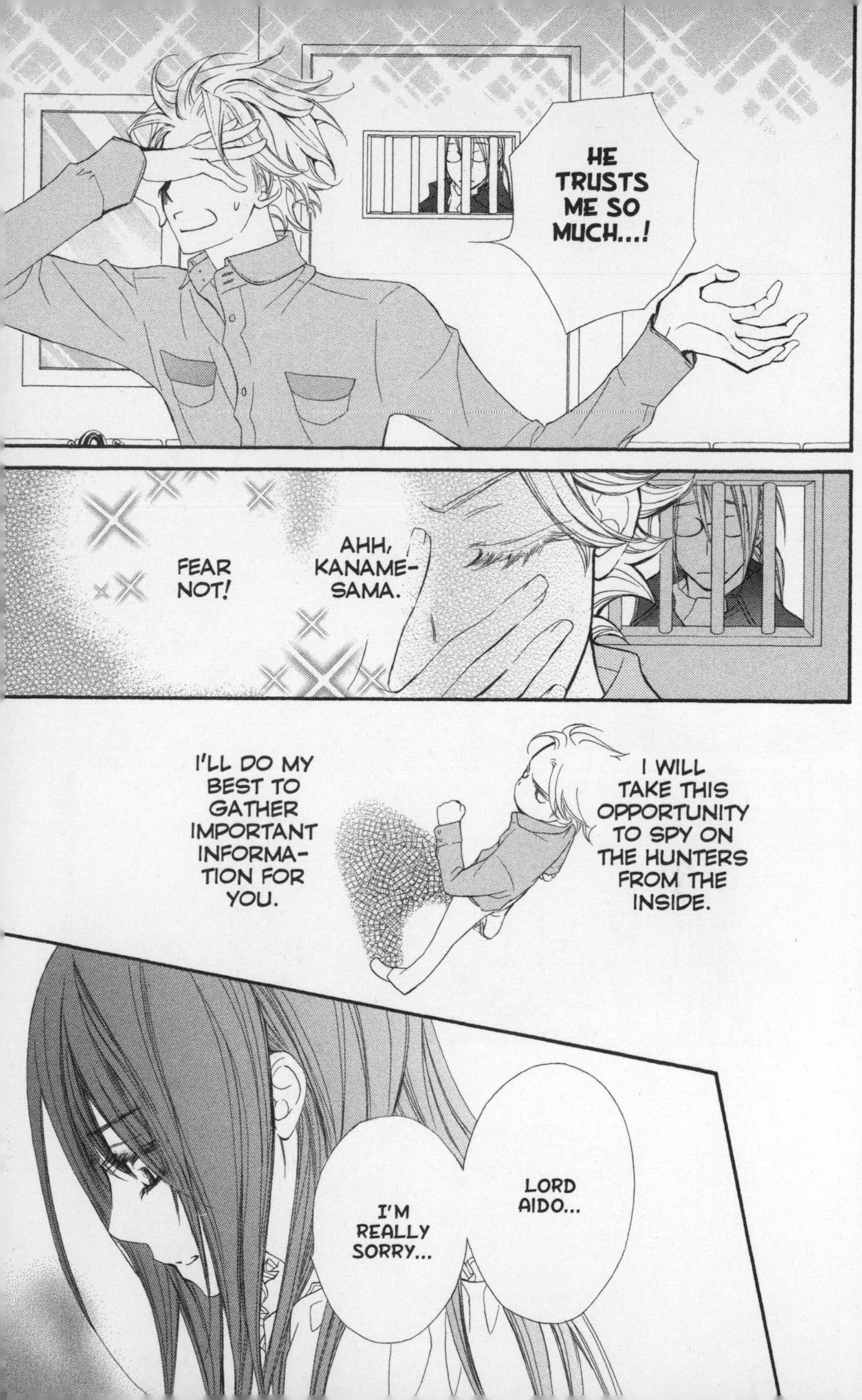
HE TRUSTS ME SO MUCH...!
AHH, KANAME-SAMA.
FEAR NOT!
I WILL TAKE THIS OPPORTUNITY TO SPY ON THE HUNTERS FROM THE INSIDE.
I'LL DO MY BEST TO GATHER IMPORTANT INFORMATION FOR YOU.
LORD AIDO...
I'M REALLY SORRY...

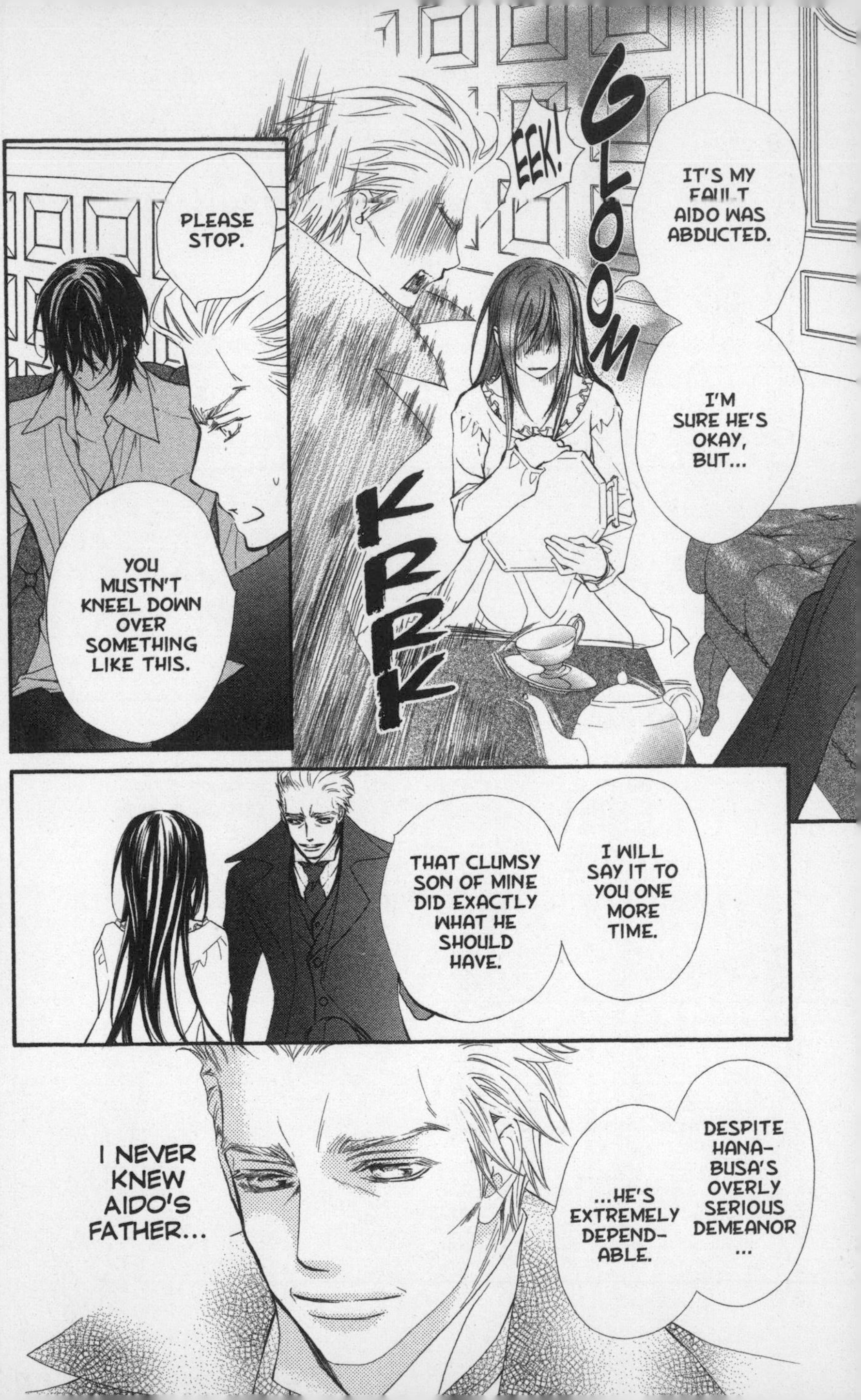
IT'S MY FAULT AIDO WAS ABDUCTED.
GLOOM
EEK!
I'M SURE HE'S OKAY, BUT...
KRRK
PLEASE STOP.
YOU MUSTN'T KNEEL DOWN OVER SOMETHING LIKE THIS.
I WILL SAY IT TO YOU ONE MORE TIME.
THAT CLUMSY SON OF MINE DID EXACTLY WHAT HE SHOULD HAVE.
DESPITE HANA-BUSA'S OVERLY SERIOUS DEMEANOR...
...HE'S EXTREMELY DEPEND-ABLE.
I NEVER KNEW AIDO'S FATHER...

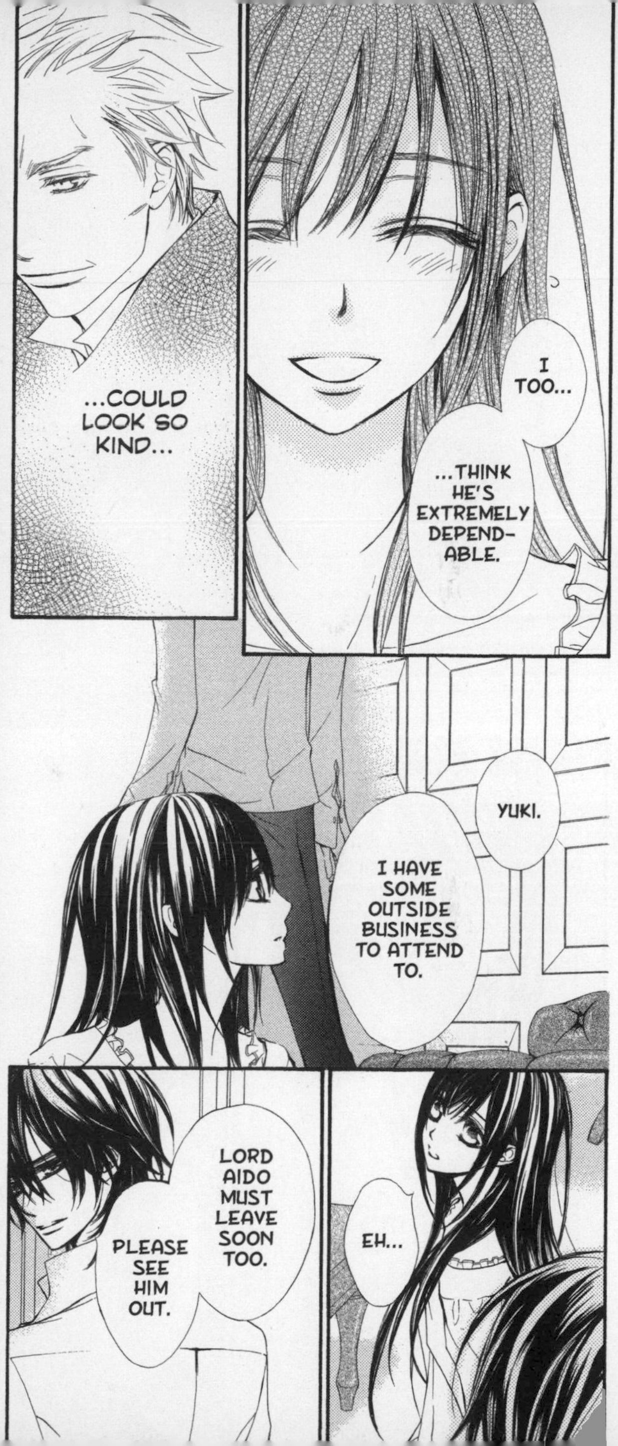
I TOO...
...THINK HE'S EXTREMELY DEPEND-ABLE.
...COULD LOOK SO KIND...
YUKI.
I HAVE SOME OUTSIDE BUSINESS TO ATTEND TO.
EH...
LORD AIDO MUST LEAVE SOON TOO.
PLEASE SEE HIM OUT.

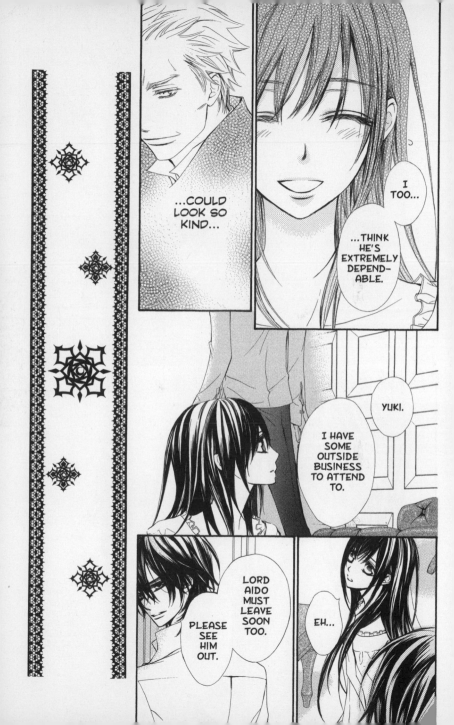

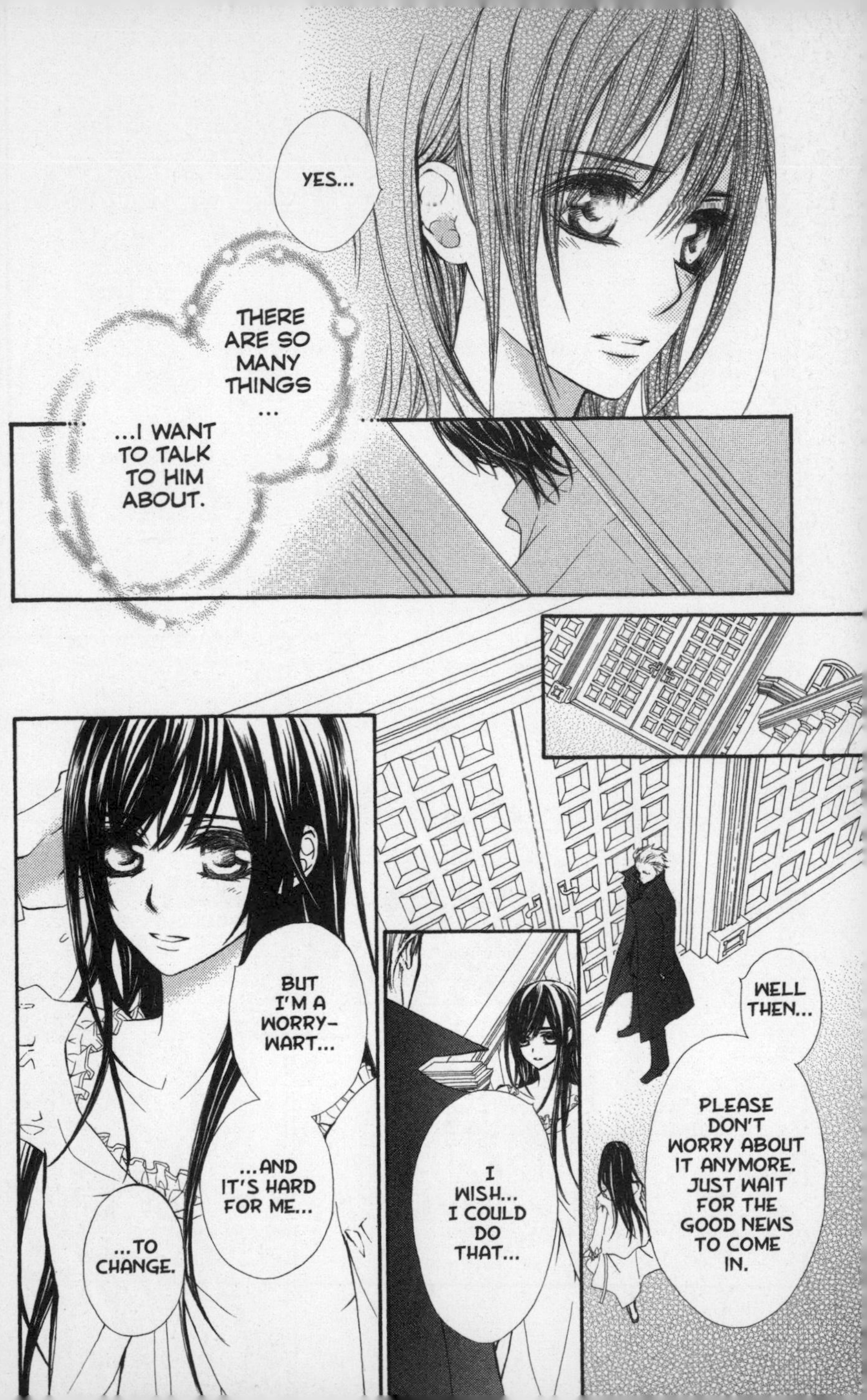
YES...
THERE ARE SO MANY THINGS...
...I WANT TO TALK TO HIM ABOUT.
WELL THEN...
PLEASE DON'T WORRY ABOUT IT ANYMORE. JUST WAIT FOR THE GOOD NEWS TO COME IN.
I WISH... I COULD DO THAT...
BUT I'M A WORRY-WART...
...AND IT'S HARD FOR ME...
...TO CHANGE.

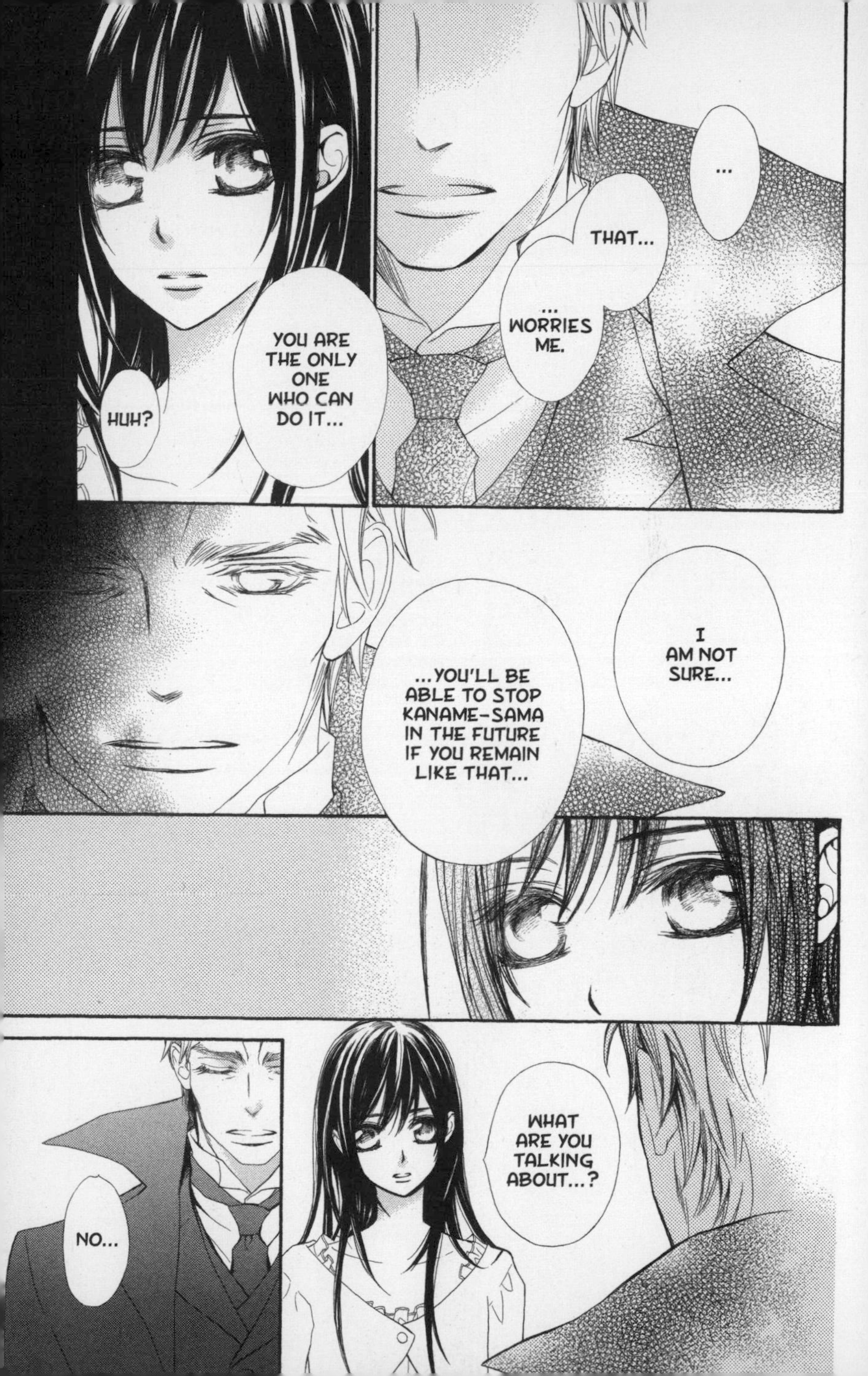
...
THAT...
... WORRIES ME.
YOU ARE THE ONLY ONE WHO CAN DO IT...
HUH?
I AM NOT SURE...
...YOU'LL BE ABLE TO STOP KANAME-SAMA IN THE FUTURE IF YOU REMAIN LIKE THAT...
WHAT ARE YOU TALKING ABOUT...?
NO...

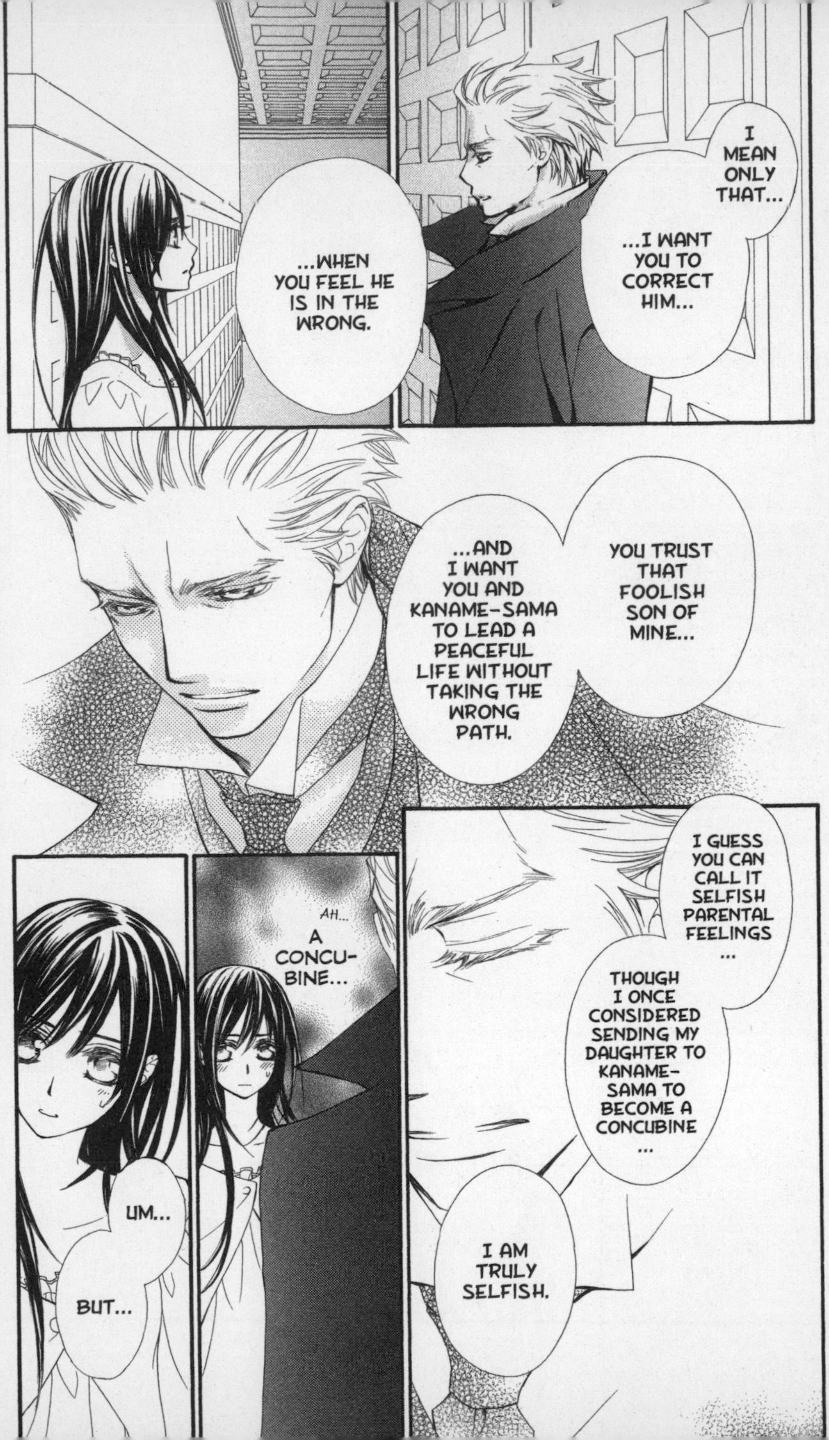
I MEAN ONLY THAT...
...I WANT YOU TO CORRECT HIM...
...WHEN YOU FEEL HE IS IN THE WRONG.
YOU TRUST THAT FOOLISH SON OF MINE...
...AND I WANT YOU AND KANAME-SAMA TO LEAD A PEACEFUL LIFE WITHOUT TAKING THE WRONG PATH.
I GUESS YOU CAN CALL IT SELFISH PARENTAL FEELINGS ...
THOUGH I ONCE CONSIDERED SENDING MY DAUGHTER TO KANAME-SAMA TO BECOME A CONCUBINE ...
I AM TRULY SELFISH.
AH... A CONCUBINE...
UM...
BUT...

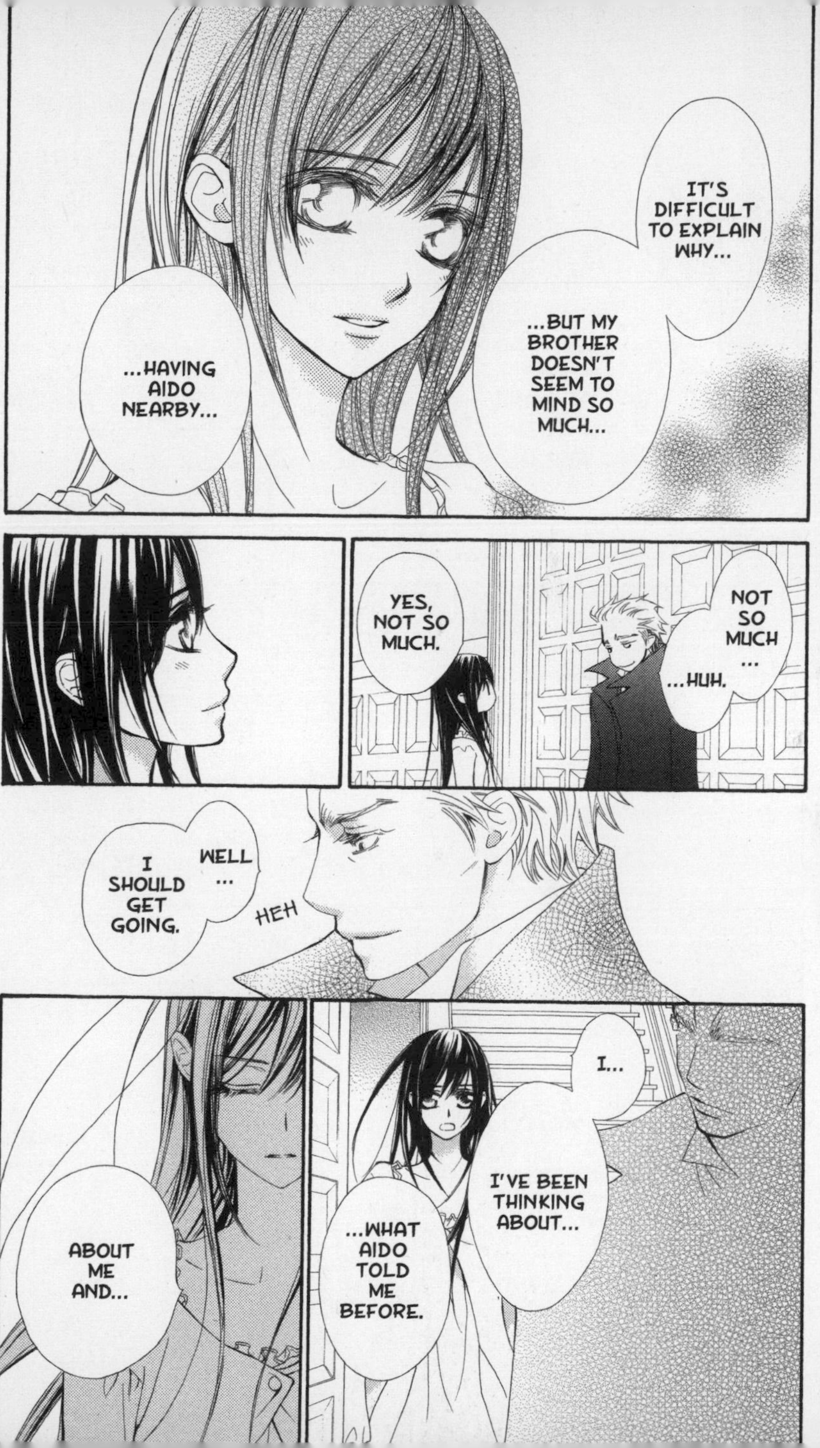
IT'S DIFFICULT TO EXPLAIN WHY...
...BUT MY BROTHER DOESN'T SEEM TO MIND SO MUCH...
...HAVING AIDO NEARBY...
NOT SO MUCH ... ...HUH.
YES, NOT SO MUCH.
WELL ...
HEH
I SHOULD GET GOING.
I...
I'VE BEEN THINKING ABOUT...
...WHAT AIDO TOLD ME BEFORE.
ABOUT ME AND...

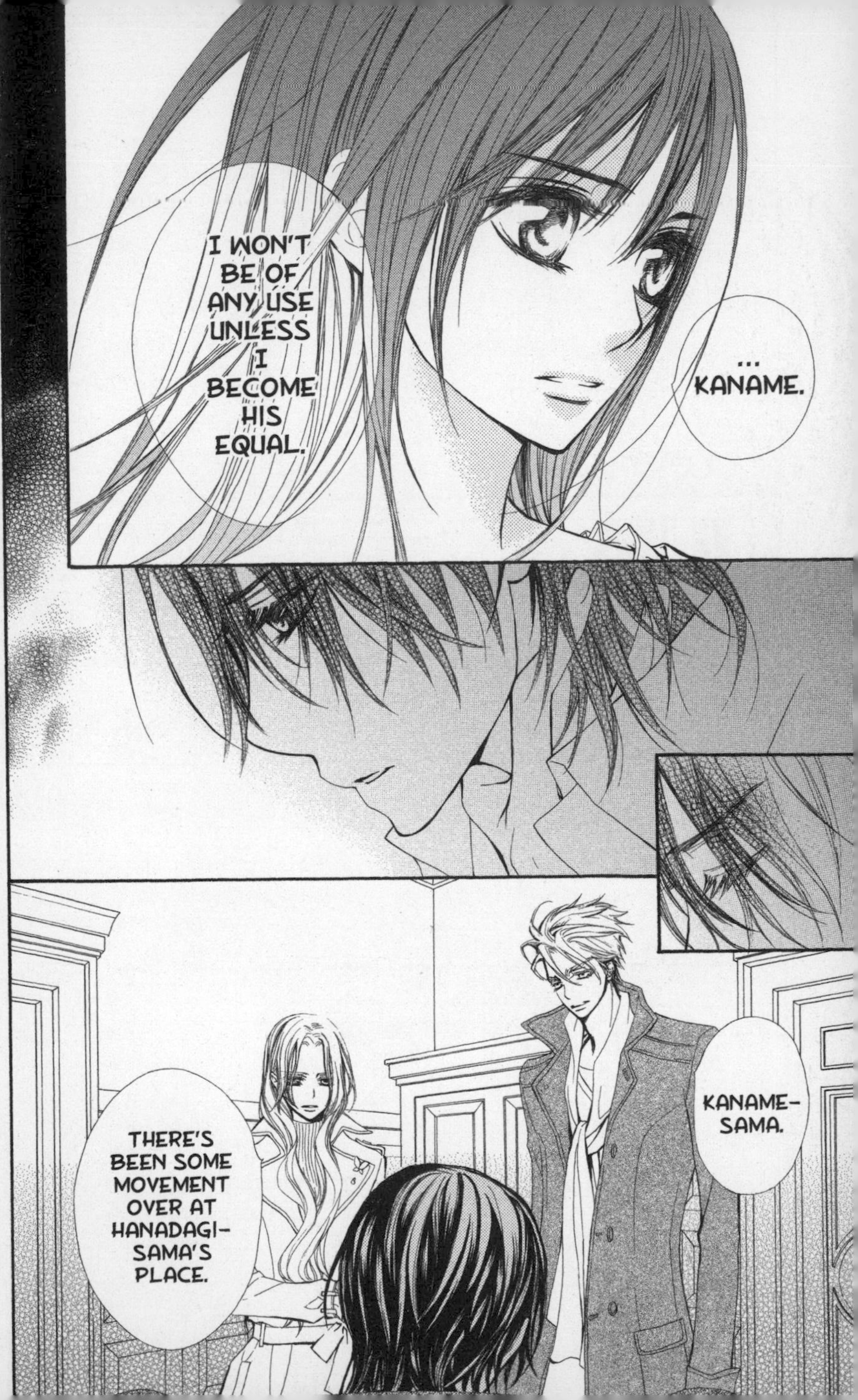
...KANAME.
I WON'T BE OF ANY USE UNLESS I BECOME HIS EQUAL.
KANAME-SAMA.
THERE'S BEEN SOME MOVEMENT OVER AT HANADAGI-SAMA'S PLACE.

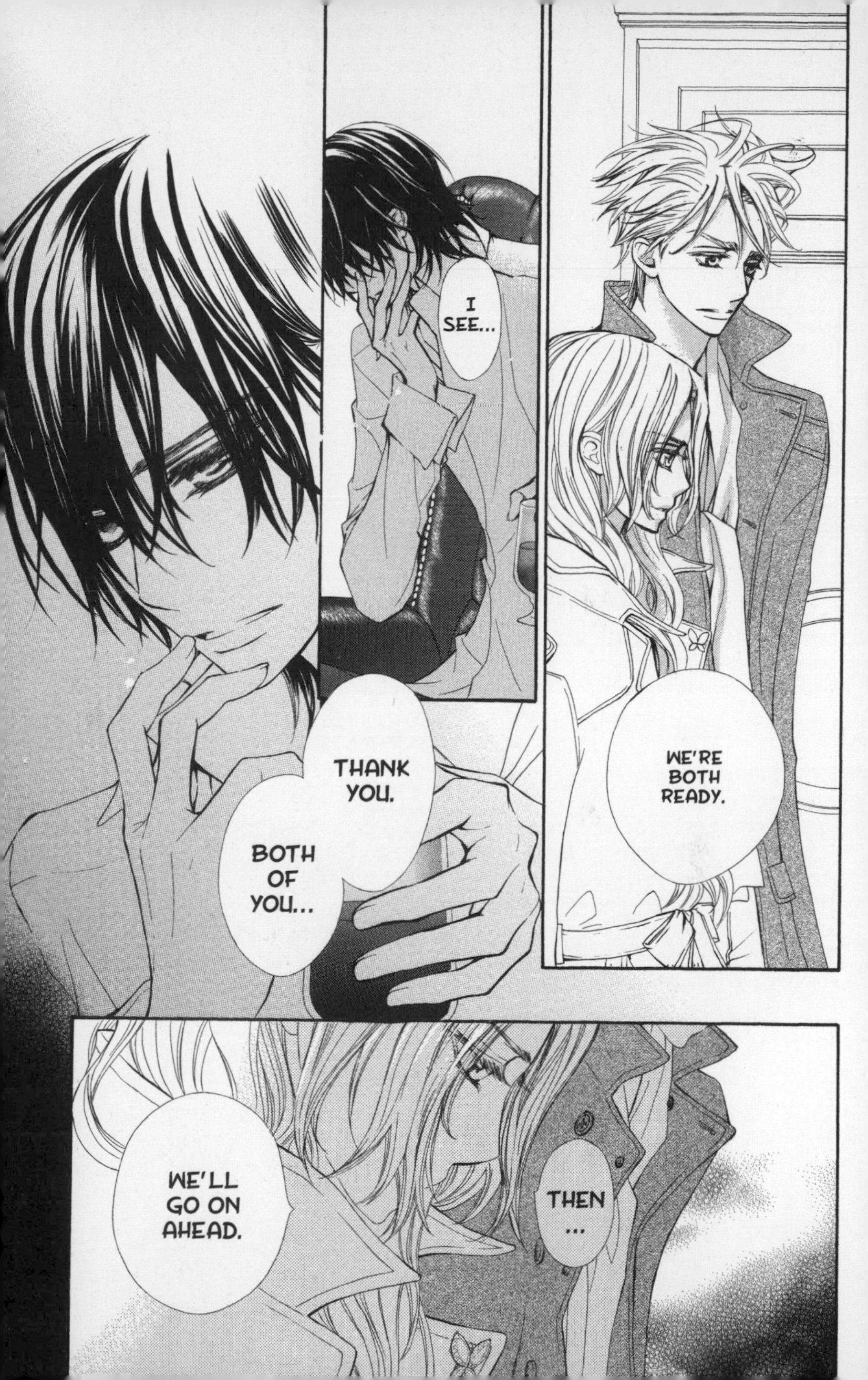
WE'RE BOTH READY.
I SEE...
THANK YOU.
BOTH OF YOU...
THEN ...
WE'LL GO ON AHEAD.

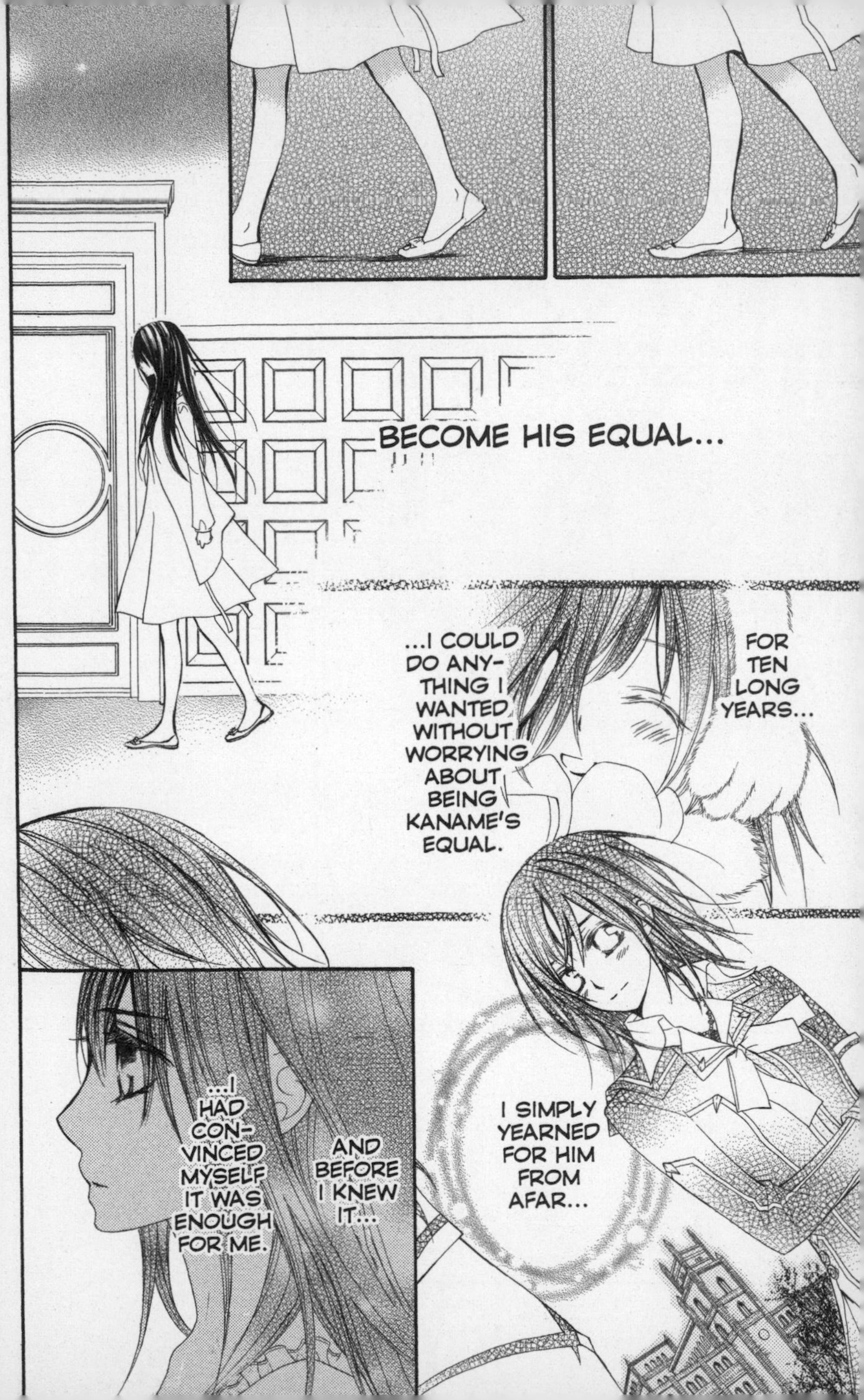
BECOME HIS EQUAL...
FOR TEN LONG YEARS...
...I COULD DO ANYTHING I WANTED WITHOUT WORRYING ABOUT BEING KANAME'S EQUAL.
I SIMPLY YEARNED FOR HIM FROM AFAR...
AND BEFORE I KNEW IT...
...I HAD CONVINCED MYSELF IT WAS ENOUGH FOR ME.

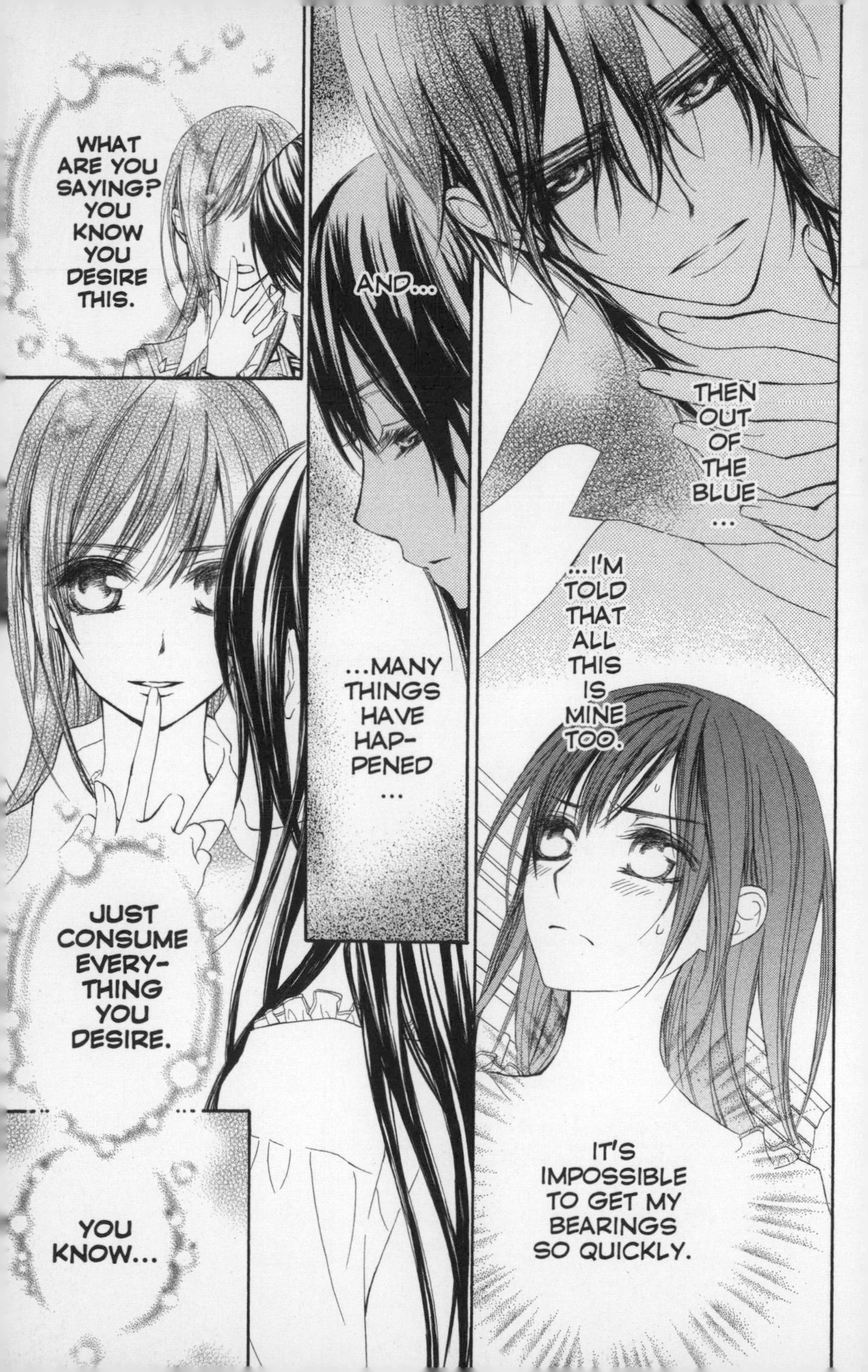
THEN OUT OF THE BLUE...
...I'M TOLD THAT ALL THIS IS MINE TOO.
IT'S IMPOSSIBLE TO GET MY BEARINGS SO QUICKLY.
AND...
...MANY THINGS HAVE HAP-PENED...
WHAT ARE YOU SAYING? YOU KNOW YOU DESIRE THIS.
JUST CONSUME EVERY-THING YOU DESIRE.
... ...
YOU KNOW...

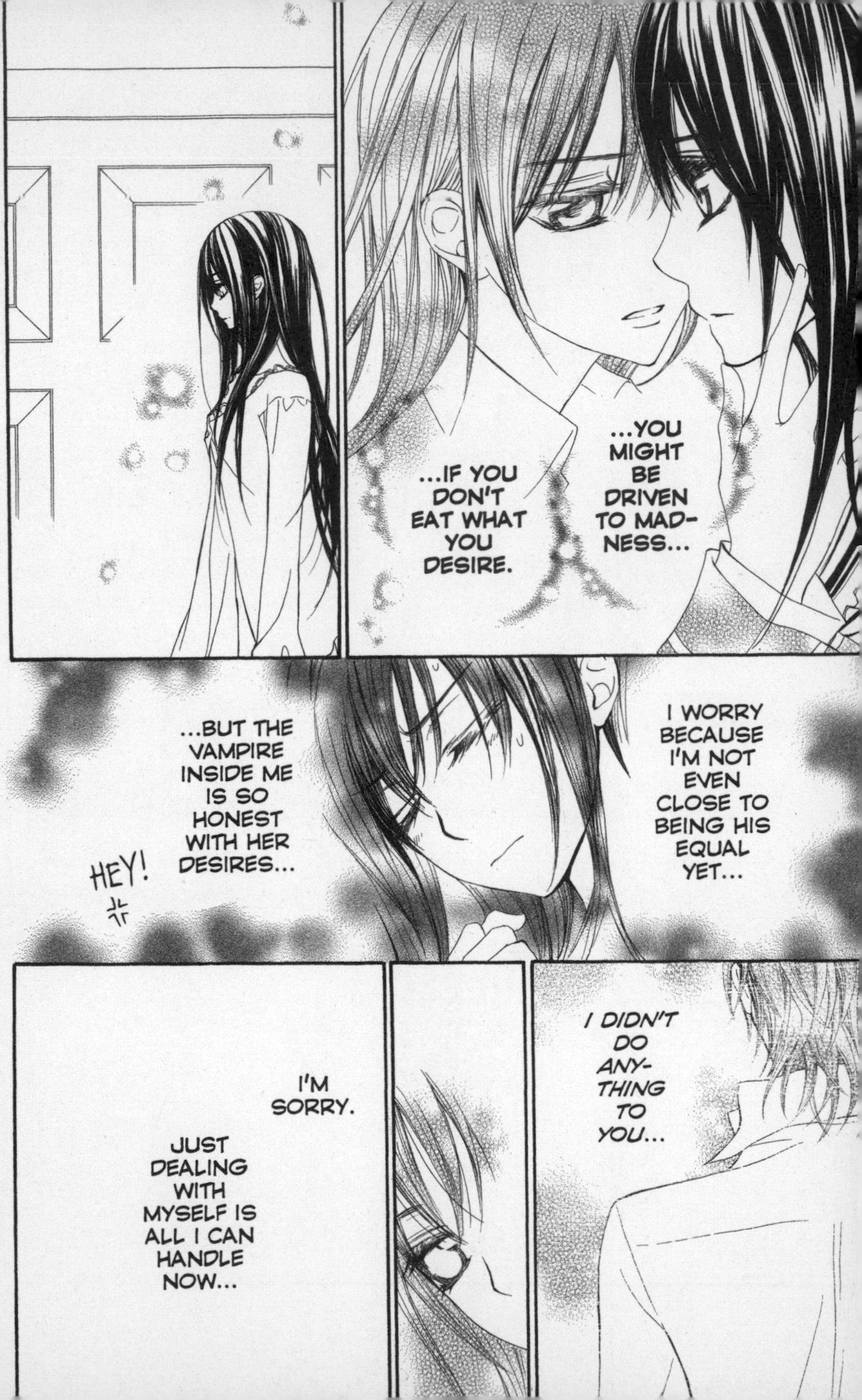
...YOU MIGHT BE DRIVEN TO MADNESS...
...IF YOU DON'T EAT WHAT YOU DESIRE.
I WORRY BECAUSE I'M NOT EVEN CLOSE TO BEING HIS EQUAL YET...
...BUT THE VAMPIRE INSIDE ME IS SO HONEST WITH HER DESIRES...
HEY!
I DIDN'T DO ANYTHING TO YOU...
I'M SORRY.
JUST DEALING WITH MYSELF IS ALL I CAN HANDLE NOW...

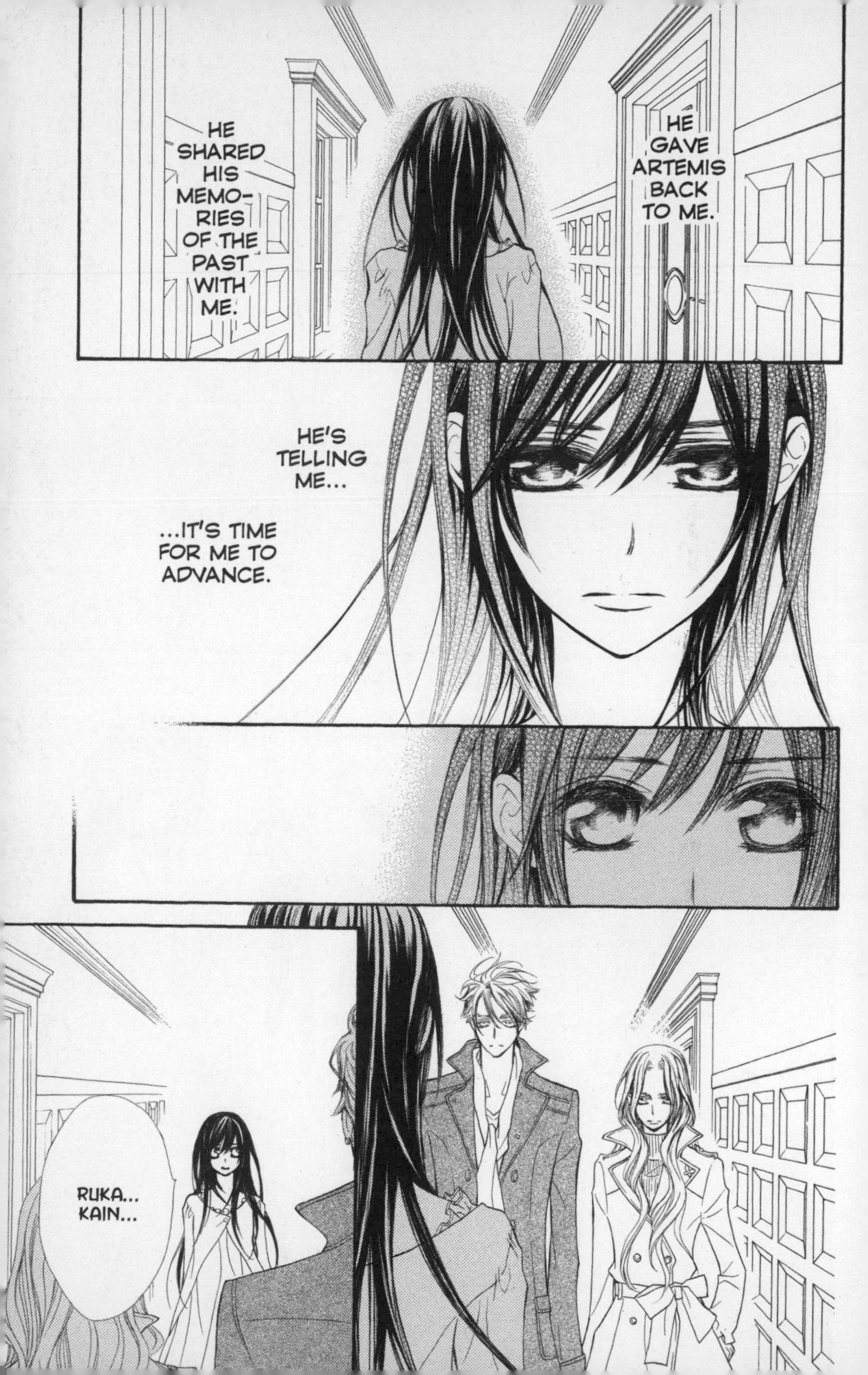
HE GAVE ARTEMIS BACK TO ME.
HE SHARED HIS MEMORIES OF THE PAST WITH ME.
HE'S TELLING ME...
...IT'S TIME FOR ME TO ADVANCE.
RUKA... KAIN...

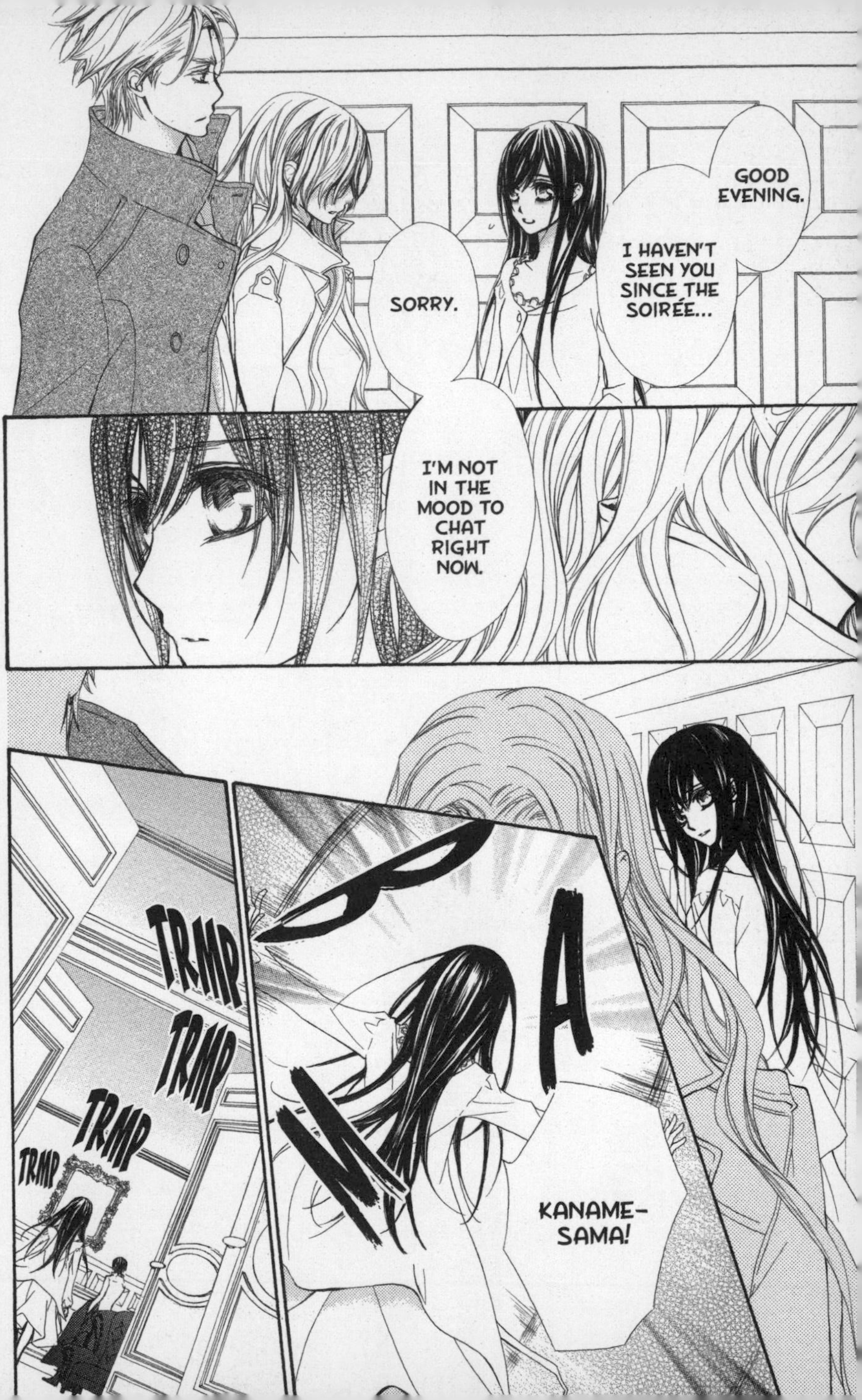
GOOD EVENING.
I HAVEN'T SEEN YOU SINCE THE SOIRÉE...
SORRY.
I'M NOT IN THE MOOD TO CHAT RIGHT NOW.
KANAME-SAMA!
BAM
TRMP
TRMP
TRMP
TRMP

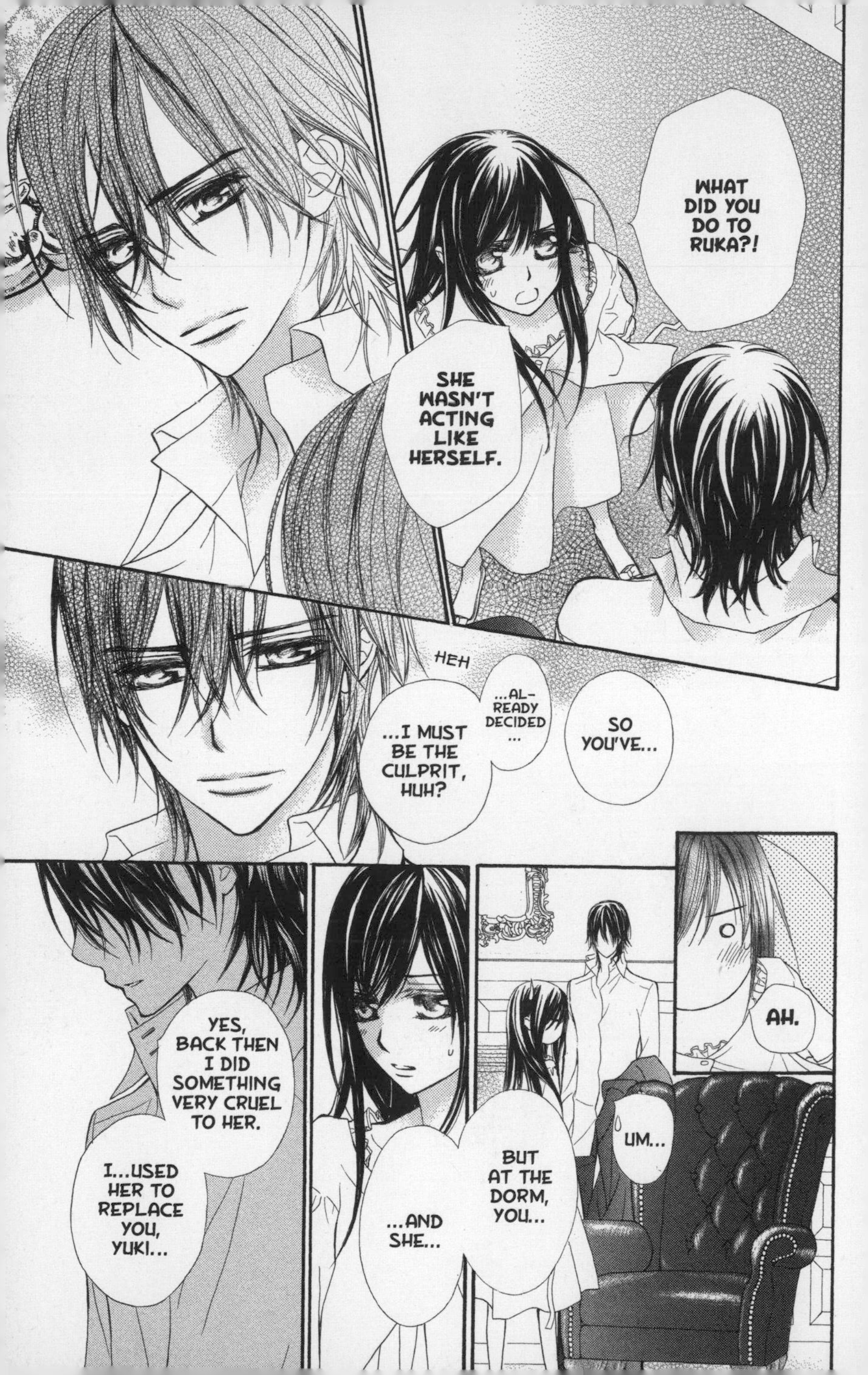
WHAT DID YOU DO TO RUKA?!
SHE WASN'T ACTING LIKE HERSELF.
SO YOU'VE...
...AL-READY DECIDED...
HEH
...I MUST BE THE CULPRIT, HUH?
AH.
UM...
BUT AT THE DORM, YOU...
...AND SHE...
YES, BACK THEN I DID SOMETHING VERY CRUEL TO HER.
I...USED HER TO REPLACE YOU, YUKI...

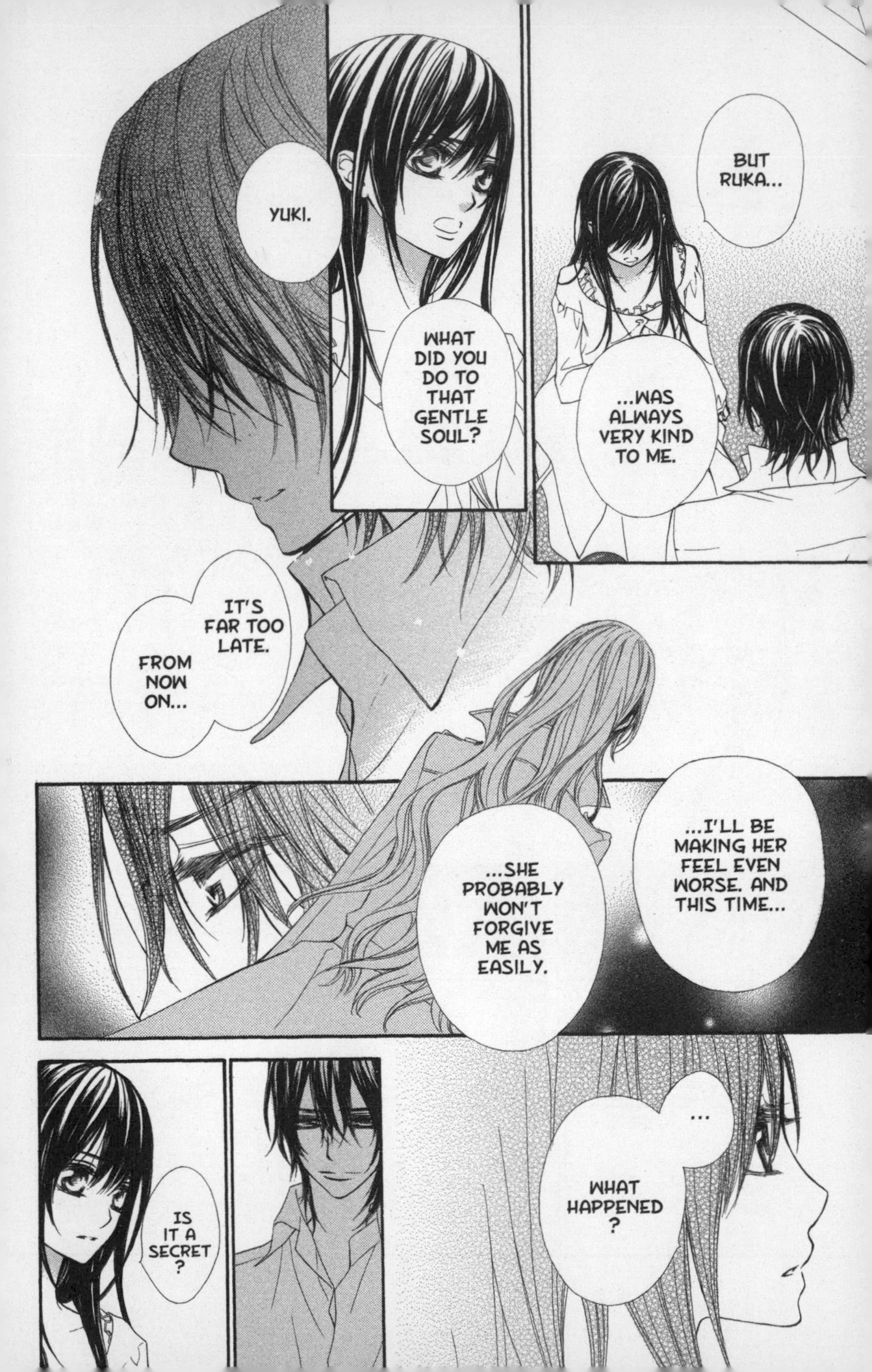
BUT RUKA...
...WAS ALWAYS VERY KIND TO ME.
WHAT DID YOU DO TO THAT GENTLE SOUL?
YUKI.
IT'S FAR TOO LATE.
FROM NOW ON...
...I'LL BE MAKING HER FEEL EVEN WORSE. AND THIS TIME...
...SHE PROBABLY WON'T FORGIVE ME AS EASILY.
...
WHAT HAPPENED?
IS IT A SECRET?

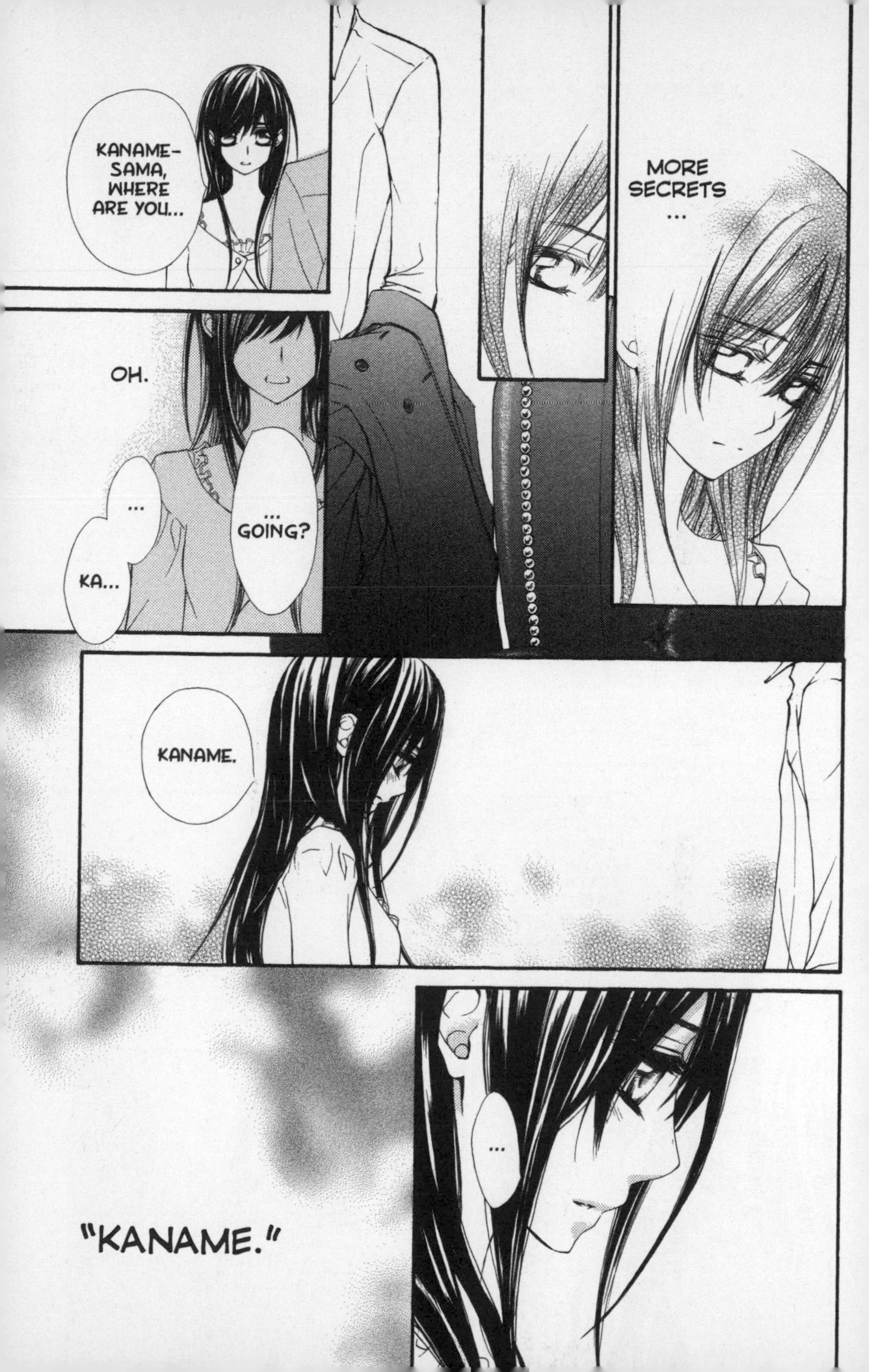
MORE SECRETS ...
KANAME-SAMA, WHERE ARE YOU...
... GOING?
OH.
... KA...
KANAME.
...
"KANAME."

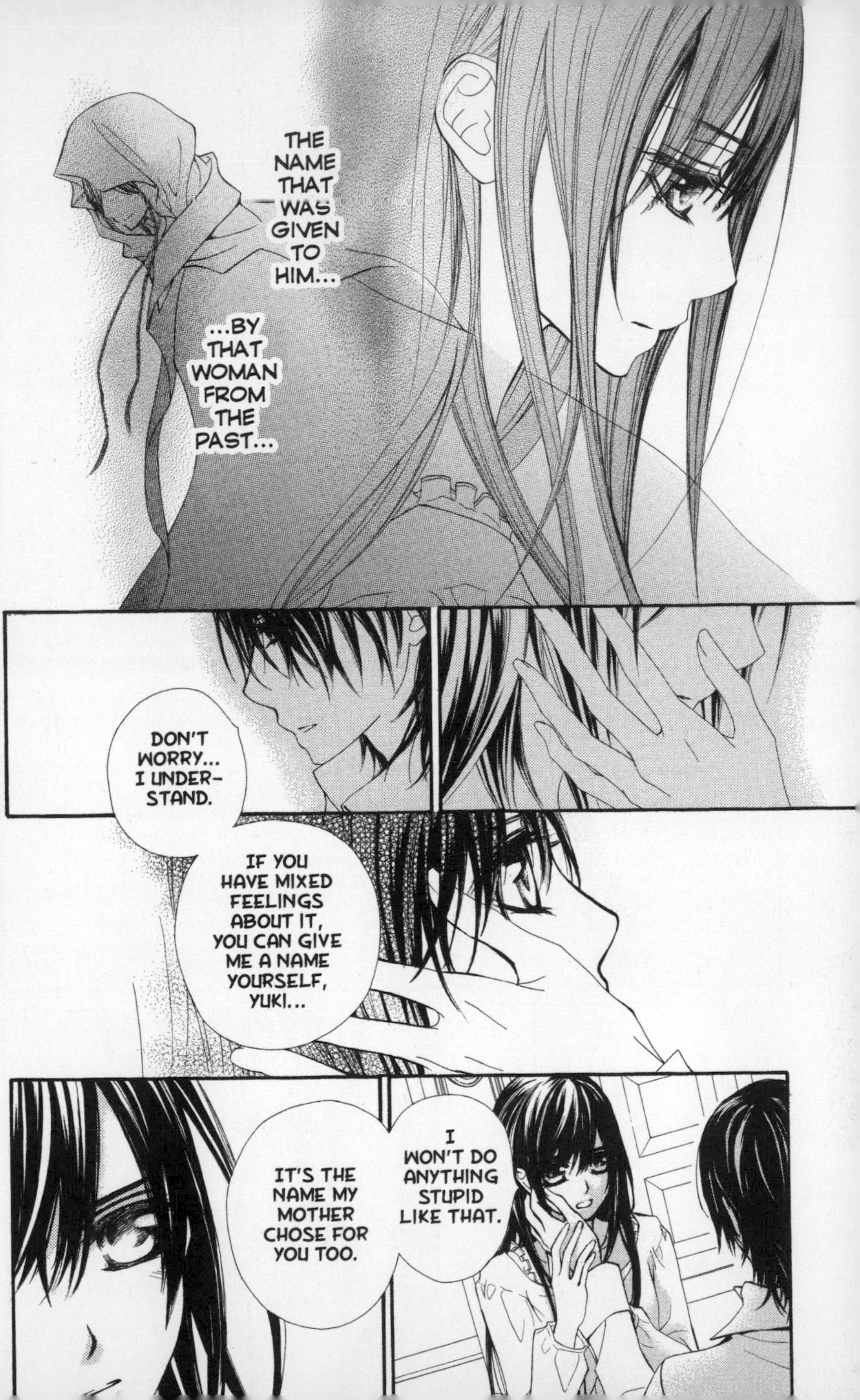
THE NAME THAT WAS GIVEN TO HIM...
...BY THAT WOMAN FROM THE PAST...
DON'T WORRY... I UNDERSTAND.
IF YOU HAVE MIXED FEELINGS ABOUT IT, YOU CAN GIVE ME A NAME YOURSELF, YUKI...
I WON'T DO ANYTHING STUPID LIKE THAT.
IT'S THE NAME MY MOTHER CHOSE FOR YOU TOO.

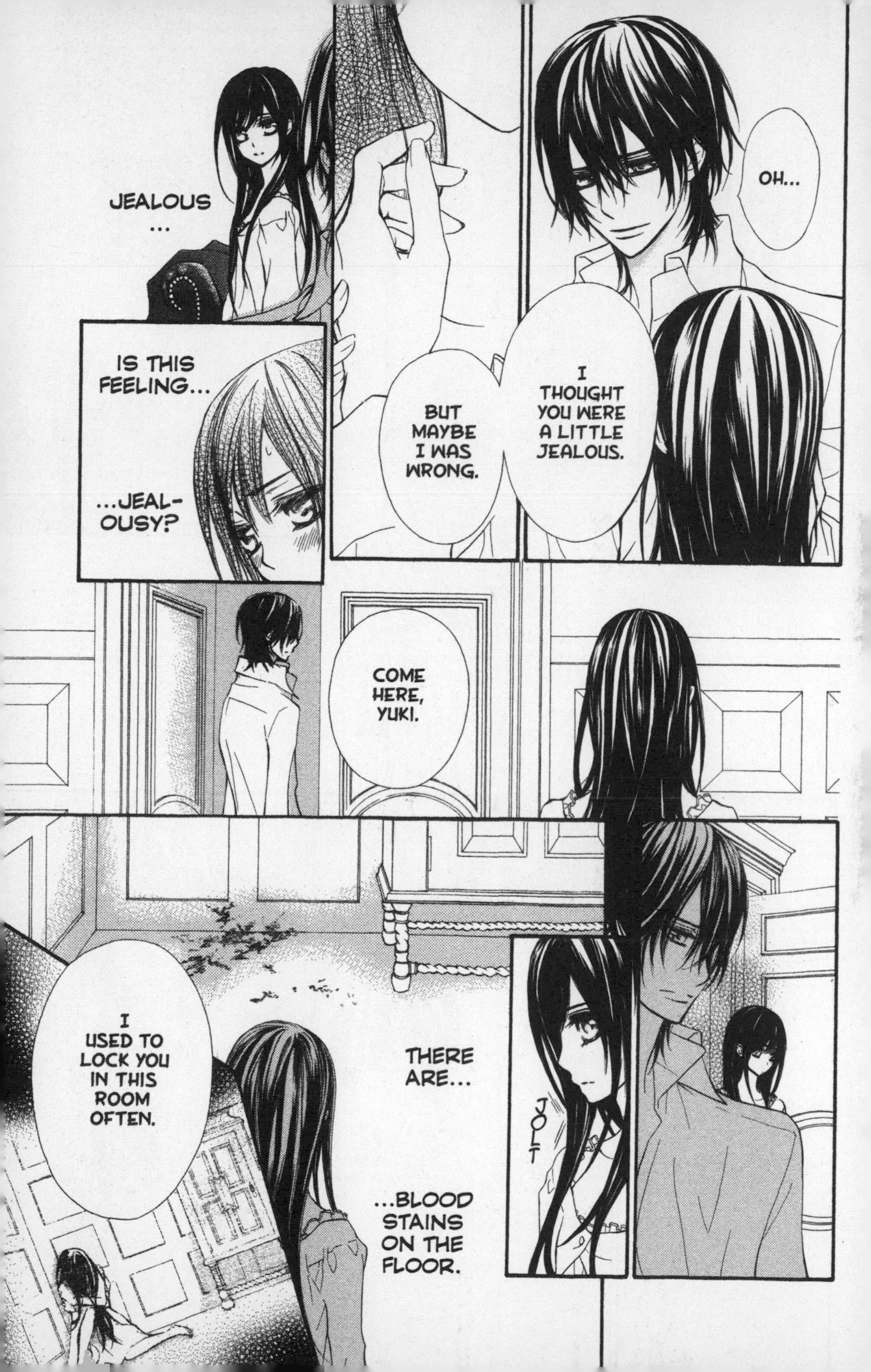
OH...
I THOUGHT YOU WERE A LITTLE JEALOUS.
BUT MAYBE I WAS WRONG.
JEALOUS ...
IS THIS FEELING...
...JEAL-OUSY?
COME HERE, YUKI.
JOLT
I USED TO LOCK YOU IN THIS ROOM OFTEN.
THERE ARE...
...BLOOD STAINS ON THE FLOOR.

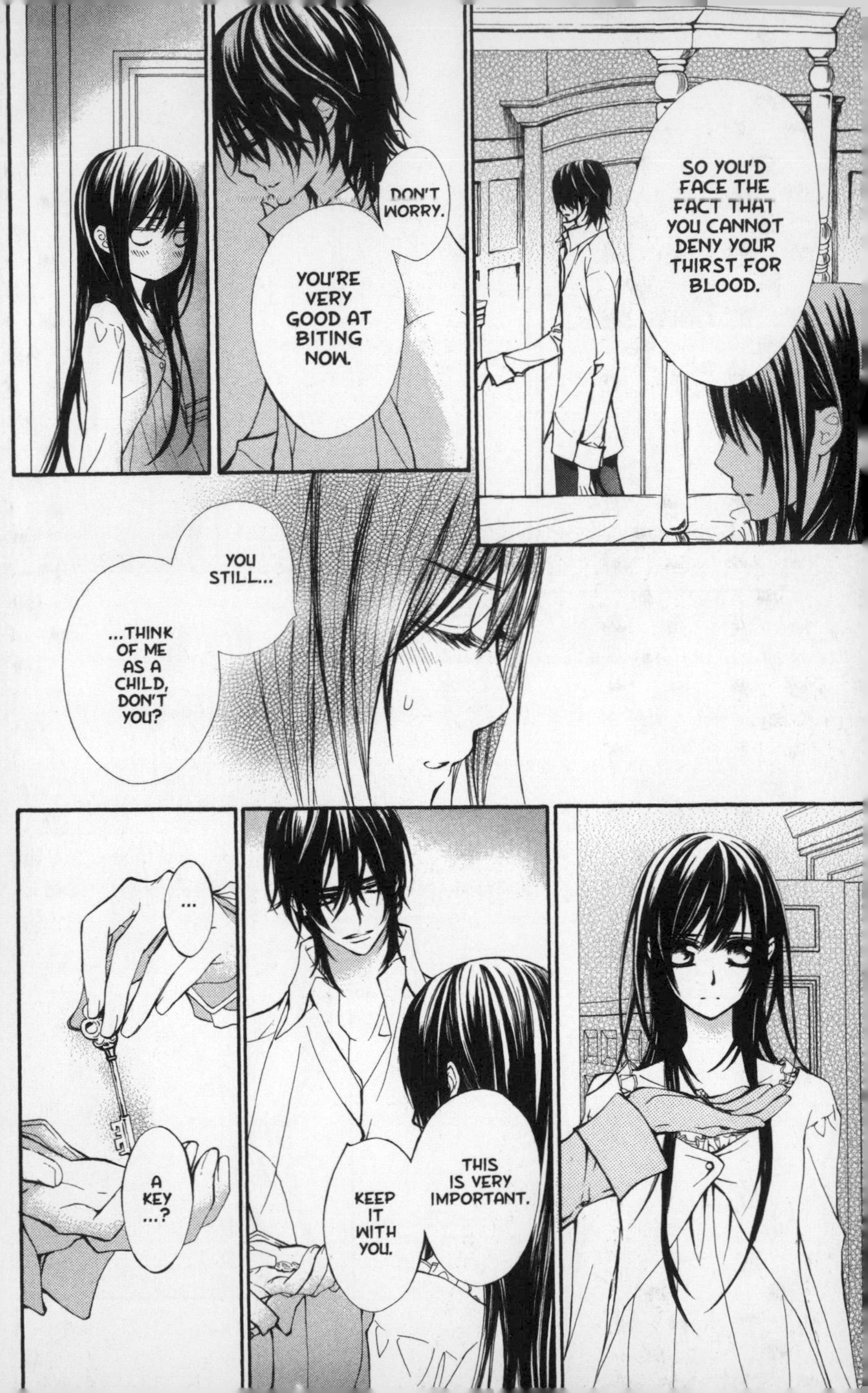
SO YOU'D FACE THE FACT THAT YOU CANNOT DENY YOUR THIRST FOR BLOOD.
DON'T WORRY.
YOU'RE VERY GOOD AT BITING NOW.
YOU STILL...
...THINK OF ME AS A CHILD, DON'T YOU?
THIS IS VERY IMPORTANT.
KEEP IT WITH YOU.
...
A KEY ...?

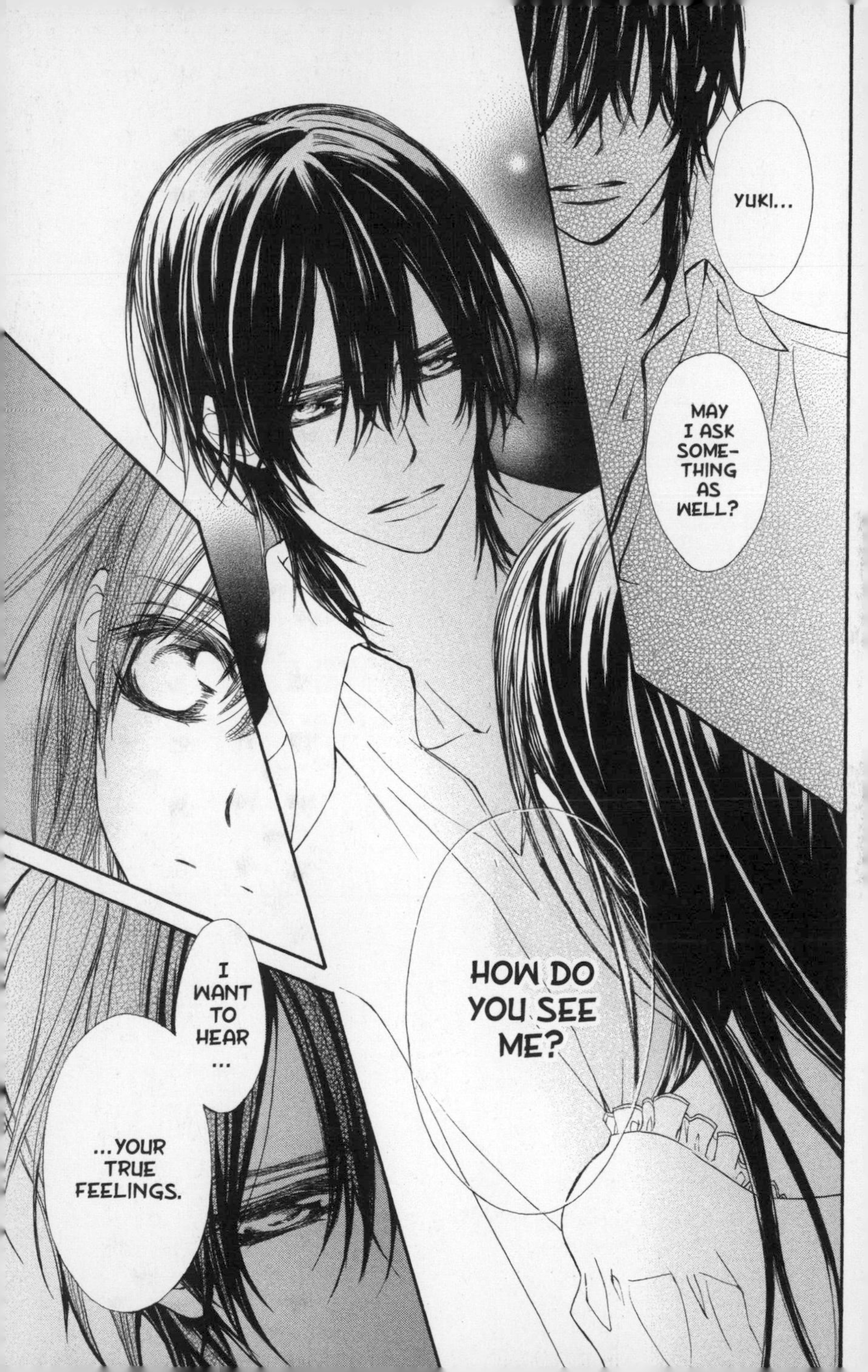
YUKI...
MAY I ASK SOMETHING AS WELL?
HOW DO YOU SEE ME?
I WANT TO HEAR...
...YOUR TRUE FEELINGS.

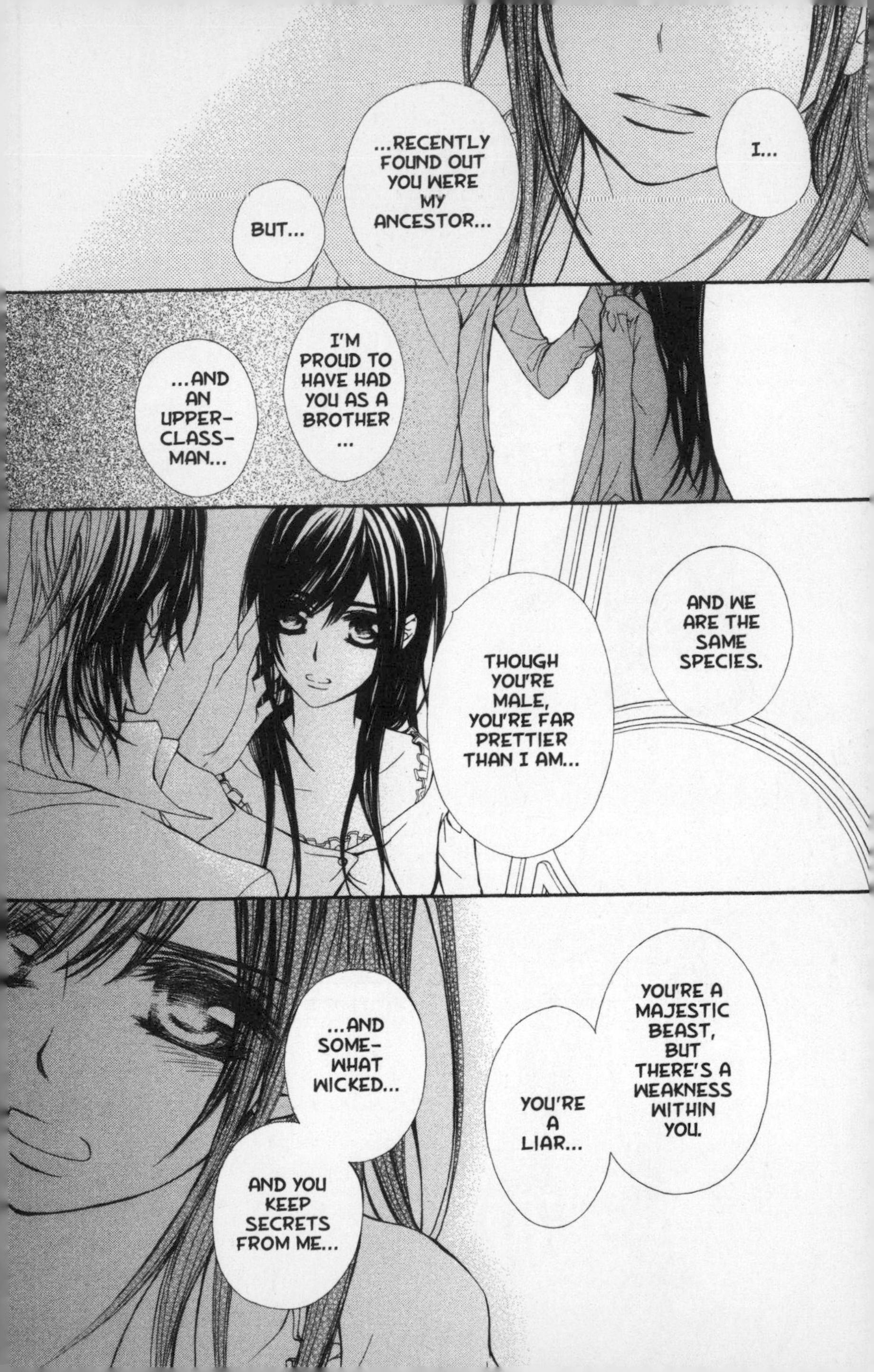
I...
...RECENTLY FOUND OUT YOU WERE MY ANCESTOR...
BUT...
I'M PROUD TO HAVE HAD YOU AS A BROTHER ...
...AND AN UPPER-CLASSMAN...
AND WE ARE THE SAME SPECIES.
THOUGH YOU'RE MALE, YOU'RE FAR PRETTIER THAN I AM...
YOU'RE A MAJESTIC BEAST, BUT THERE'S A WEAKNESS WITHIN YOU.
YOU'RE A LIAR...
...AND SOME-WHAT WICKED...
AND YOU KEEP SECRETS FROM ME...

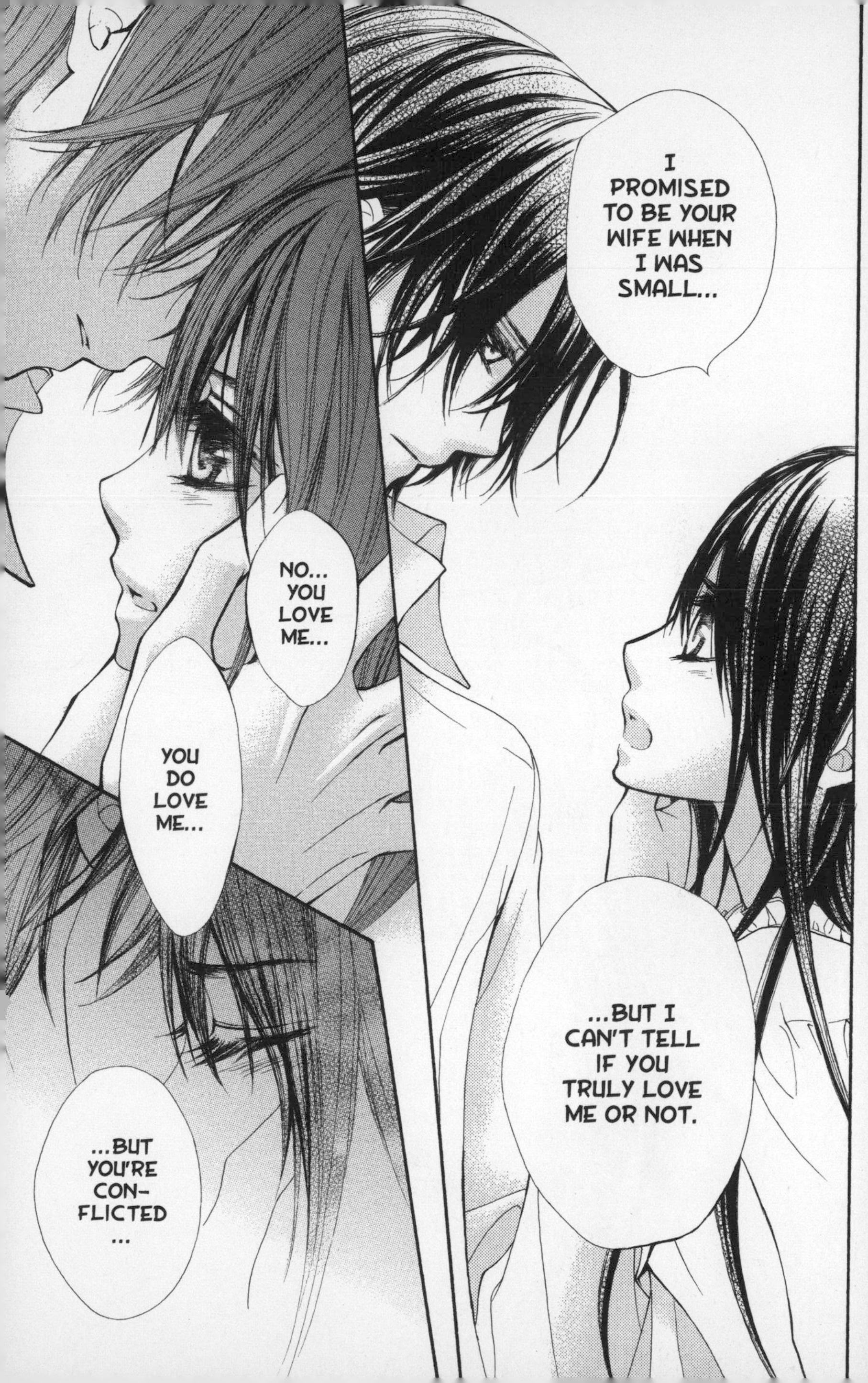
I PROMISED TO BE YOUR WIFE WHEN I WAS SMALL...
...BUT I CAN'T TELL IF YOU TRULY LOVE ME OR NOT.
NO... YOU LOVE ME...
YOU DO LOVE ME...
...BUT YOU'RE CON-FLICTED ...

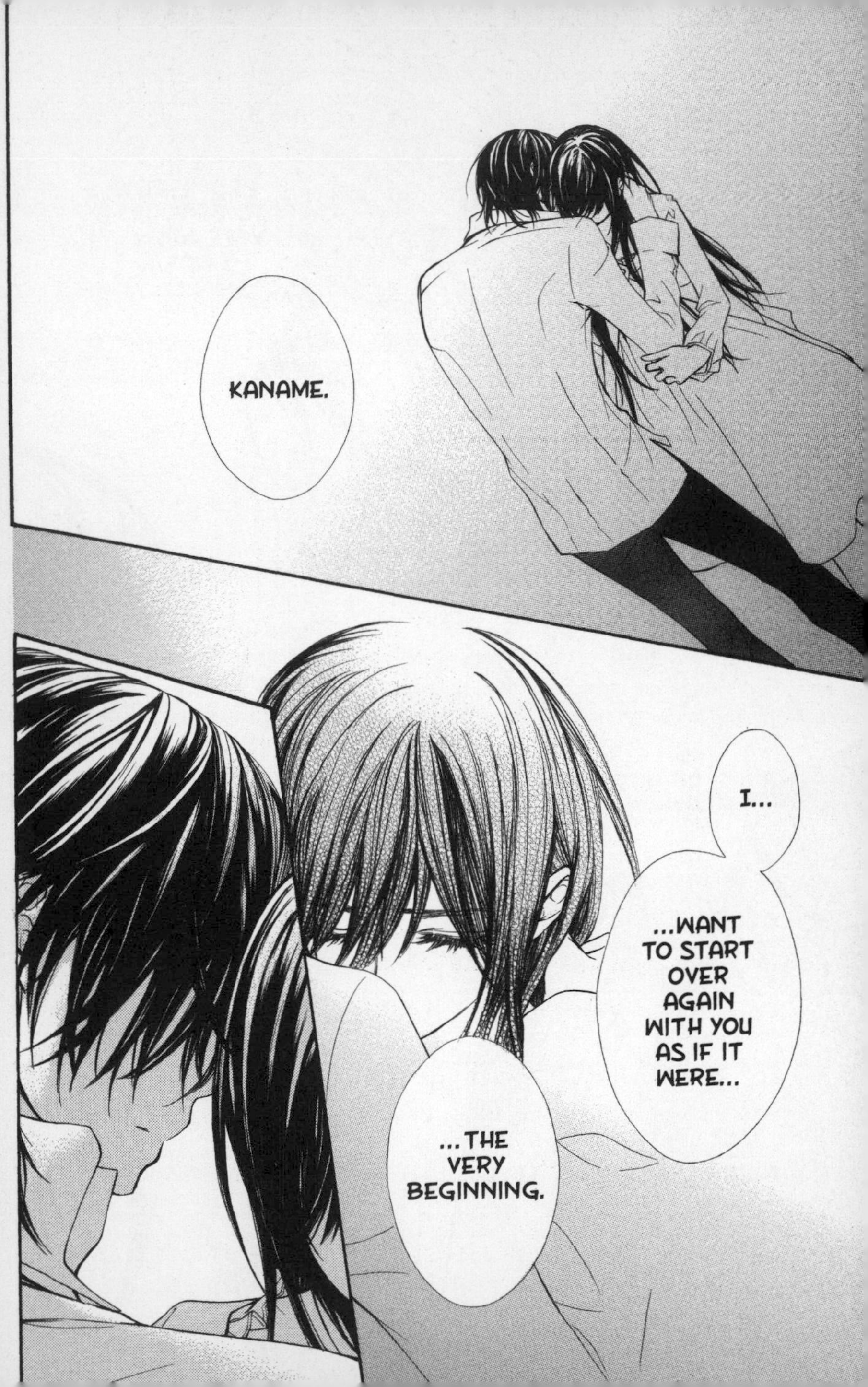
KANAME.
I...
...WANT TO START OVER AGAIN WITH YOU AS IF IT WERE...
...THE VERY BEGINNING.

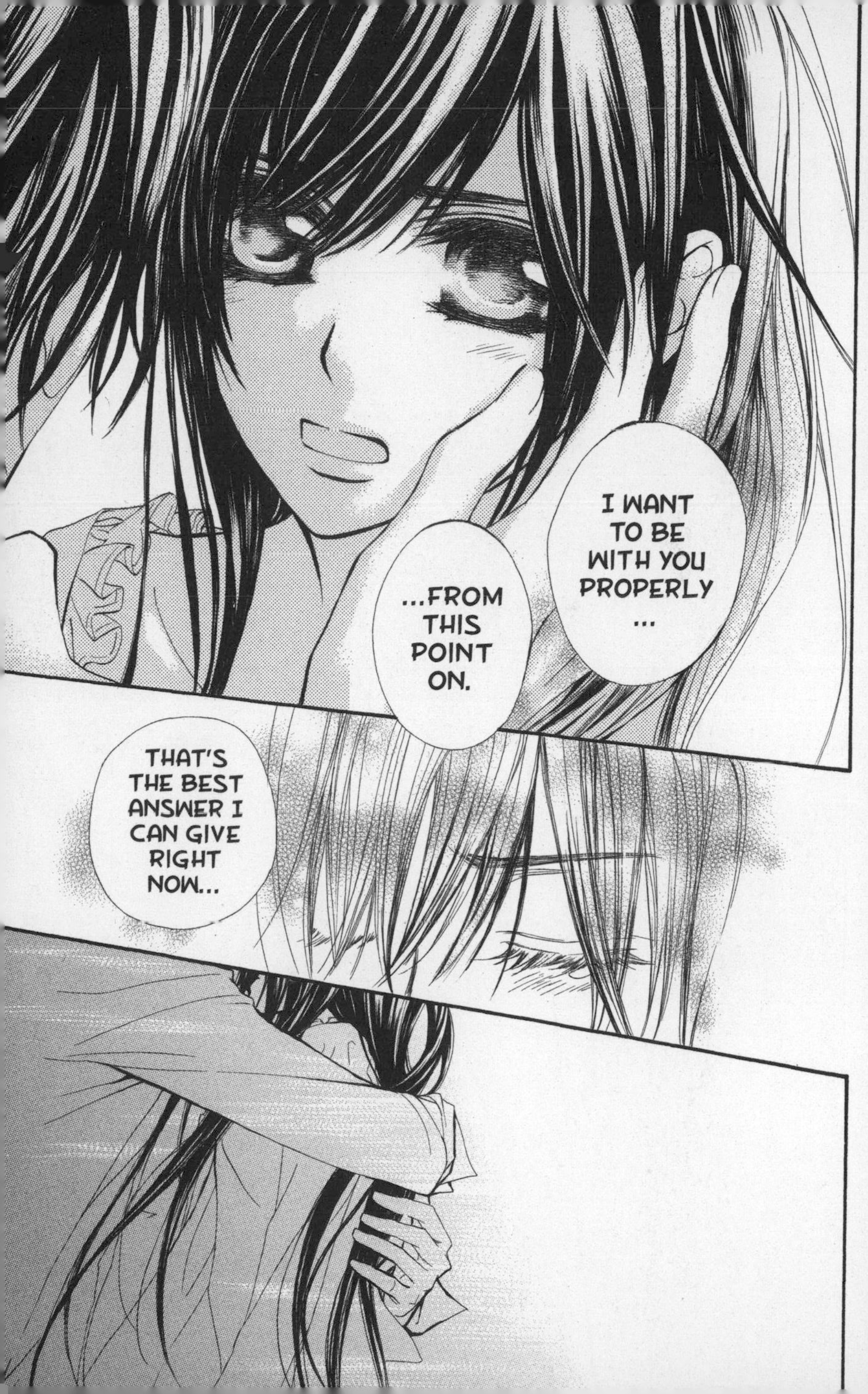
I WANT TO BE WITH YOU PROPERLY ...
...FROM THIS POINT ON.
THAT'S THE BEST ANSWER I CAN GIVE RIGHT NOW...

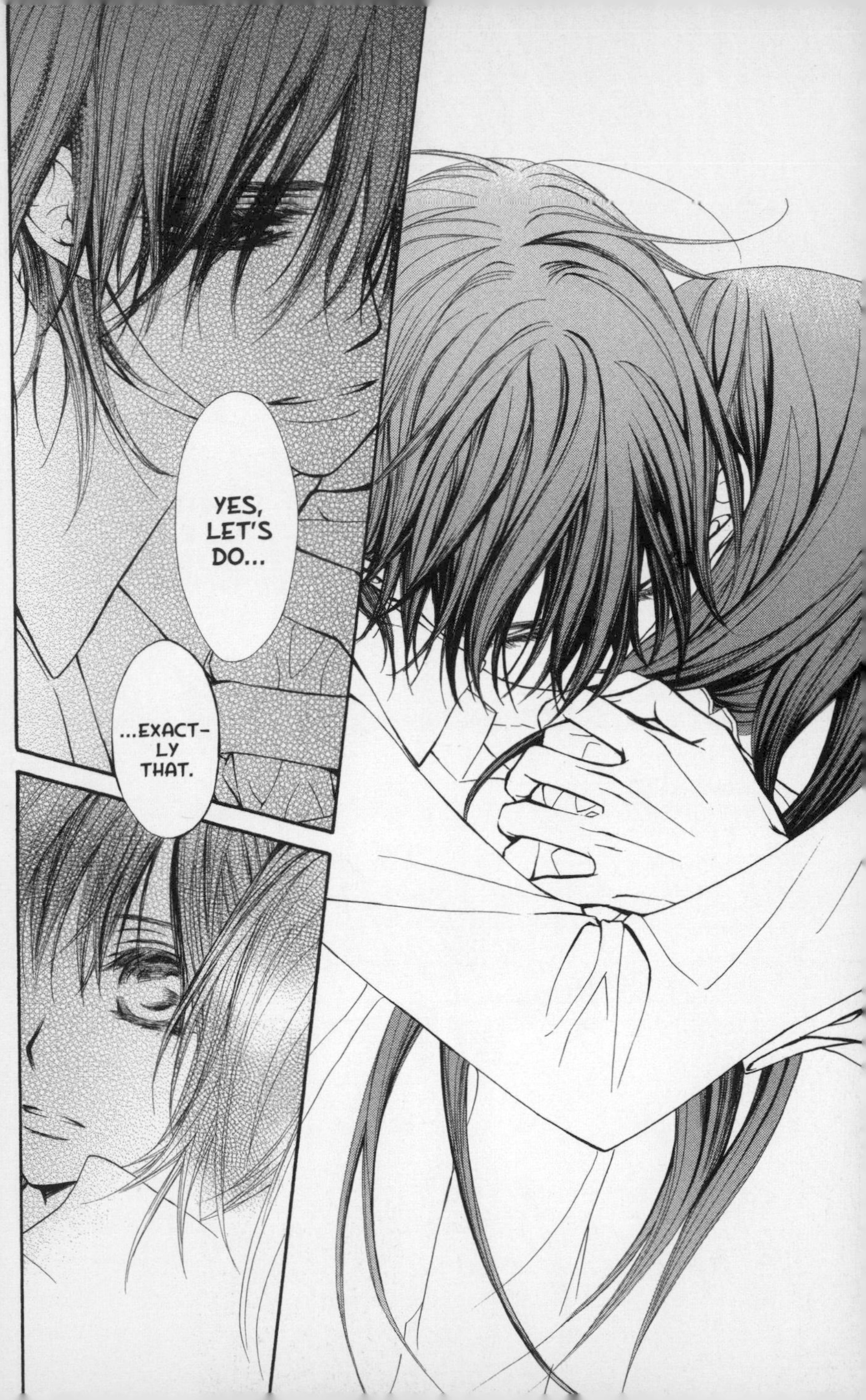
YES, LET'S DO...
...EXACT-LY THAT.

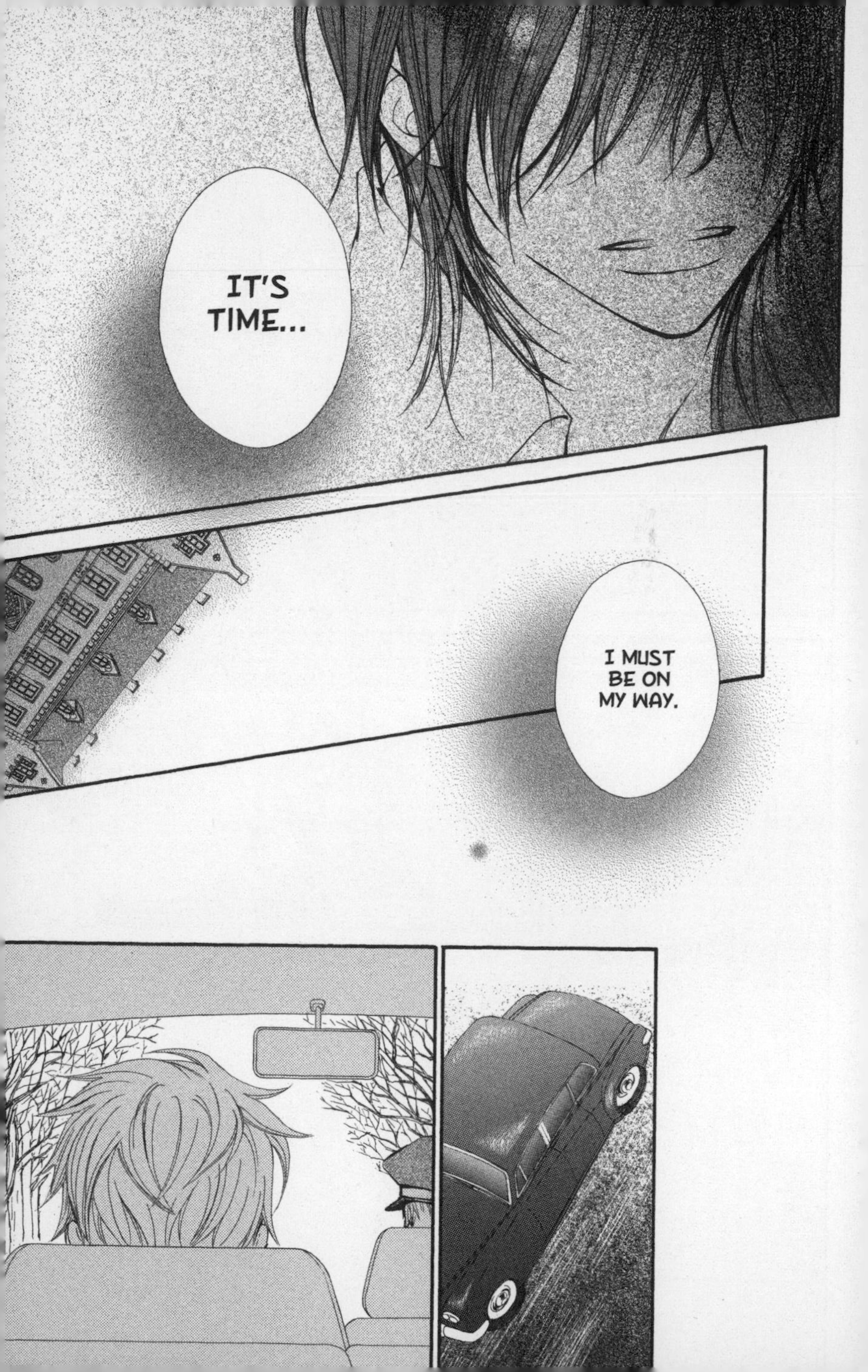
IT'S TIME...
I MUST BE ON MY WAY.

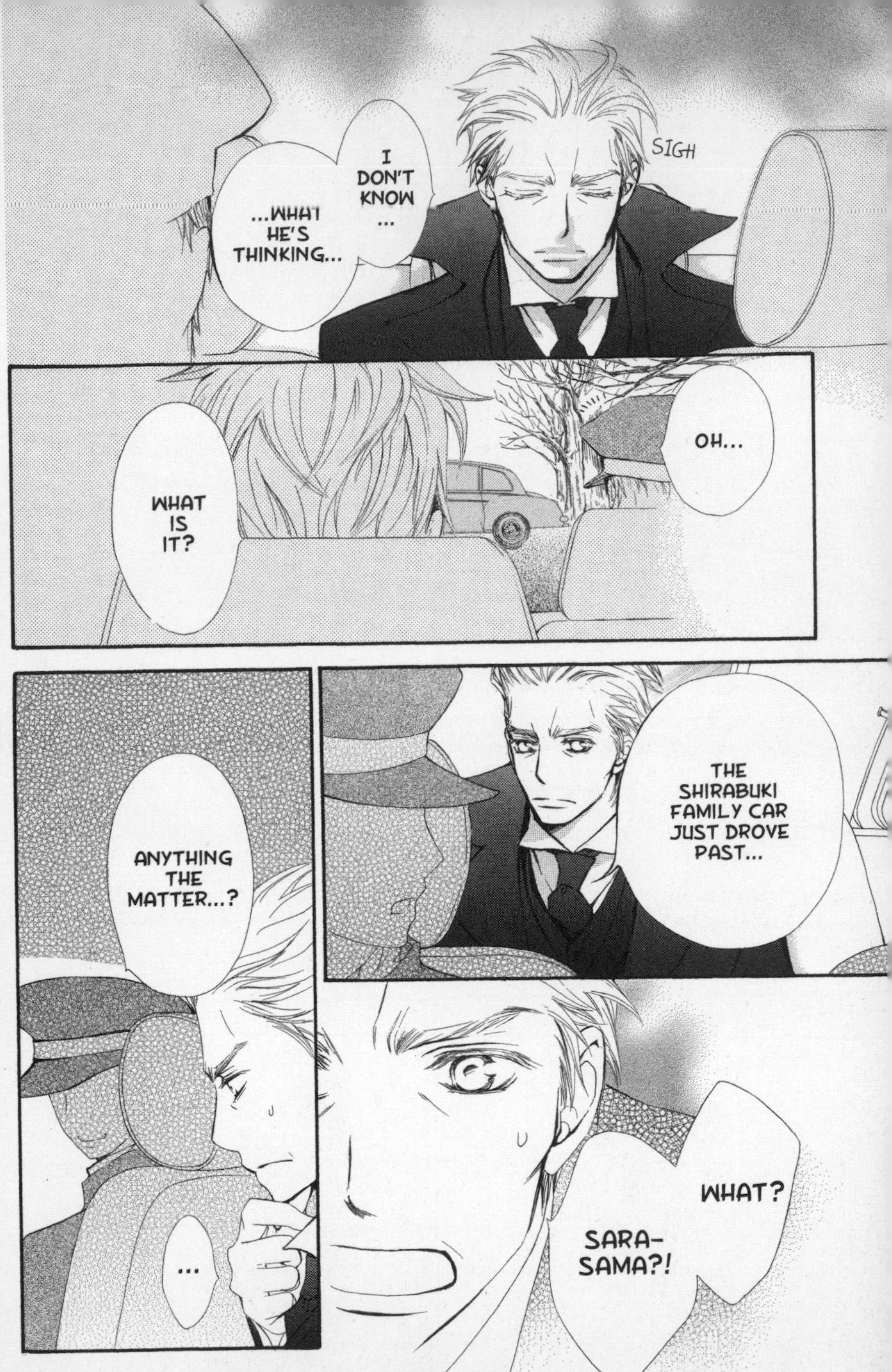
SIGH
I DON'T KNOW ...
...WHAT HE'S THINKING...
OH...
WHAT IS IT?
THE SHIRABUKI FAMILY CAR JUST DROVE PAST...
WHAT?
SARA-SAMA?!
ANYTHING THE MATTER...?
...

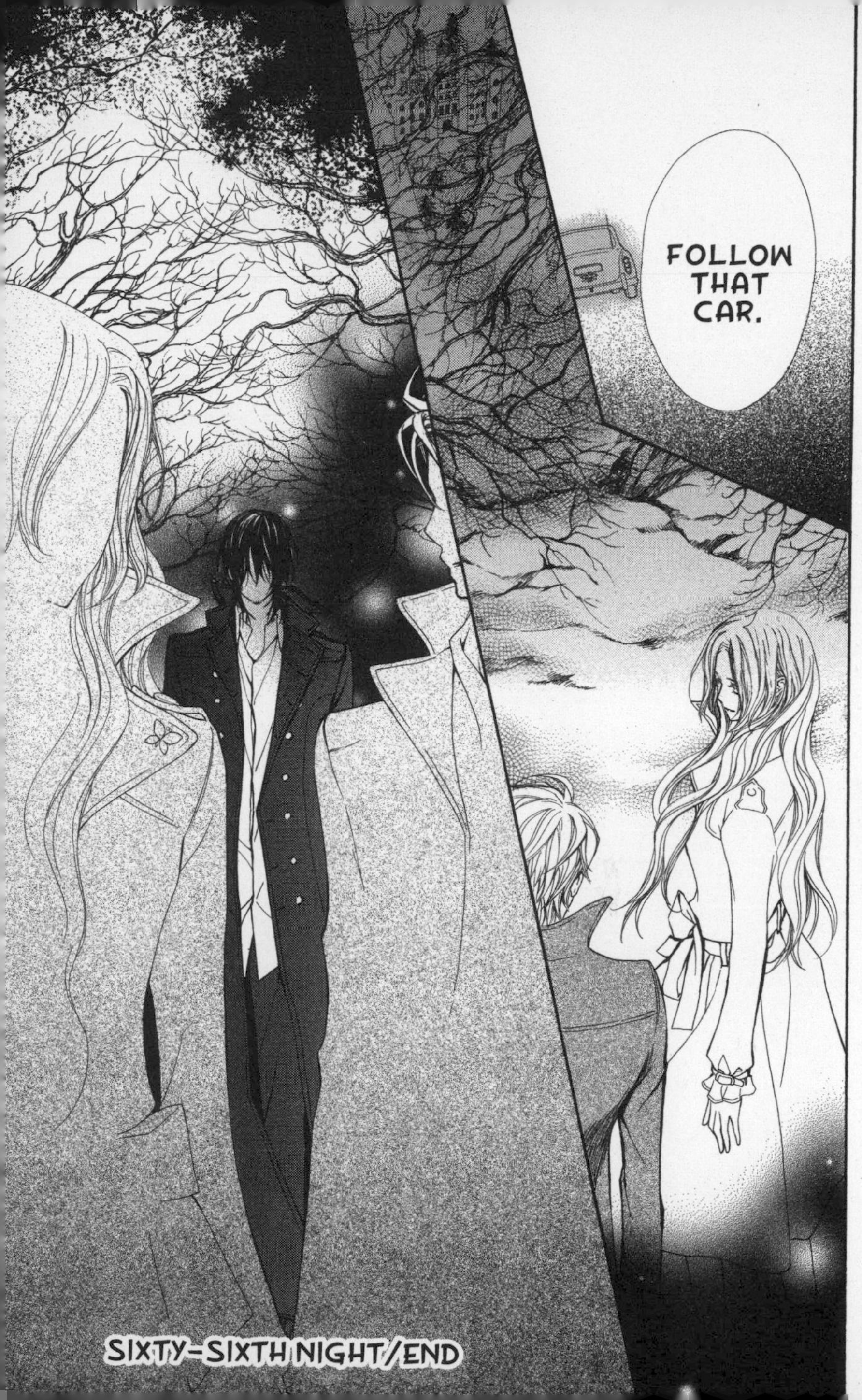
FOLLOW THAT CAR.
SIXTY-SIXTH NIGHT/END

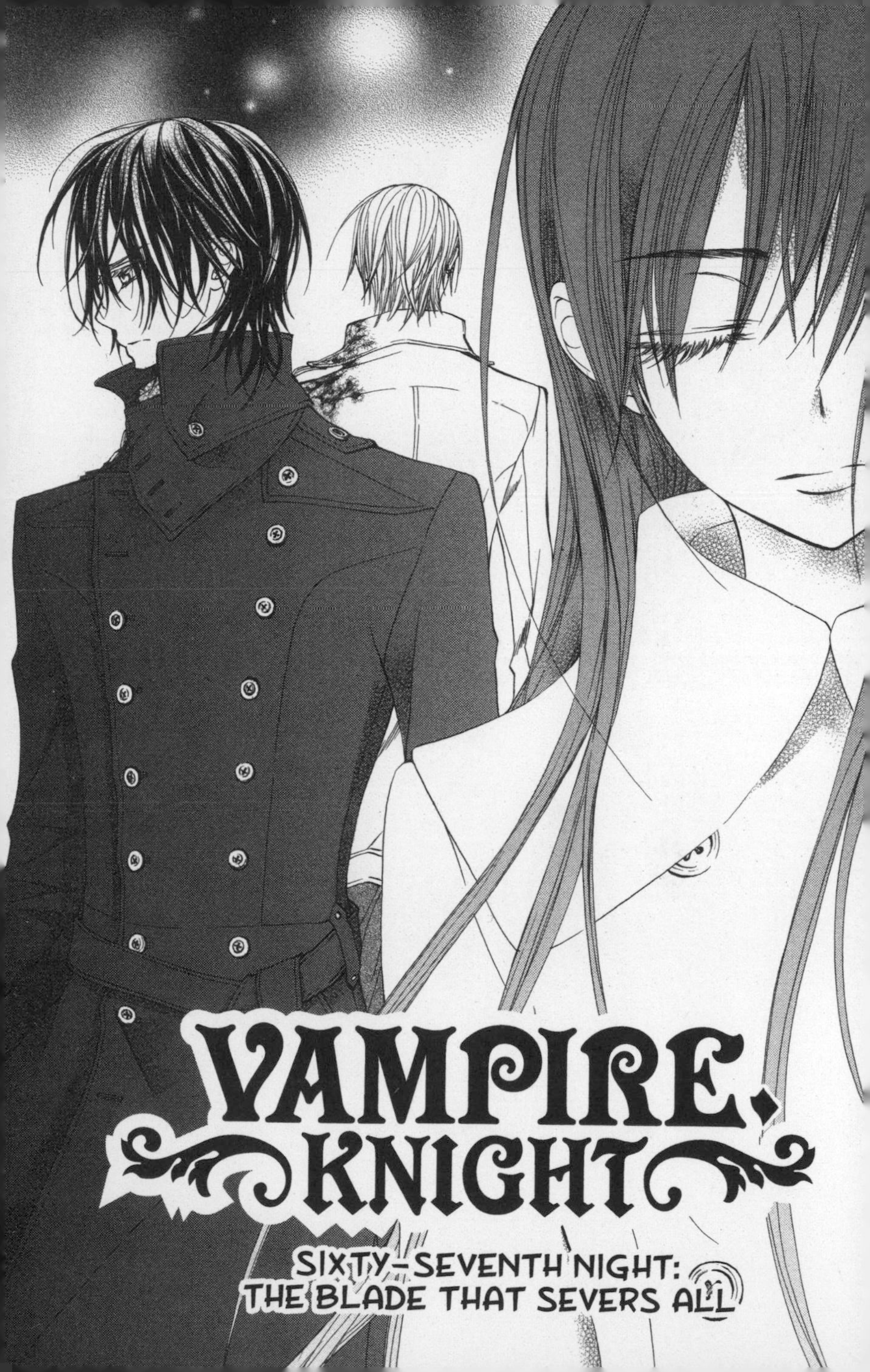
VAMPIRE KNIGHT
SIXTY-SEVENTH NIGHT:
THE BLADE THAT SEVERS ALL

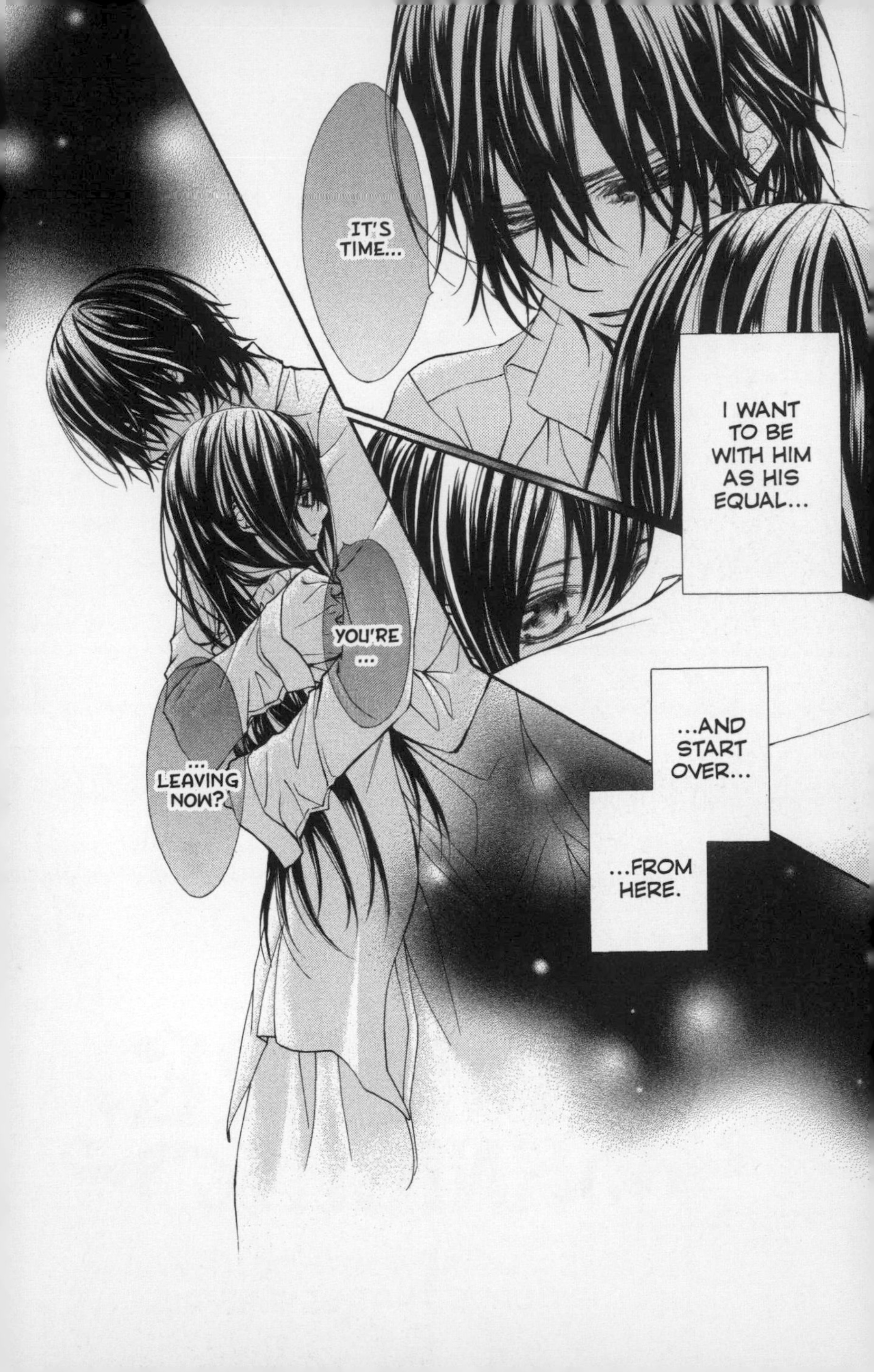
IT'S TIME...
I WANT TO BE WITH HIM AS HIS EQUAL...
YOU'RE ...
... LEAVING NOW?
...AND START OVER...
...FROM HERE.

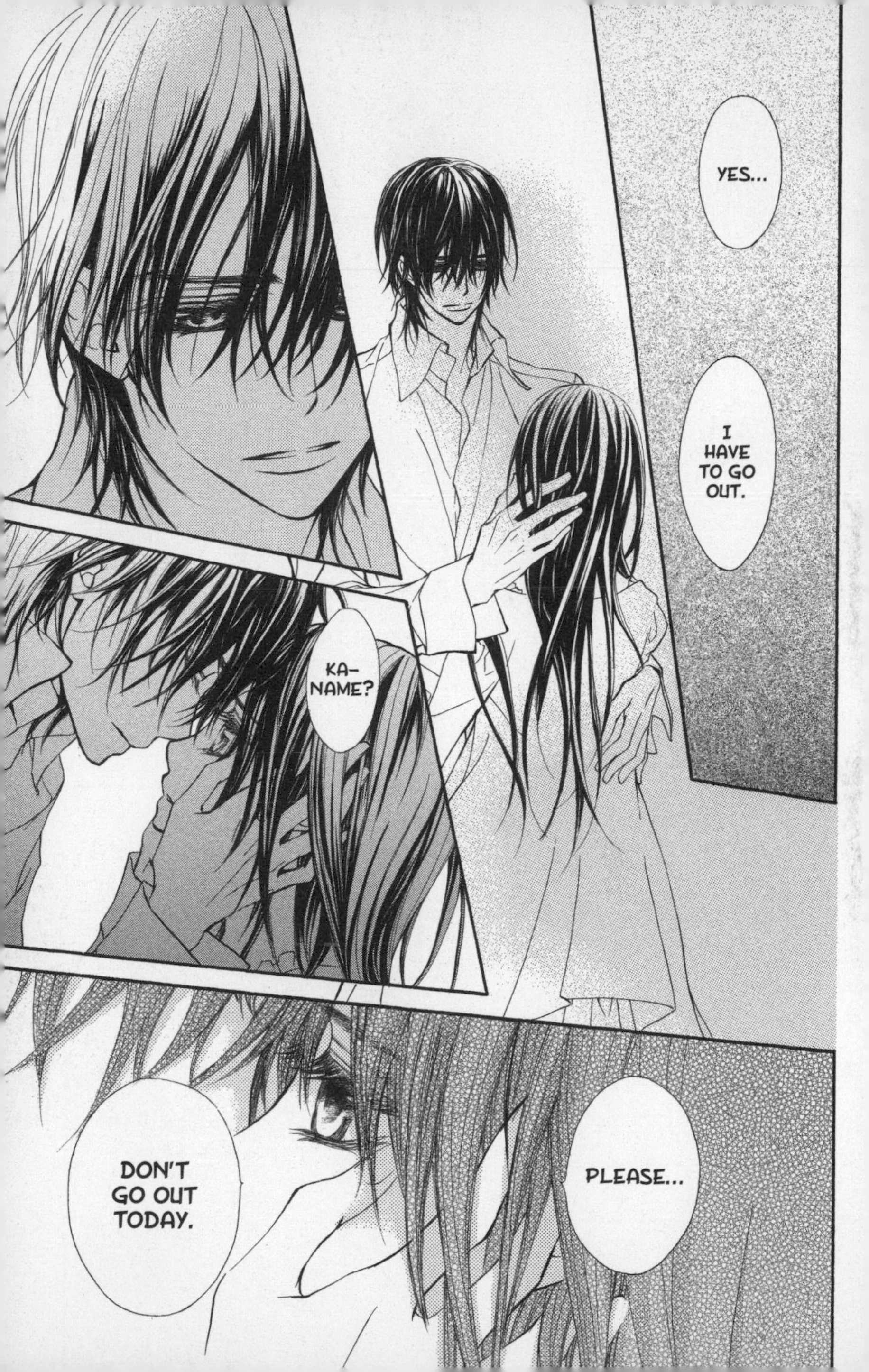
YES...
I HAVE TO GO OUT.
KA-NAME?
PLEASE...
DON'T GO OUT TODAY.

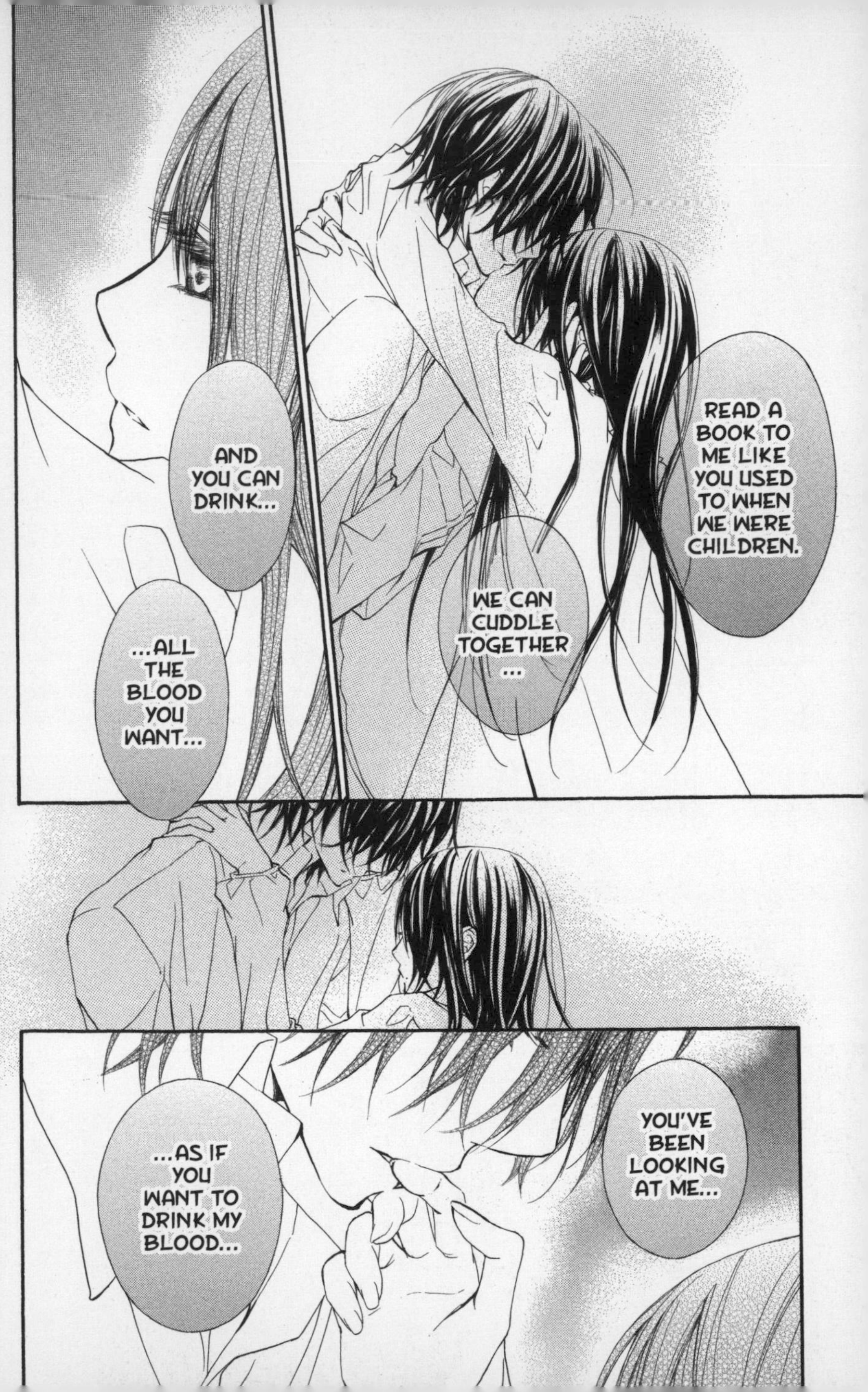
READ A BOOK TO ME LIKE YOU USED TO WHEN WE WERE CHILDREN.
WE CAN CUDDLE TOGETHER...
AND YOU CAN DRINK...
...ALL THE BLOOD YOU WANT...
YOU'VE BEEN LOOKING AT ME...
...AS IF YOU WANT TO DRINK MY BLOOD...

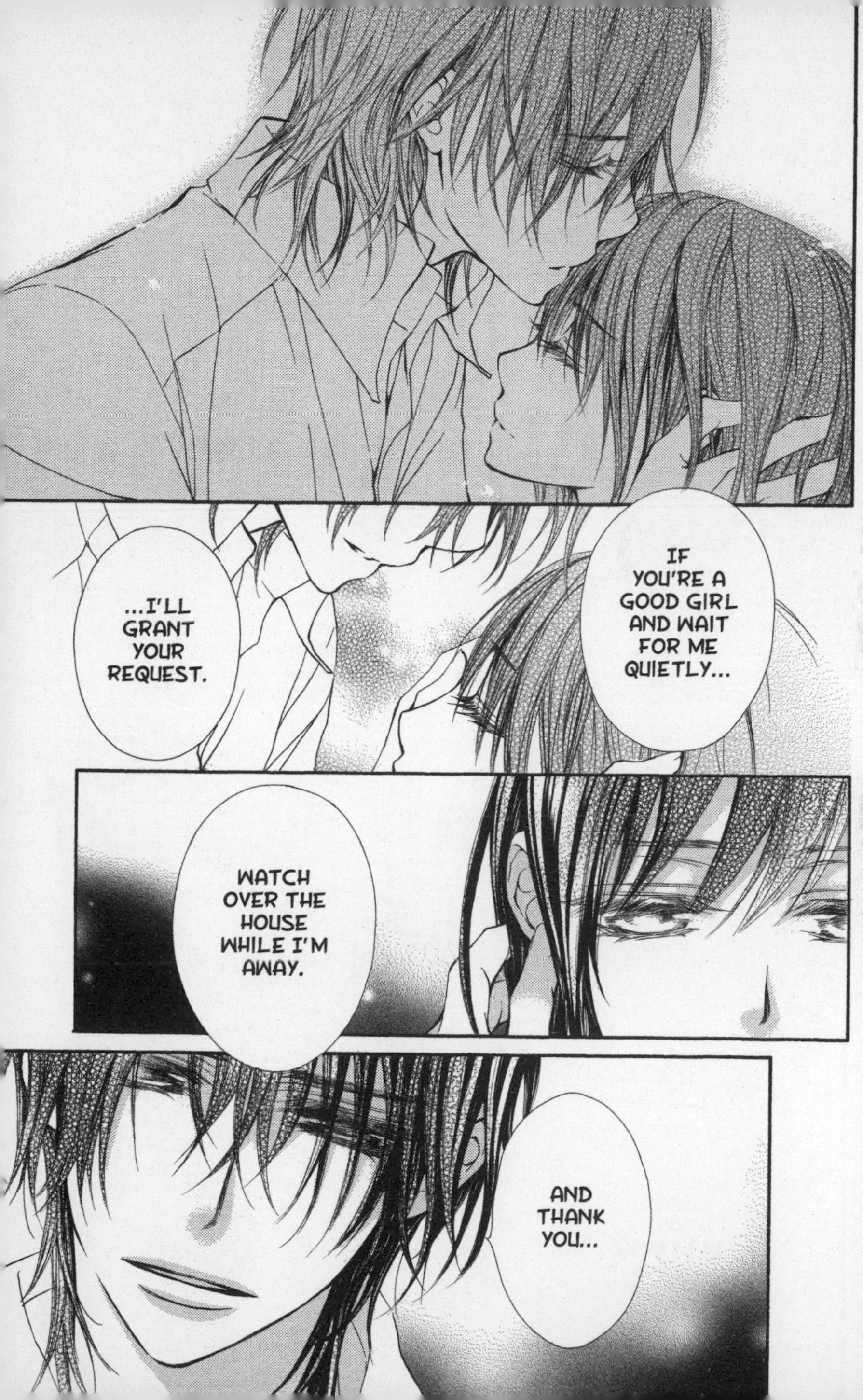
IF YOU'RE A GOOD GIRL AND WAIT FOR ME QUIETLY...
...I'LL GRANT YOUR REQUEST.
WATCH OVER THE HOUSE WHILE I'M AWAY.
AND THANK YOU...

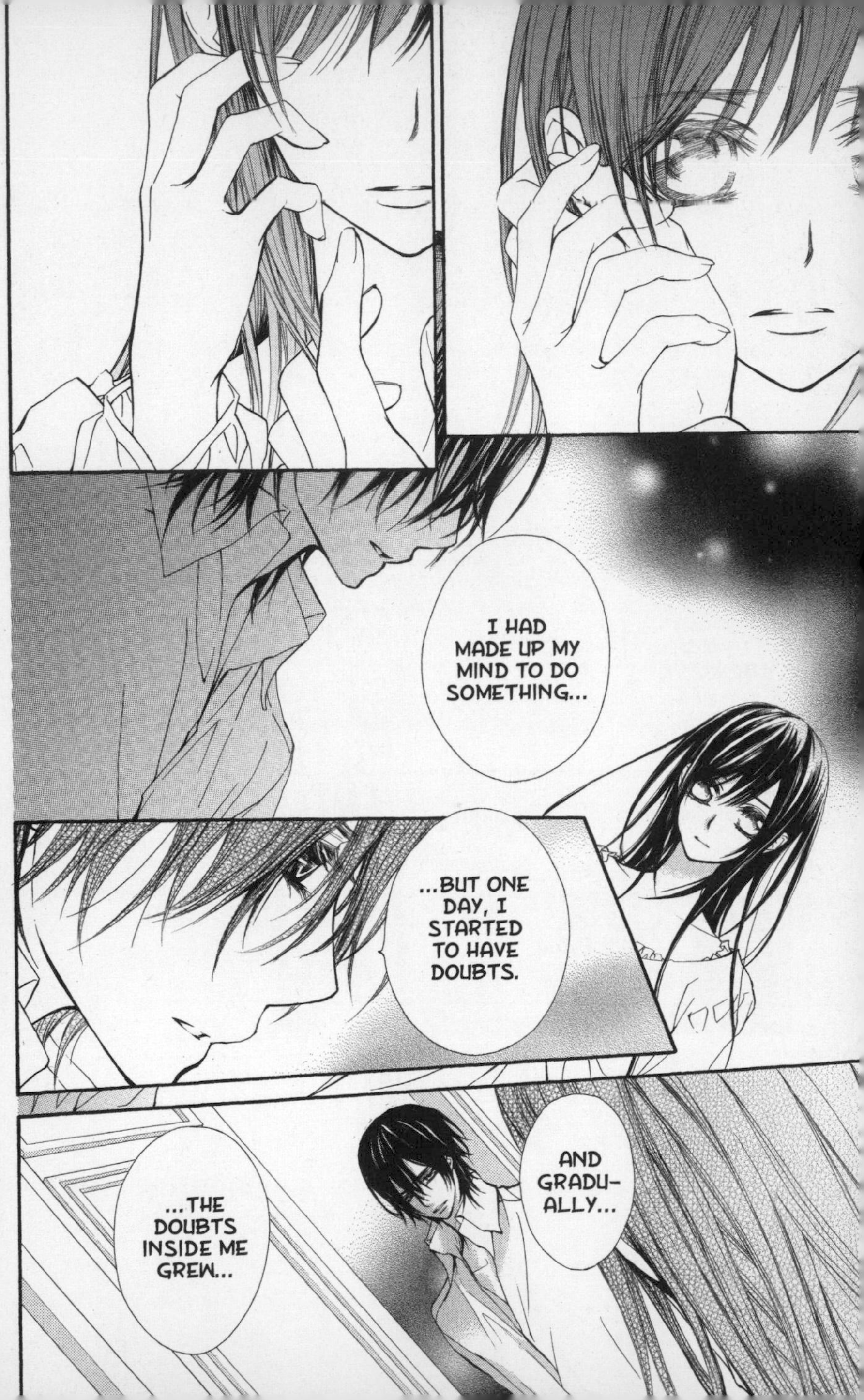
I HAD MADE UP MY MIND TO DO SOMETHING...
...BUT ONE DAY, I STARTED TO HAVE DOUBTS.
AND GRADU-ALLY...
...THE DOUBTS INSIDE ME GREW...

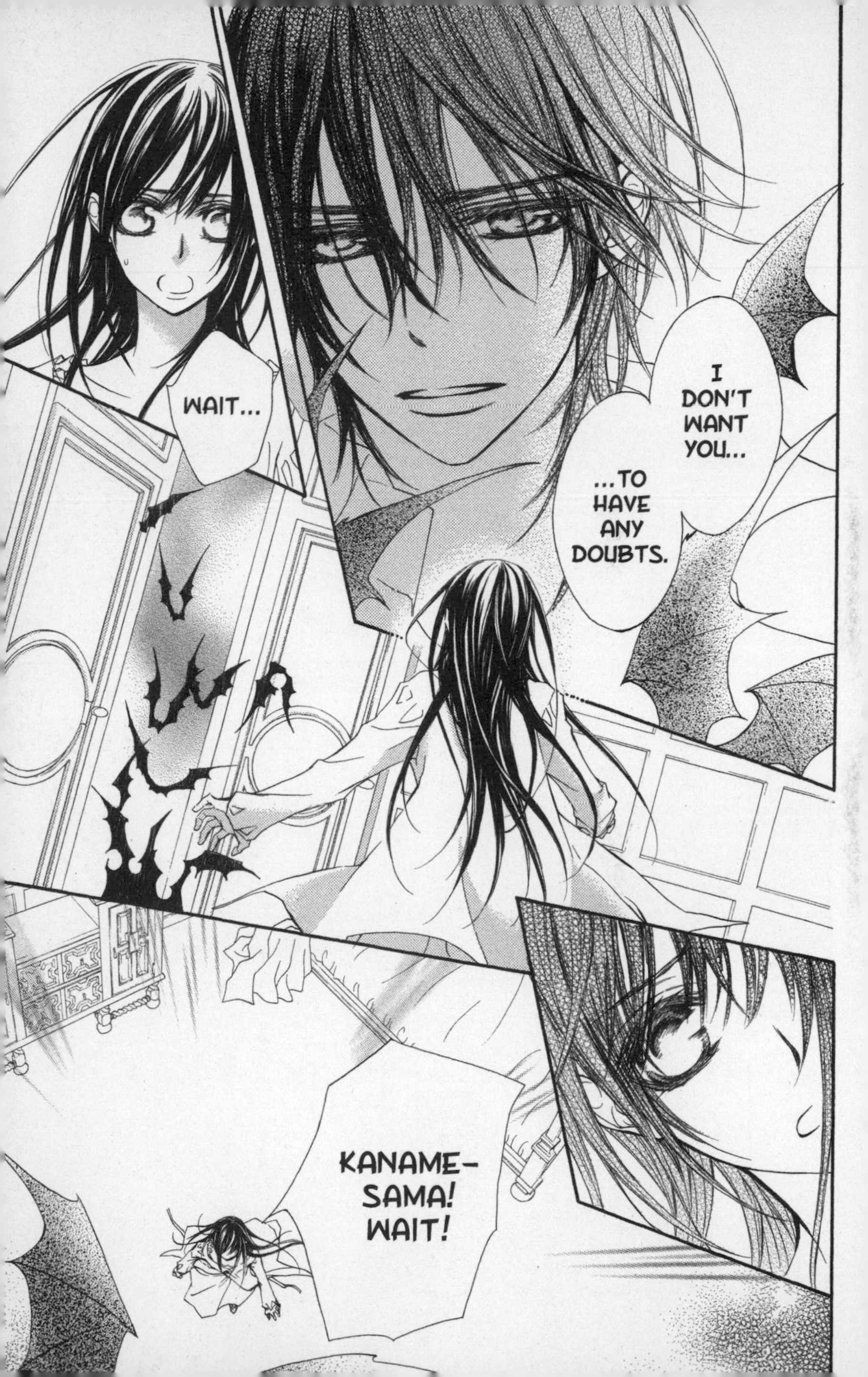
I DON'T WANT YOU...
...TO HAVE ANY DOUBTS.
WAIT...
KANAME-SAMA! WAIT!

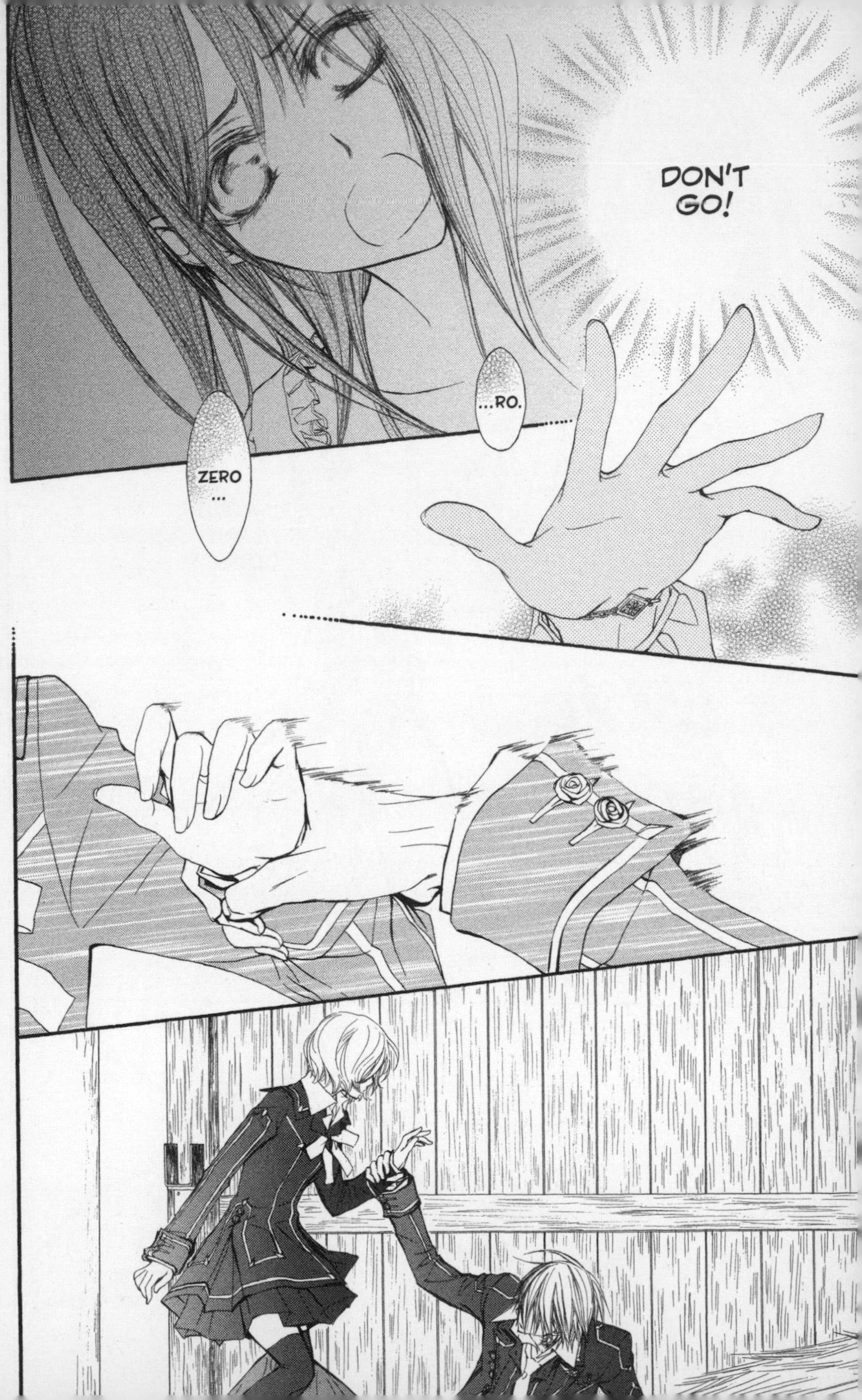
DON'T GO!
...RO.
ZERO ...

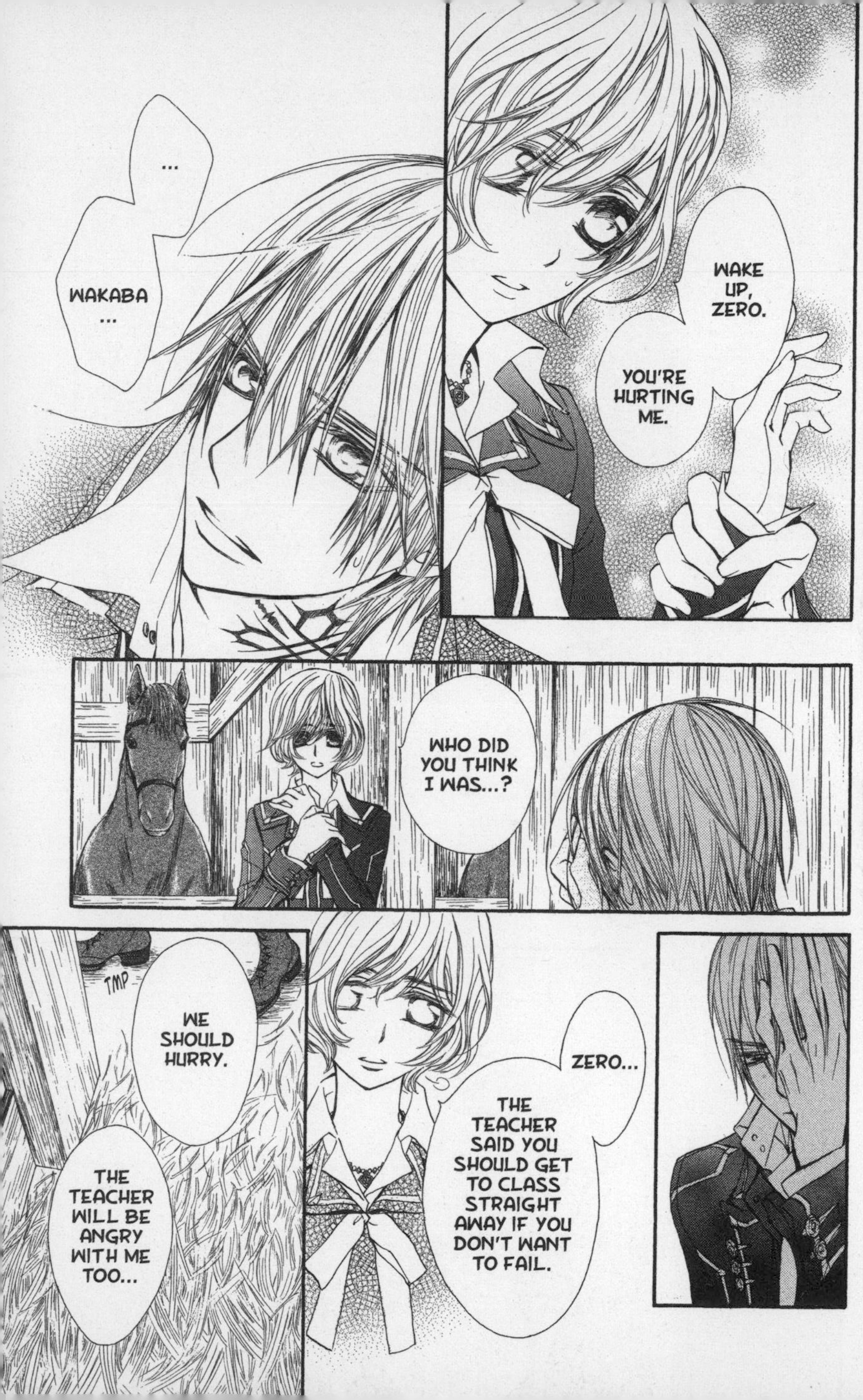
WAKE UP, ZERO.
YOU'RE HURTING ME.
...
WAKABA ...
WHO DID YOU THINK I WAS...?
ZERO...
THE TEACHER SAID YOU SHOULD GET TO CLASS STRAIGHT AWAY IF YOU DON'T WANT TO FAIL.
TMP
WE SHOULD HURRY.
THE TEACHER WILL BE ANGRY WITH ME TOO...

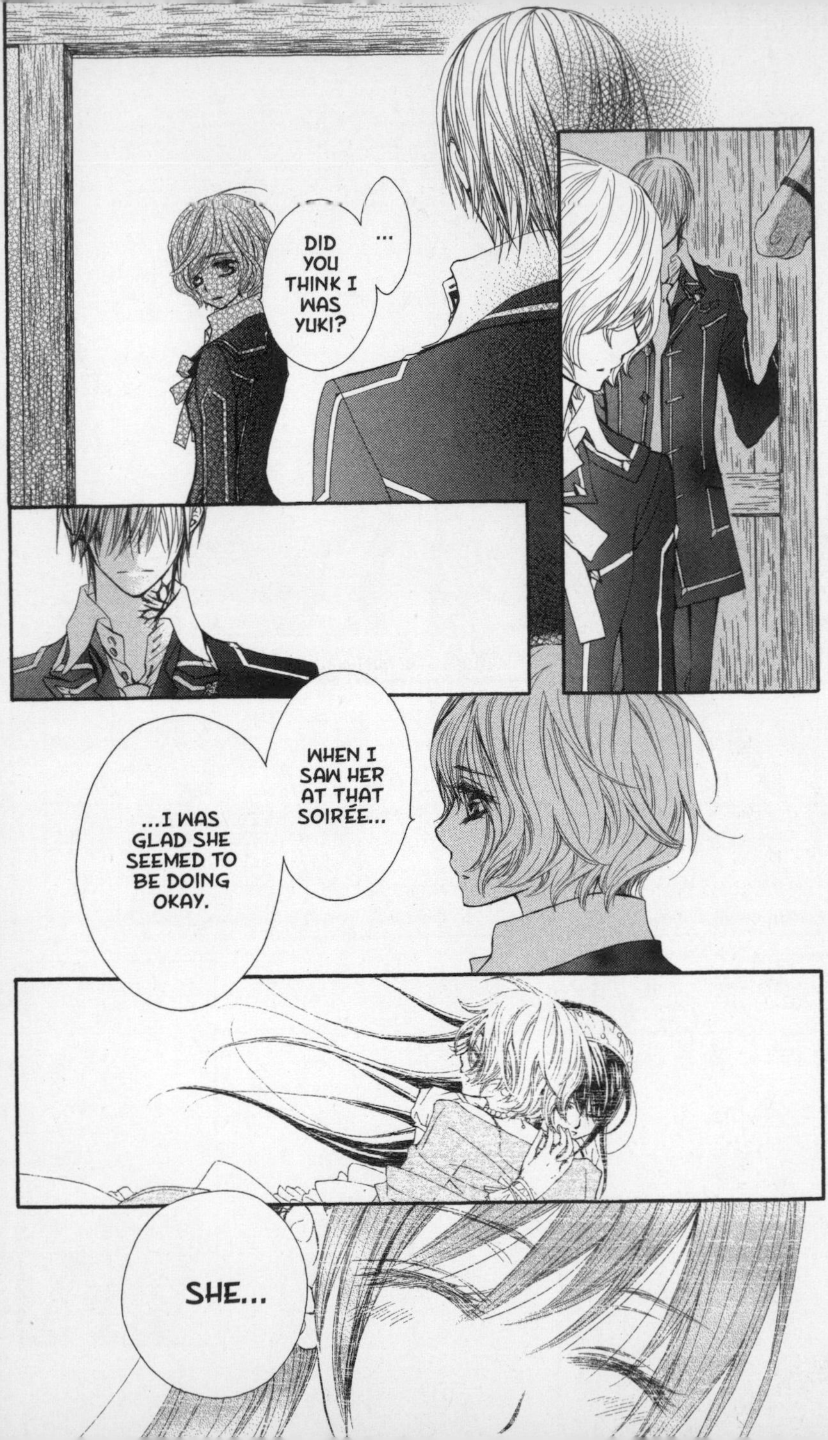
...
DID YOU THINK I WAS YUKI?
WHEN I SAW HER AT THAT SOIRÉE...
...I WAS GLAD SHE SEEMED TO BE DOING OKAY.
SHE...

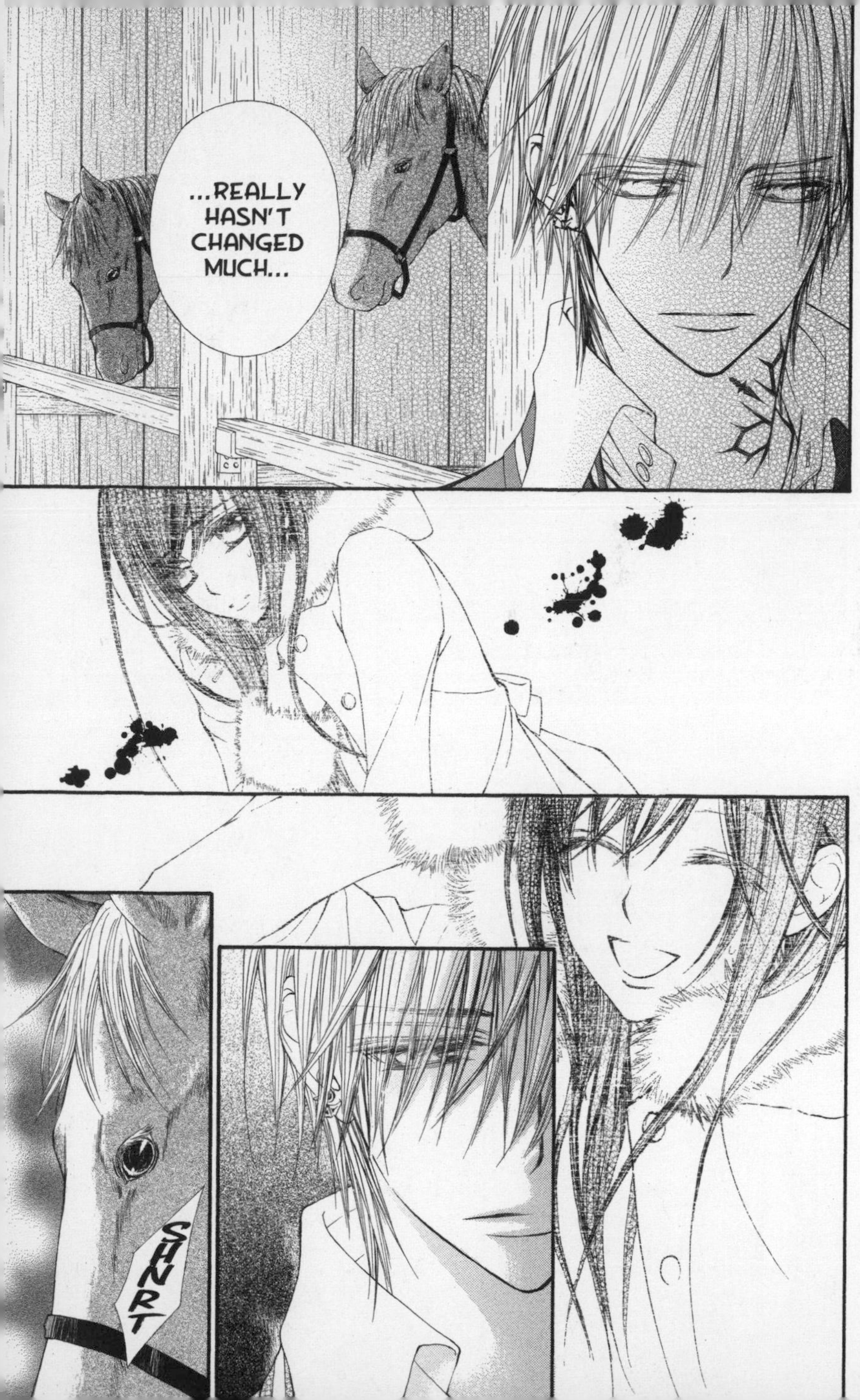
...REALLY HASN'T CHANGED MUCH...
SHNRT

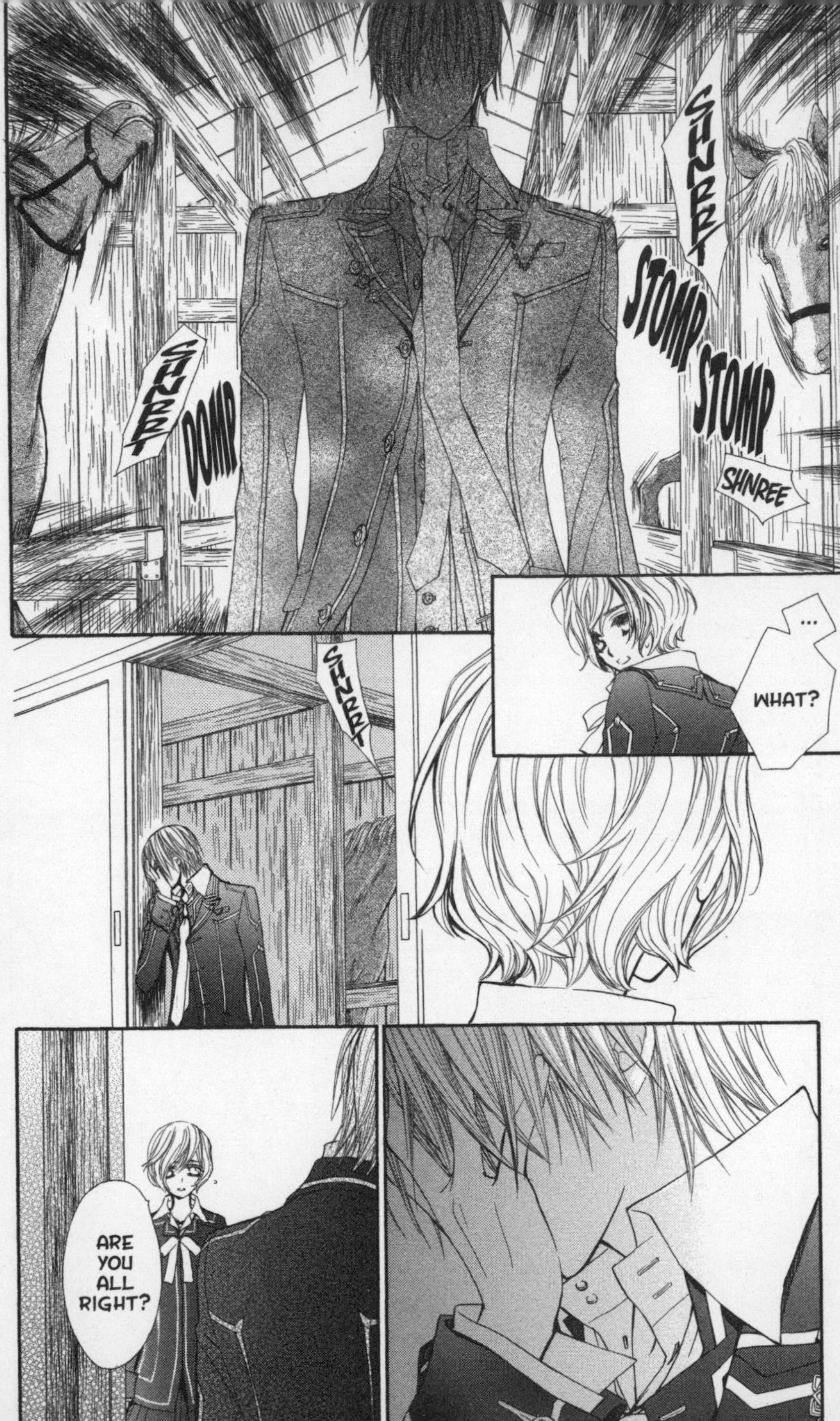
SHNRRT
STOMP STOMP
SHNREE
SHNRRT
DOMP
...
WHAT?
SHNRRT
ARE YOU ALL RIGHT?

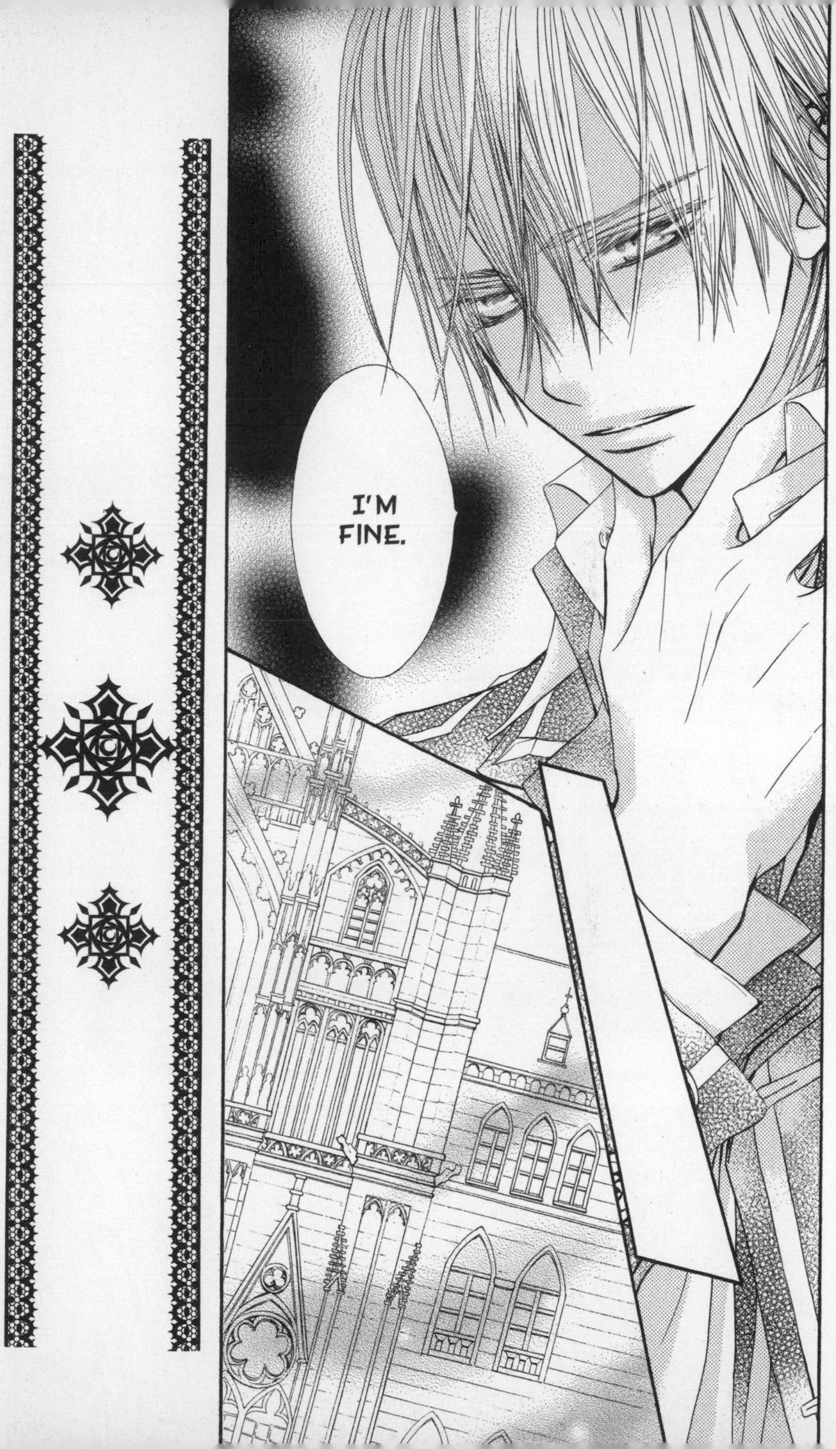
I'M FINE.

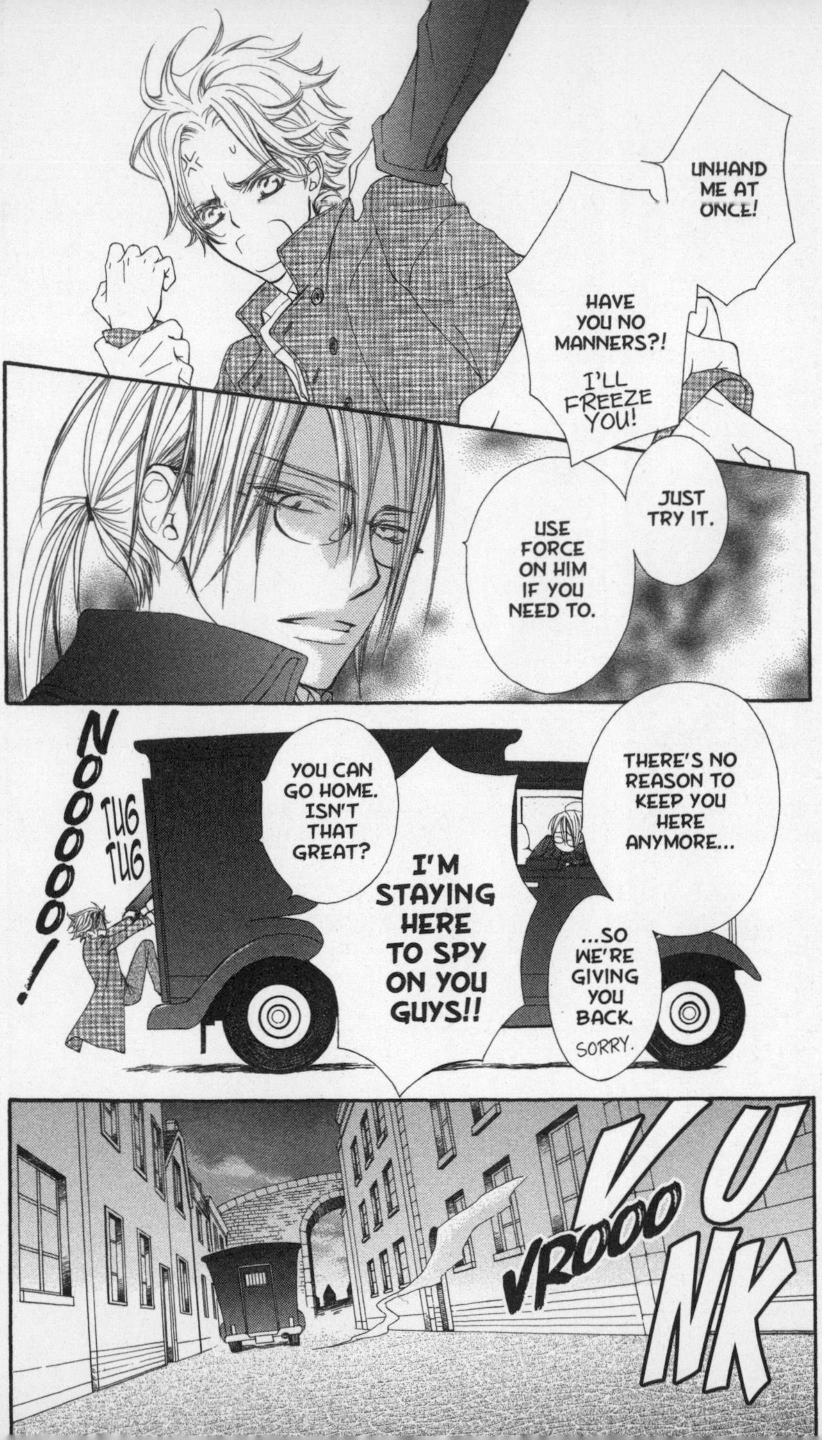
UNHAND ME AT ONCE!
HAVE YOU NO MANNERS?!
I'LL FREEZE YOU!
JUST TRY IT.
USE FORCE ON HIM IF YOU NEED TO.
THERE'S NO REASON TO KEEP YOU HERE ANYMORE...
...SO WE'RE GIVING YOU BACK.
SORRY.
YOU CAN GO HOME. ISN'T THAT GREAT?
I'M STAYING HERE TO SPY ON YOU GUYS!!
TUG TUG
NOOOOOO!
VUNK
VROOOO

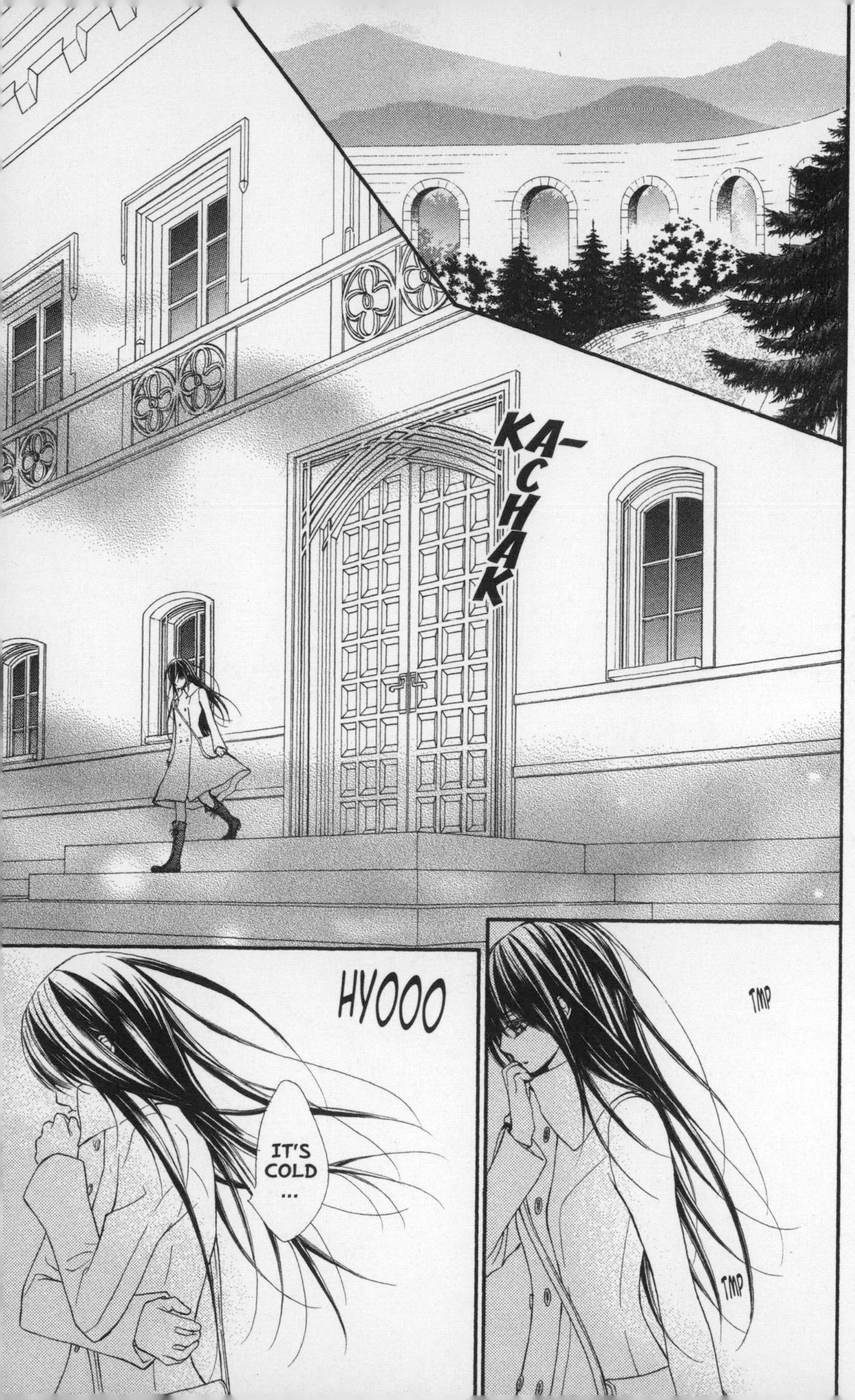
KA-CHAK
TMP
TMP
HYOOO
IT'S COLD ...

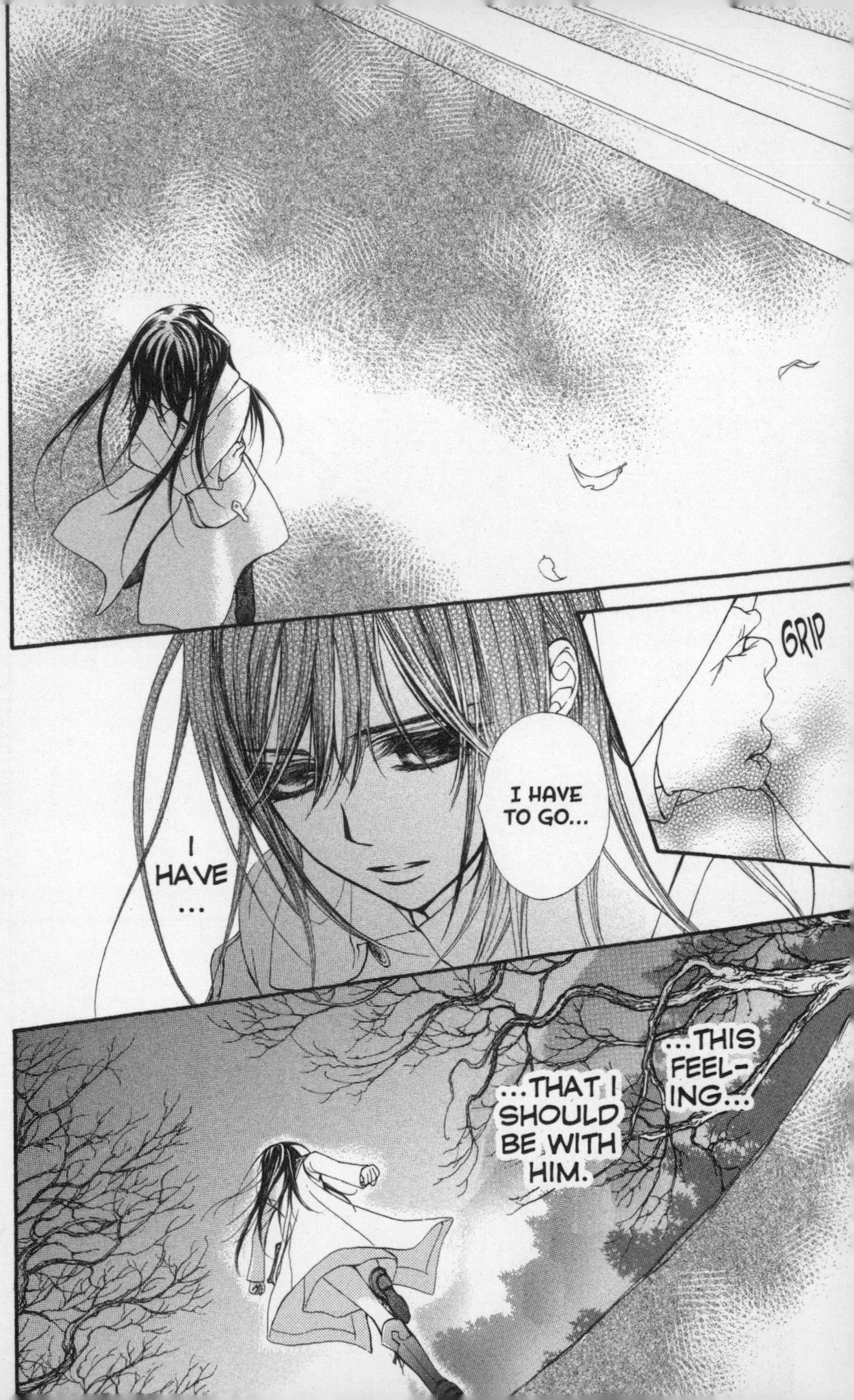
GRIP
I HAVE TO GO...
I HAVE ...
...THIS FEEL- ING...
...THAT I SHOULD BE WITH HIM.

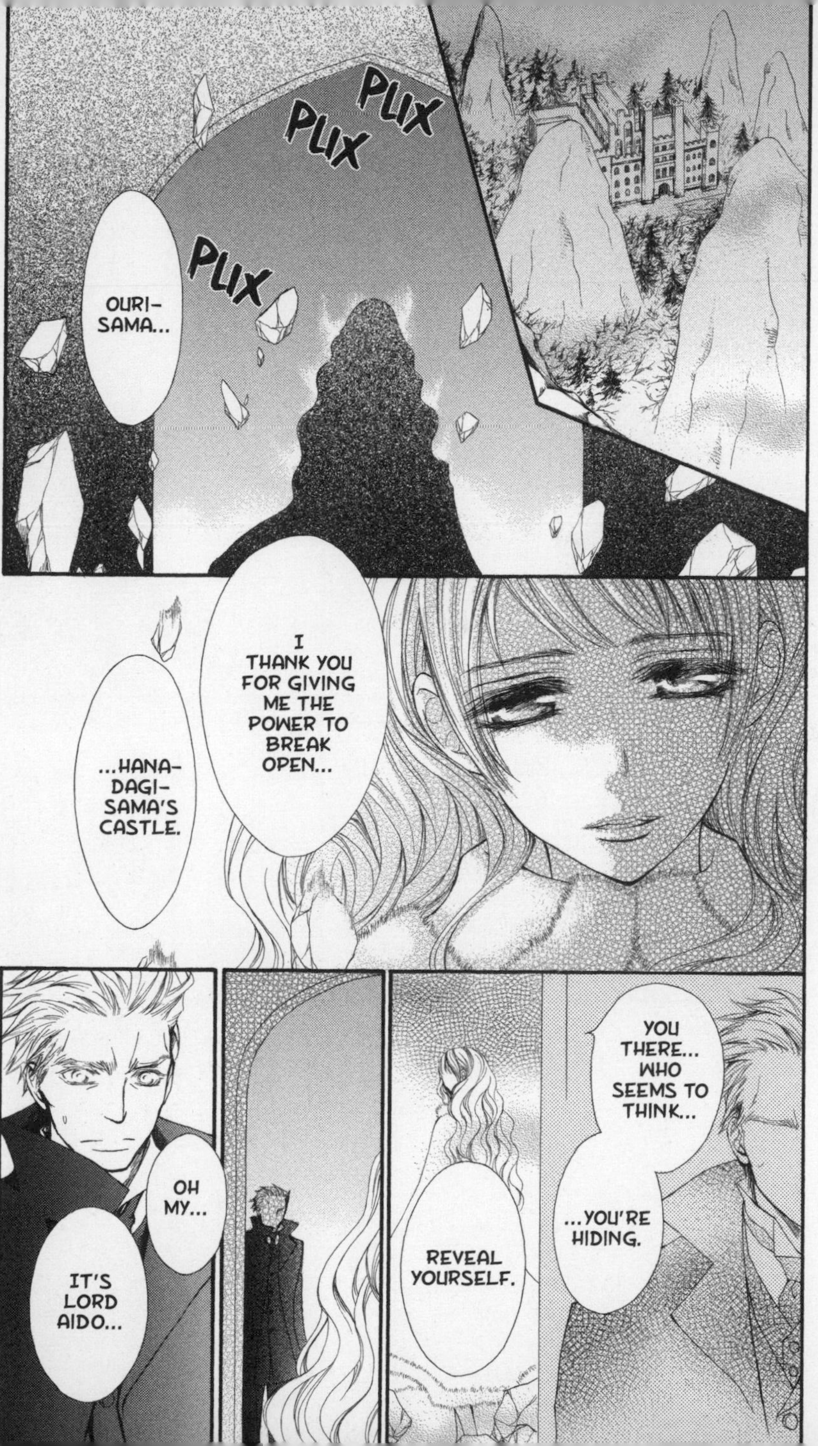
PLIX
PLIX
PLIX
OURI-SAMA...
I THANK YOU FOR GIVING ME THE POWER TO BREAK OPEN...
...HANA-DAGI-SAMA'S CASTLE.
YOU THERE... WHO SEEMS TO THINK...
...YOU'RE HIDING.
REVEAL YOURSELF.
OH MY...
IT'S LORD AIDO...

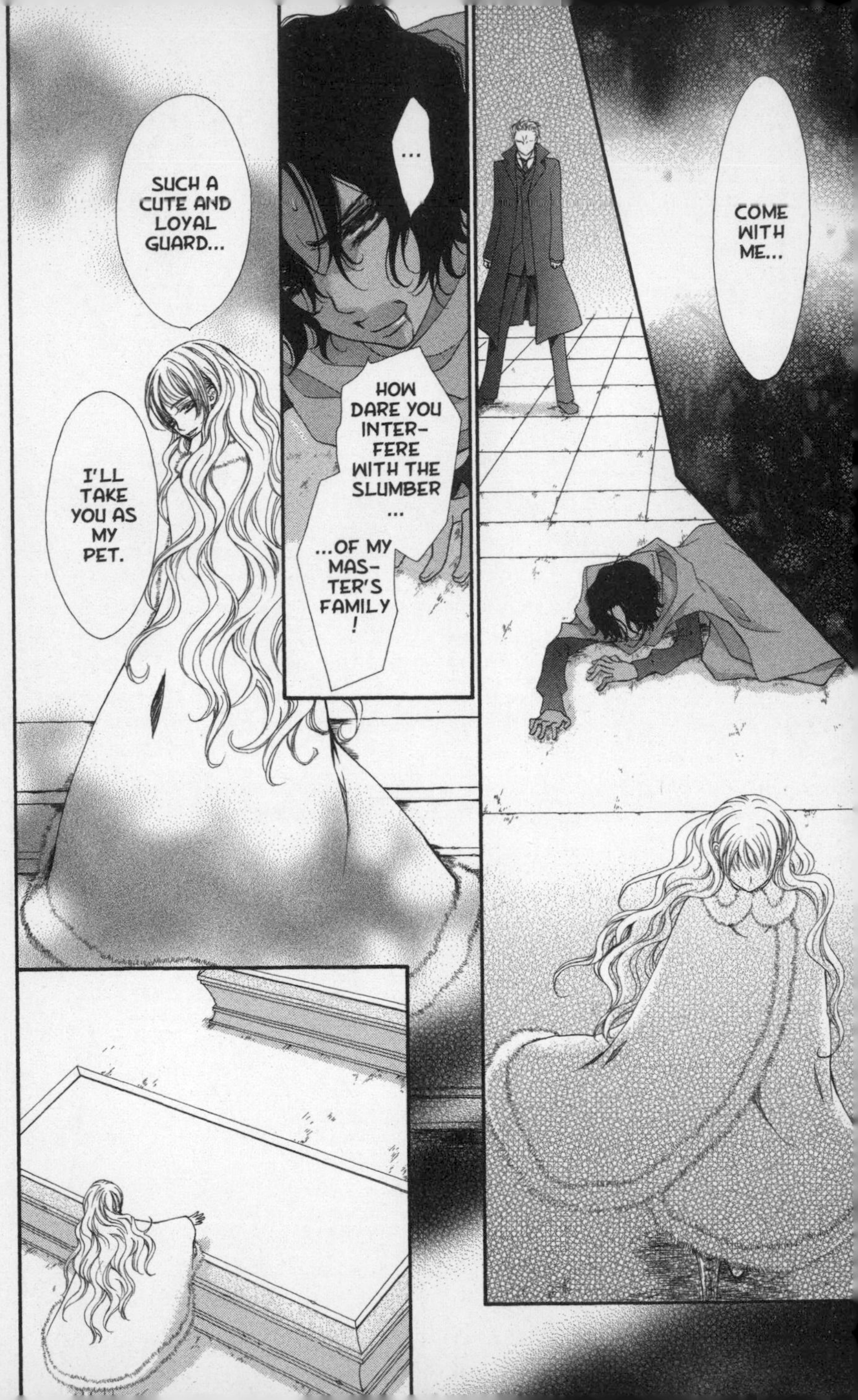
COME WITH ME...
...
HOW DARE YOU INTERFERE WITH THE SLUMBER...
...OF MY MASTER'S FAMILY!
SUCH A CUTE AND LOYAL GUARD...
I'LL TAKE YOU AS MY PET.

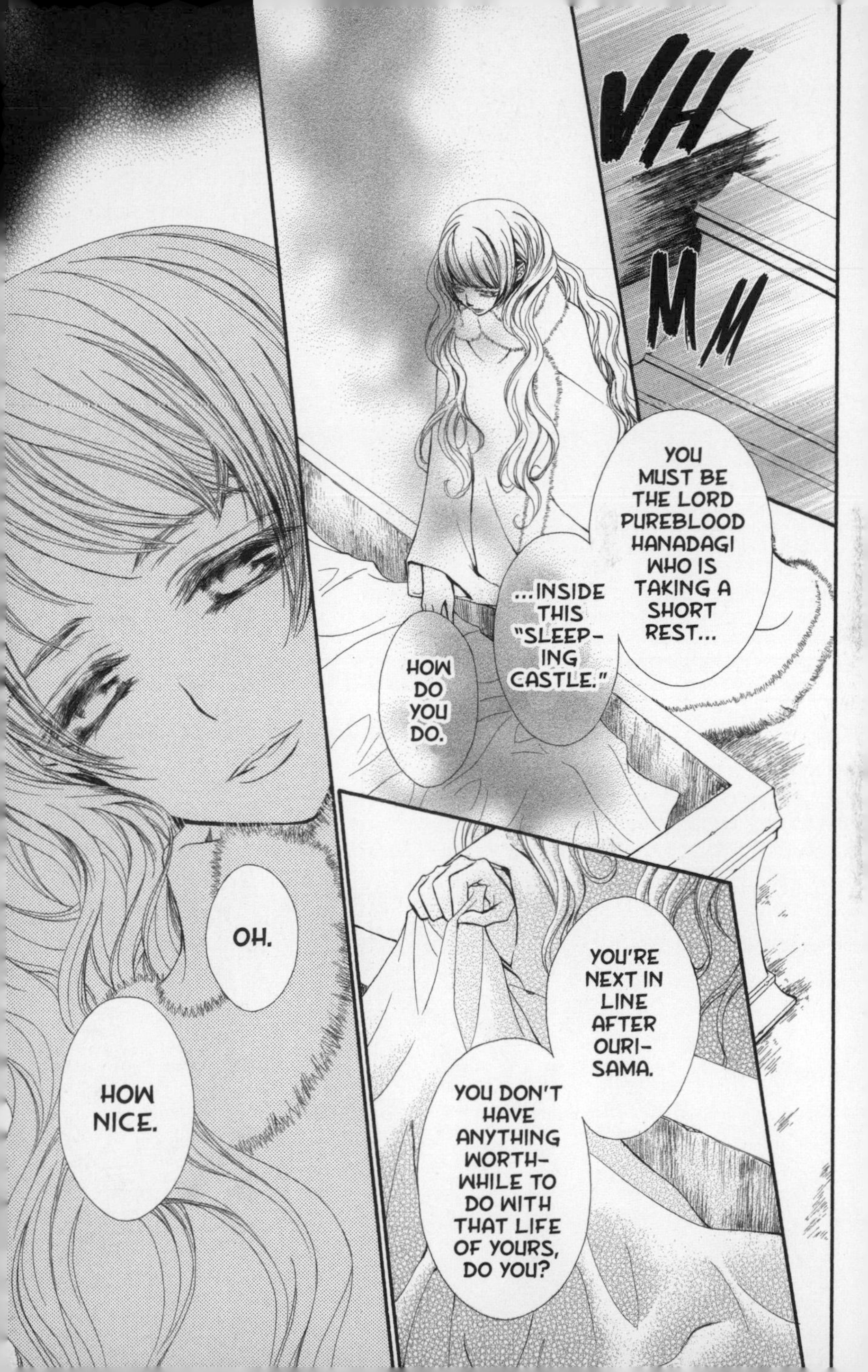
VHMM
YOU MUST BE THE LORD PUREBLOOD HANADAGI WHO IS TAKING A SHORT REST...
...INSIDE THIS "SLEEPING CASTLE."
HOW DO YOU DO.
YOU'RE NEXT IN LINE AFTER OURI-SAMA.
YOU DON'T HAVE ANYTHING WORTHWHILE TO DO WITH THAT LIFE OF YOURS, DO YOU?
OH.
HOW NICE.

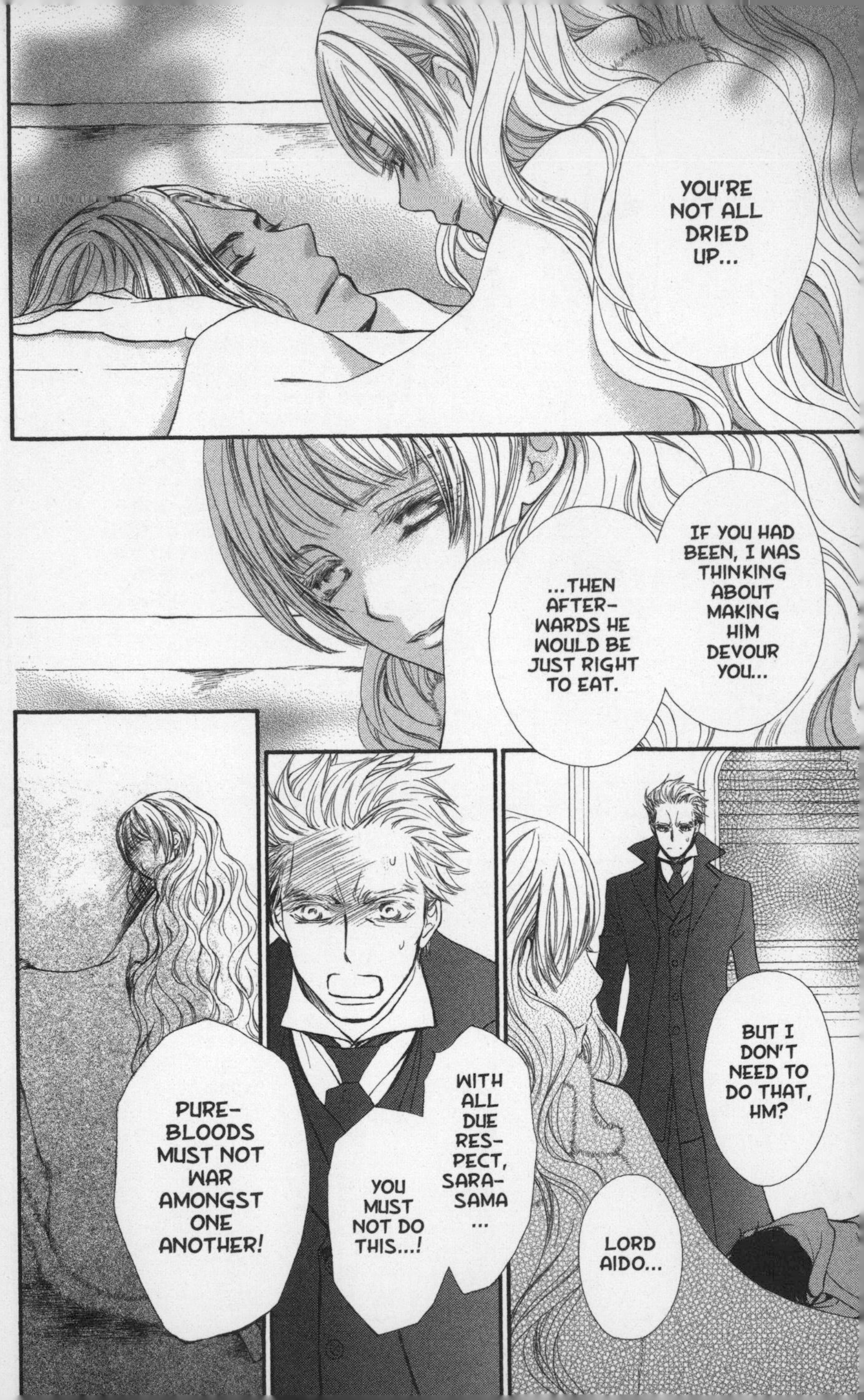
YOU'RE NOT ALL DRIED UP...
IF YOU HAD BEEN, I WAS THINKING ABOUT MAKING HIM DEVOUR YOU...
...THEN AFTER-WARDS HE WOULD BE JUST RIGHT TO EAT.
BUT I DON'T NEED TO DO THAT, HM?
LORD AIDO...
WITH ALL DUE RES-PECT, SARA-SAMA...
YOU MUST NOT DO THIS...!
PURE-BLOODS MUST NOT WAR AMONGST ONE ANOTHER!

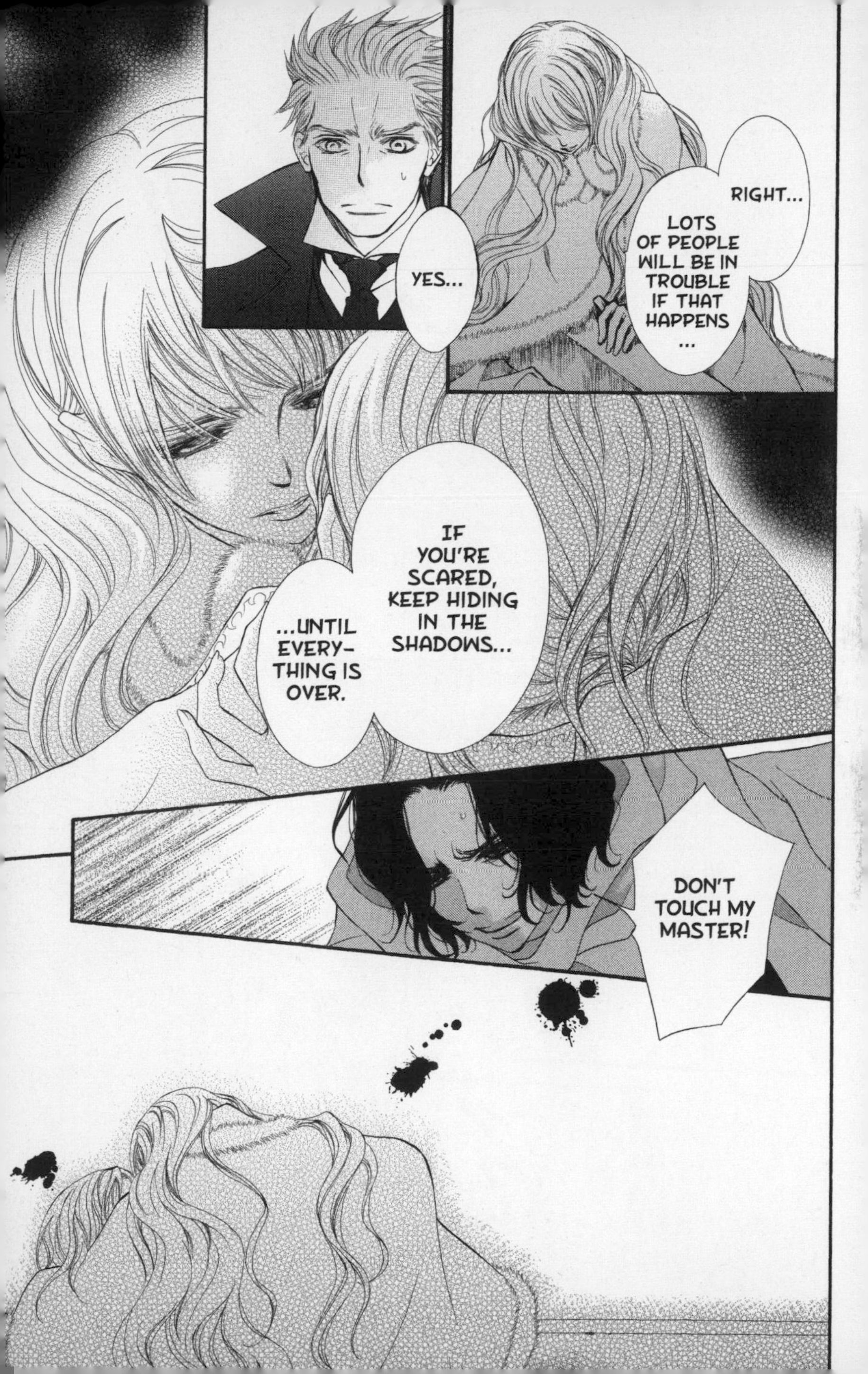
RIGHT...
LOTS OF PEOPLE WILL BE IN TROUBLE IF THAT HAPPENS ...
YES...
IF YOU'RE SCARED, KEEP HIDING IN THE SHADOWS...
...UNTIL EVERY-THING IS OVER.
DON'T TOUCH MY MASTER!

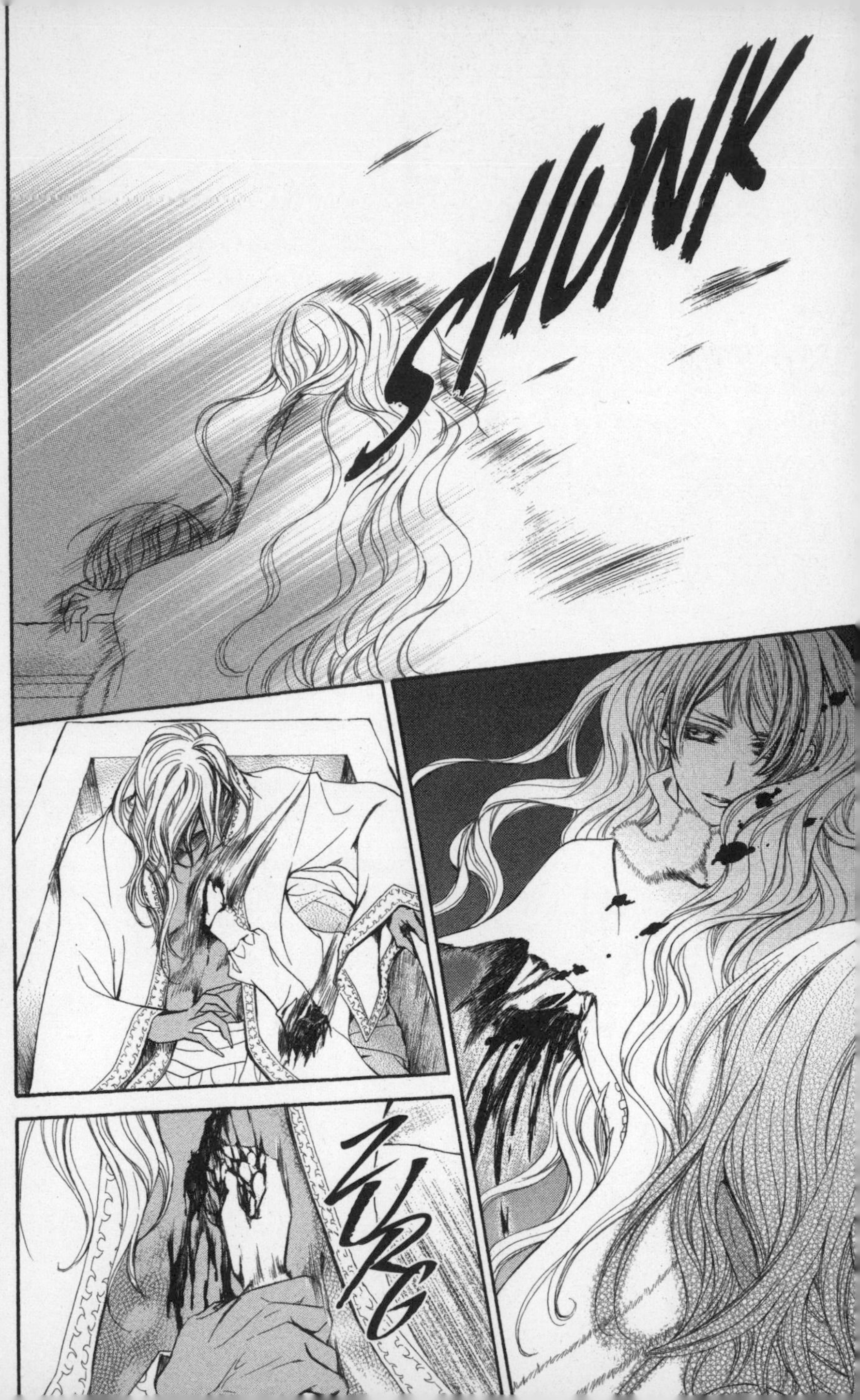
SHUNK
ZING

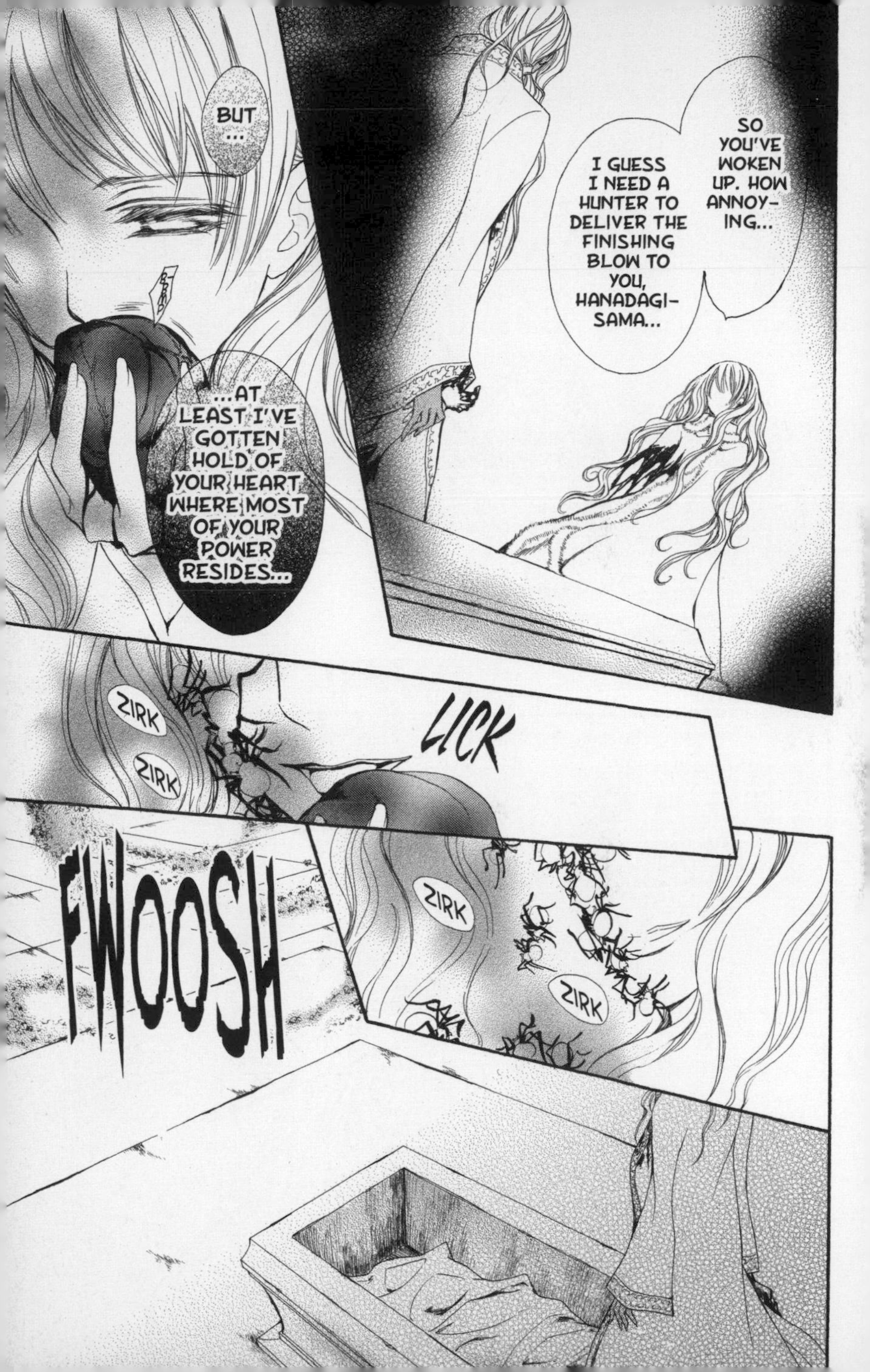
SO YOU'VE WOKEN UP. HOW ANNOY-ING...
I GUESS I NEED A HUNTER TO DELIVER THE FINISHING BLOW TO YOU, HANADAGI-SAMA...
BUT...
...AT LEAST I'VE GOTTEN HOLD OF YOUR HEART WHERE MOST OF YOUR POWER RESIDES...
LICK
ZIRK
ZIRK
ZIRK
ZIRK
FWOOSH

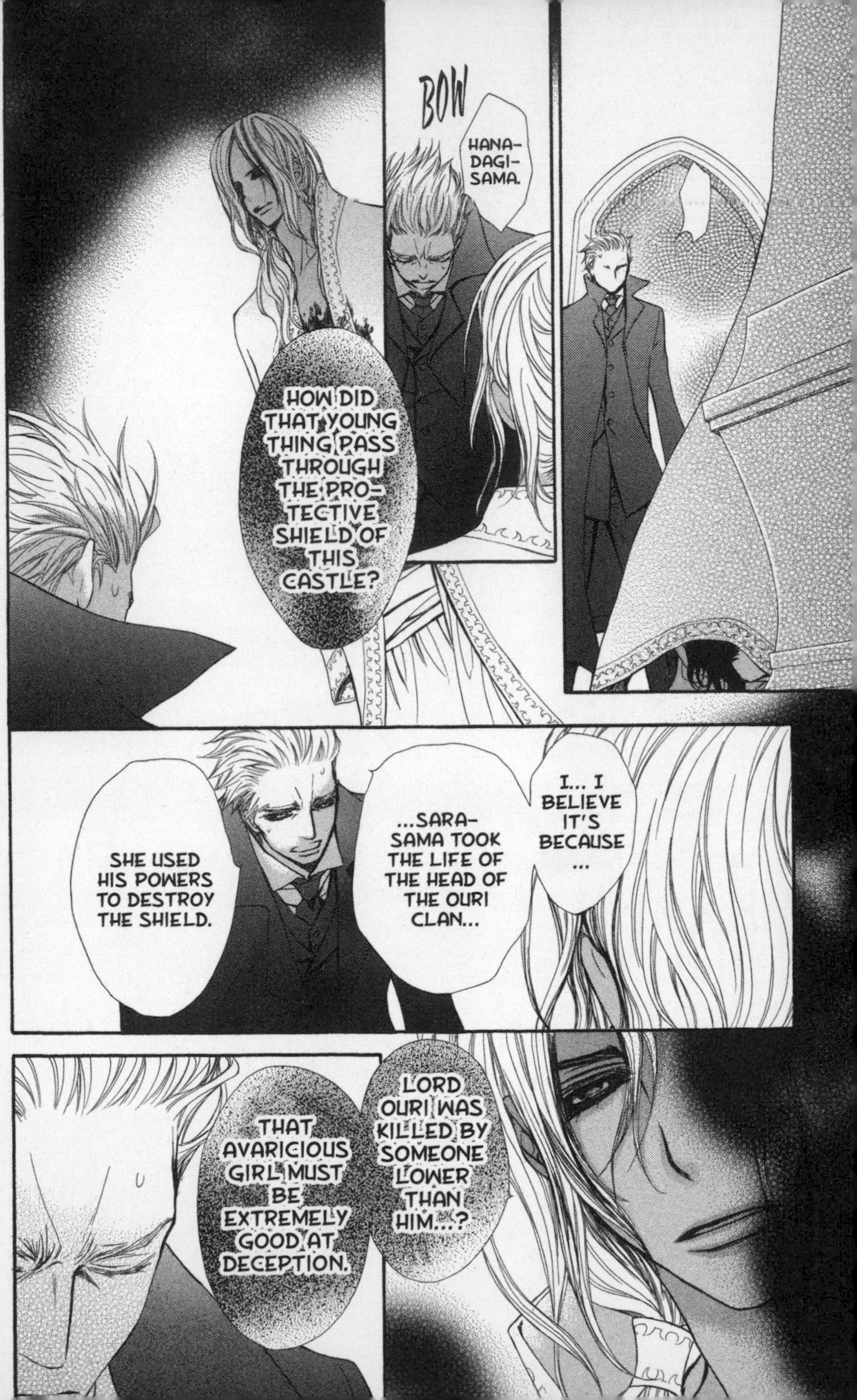
BOW
HANA-DAGI-SAMA.
HOW DID THAT YOUNG THING PASS THROUGH THE PRO-TECTIVE SHIELD OF THIS CASTLE?
I... I BELIEVE IT'S BECAUSE ...
...SARA-SAMA TOOK THE LIFE OF THE HEAD OF THE OURI CLAN...
SHE USED HIS POWERS TO DESTROY THE SHIELD.
LORD OURI WAS KILLED BY SOMEONE LOWER THAN HIM...?
THAT AVARICIOUS GIRL MUST BE EXTREMELY GOOD AT DECEPTION.

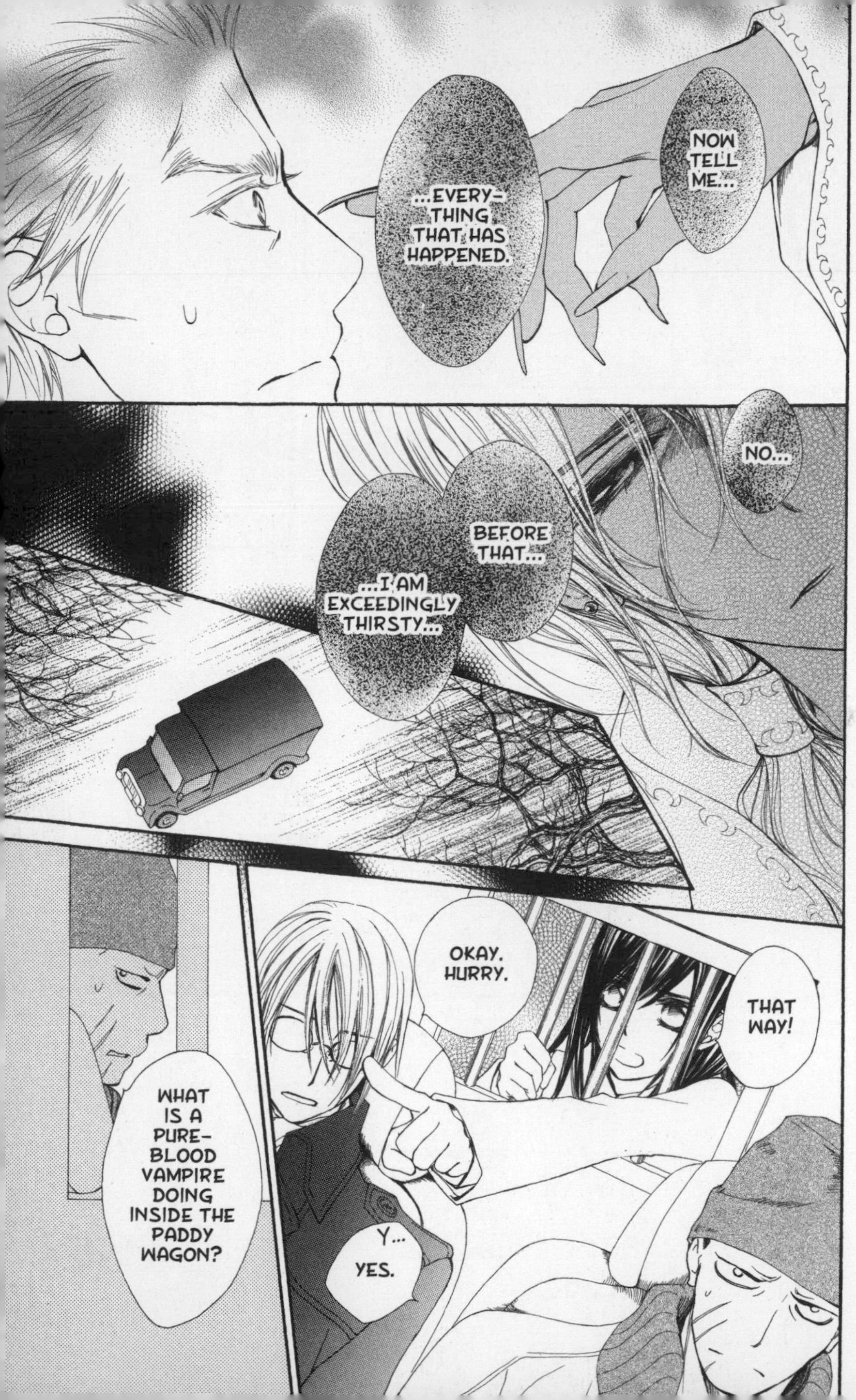
NOW TELL ME...
...EVERYTHING THAT HAS HAPPENED.
NO...
BEFORE THAT...
...I AM EXCEEDINGLY THIRSTY...
THAT WAY!
OKAY. HURRY.
Y... YES.
WHAT IS A PURE-BLOOD VAMPIRE DOING INSIDE THE PADDY WAGON?

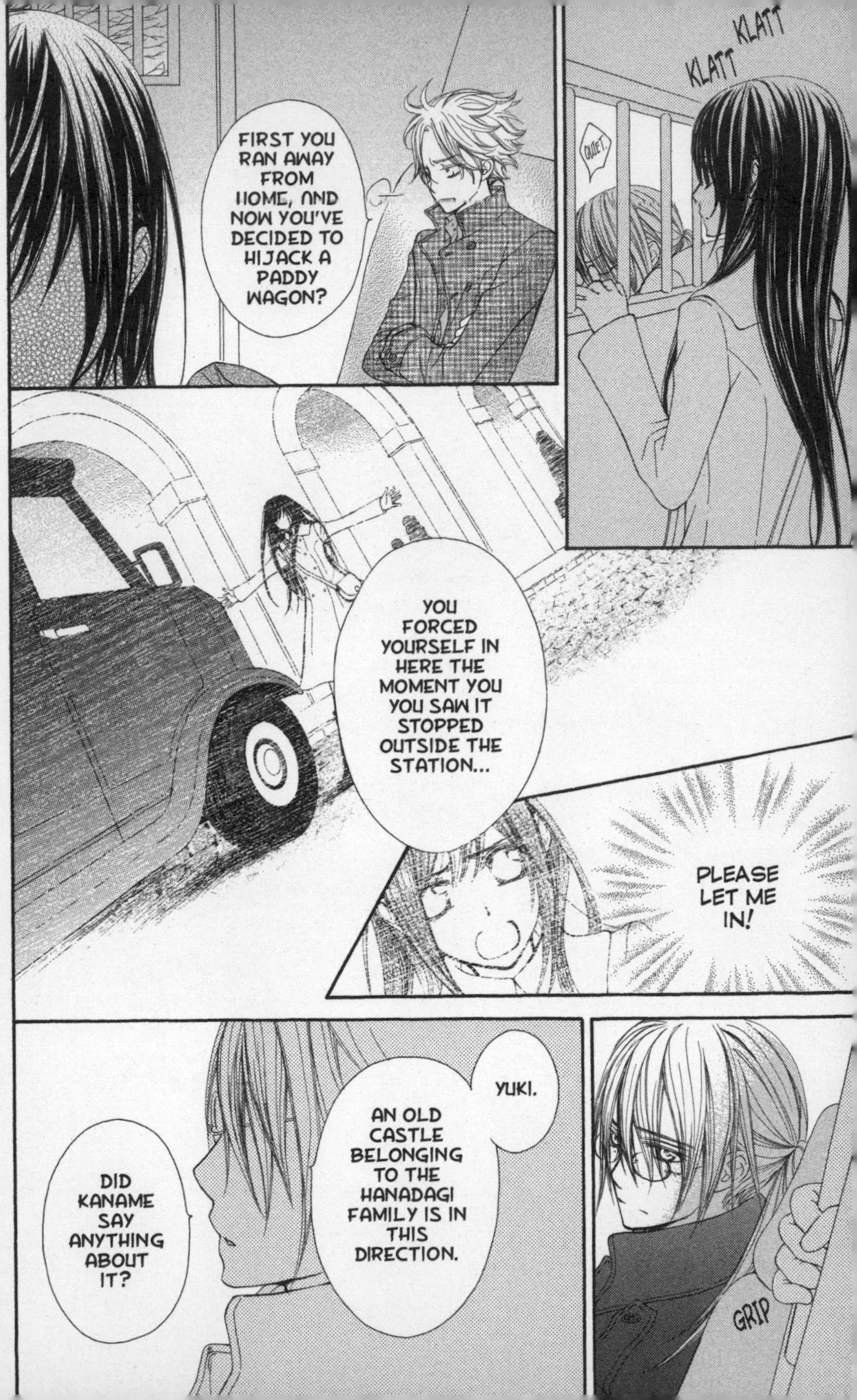
KLATT KLATT
QUIET.
FIRST YOU RAN AWAY FROM HOME, AND NOW YOU'VE DECIDED TO HIJACK A PADDY WAGON?
YOU FORCED YOURSELF IN HERE THE MOMENT YOU YOU SAW IT STOPPED OUTSIDE THE STATION...
PLEASE LET ME IN!
GRIP
YUKI.
AN OLD CASTLE BELONGING TO THE HANADAGI FAMILY IS IN THIS DIRECTION.
DID KANAME SAY ANYTHING ABOUT IT?

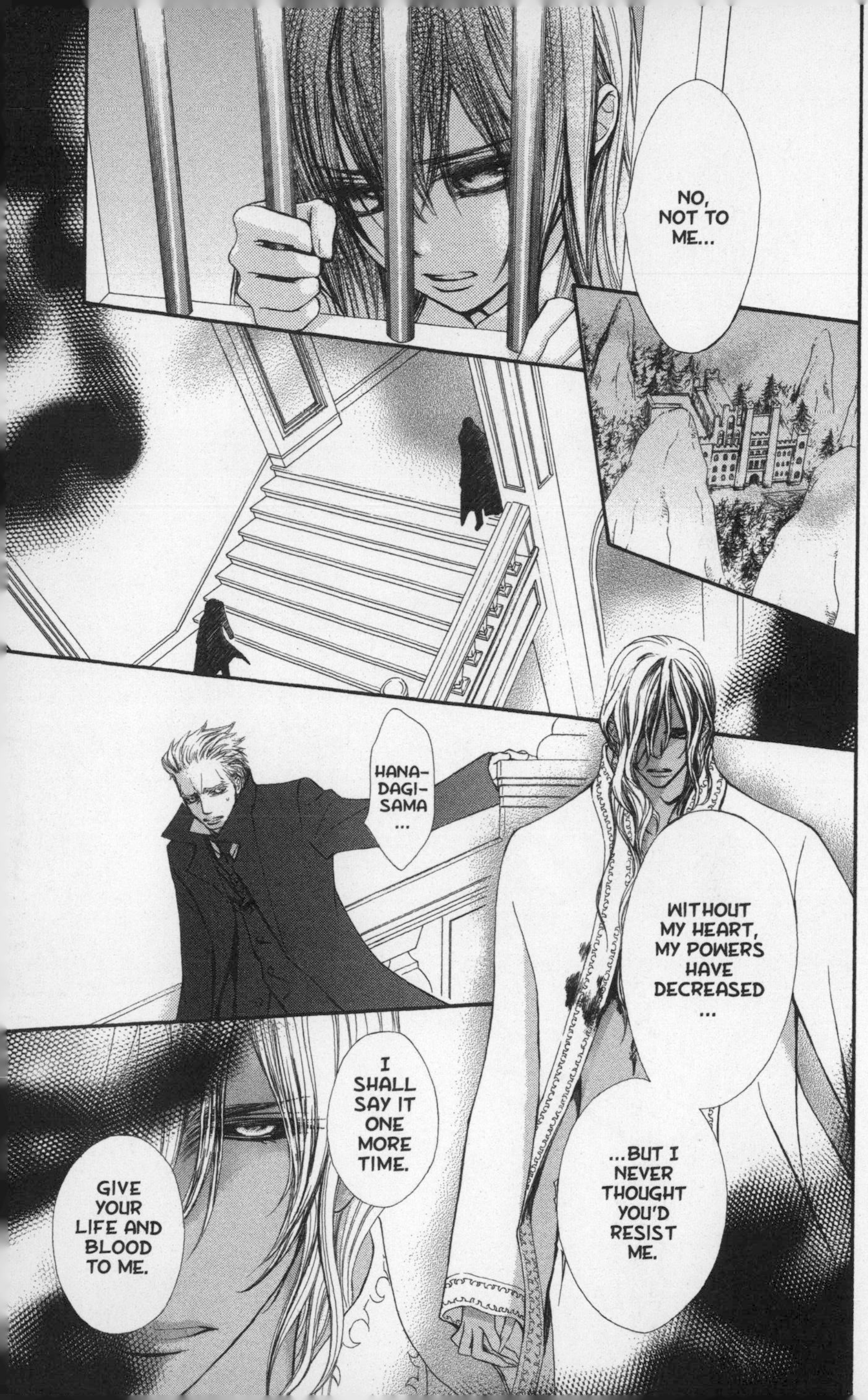
NO, NOT TO ME...
WITHOUT MY HEART, MY POWERS HAVE DECREASED ...
...BUT I NEVER THOUGHT YOU'D RESIST ME.
HANA-DAGI-SAMA ...
I SHALL SAY IT ONE MORE TIME.
GIVE YOUR LIFE AND BLOOD TO ME.

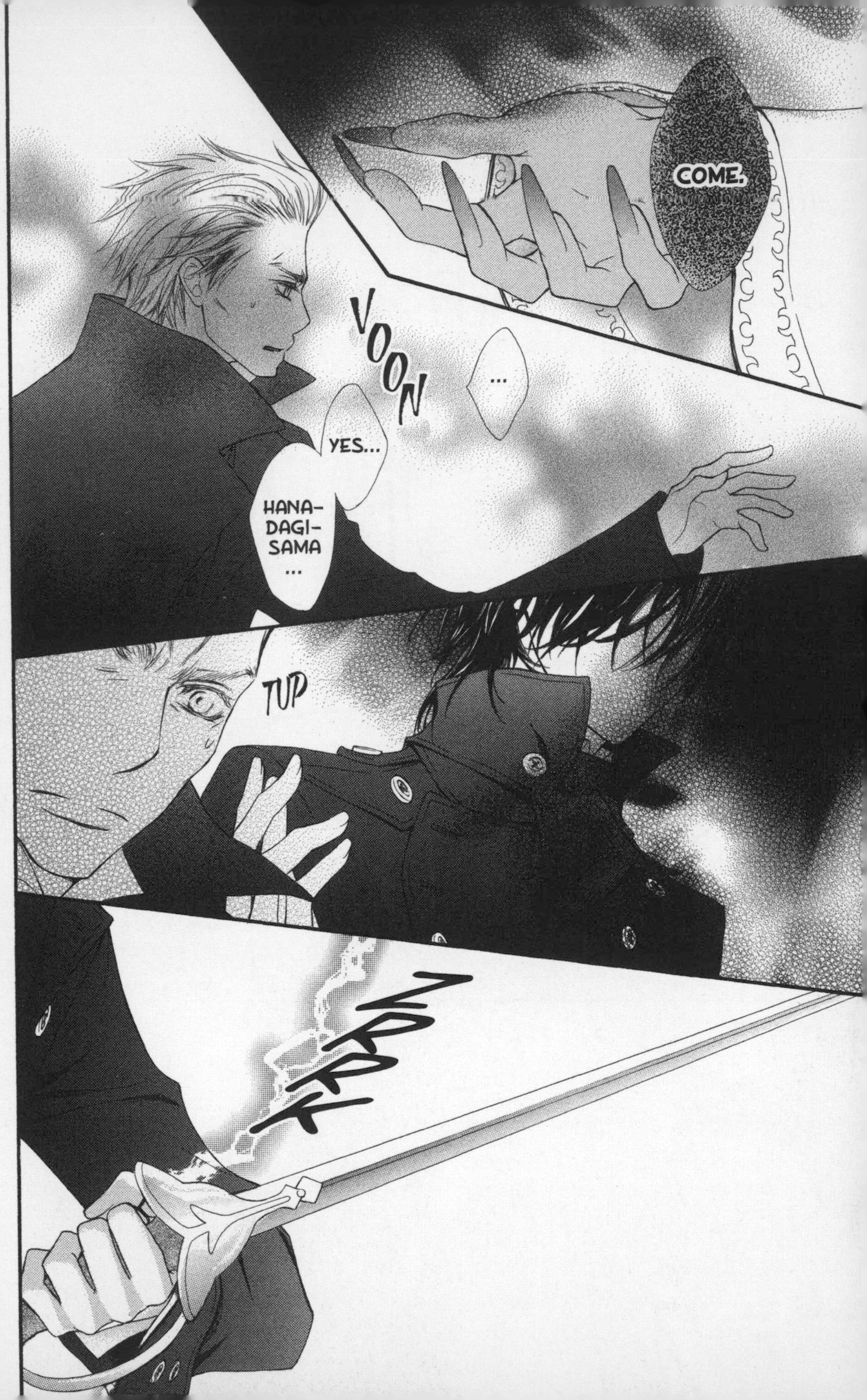
COME.
VOON
...
YES...
HANA-DAGI-SAMA ...
TUP
ZORRK

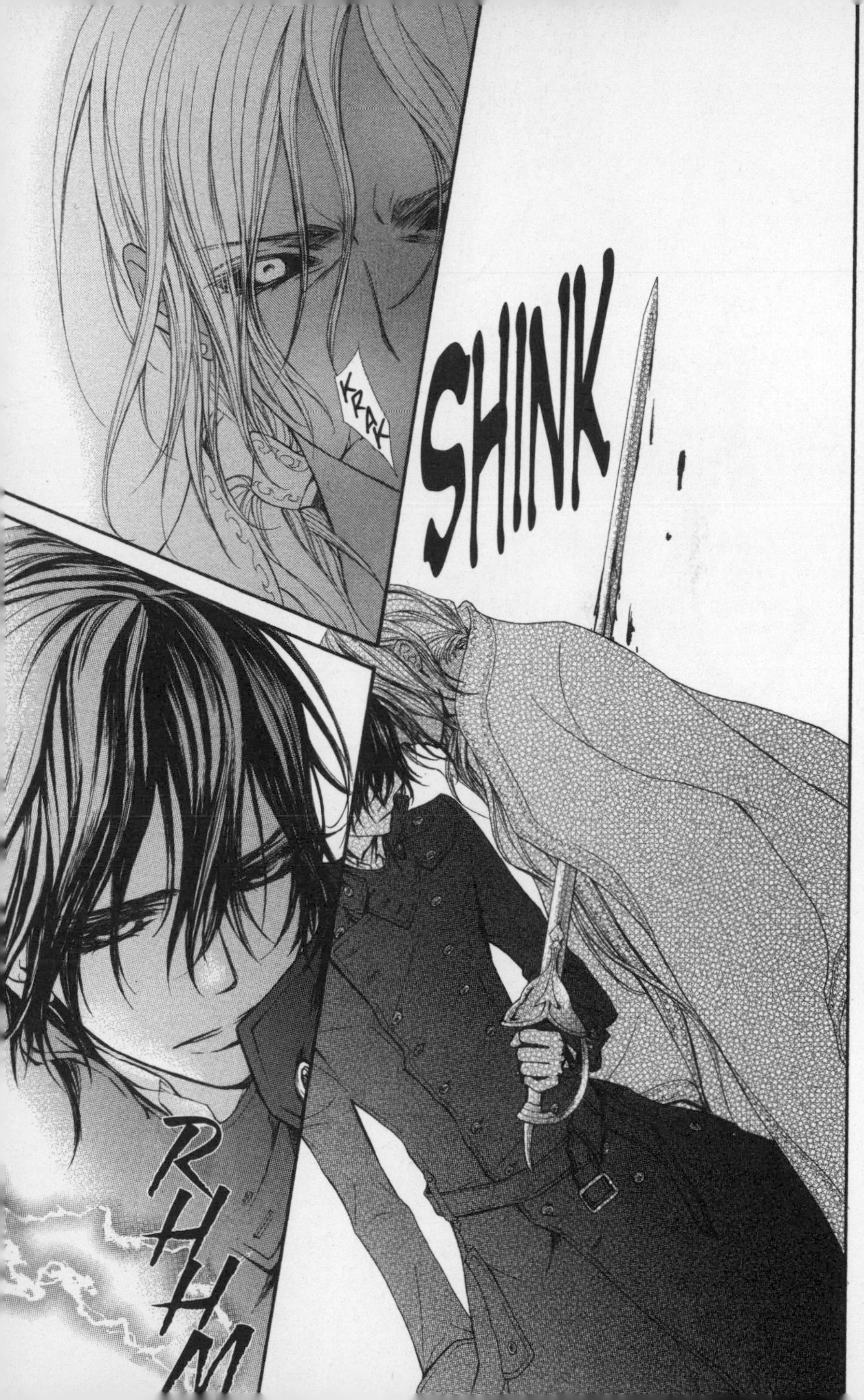
SHINK
KRAK
RHHM

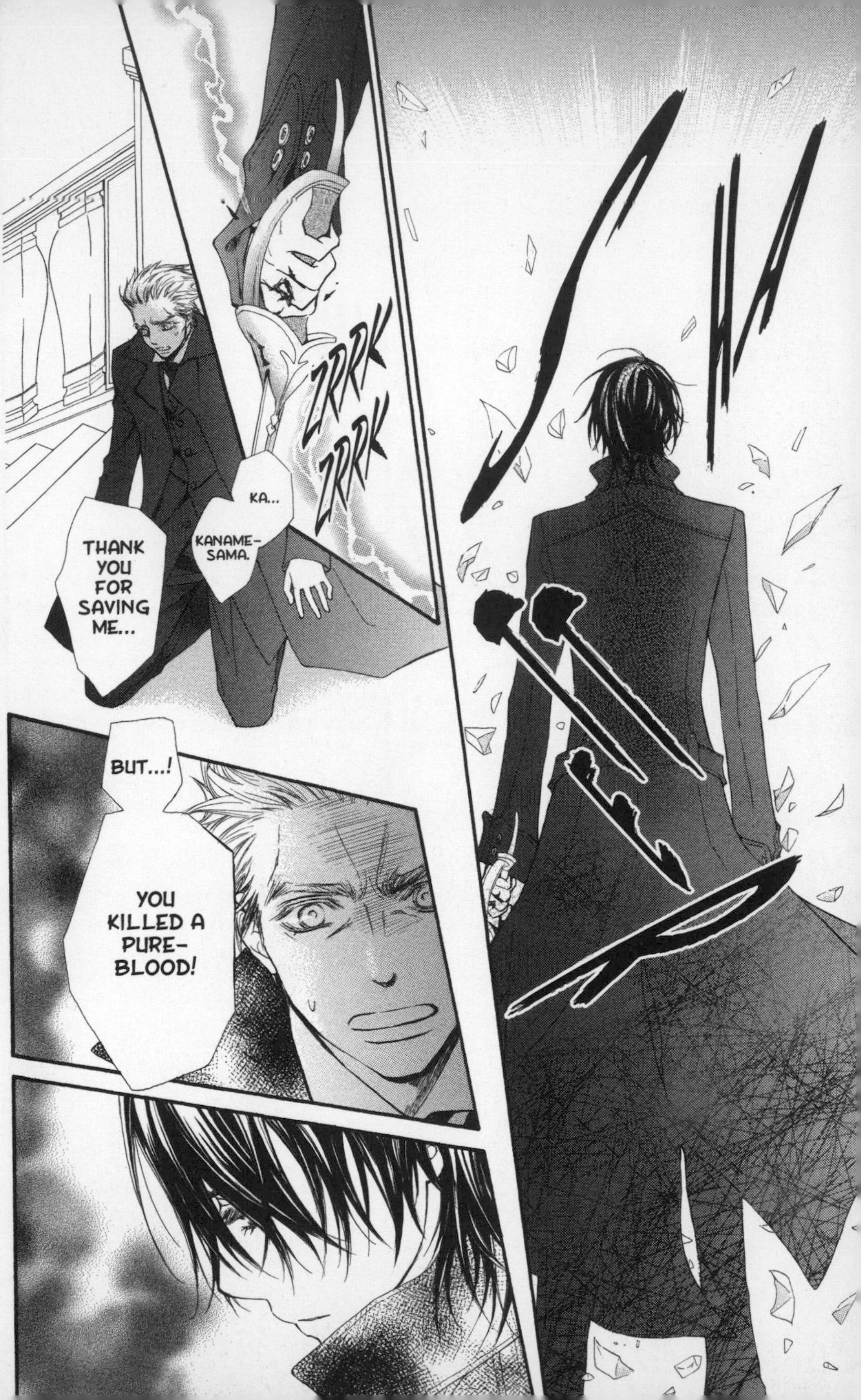
ZRRK
ZRRK
KA...
KANAME-SAMA.
THANK YOU FOR SAVING ME...
BUT...!
YOU KILLED A PURE-BLOOD!

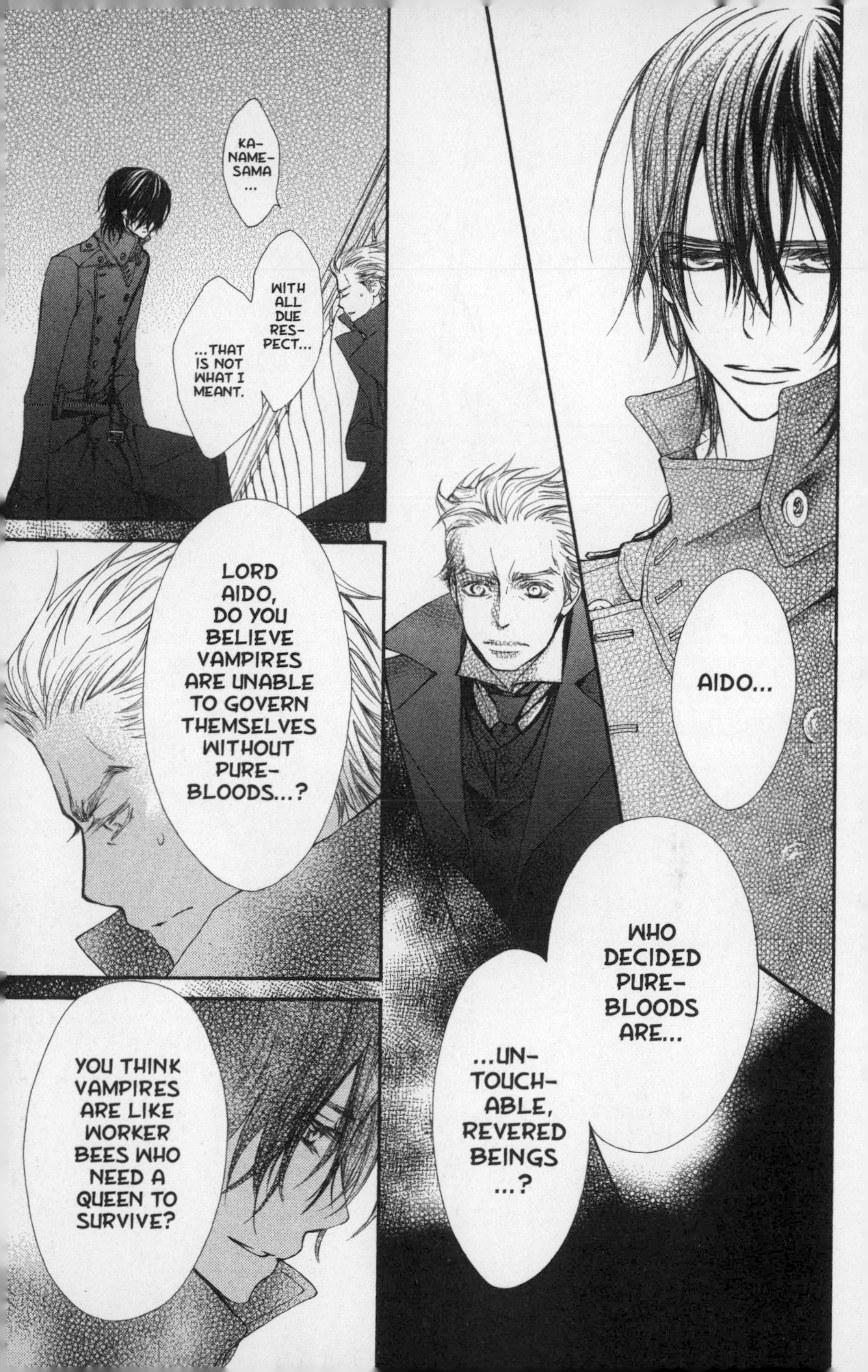
AIDO...
WHO DECIDED PURE-BLOODS ARE...
...UN-TOUCH-ABLE, REVERED BEINGS ...?
KA-NAME-SAMA ...
WITH ALL DUE RES-PECT...
...THAT IS NOT WHAT I MEANT.
LORD AIDO, DO YOU BELIEVE VAMPIRES ARE UNABLE TO GOVERN THEMSELVES WITHOUT PURE-BLOODS...?
YOU THINK VAMPIRES ARE LIKE WORKER BEES WHO NEED A QUEEN TO SURVIVE?

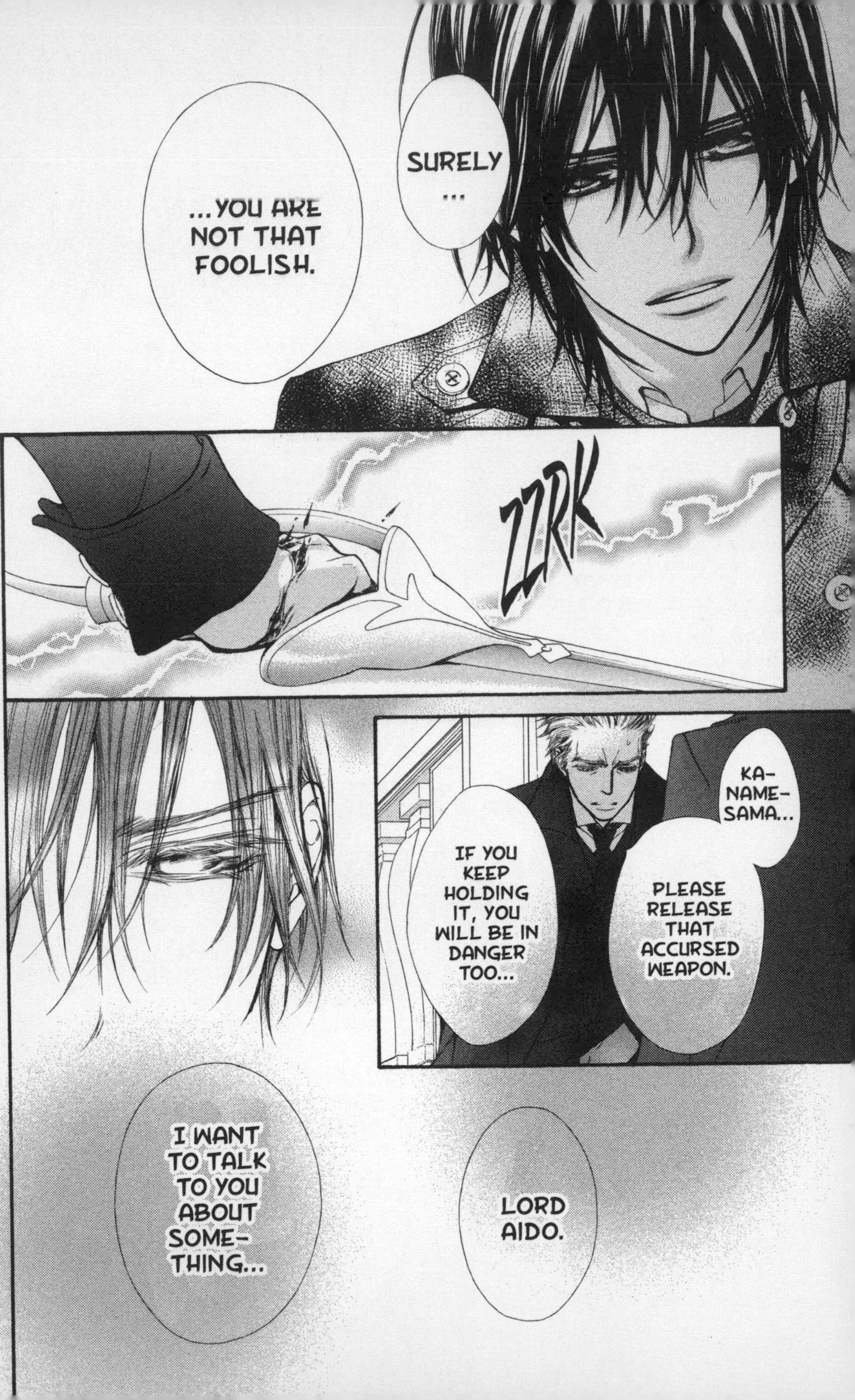
SURELY...
...YOU ARE NOT THAT FOOLISH.
ZZRK
KA-NAME-SAMA...
PLEASE RELEASE THAT ACCURSED WEAPON.
IF YOU KEEP HOLDING IT, YOU WILL BE IN DANGER TOO...
LORD AIDO.
I WANT TO TALK TO YOU ABOUT SOME-THING...

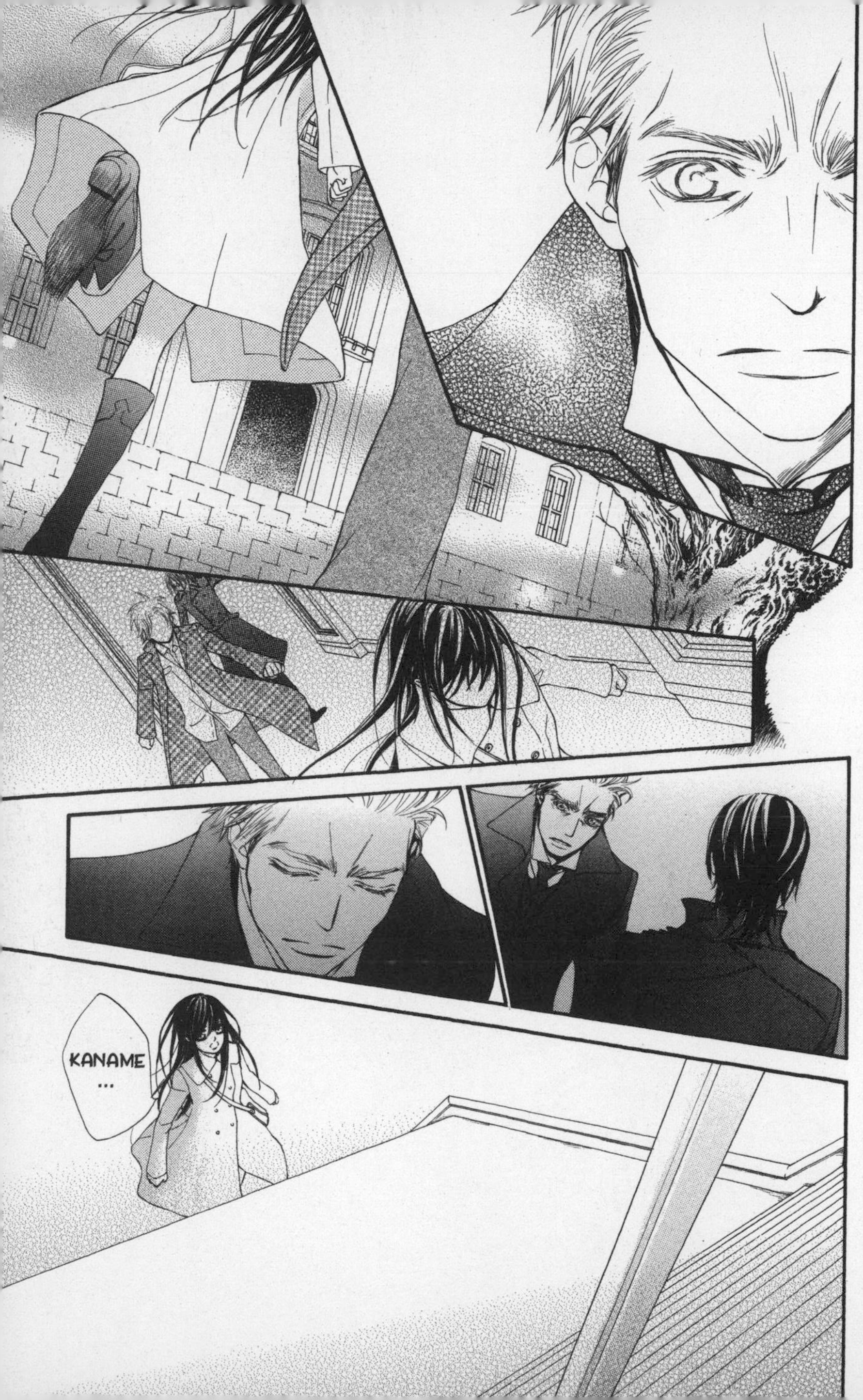
KANAME ...

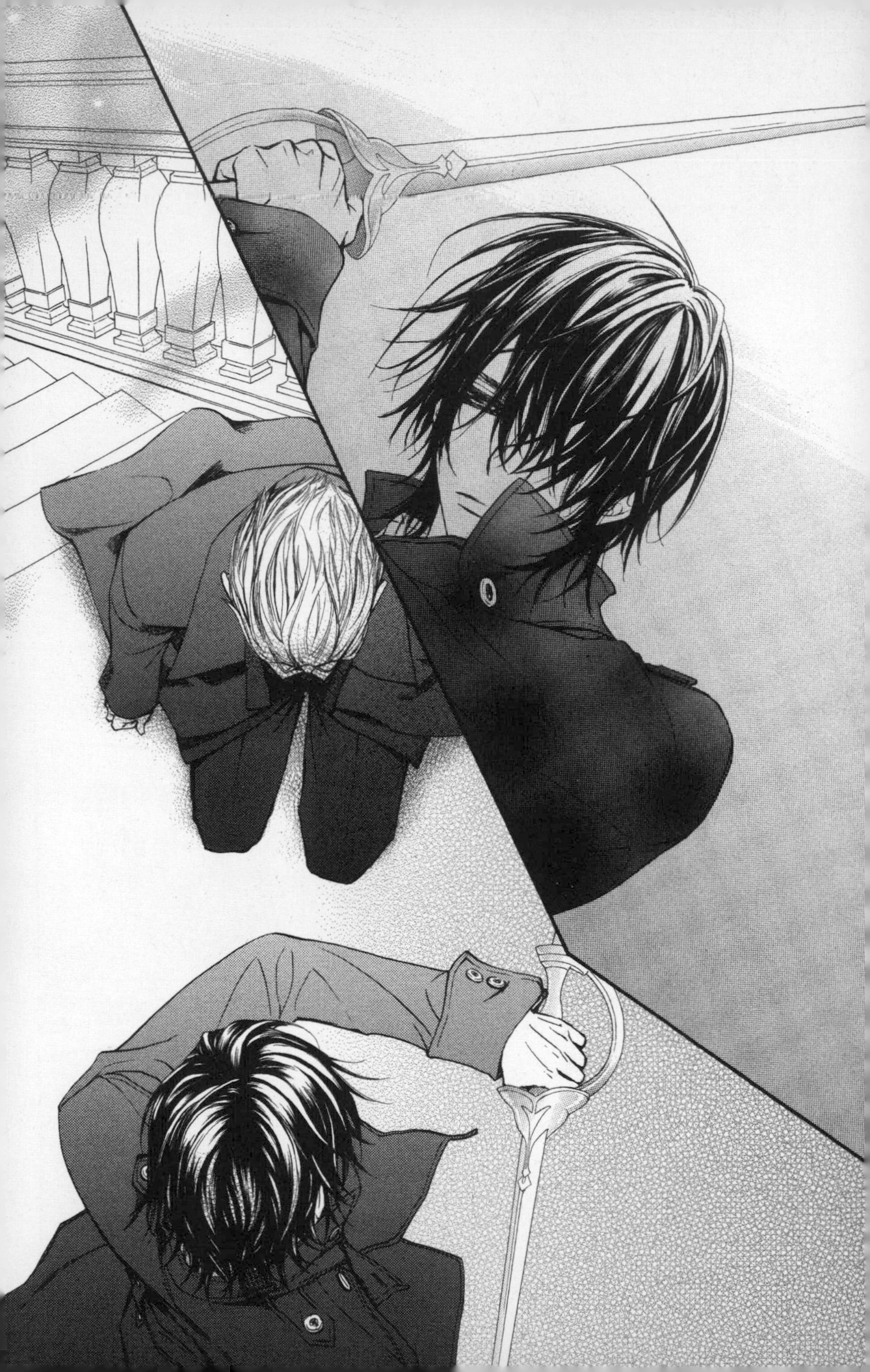

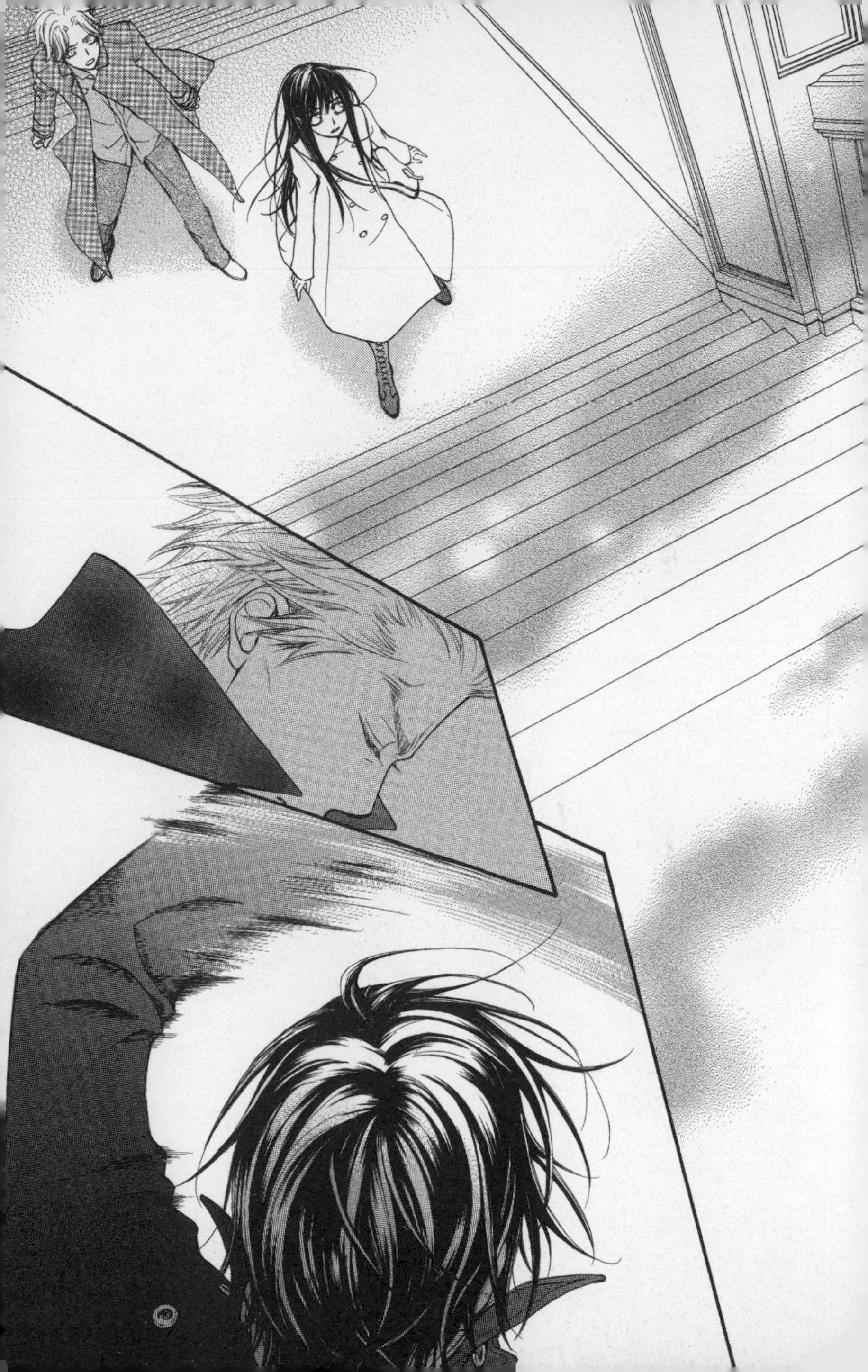

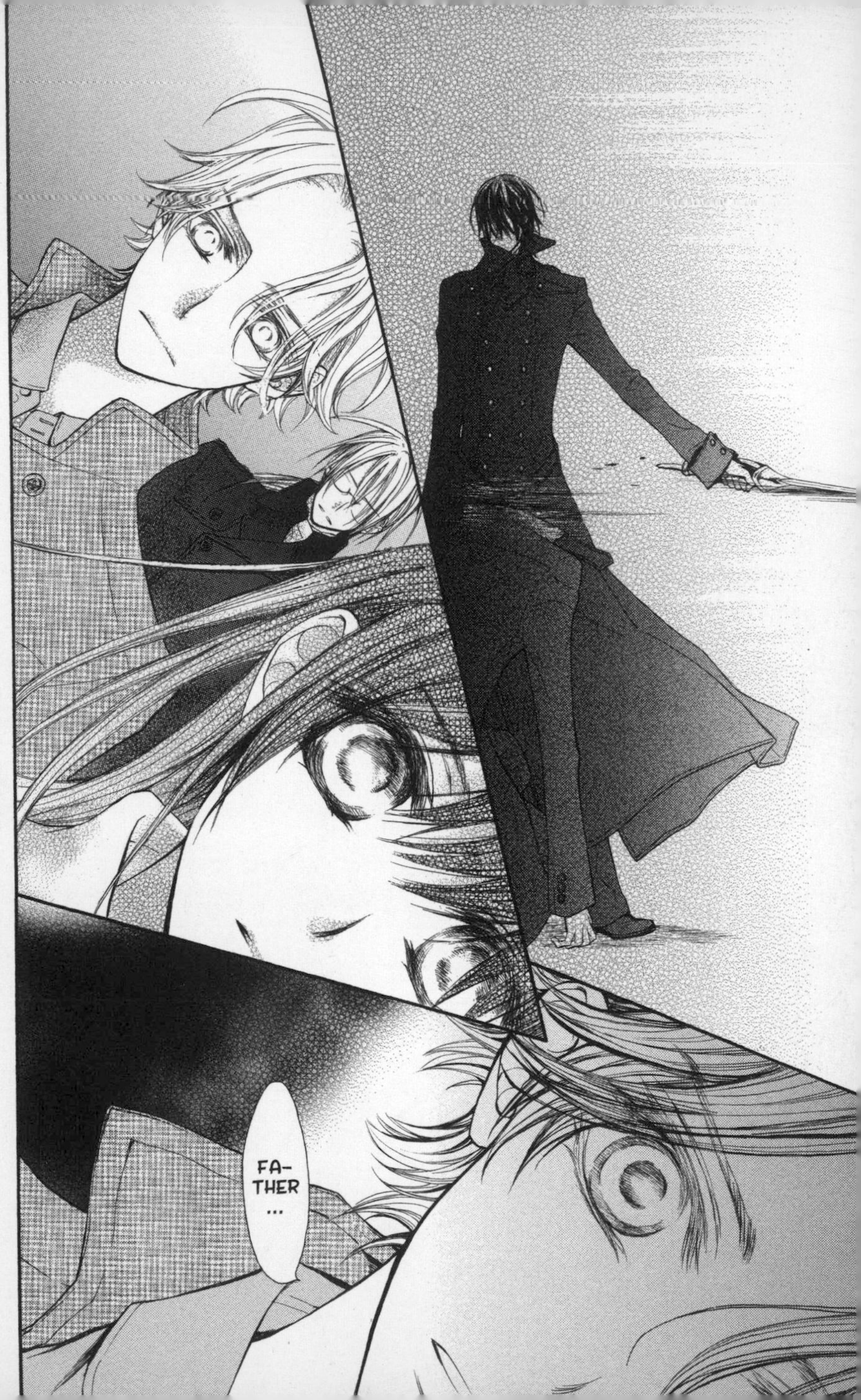
FA-
THER
...

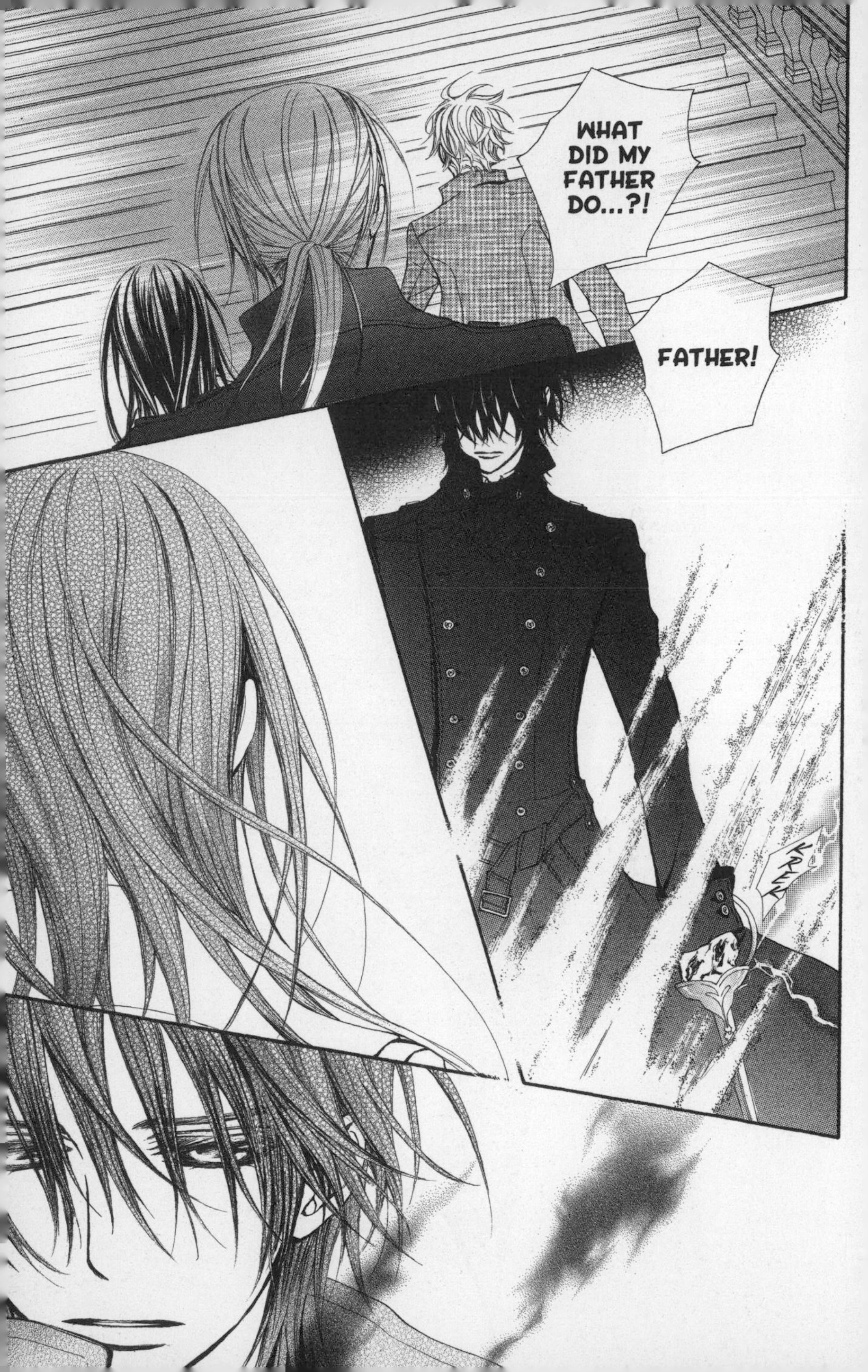
WHAT DID MY FATHER DO...?!
FATHER!
KREEK

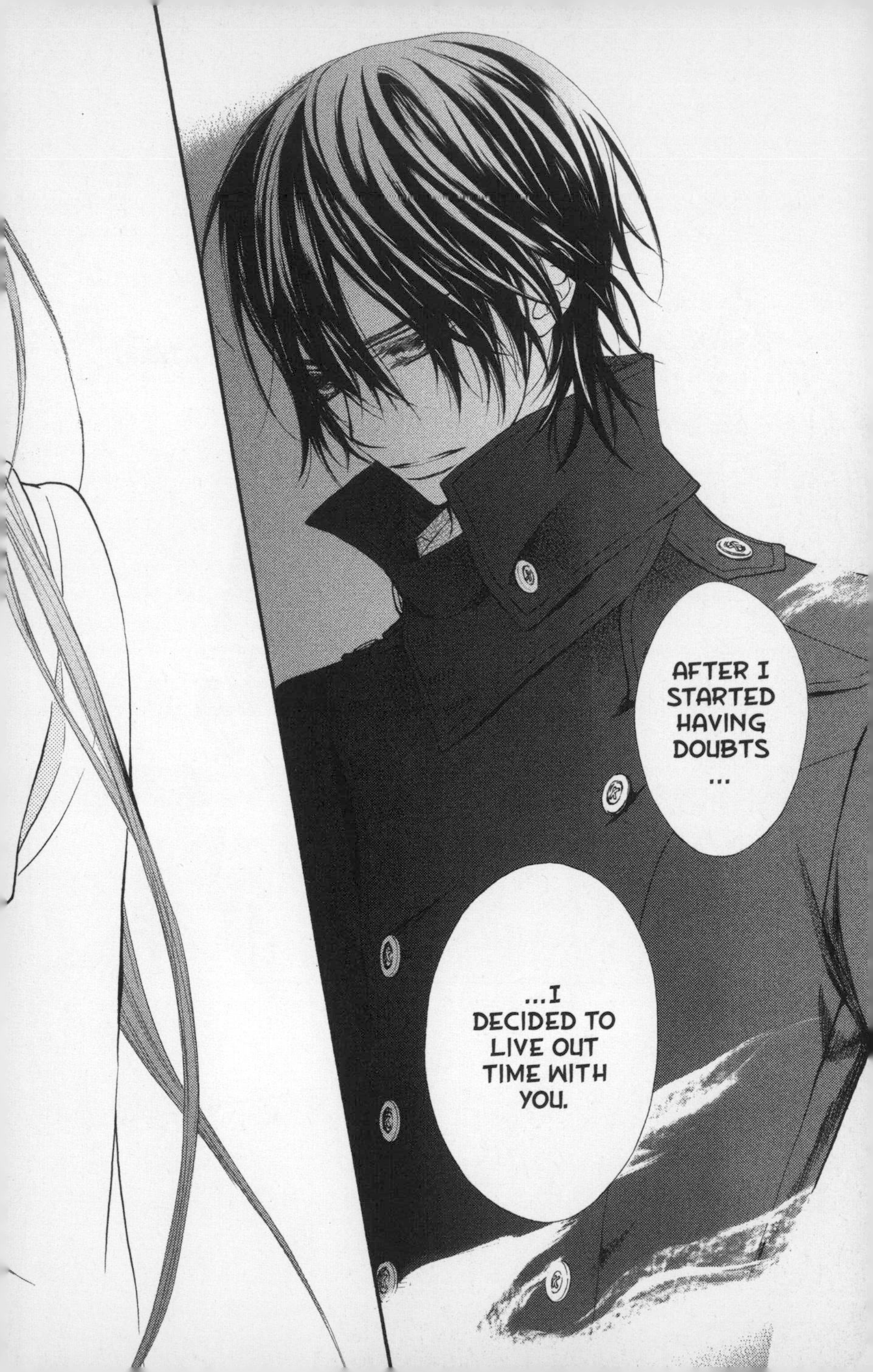
AFTER I STARTED HAVING DOUBTS ...
...I DECIDED TO LIVE OUT TIME WITH YOU.

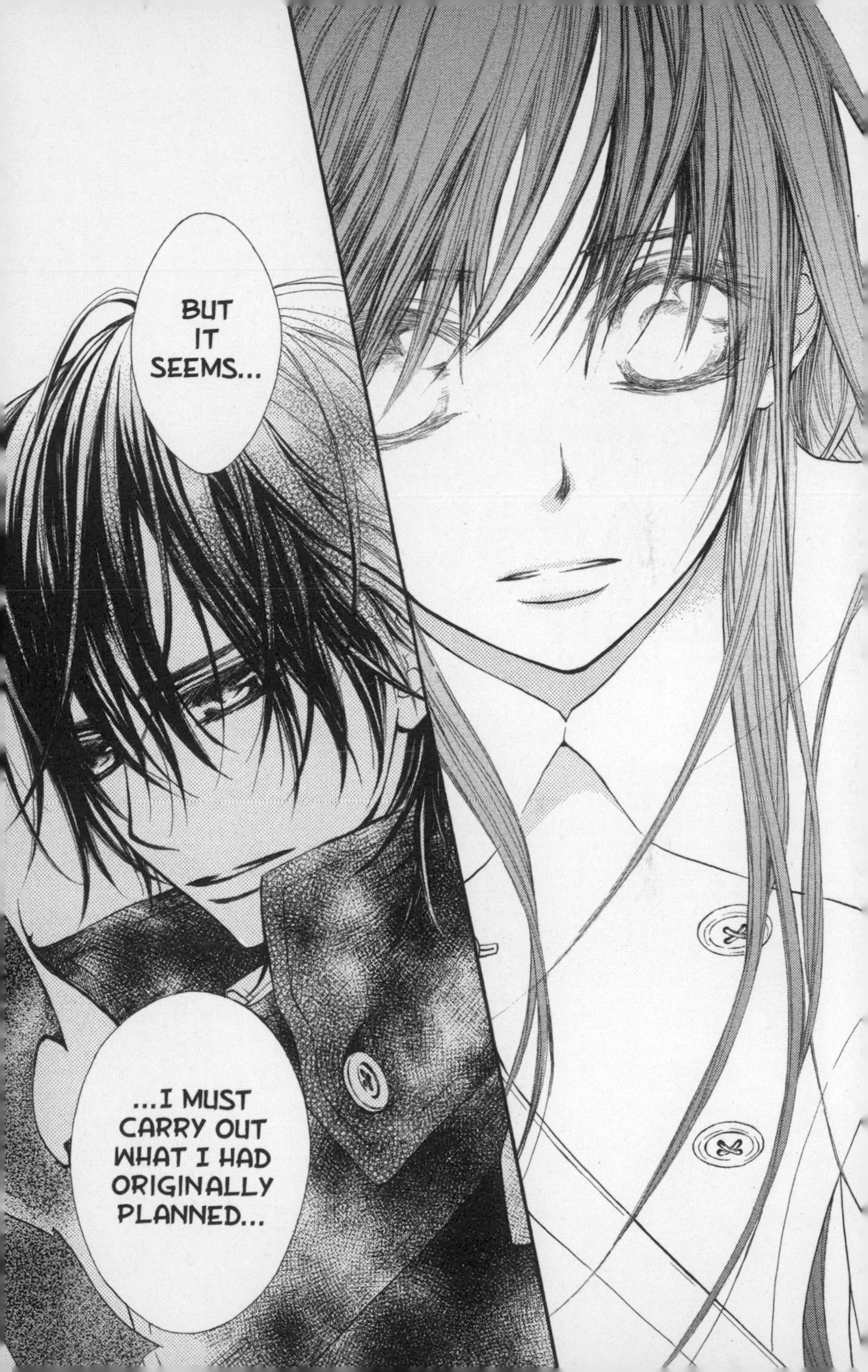
BUT IT SEEMS...
...I MUST CARRY OUT WHAT I HAD ORIGINALLY PLANNED...

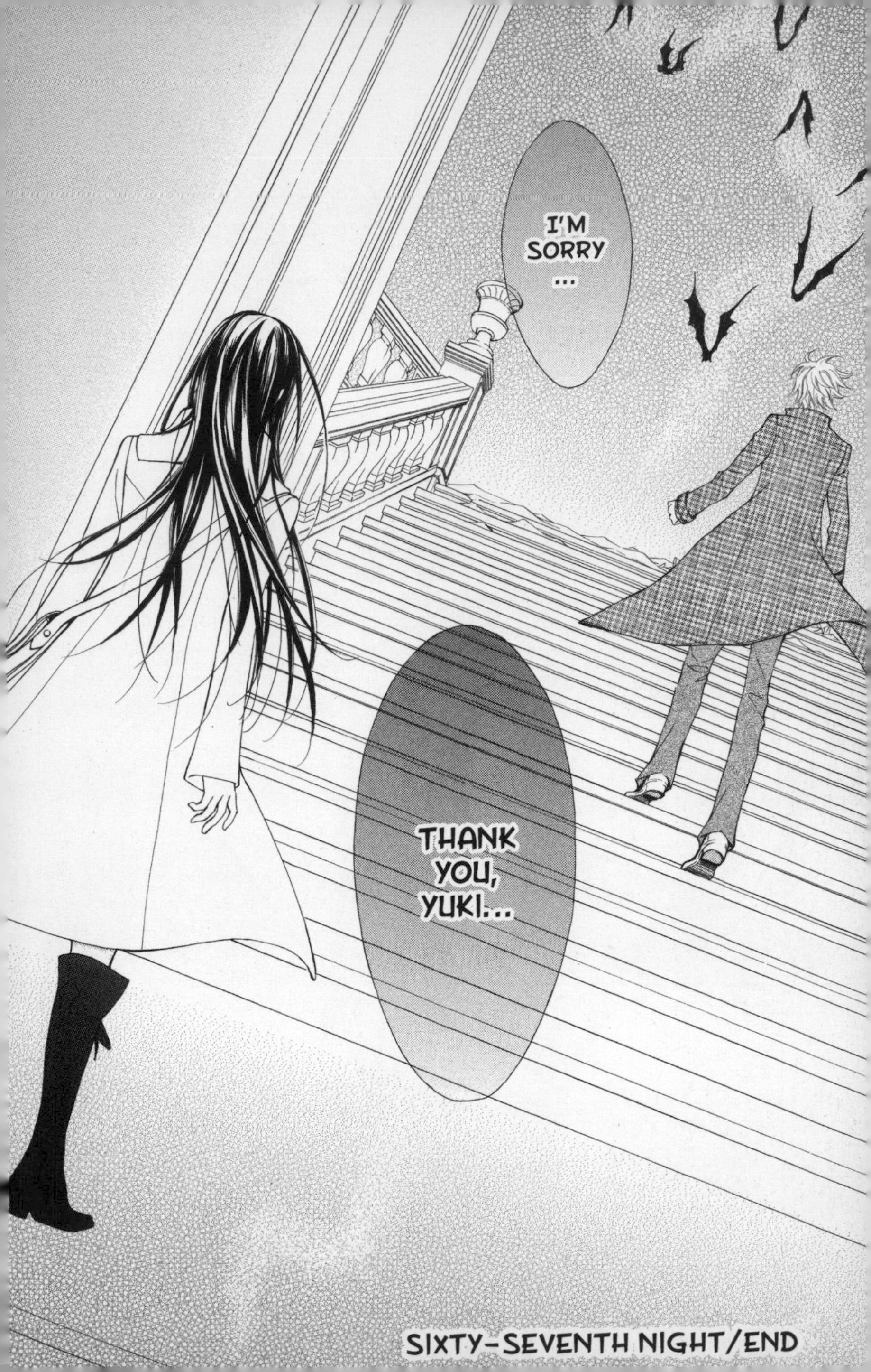
I'M SORRY ...
THANK YOU, YUKI...
SIXTY-SEVENTH NIGHT/END

VAMPIRE KNIGHT

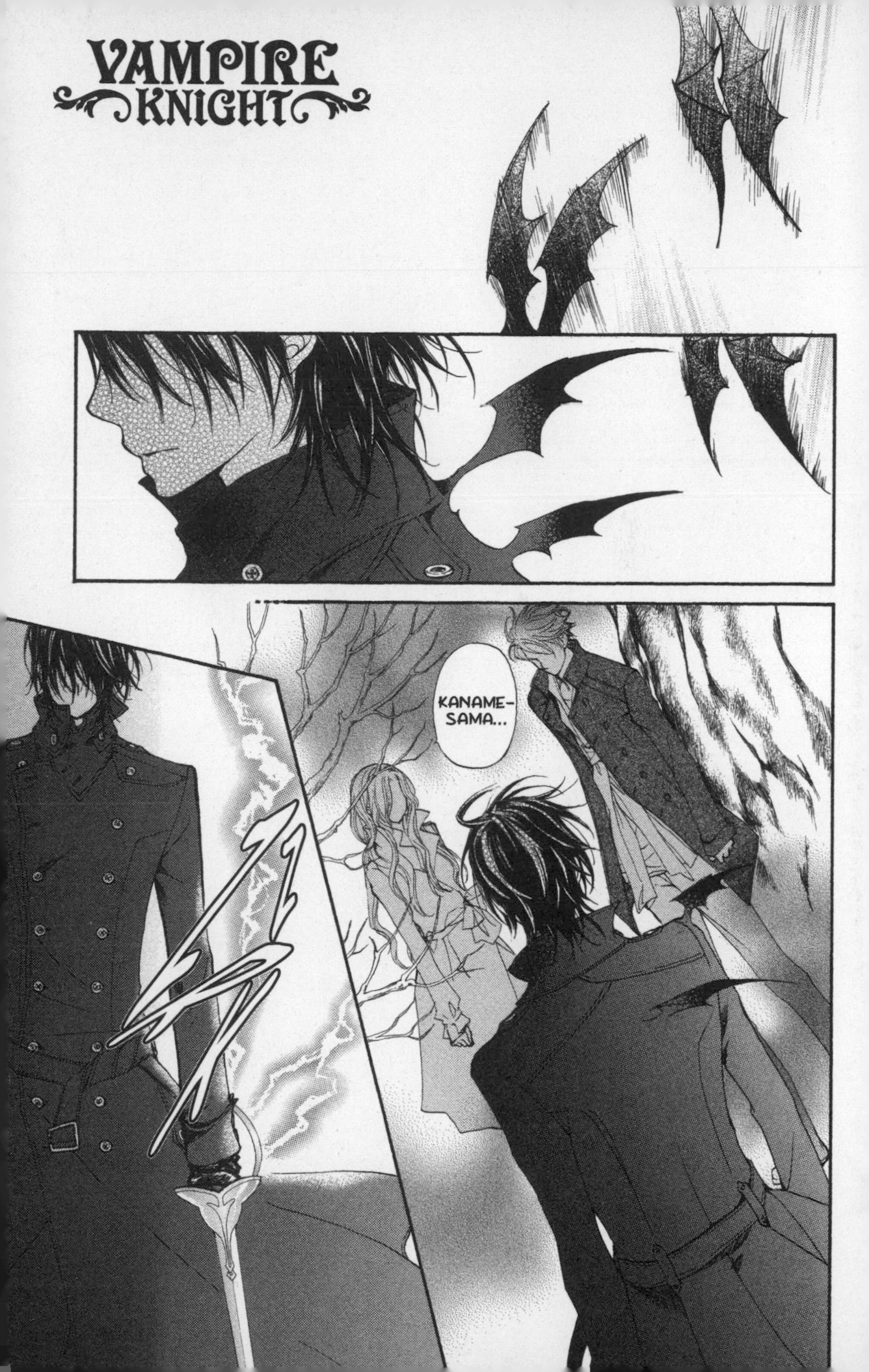
KANAME-SAMA...

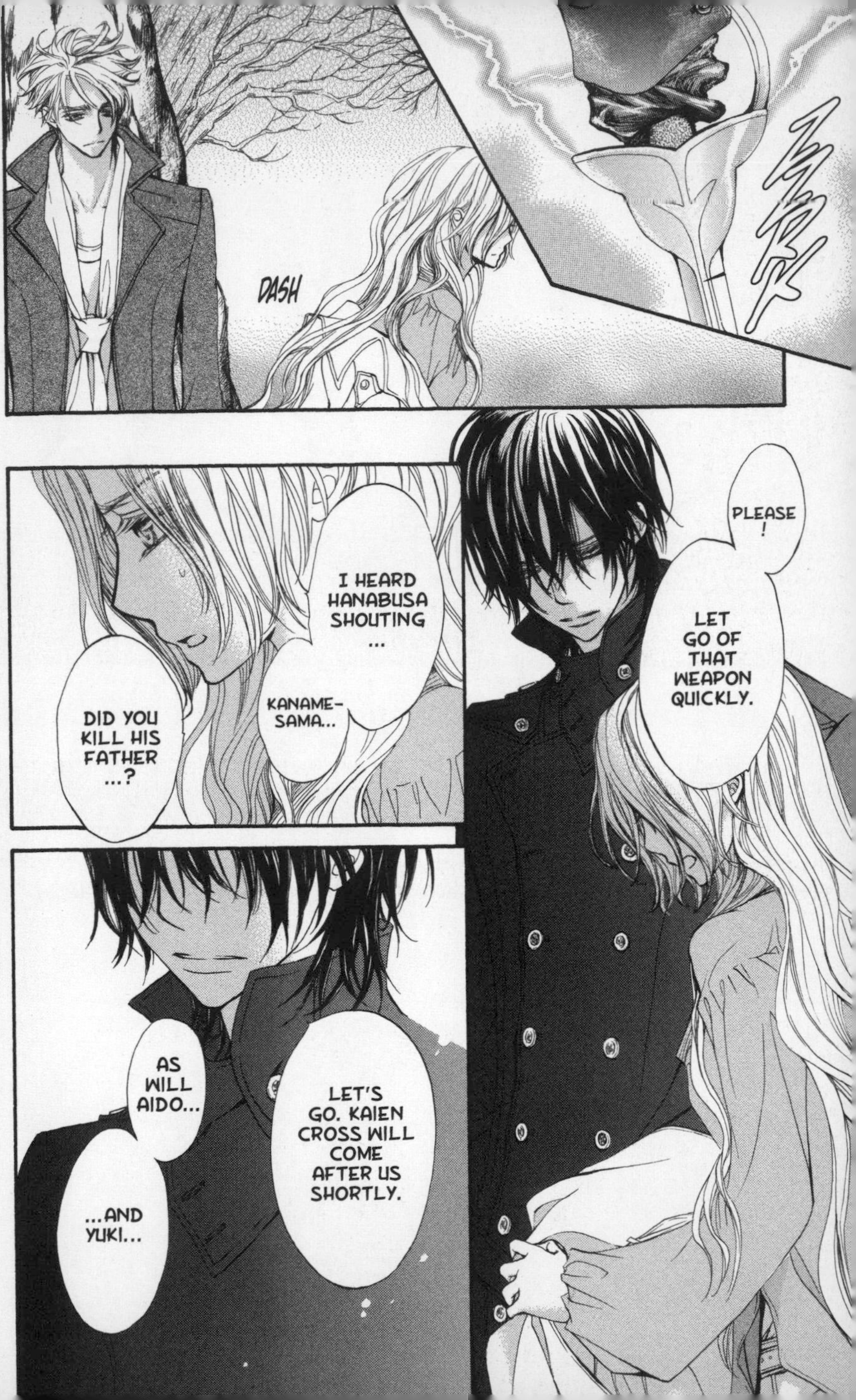
DASH
PLEASE!
LET GO OF THAT WEAPON QUICKLY.
I HEARD HANABUSA SHOUTING...
KANAME-SAMA...
DID YOU KILL HIS FATHER...?
LET'S GO. KAIEN CROSS WILL COME AFTER US SHORTLY.
AS WILL AIDO...
...AND YUKI...

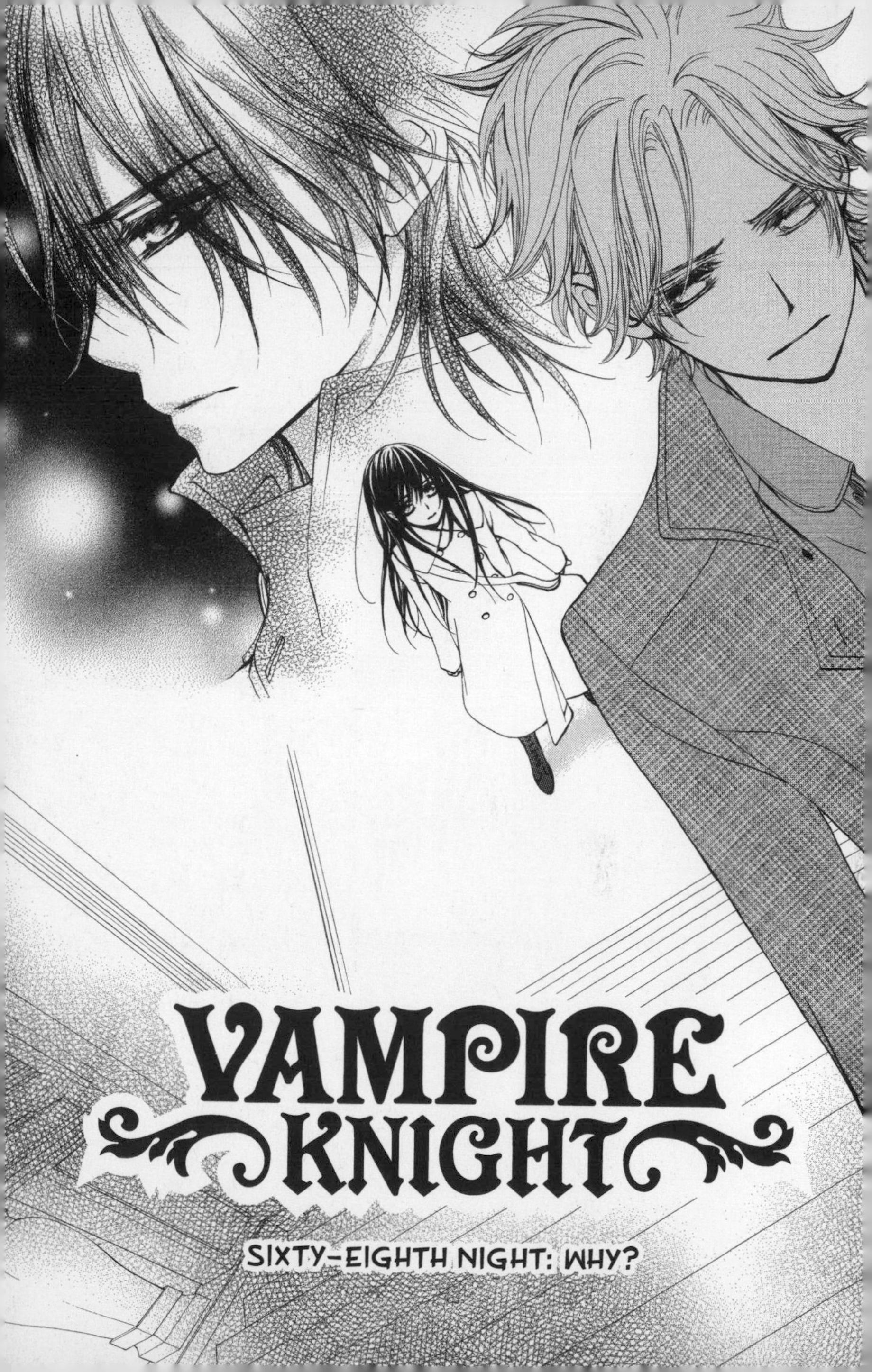
VAMPIRE
KNIGHT
SIXTY-EIGHTH NIGHT: WHY?

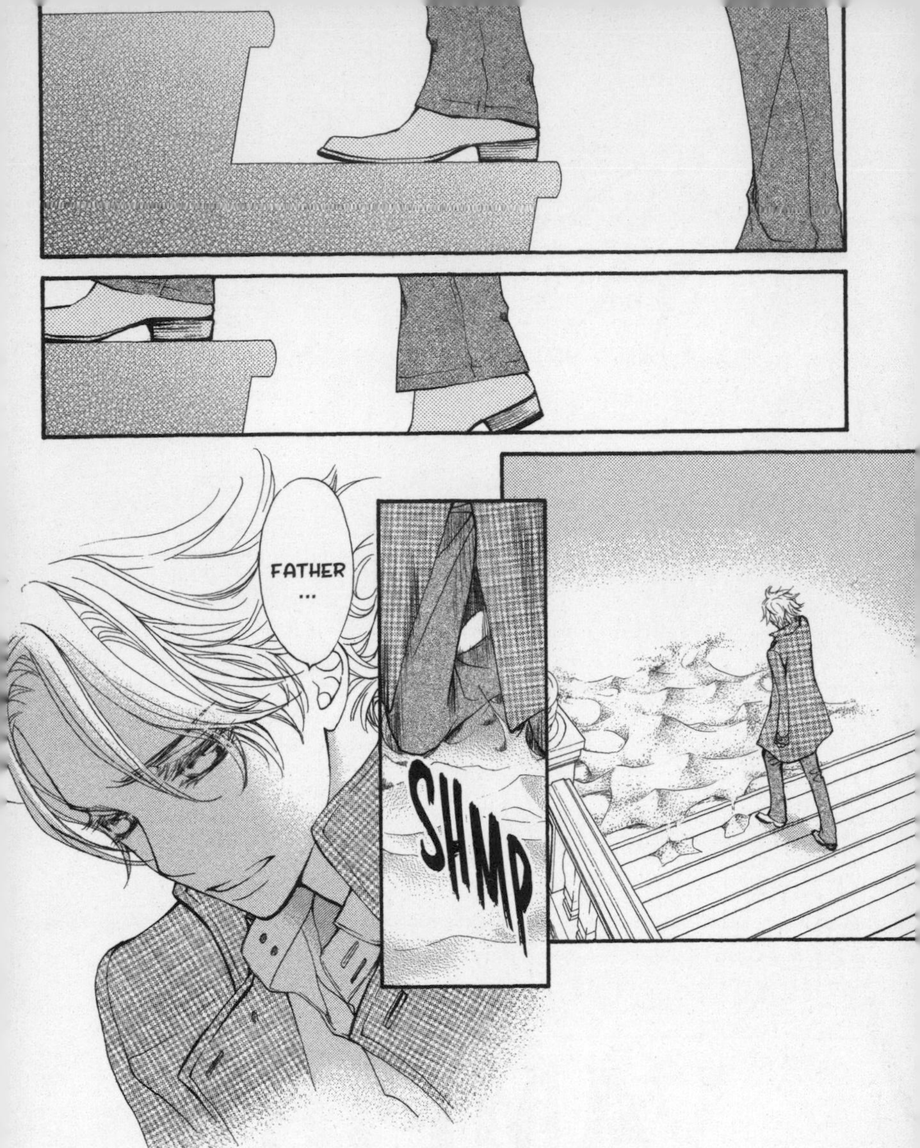
SHMP
FATHER
...

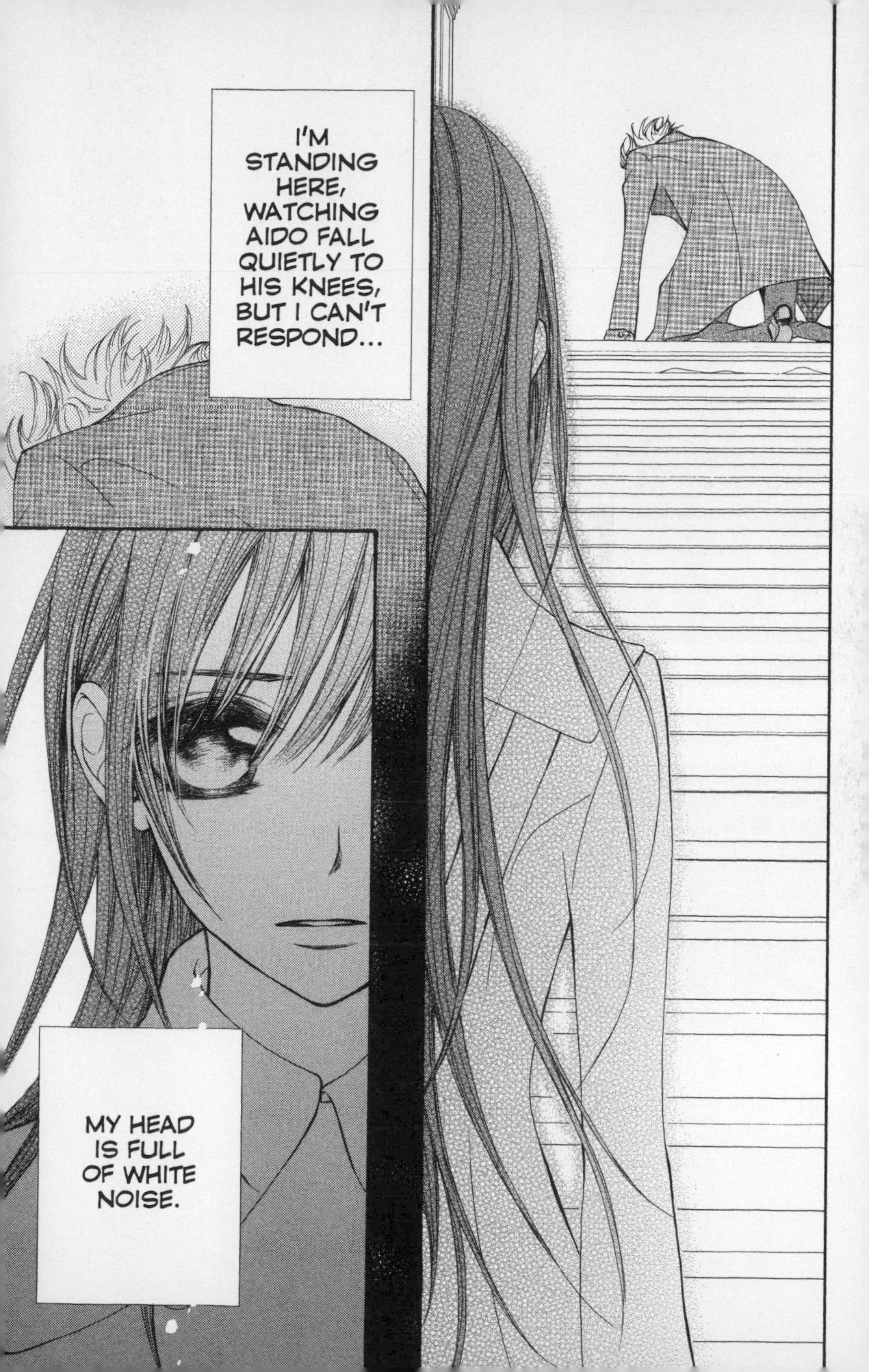
I'M STANDING HERE, WATCHING AIDO FALL QUIETLY TO HIS KNEES, BUT I CAN'T RESPOND...
MY HEAD IS FULL OF WHITE NOISE.

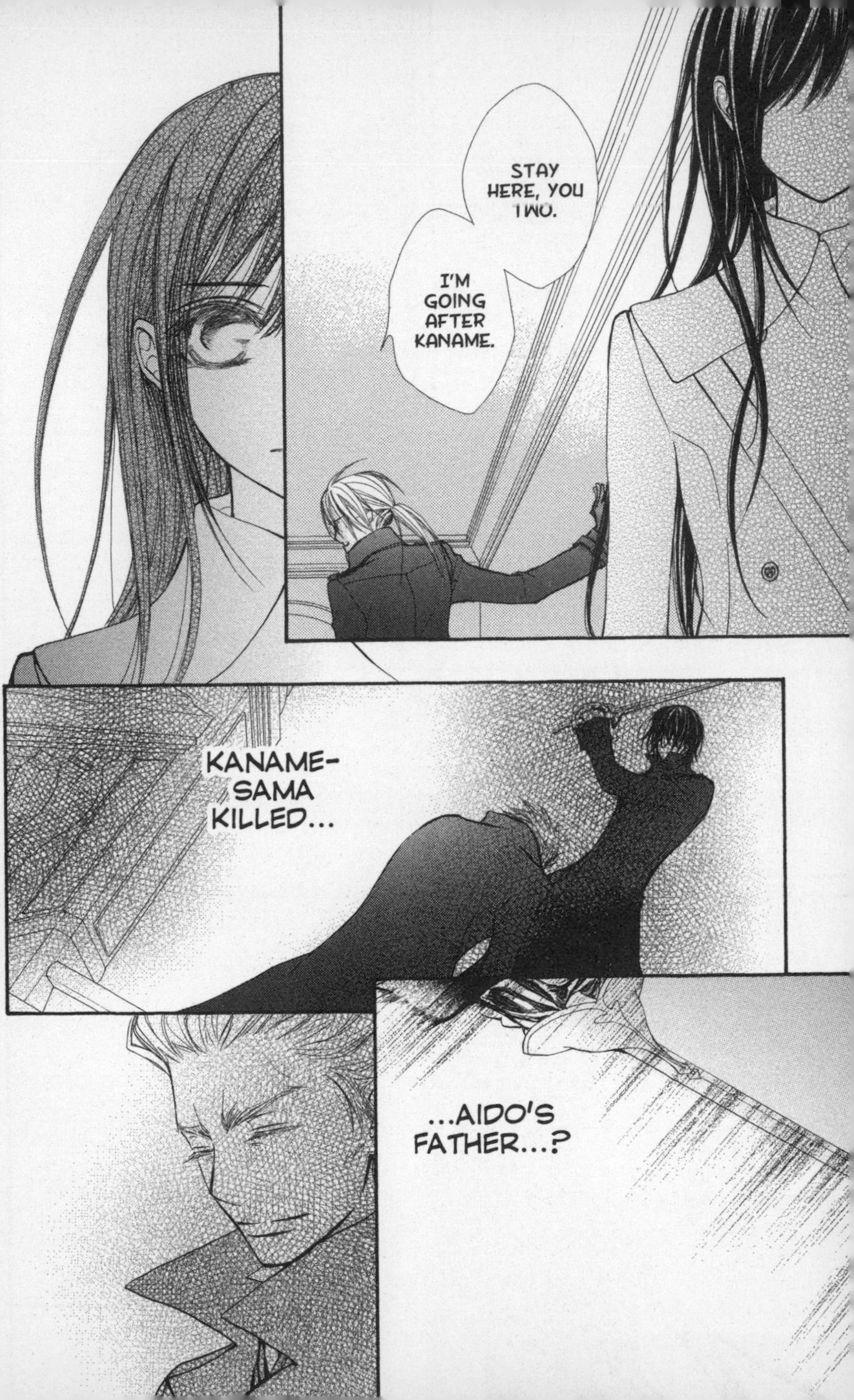
STAY HERE, YOU TWO.
I'M GOING AFTER KANAME.
KANAME-SAMA KILLED...
...AIDO'S FATHER...?

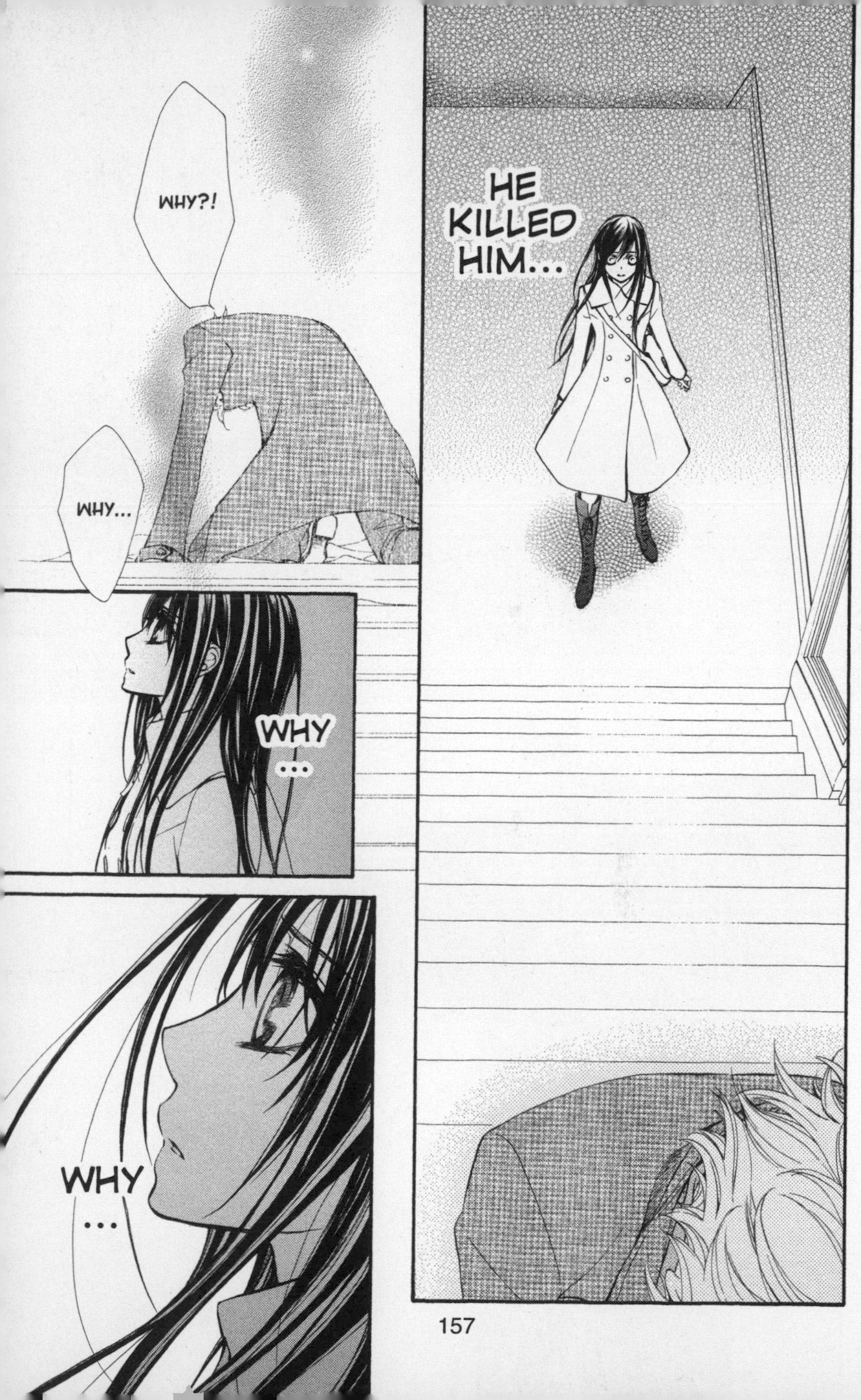
HE KILLED HIM...
WHY?!
WHY...
WHY ...
WHY ...

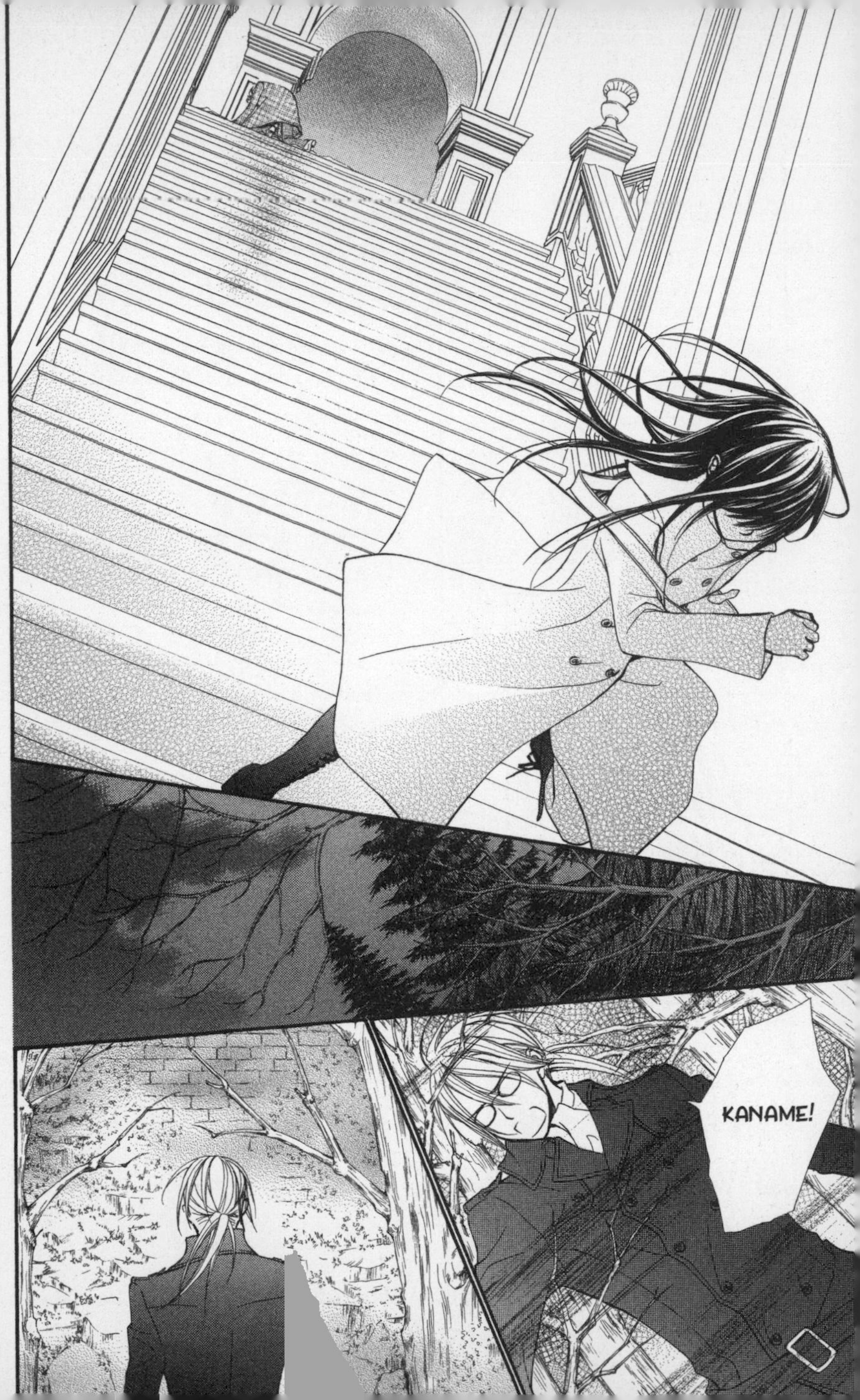
KANAME!

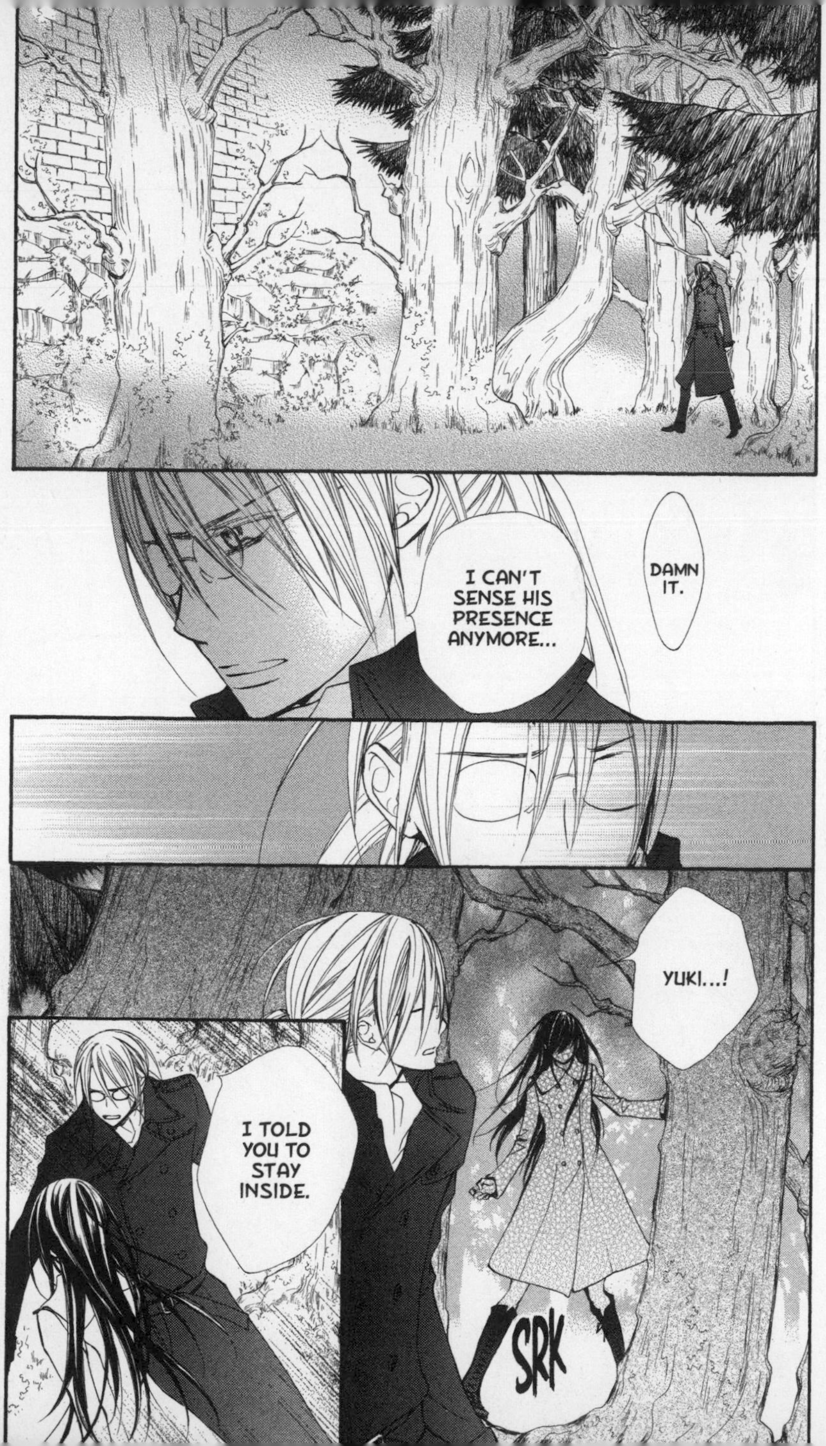
DAMN IT.
I CAN'T SENSE HIS PRESENCE ANYMORE...
YUKI...!
SRK
I TOLD YOU TO STAY INSIDE.

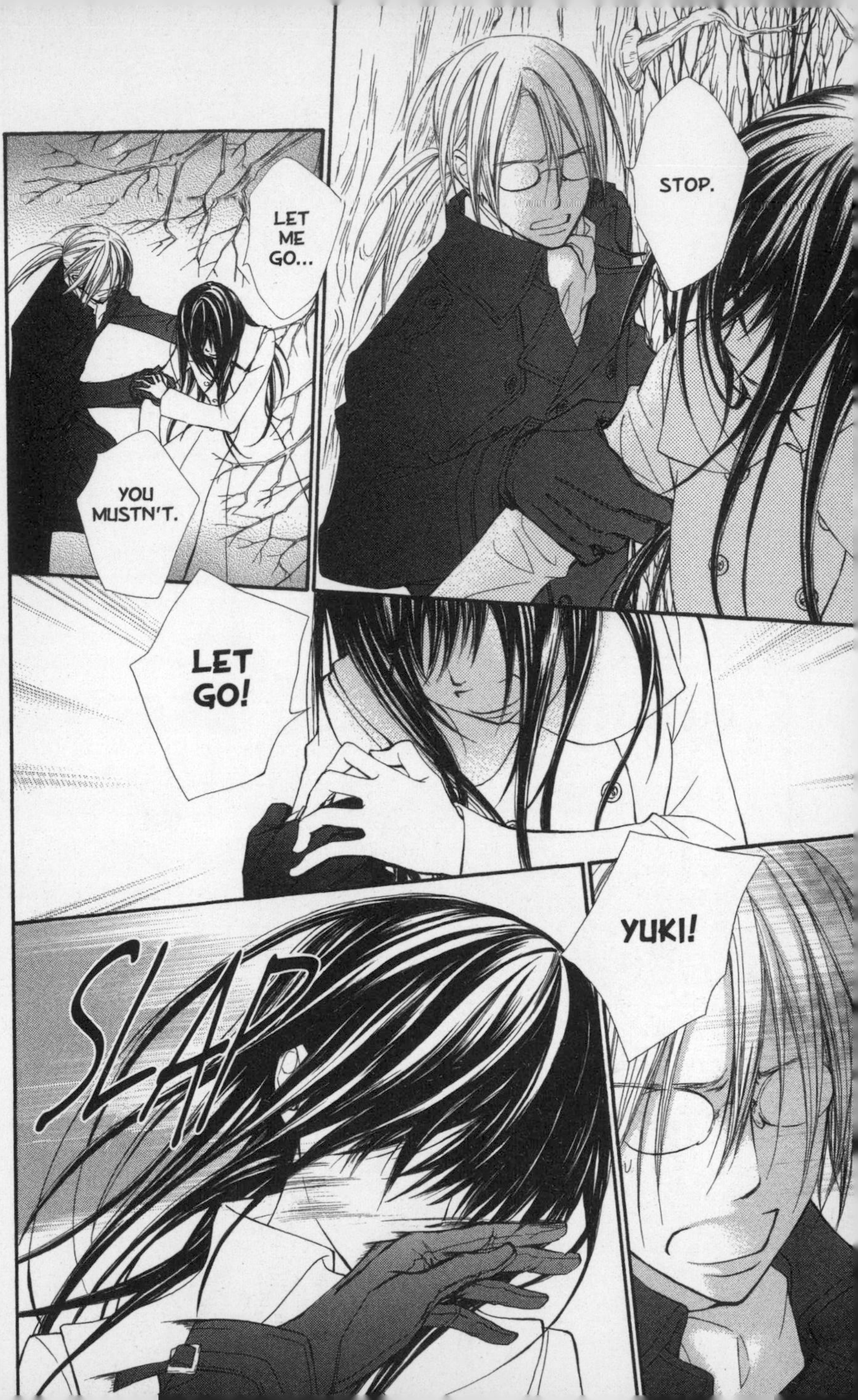
STOP.
LET ME GO...
YOU MUSTN'T.
LET GO!
YUKI!
SLAP

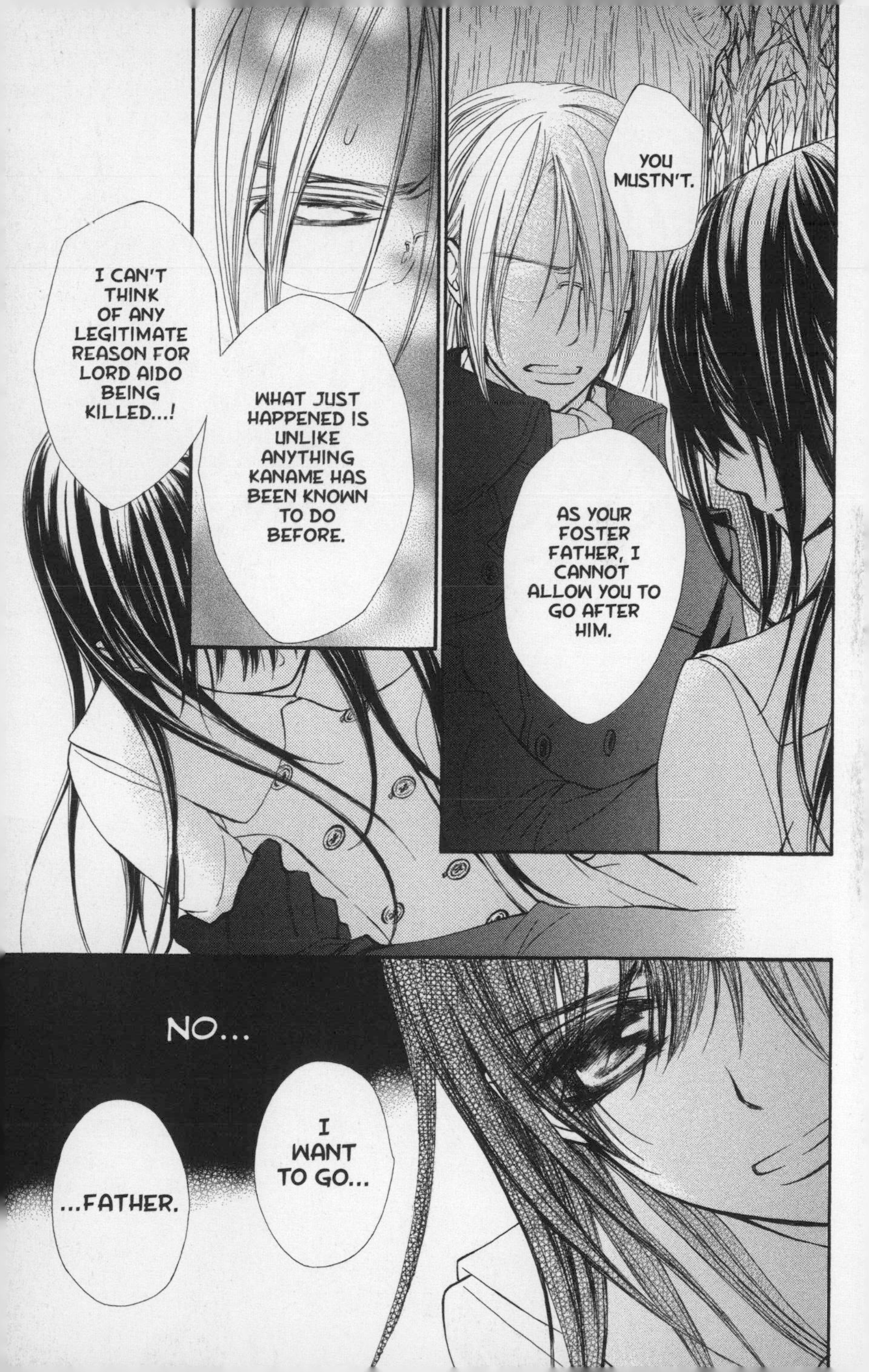
YOU MUSTN'T.
AS YOUR FOSTER FATHER, I CANNOT ALLOW YOU TO GO AFTER HIM.
WHAT JUST HAPPENED IS UNLIKE ANYTHING KANAME HAS BEEN KNOWN TO DO BEFORE.
I CAN'T THINK OF ANY LEGITIMATE REASON FOR LORD AIDO BEING KILLED...!
NO...
I WANT TO GO...
...FATHER.

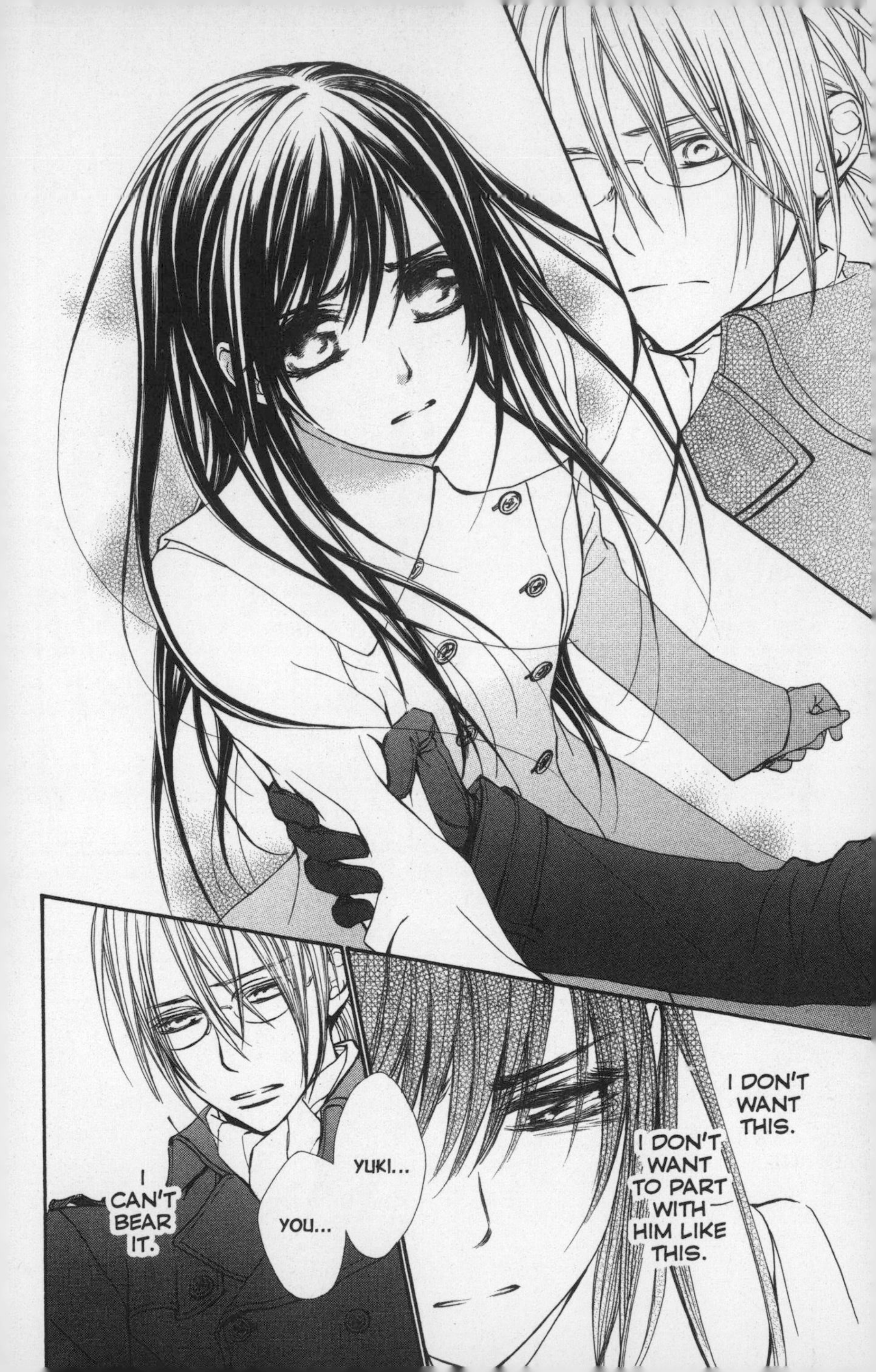
I DON'T WANT THIS.
I DON'T WANT TO PART WITH HIM LIKE THIS.
YUKI...
YOU...
I CAN'T BEAR IT.

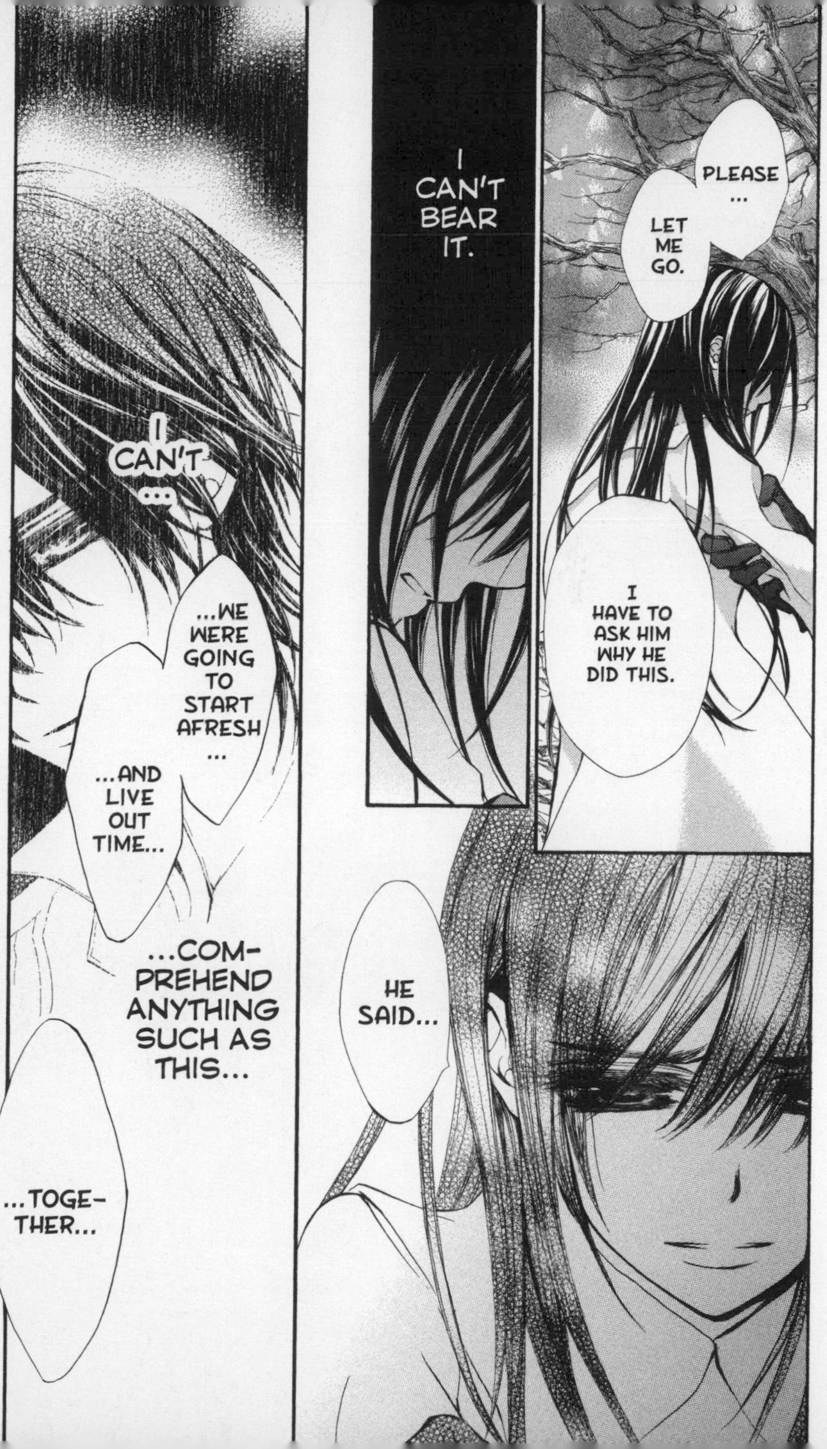
PLEASE...
LET ME GO.
I HAVE TO ASK HIM WHY HE DID THIS.
I CAN'T BEAR IT.
HE SAID...
I CAN'T...
...WE WERE GOING TO START AFRESH...
...AND LIVE OUT TIME...
...COM-PREHEND ANYTHING SUCH AS THIS...
...TOGE-THER...

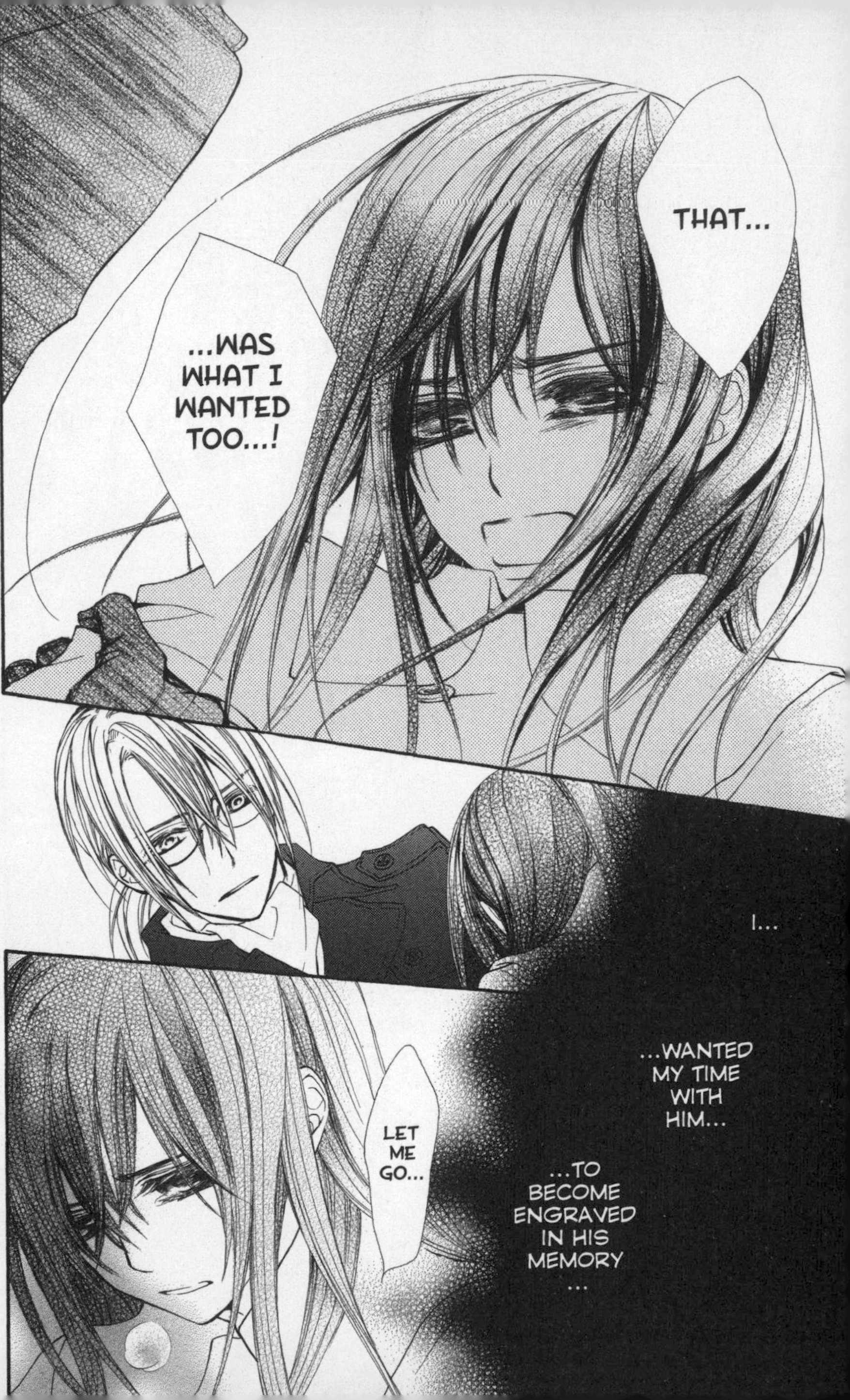
THAT...
...WAS WHAT I WANTED TOO...!
I...
...WANTED MY TIME WITH HIM...
...TO BECOME ENGRAVED IN HIS MEMORY...
LET ME GO...

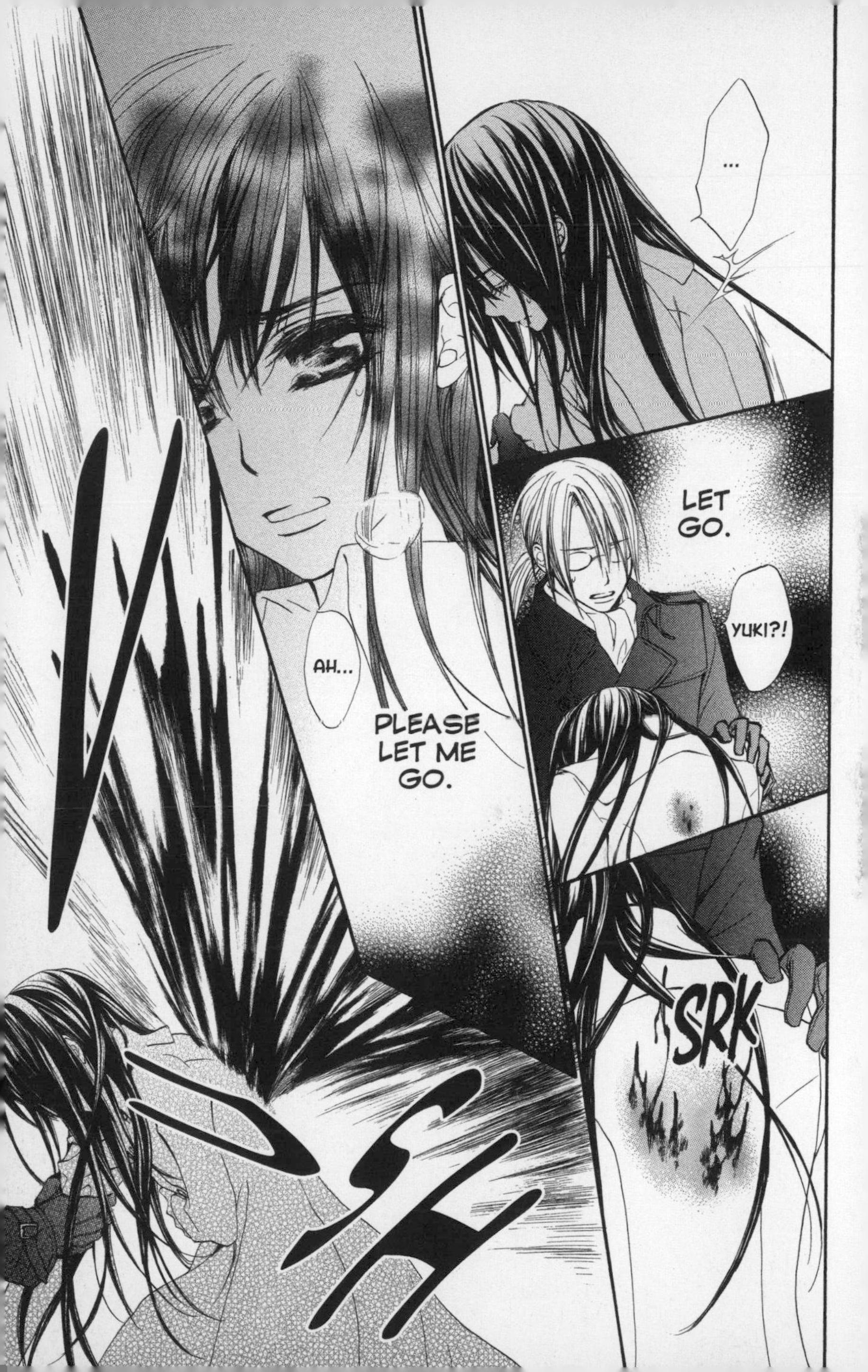
...
LET GO.
YUKI?!
SRK
AH...
PLEASE LET ME GO.

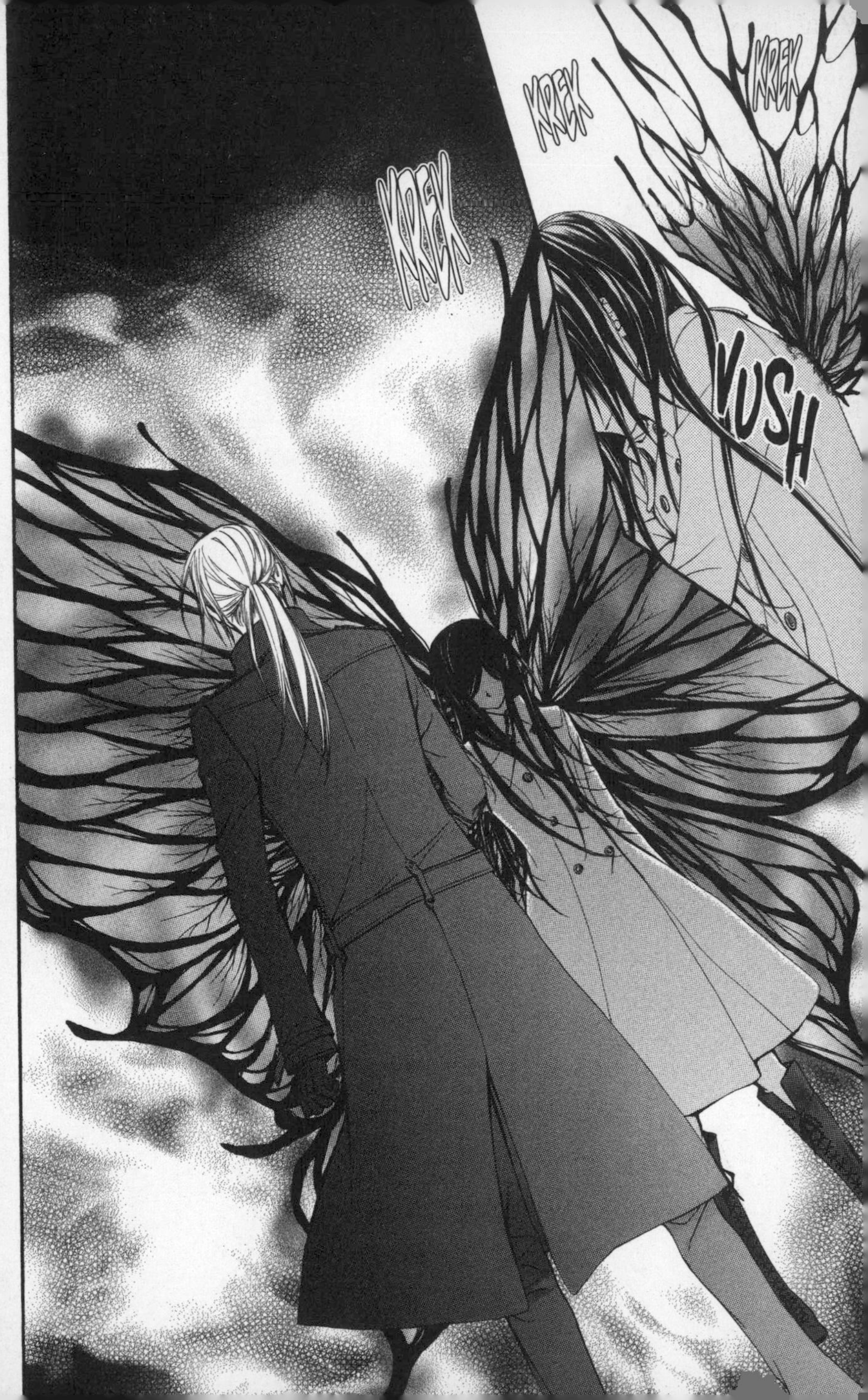
KREK
KREK
KREK
VUSH

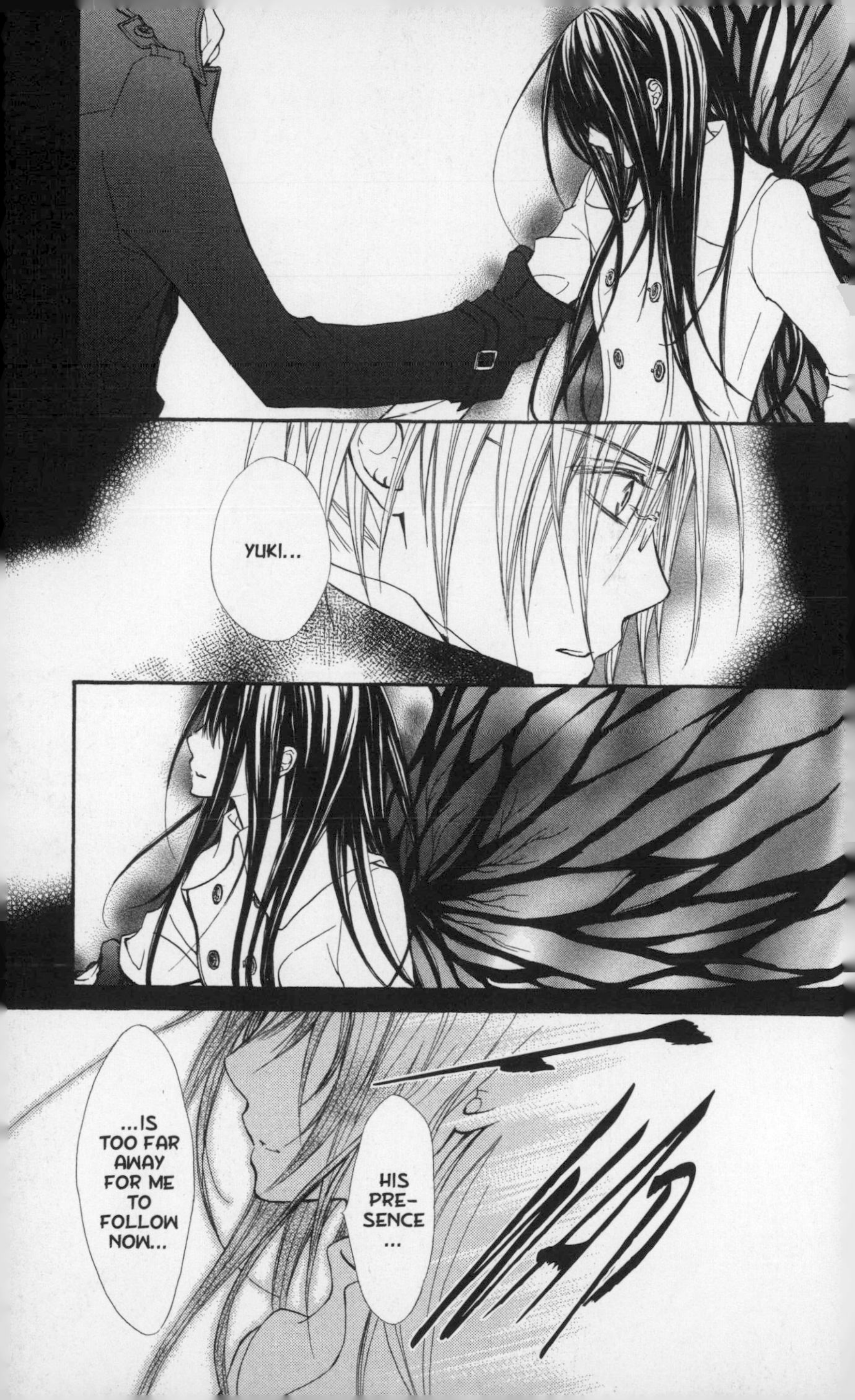
YUKI...
HIS PRESENCE...
...IS TOO FAR AWAY FOR ME TO FOLLOW NOW...

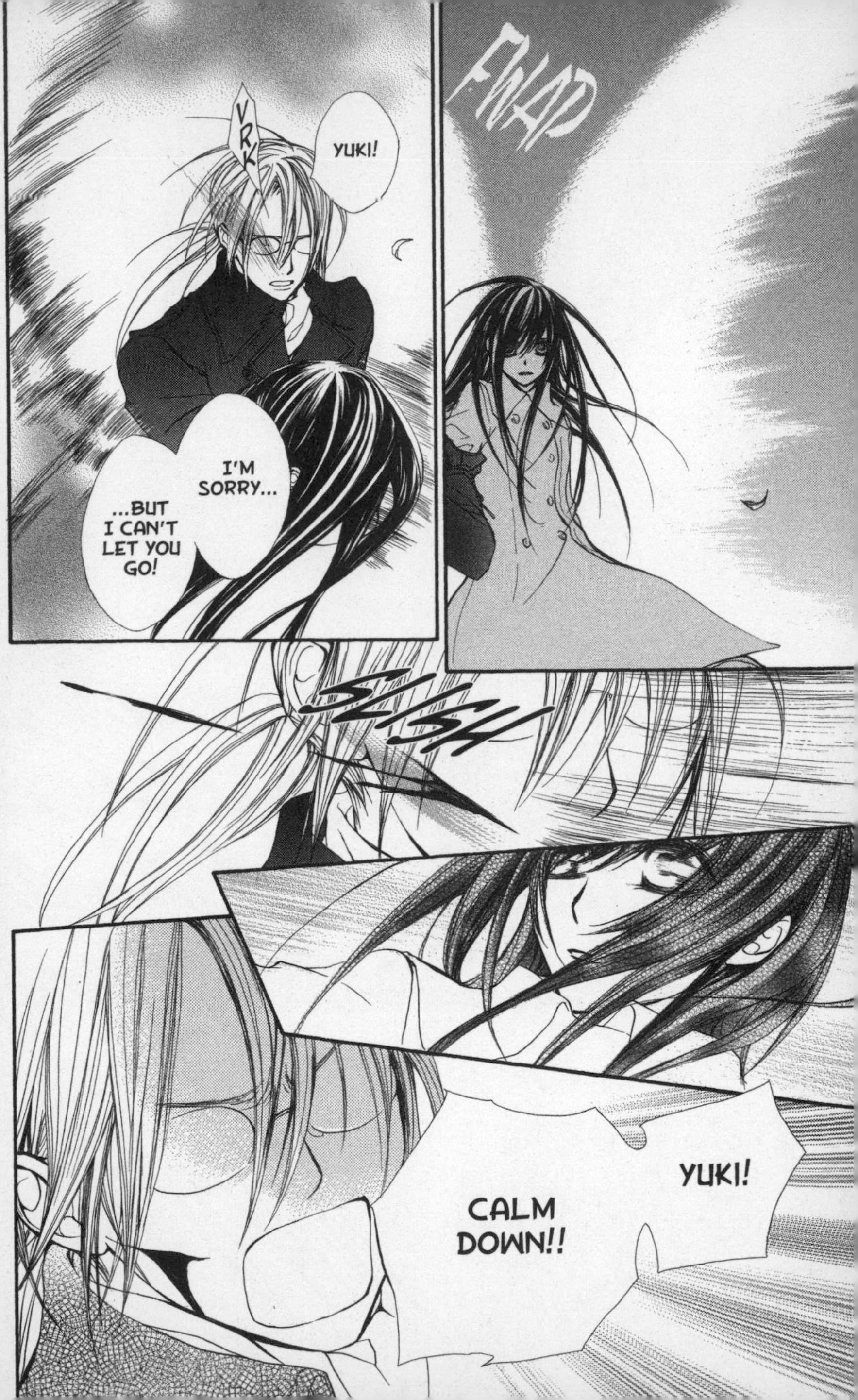
FWAP
YUKI!
VRK
I'M SORRY...
...BUT I CAN'T LET YOU GO!
SWISH
YUKI!
CALM DOWN!!

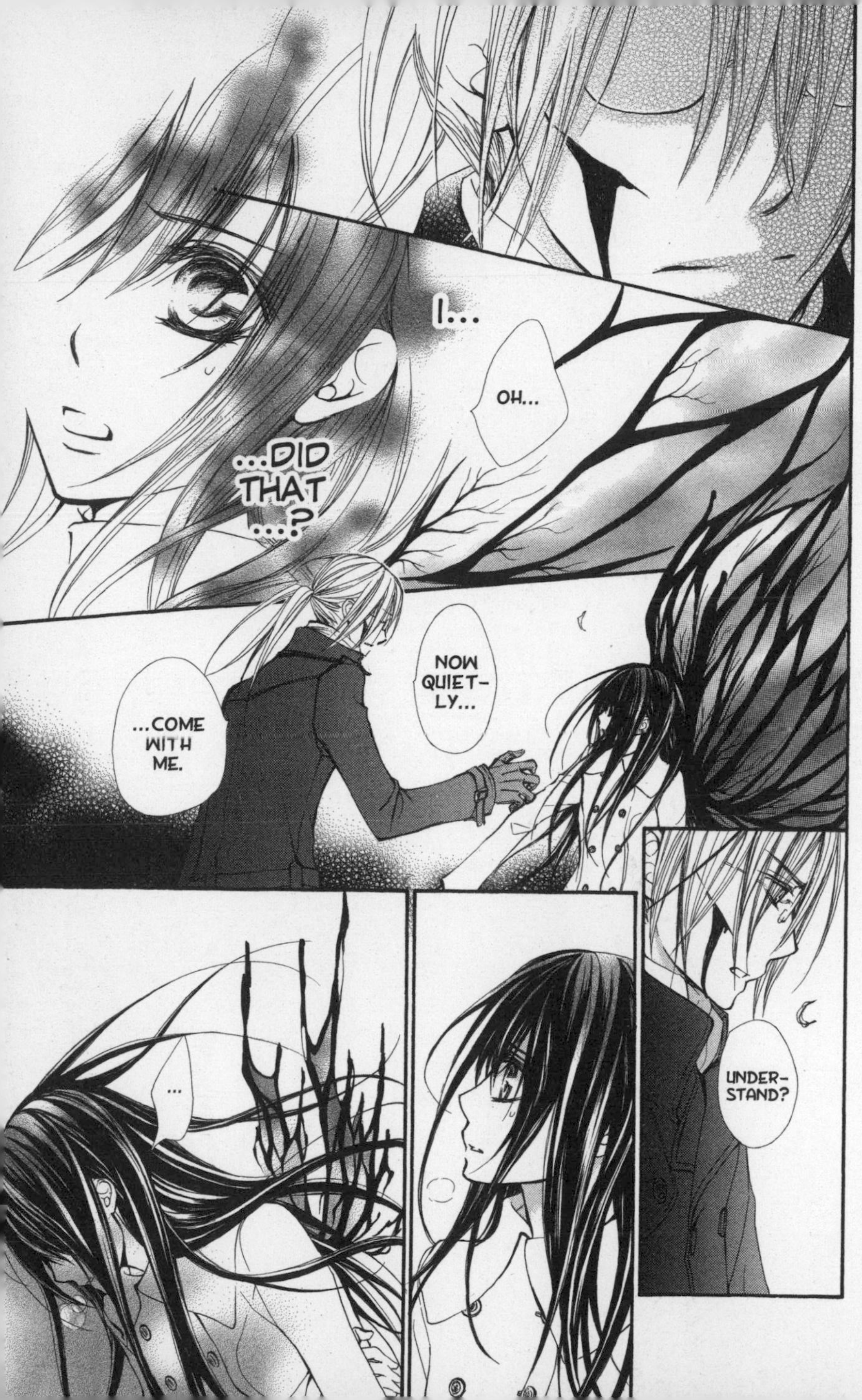
I...
OH...
...DID THAT ...?
NOW QUIET-LY...
...COME WITH ME.
UNDER-STAND?
...

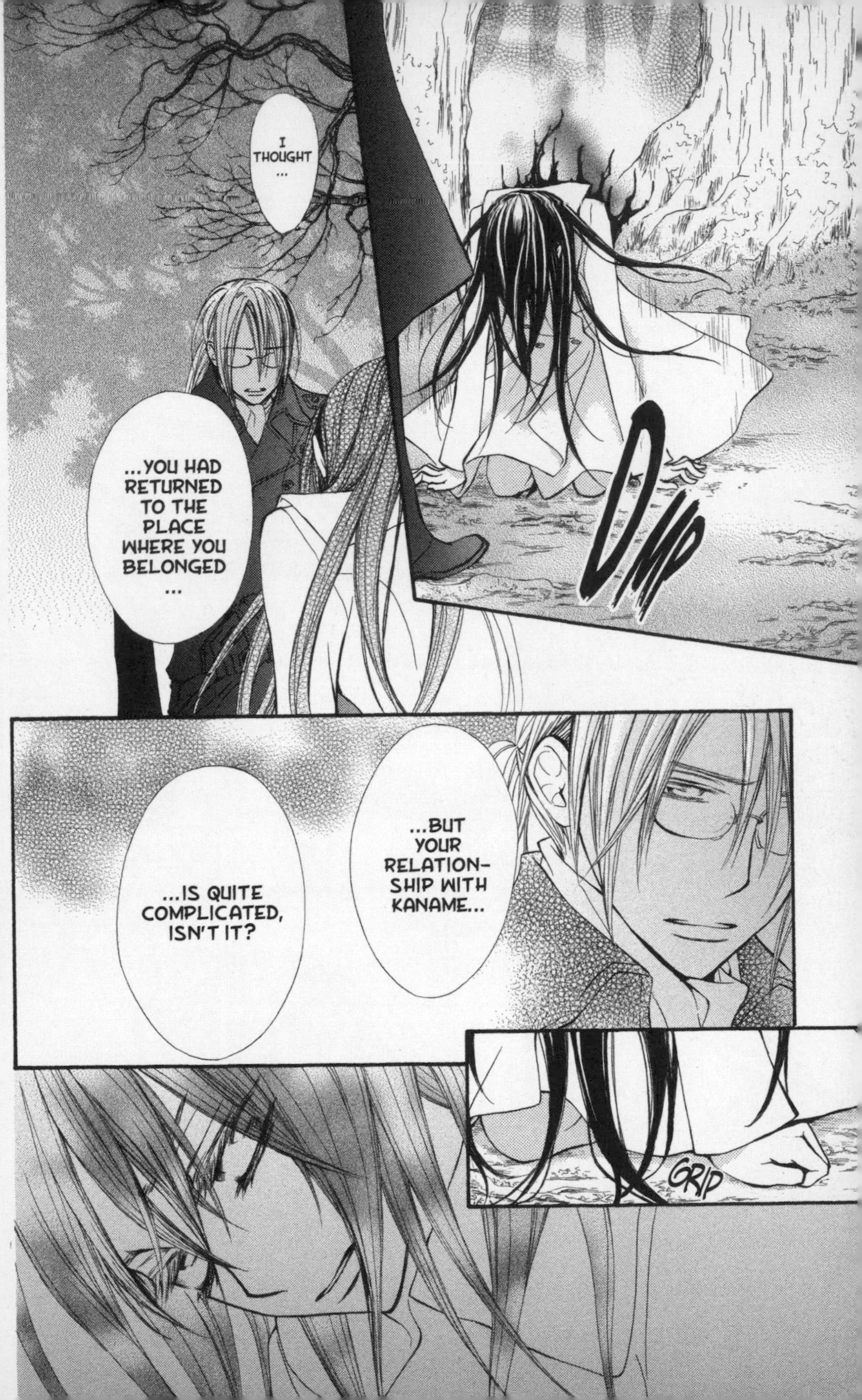
DMP
I THOUGHT ...
...YOU HAD RETURNED TO THE PLACE WHERE YOU BELONGED ...
...BUT YOUR RELATION-SHIP WITH KANAME...
...IS QUITE COMPLICATED, ISN'T IT?
GRIP

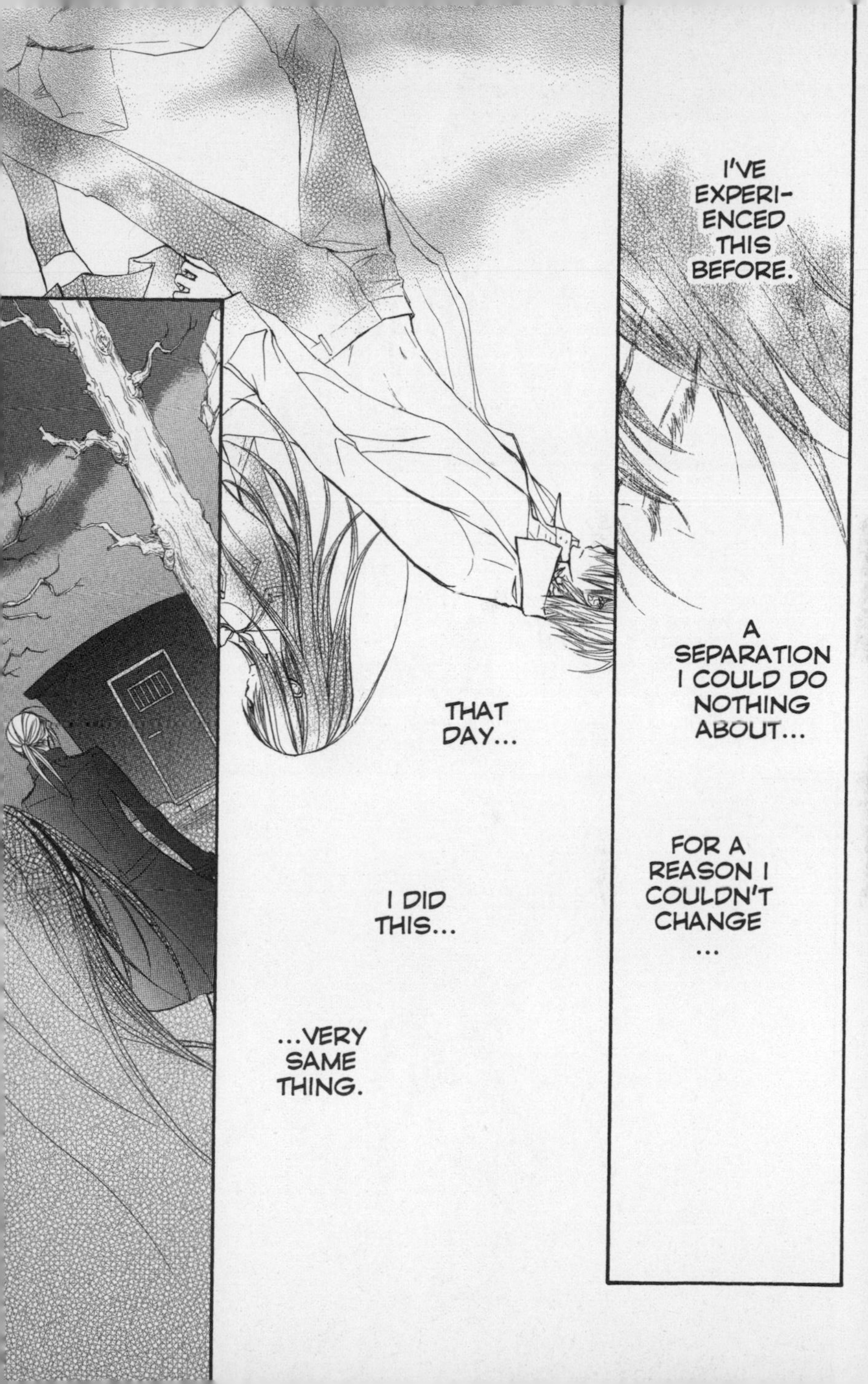
I'VE EXPERIENCED THIS BEFORE.
A SEPARATION I COULD DO NOTHING ABOUT...
FOR A REASON I COULDN'T CHANGE...
THAT DAY...
I DID THIS...
...VERY SAME THING.

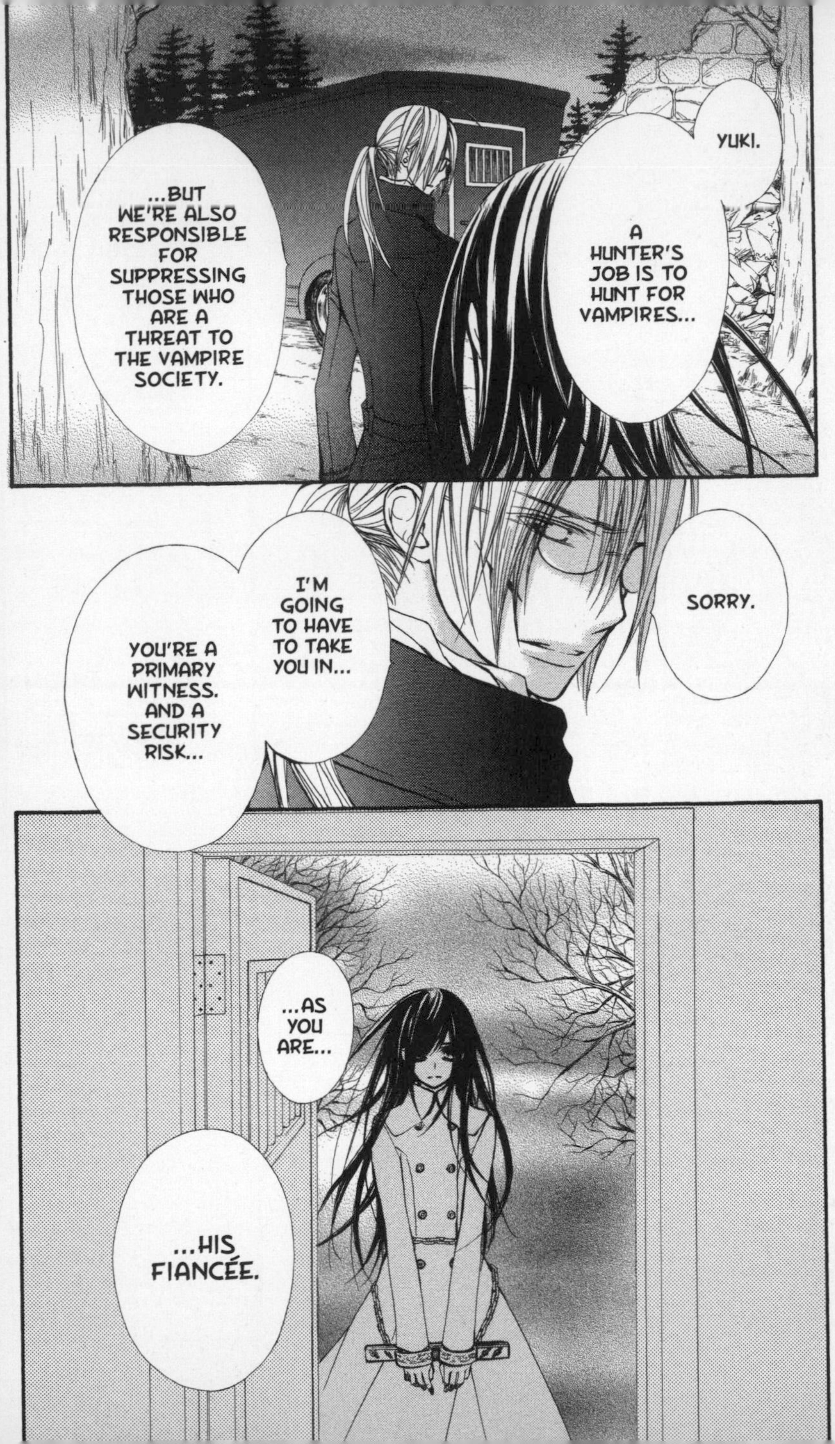
YUKI.
A HUNTER'S JOB IS TO HUNT FOR VAMPIRES...
...BUT WE'RE ALSO RESPONSIBLE FOR SUPPRESSING THOSE WHO ARE A THREAT TO THE VAMPIRE SOCIETY.
SORRY.
I'M GOING TO HAVE TO TAKE YOU IN...
YOU'RE A PRIMARY WITNESS. AND A SECURITY RISK...
...AS YOU ARE...
...HIS FIANCÉE.

Many Thanks!

O. Mio-sama
K. Midori-sama
I. Asami-sama
A. Ichiya-sama

And my mother, family & friends.

And to my editor and the members of the Editorial Office... I apologize for not being able to become "a manga artist who doesn't cause too much trouble." I'll do my best...

And most of all, I would like to thank all the readers. It's because of your existence that I get to put my work in a magazine, and you give me the support to continue working on this series. Thank you very much. I read all of your letters too!!

I hope to see you in volume 15.

樋野まつり。
Matsuri Hino

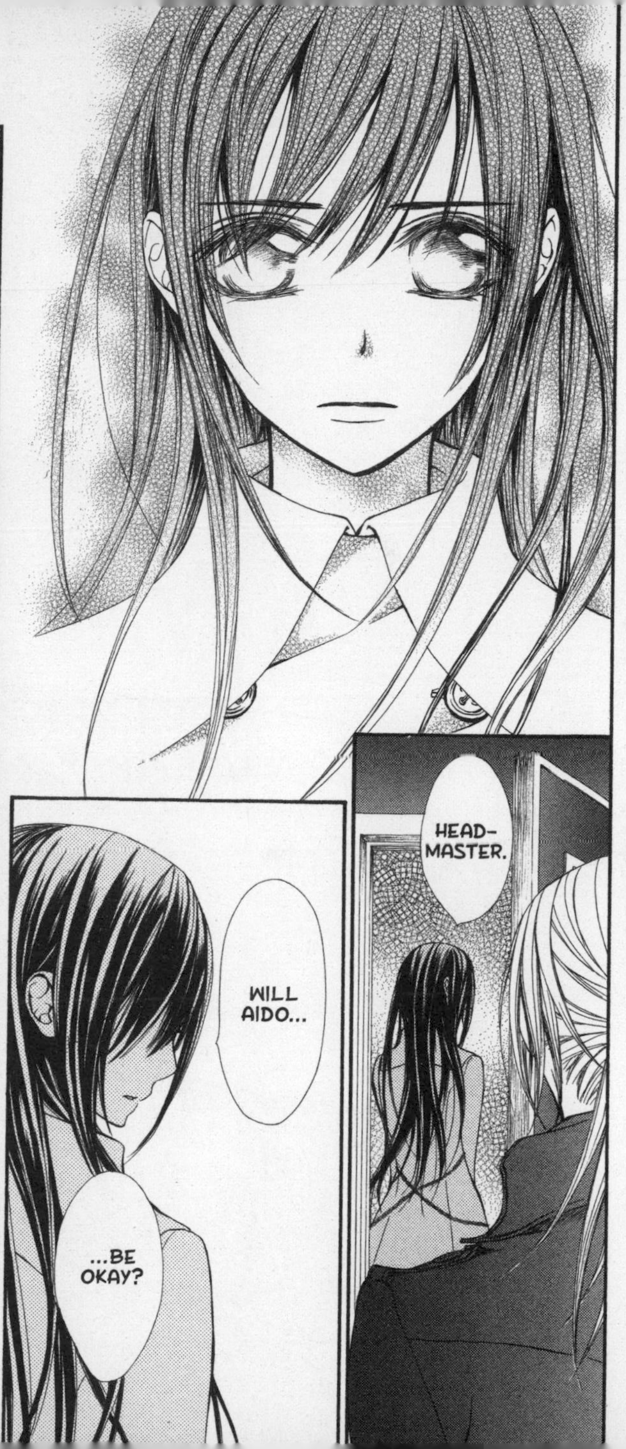
HEAD-MASTER.
WILL AIDO...
...BE OKAY?

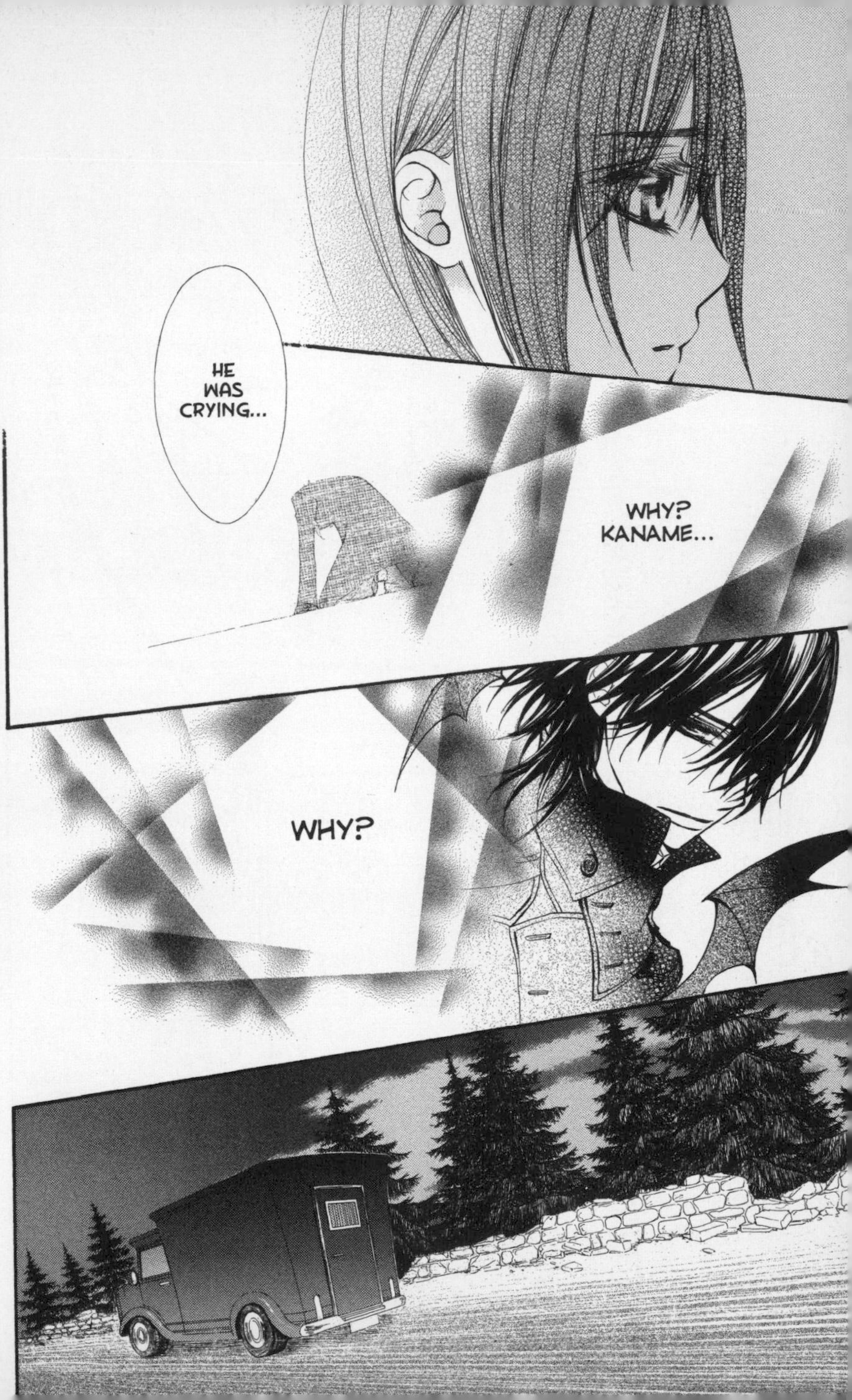
HE WAS CRYING...
WHY? KANAME...
WHY?

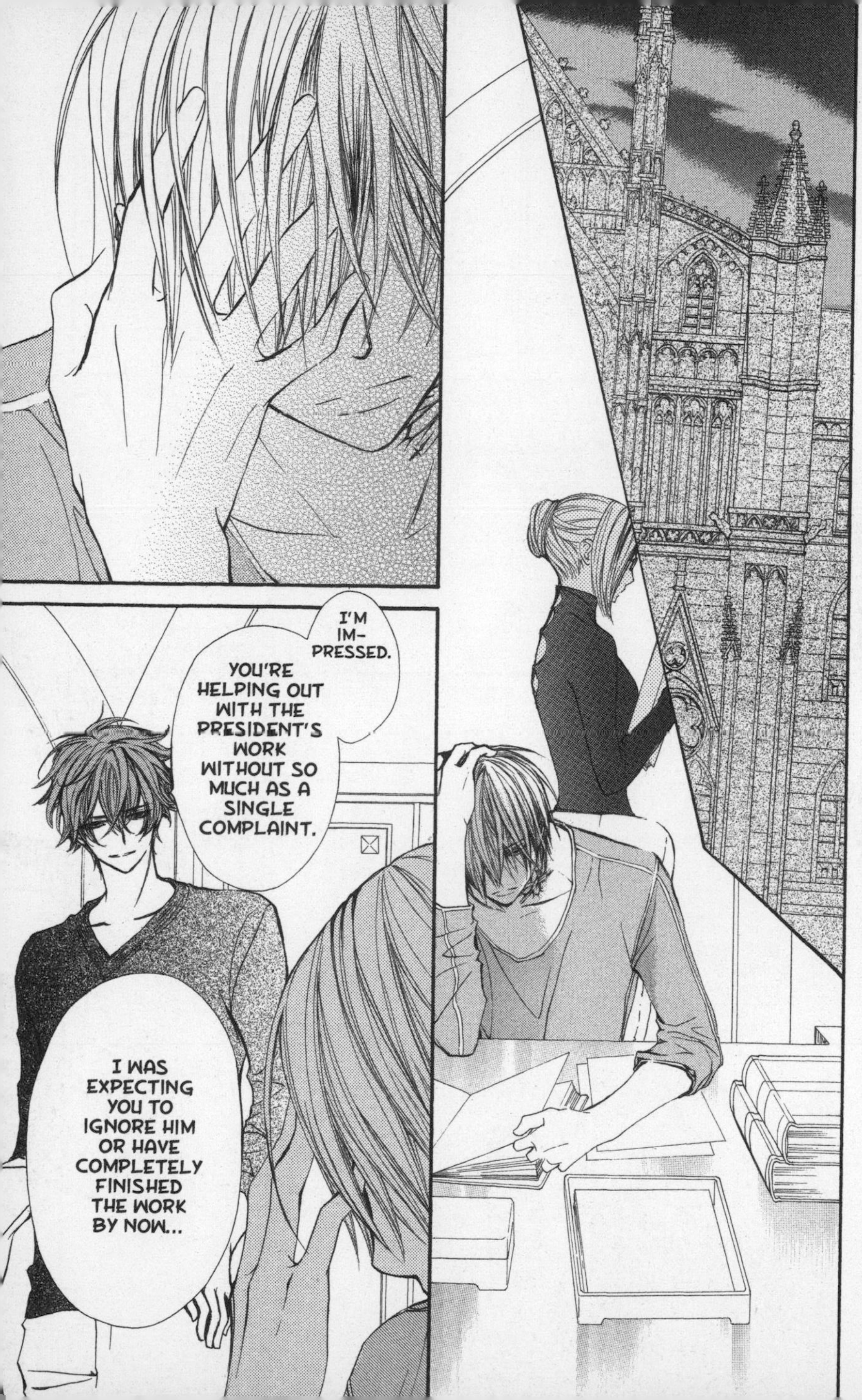
I'M IM-PRESSED.
YOU'RE HELPING OUT WITH THE PRESIDENT'S WORK WITHOUT SO MUCH AS A SINGLE COMPLAINT.
I WAS EXPECTING YOU TO IGNORE HIM OR HAVE COMPLETELY FINISHED THE WORK BY NOW...

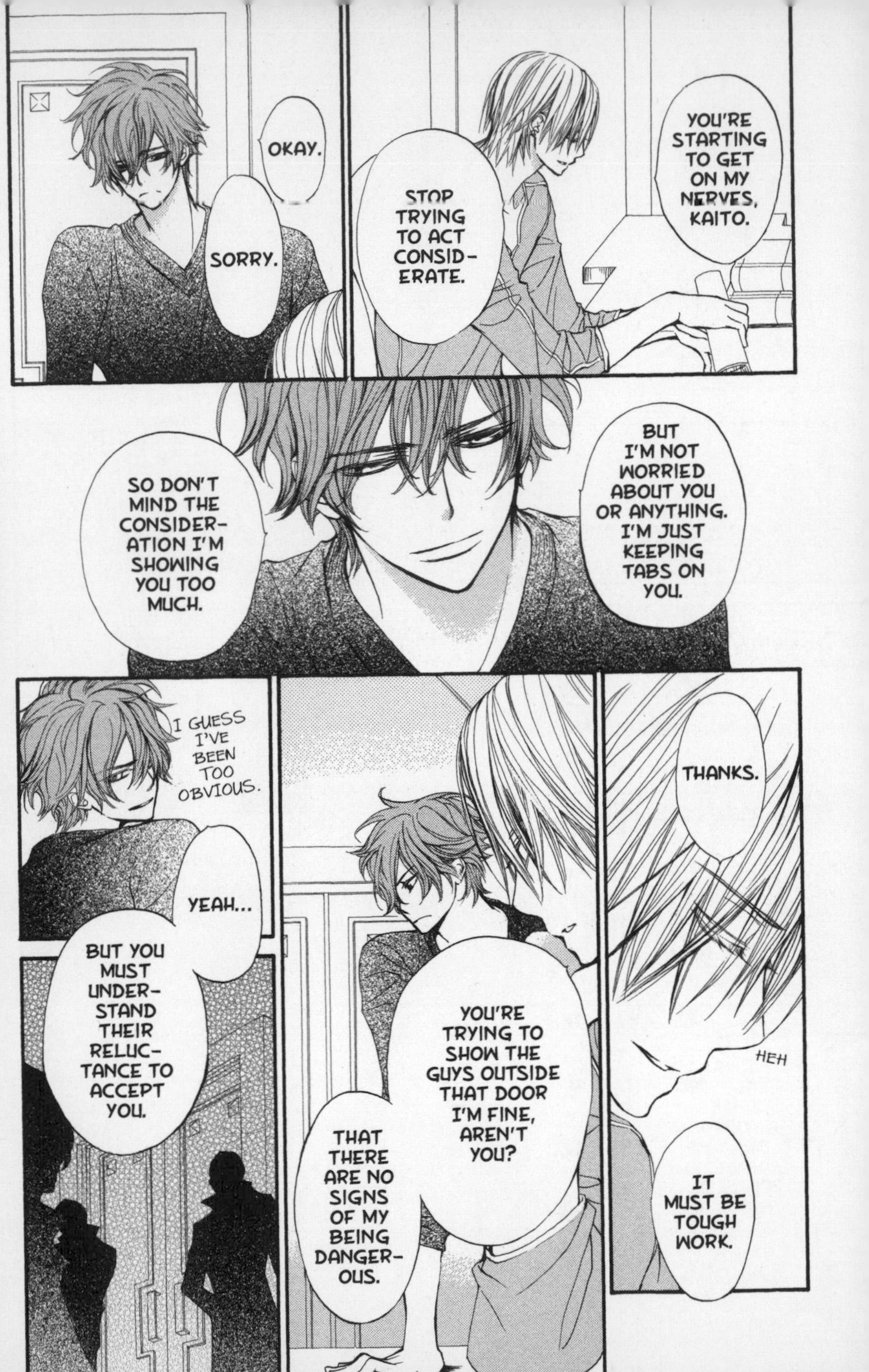
YOU'RE STARTING TO GET ON MY NERVES, KAITO.
STOP TRYING TO ACT CONSID-ERATE.
OKAY.
SORRY.
BUT I'M NOT WORRIED ABOUT YOU OR ANYTHING. I'M JUST KEEPING TABS ON YOU.
SO DON'T MIND THE CONSIDER-ATION I'M SHOWING YOU TOO MUCH.
THANKS.
HEH
IT MUST BE TOUGH WORK.
YOU'RE TRYING TO SHOW THE GUYS OUTSIDE THAT DOOR I'M FINE, AREN'T YOU?
THAT THERE ARE NO SIGNS OF MY BEING DANGER-OUS.
I GUESS I'VE BEEN TOO OBVIOUS.
YEAH...
BUT YOU MUST UNDER-STAND THEIR RELUC-TANCE TO ACCEPT YOU.

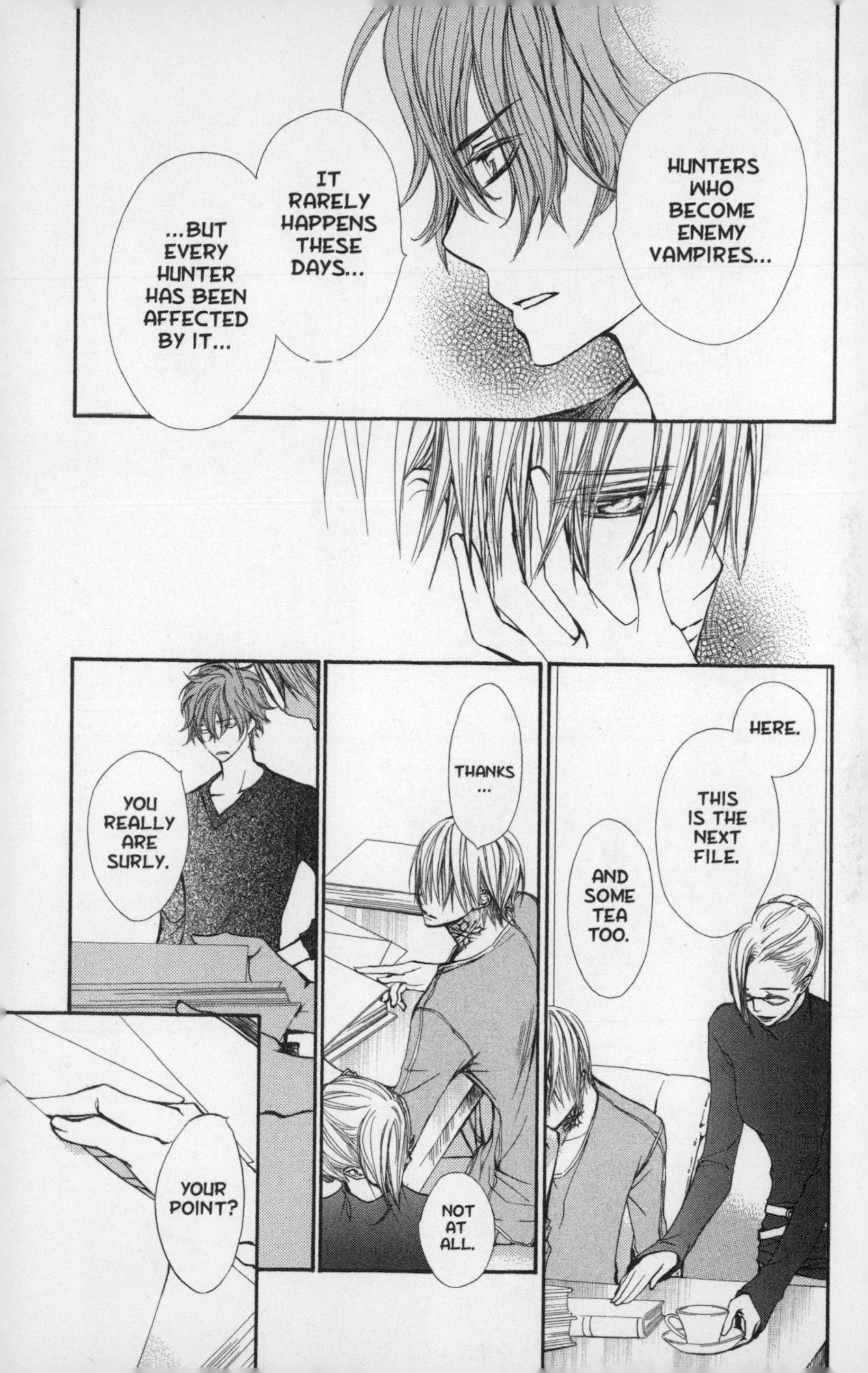
HUNTERS WHO BECOME ENEMY VAMPIRES...
IT RARELY HAPPENS THESE DAYS...
...BUT EVERY HUNTER HAS BEEN AFFECTED BY IT...
HERE.
THIS IS THE NEXT FILE.
AND SOME TEA TOO.
THANKS ...
NOT AT ALL.
YOU REALLY ARE SURLY.
YOUR POINT?

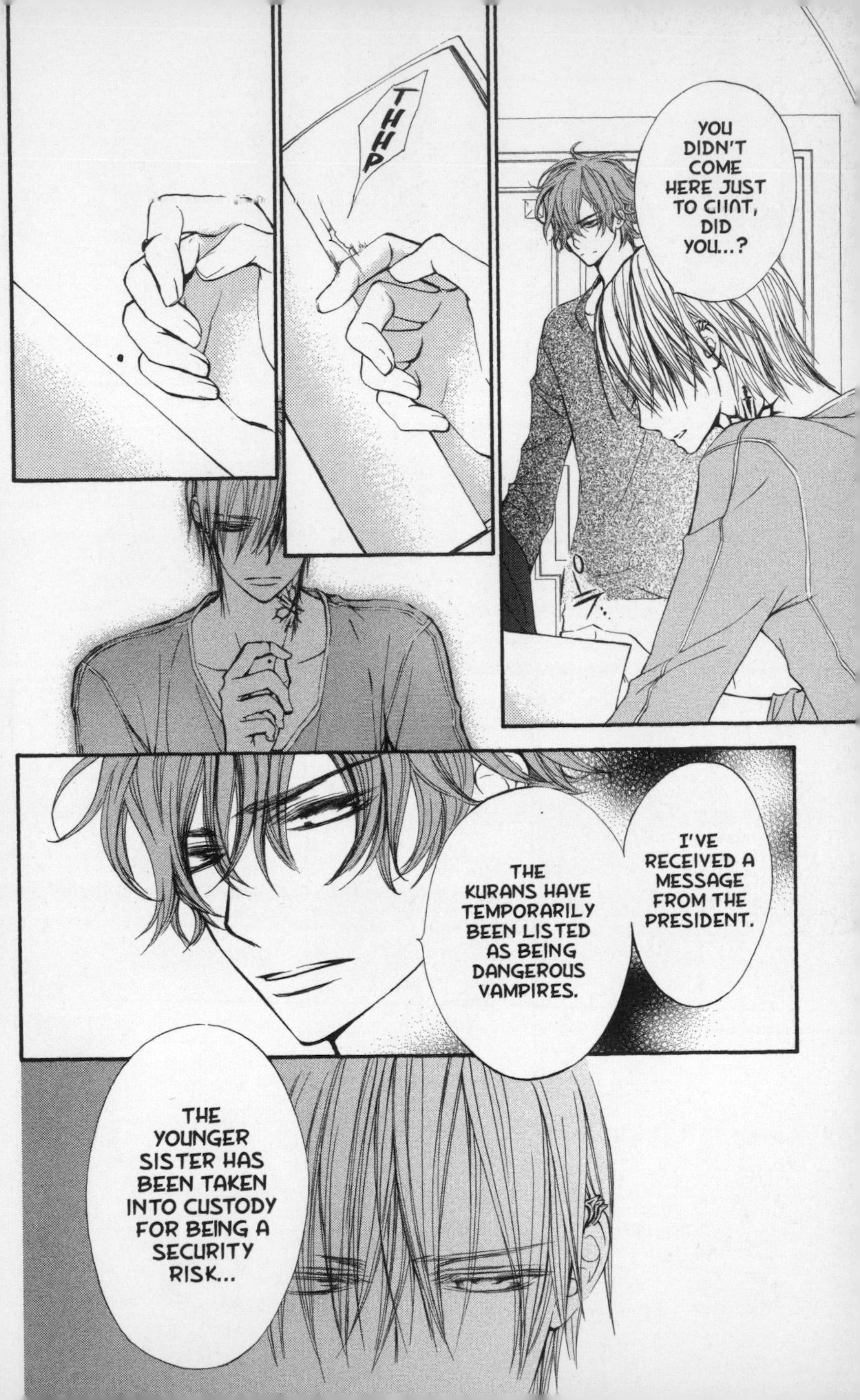
YOU DIDN'T COME HERE JUST TO CHAT, DID YOU...?
THHP
I'VE RECEIVED A MESSAGE FROM THE PRESIDENT.
THE KURANS HAVE TEMPORARILY BEEN LISTED AS BEING DANGEROUS VAMPIRES.
THE YOUNGER SISTER HAS BEEN TAKEN INTO CUSTODY FOR BEING A SECURITY RISK...

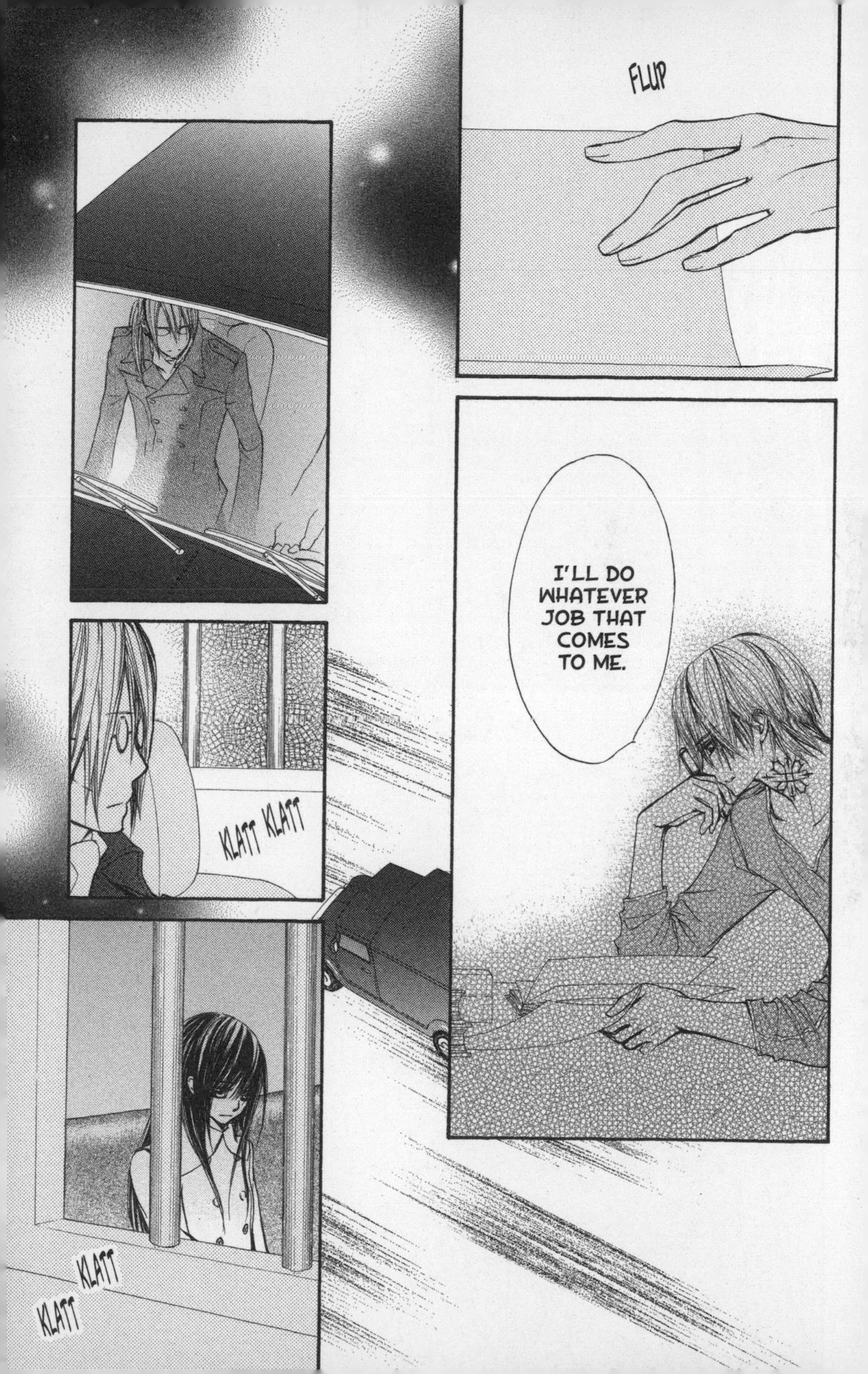
FLUP
I'LL DO WHATEVER JOB THAT COMES TO ME.
KLATT KLATT
KLATT
KLATT

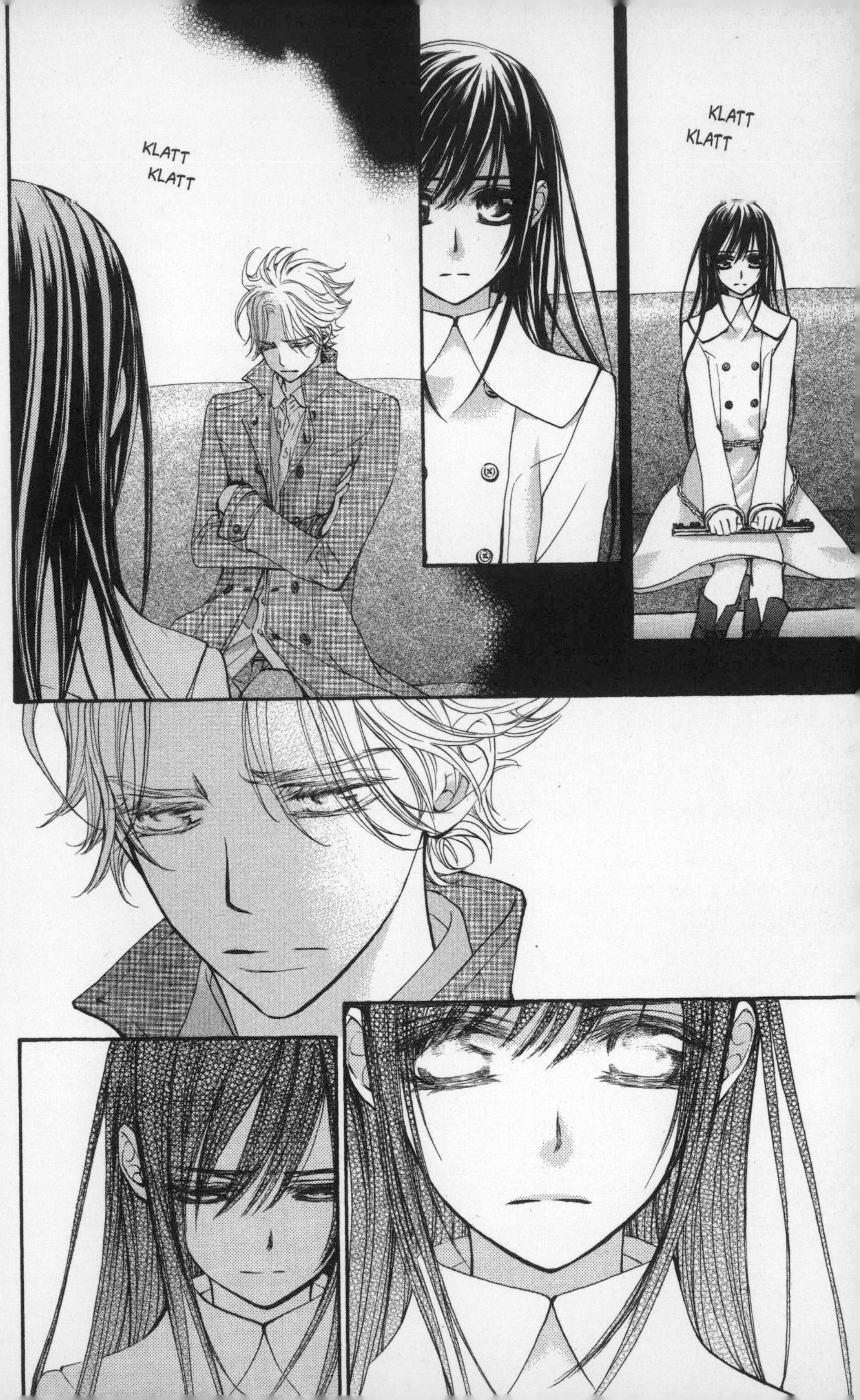
KLATT
KLATT
KLATT
KLATT

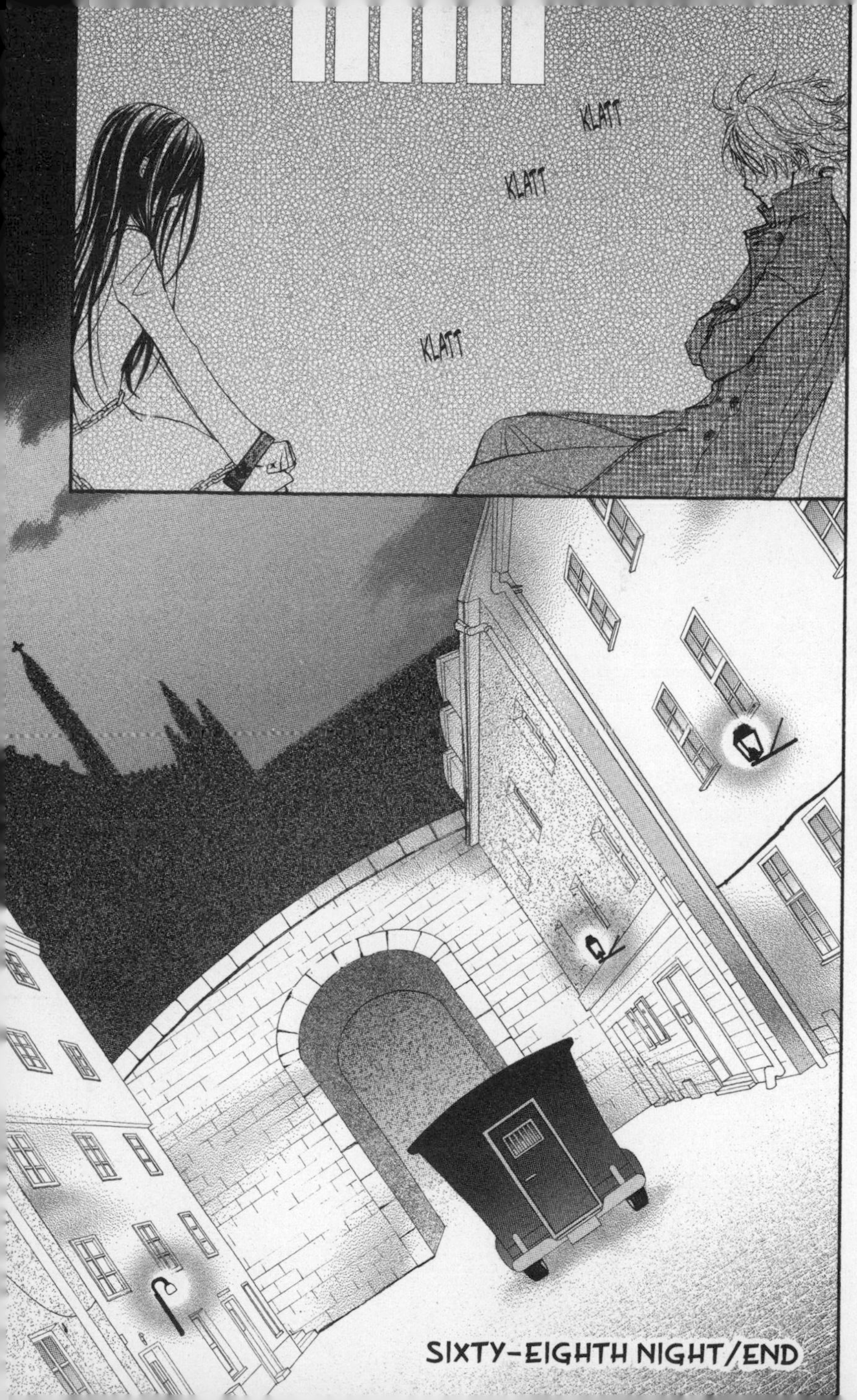
KLATT
KLATT
KLATT
SIXTY-EIGHTH NIGHT/END

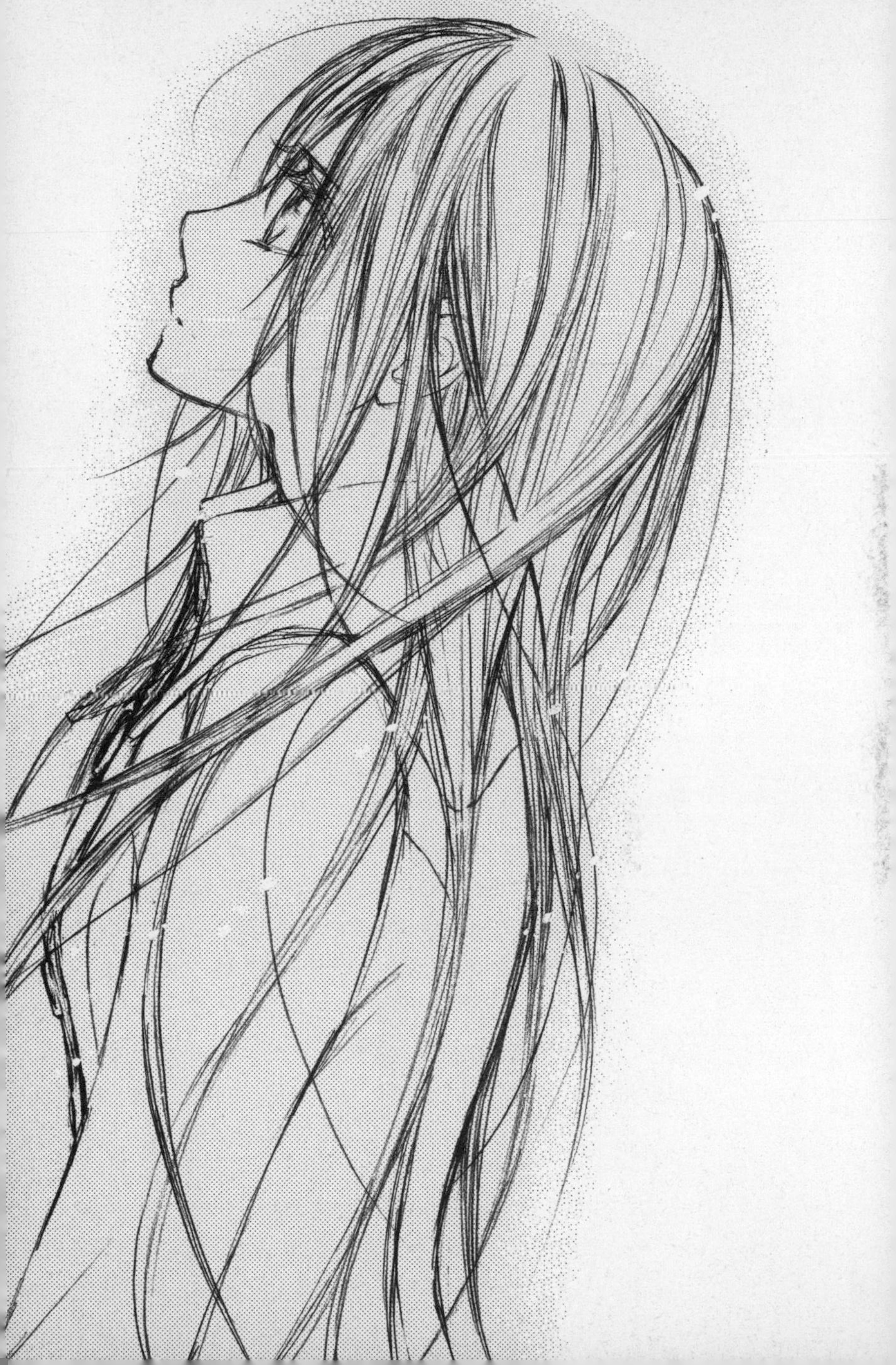

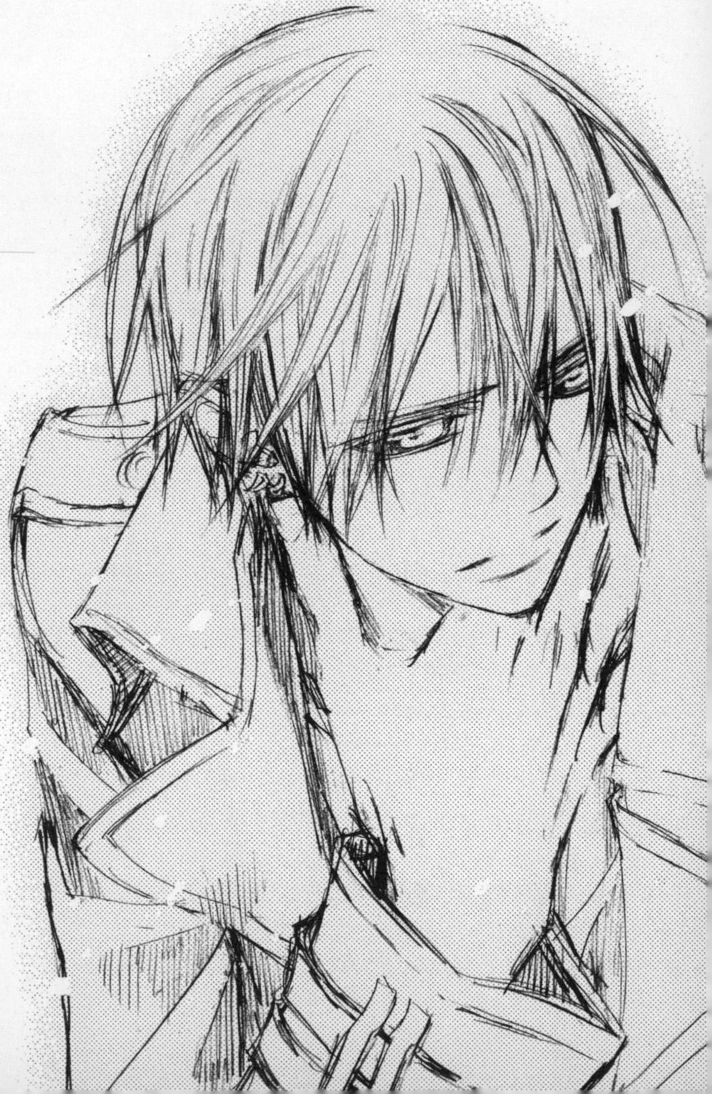

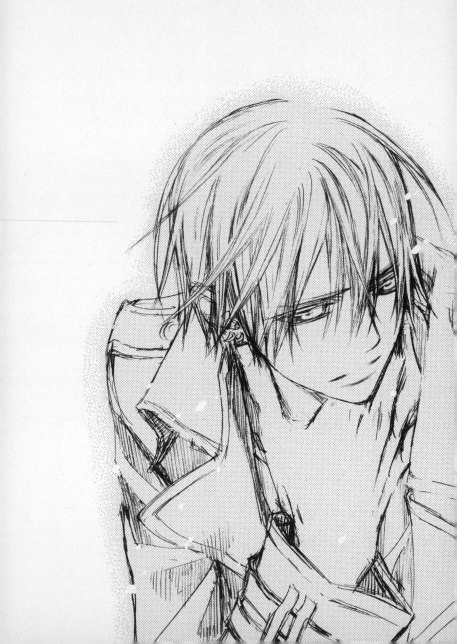

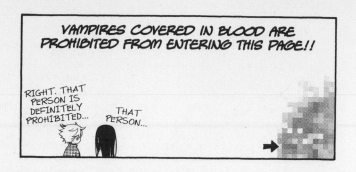

VAMPIRES COVERED IN BLOOD ARE PROHIBITED FROM ENTERING THIS PAGE!!

RIGHT. THAT PERSON IS DEFINITELY PROHIBITED...

THAT PERSON...

SURVEILLANCE CAMERA

TMP   TMP   TMP   TMP

SURVEILLANCE CAMERA

TMP

TMP

TMP

SURVEILLANCE CAMERA

YOU'RE LIKE A LITTLE DUCKLING ...

IT'S MY JOB.

TMP

ONE DAY, KAITO TAKAMIYA THOUGHT ...
IN HIS OFFICE
WHY DOES ZERO ...
GRADE REPORT
...GET SUCH GOOD GRADES EVEN THOUGH HE SLEEPS THROUGH CLASS?
HE DOESN'T HAVE TIME TO STUDY, DOES HE?
OH
ZERO'S GRADE REPORT
SLEEP-LEARNING!
IT'S THE ONLY EXPLANATION!!!
ZERO

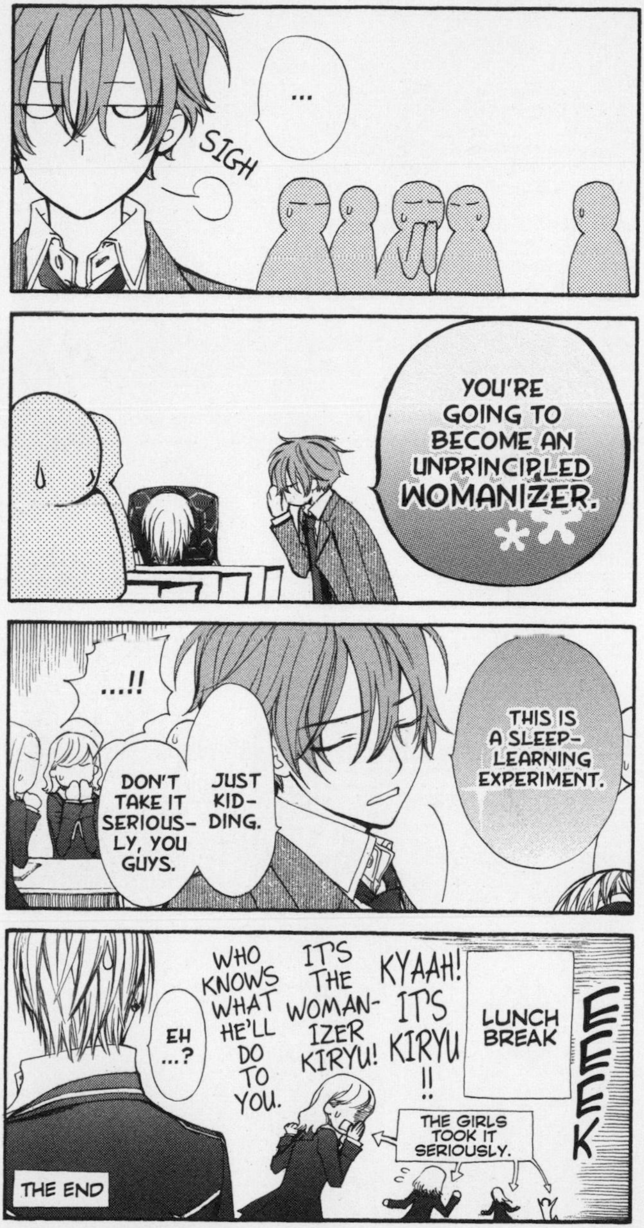
...
SIGH
YOU'RE GOING TO BECOME AN UNPRINCIPLED WOMANIZER.
THIS IS A SLEEP-LEARNING EXPERIMENT.
JUST KID-DING.
DON'T TAKE IT SERIOUS-LY, YOU GUYS.
...!!
EEEEK
LUNCH BREAK
KYAAH! IT'S KIRYU!!
IT'S THE WOMAN-IZER KIRYU!
WHO KNOWS WHAT HE'LL DO TO YOU.
EH ...?
THE GIRLS TOOK IT SERIOUSLY.
THE END

SHE ARRIVED AT THE HUNTER SOCIETY. BUT...

LOOK AT THAT GIRL IN FRONT OF THE DOOR.
OH, HER. I'VE HEARD SHE CAN'T GO INSIDE FOR SIX MONTHS.
SHE LOOKS LIKE A JUNIOR HIGH STUDENT... MAYBE I SHOULD CALL THE POLICE...?
IN

CONTINUED IN VOLUME 15!

[YUKI WILL HAVE TO WAIT ONLY FOUR MONTHS FOR THE SHOJO BEAT RELEASE. ;) —ED]

EDITOR'S NOTES

Characters

Matsuri Hino puts careful thought into the names of her characters in *Vampire Knight*. Below is the collection of characters through volume 14. Each character's name is presented family name first, per the kanji reading.

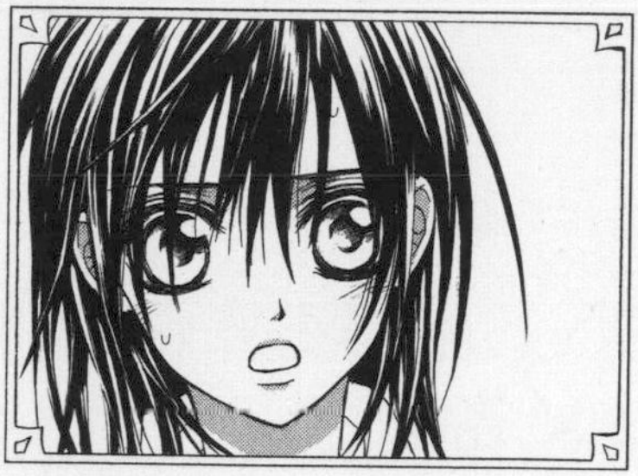

黒主優姫

Cross Yuki

Yuki's last name, *Kurosu*, is the Japanese pronunciation of the English word "cross." However, the kanji has a different meaning—*kuro* means "black" and *su* means "master." Her first name is a combination of *yuu*, meaning "tender" or "kind," and *ki*, meaning "princess."

錐生零

Kiryu Zero

Zero's first name is the kanji for *rei*, meaning "zero." In his last name, *Kiryu*, the *ki* means "auger" or "drill," and the *ryu* means "life."

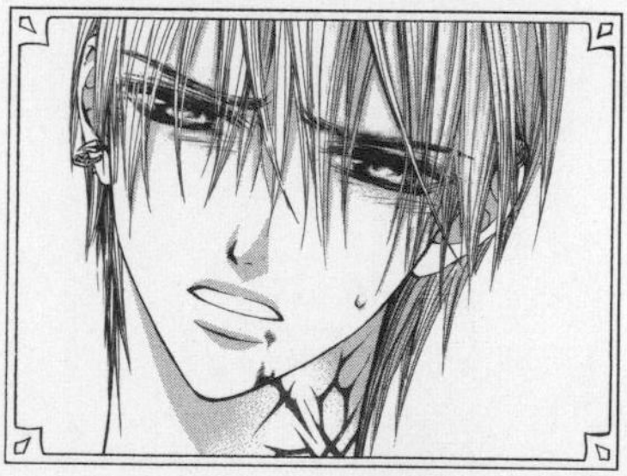

玖蘭枢

Kuran Kaname

Kaname means "hinge" or "door."
The kanji for his last name is a
combination of the old-fashioned
way of writing *ku*, meaning "nine,"
and *ran*, meaning "orchid": "nine
orchids."

藍堂英

Aido Hanabusa

Hanabusa means "petals of a flower."
Aido means "indigo temple." In
Japanese, the pronunciation of *Aido* is
very close to the pronunciation of the
English word *idol*.

架院暁

Kain Akatsuki

Akatsuki means "dawn" or "day-
break." In *Kain*, *ka* is a base or
support, while *in* denotes a building
that has high fences around it, such
as a temple or school.

早園瑠佳

Souen Ruka

In *Ruka*, the *ru* means "lapis lazuli" while the *ka* means "good-looking" or "beautiful." The *sou* in Ruka's surname, *Souen*, means "early," but this kanji also has an obscure meaning of "strong fragrance." The *en* means "garden."

一条拓麻

Ichijo Takuma

Ichijo can mean a "ray" or "streak." The kanji for *Takuma* is a combination of *taku*, meaning "to cultivate" and *ma*, which is the kanji for *asa*, meaning "hemp" or "flax," a plant with blue flowers.

支葵千里

Shiki Senri

Shiki's last name is a combination of *shi*, meaning "to support" and *ki*, meaning "mallow"—a flowering plant with pink or white blossoms. The *ri* in *Senri* is a traditional Japanese unit of measure for distance, and one *ri* is about 2.44 miles. *Senri* means "1,000 *ri*."

夜刈十牙

Yagari Toga

Yagari is a combination of *ya*, meaning "night," and *gari*, meaning "to harvest." *Toga* means "ten fangs."

一条麻遠, 一翁

Ichijo Asato, aka "Ichio"

Ichijo can mean a "ray" or "streak." Asato's first name is comprised of *asa*, meaning "hemp" or "flax," and *tou*, meaning "far off." His nickname is *ichi*, or "one," combined with *ou*, which can be used as an honorific when referring to an older man.

若葉沙頼

Wakaba Sayori

Yori's full name is Sayori Wakaba. *Wakaba* means "young leaves." Her given name, *Sayori*, is a combination of *sa*, meaning "sand," and *yori*, meaning "trust."

星煉
Seiren

Sei means "star" and *ren* means "to smelt" or "refine." *Ren* is also the same kanji used in *rengoku*, or "purgatory."

遠矢莉磨
Toya Rima

Toya means a "far-reaching arrow." Rima's first name is a combination of *ri*, or "jasmine," and *ma*, which signifies enhancement by wearing away, such as by polishing or scouring.

紅まり亜
Kurenai Maria

Kurenai means "crimson." The kanji for the last *a* in Maria's first name is the same that is used in "Asia."

錐生壱縷
Kiryu Ichiru
Ichi is the old-fashioned way of writing "one," and *ru* means "thread."

緋桜閑, 狂咲姫
Hio Shizuka, Kuruizaki-hime
Shizuka means "calm and quiet." In Shizuka's family name, *hi* is "scarlet," and *ou* is "cherry blossoms." Shizuka Hio is also referred to as the "Kuruizaki-hime." *Kuruizaki* means "flowers blooming out of season," and *hime* means "princess."

藍堂月子
Aido Tsukiko
Aido means "indigo temple." *Tsukiko* means "moon child."

白露更

Shirabuki Sara

Shira is "white," and *buki* is "butterbur," a plant with white flowers. *Sara* means "renew."

黒主灰閻

Cross Kaien

Cross, or *Kurosu*, means "black master." Kaien is a combination of *kai*, meaning "ashes," and *en*, meaning "village gate." The kanji for *en* is also used for Enma, the ruler of the Underworld in Buddhist mythology.

玖蘭李土

Kuran Rido

Kuran means "nine orchids." In *Rido*, *ri* means "plum" and *do* means "earth."

玖蘭樹里

Kuran Juri

Kuran means "nine orchids." In her first name, *ju* means "tree" and a *ri* is a traditional Japanese unit of measure for distance. The kanji for *ri* is the same as in Senri's name.

玖蘭悠

Kuran Haruka

Kuran means "nine orchids." *Haruka* means "distant" or "remote."

鷹宮海斗

Takamiya Kaito

Taka means "hawk" and *miya* means "imperial palace" or "shrine." *Kai* is "sea" and *to* means "to measure" or "grid."

菖藤依砂也

Shoto Isaya

Sho means "Siberian Iris" and *to* is "wisteria." The *I* in *Isaya* means "to rely on," while the *sa* means "sand." *Ya* is a suffix used for emphasis.

橙茉

Toma

In the family name *Toma, to* means "seville orange" and *ma* means "jasmine flower."

Terms

-sama: The suffix *sama* is used in formal address for someone who ranks higher in the social hierarchy. The vampires call their leader "Kaname-sama" only when they are among their own kind.

Matsuri Hino burst onto the manga scene with her series *Kono Yume ga Sametara* (When This Dream Is Over), which was published in *LaLa DX* magazine. Hino was a manga artist a mere nine months after she decided to become one.

With the success of her popular series *Captive Hearts* and *MeruPuri*, Hino has established herself as a major player in the world of shojo manga. *Vampire Knight* is currently serialized in *LaLa* magazine.

Hino enjoys creative activities and has commented that she would have been either an architect or an apprentice to traditional Japanese craft masters if she had not become a manga artist.

VAMPIRE KNIGHT

Vol. 14

Shojo Beat Edition

STORY AND ART BY

MATSURI HINO

Adaptation/Nancy Thistlethwaite
Translation/Tetsuichiro Miyaki
Touch-up Art & Lettering/Rina Mapa
Graphic Design/Amy Martin
Editor/Nancy Thistlethwaite

Printed in the U.S.A.

Published by VIZ Media, LLC
P.O. Box 77010
San Francisco, CA 94107

10 9 8 7 6 5 4 3 2 1
First printing, July 2012

RATED T+ FOR OLDER TEEN

PARENTAL ADVISORY
VAMPIRE KNIGHT is rated T+ for Older Teen and is recommended for ages 16 and up. This volume contains sexual themes and violence.

ratings.viz.com

www.viz.com

www.shojobeat.com

SURPRISE!

You may be reading the wrong way!

It's true: In keeping with the original Japanese comic format, this book reads from right to left—so action, sound effects, and word balloons are completely reversed. This preserves the orientation of the original artwork—plus, it's fun! Check out the diagram shown here to get the hang of things, and then turn to the other side of the book to get started!

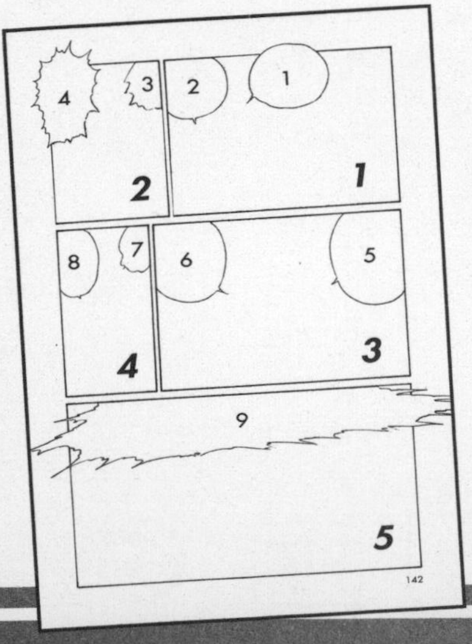
1
2
1
3
4
2
5
6
3
7
8
4
9
5
142

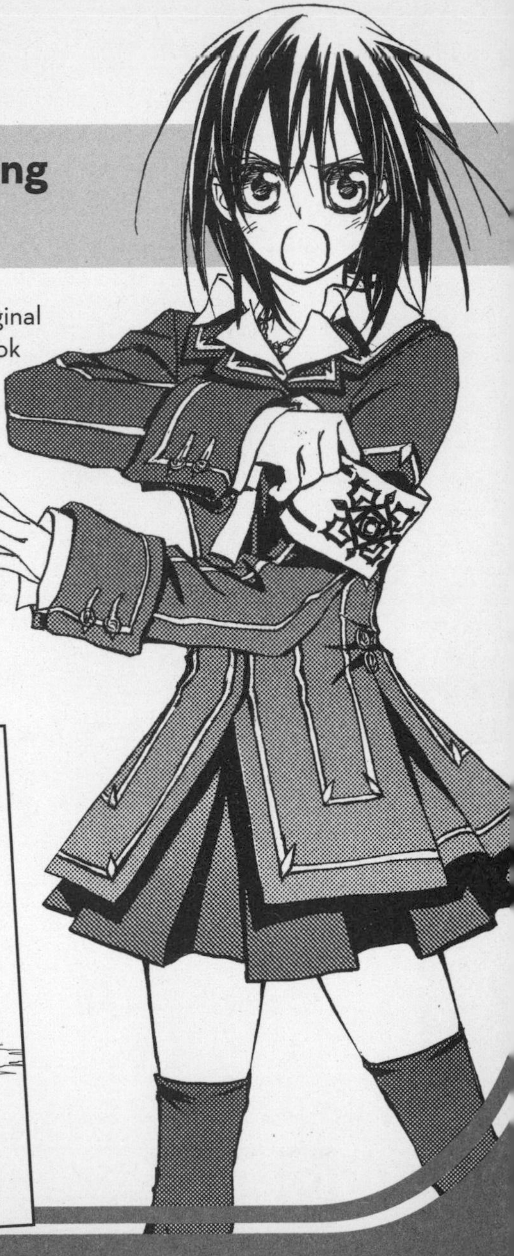